Sporting Gender

Contemporary Chinese Studies

This series provides new scholarship and perspectives on modern and contemporary China, including China's contested borderlands and minority peoples; ongoing social, cultural, and political changes; and the varied histories that animate China today.

A list of titles in this series appears at the end of this book.

Sporting Gender

Women Athletes and Celebrity-Making during China's National Crisis, 1931-45

Yunxiang Gao 高云翔

UBCPress · Vancouver · Toronto

21 20 19 18 17 16 15 14 13   5 4 3 2 1

Printed in Canada on FSC-certified ancient-forest-free paper
(100% post-consumer recycled) that is processed chlorine- and acid-free.

Library and Archives Canada Cataloguing in Publication

Gao, Yunxiang
   Sporting gender : women athletes and celebrity-making during China's national crisis, 1931-45 / Yunxiang Gao.

(Contemporary Chinese studies, ISSN 1206-9523)
Includes bibliographical references and index.
Also issued in electronic format.
ISBN 978-0-7748-2481-1 (bound); ISBN 978-0-7748-2482-8 (pbk.)

   1. Women athletes – China – Biography. 2. Sports – Social aspects – China – History – 20th century. 3. Sports – Political aspects – China – History – 20th century. 4. Women in popular culture – China – 20th century. 5. Sports in popular culture – China – 20th century. 6. Mass media and sports – China – History – 20th century. 7. Body image in women – China – History – 20th century. 8. Women – China – Social conditions. I. Title. II. Series: Contemporary Chinese studies

GV709.18.C6G26 2013   796.0951   C2012-906981-7

Canada

UBC Press gratefully acknowledges the financial support for our publishing program of the Government of Canada (through the Canada Book Fund), the Canada Council for the Arts, and the British Columbia Arts Council.

This book has been published with the help of a grant from the Canadian Federation for the Humanities and Social Sciences, through the Awards to Scholarly Publications Program, using funds provided by the Social Sciences and Humanities Research Council of Canada.

UBC Press
The University of British Columbia
2029 West Mall
Vancouver, BC V6T 1Z2
www.ubcpress.ca

To my father, Gao Zhen 高珍
  (17 November 1941 – 14 November 2011)

and mother, Du Xiuhua 杜秀花
  (1 January 1947-)

父兮生我　母兮鞠我
拊我畜我　长我育我
顾我复我　出入腹我
欲报之德　昊天罔极

Contents

List of Figures

Acknowledgments

I would like to thank the many friends and colleagues who helped over years to make this book possible. R. David Arkush, professor emeritus at the University of Iowa, deserves the deepest appreciation for his patient and consistent guidance and support throughout my graduate school years. Special thanks are due to Charles Hayford, an independent scholar and editor of the *Journal of American–East Asian Relations.* A paper on Chinese women's sports during the War of Resistance against Japan, which Dr. Hayford worked on with me in his seminar at the University of Iowa in 1999, serves as the prototype of the project. I enjoyed further talks with him about my manuscript in the ensuing years, and consider him my teacher and friend.

When I presented the seminar paper at the International Symposium on Sports and Culture in Iowa City in the summer of 1999, I benefited from the wisdom of Susan Brownell of the University of Missouri, who served on the same panel with me. The knowledge I gained from Linda Kerber, Steven Vlastos, and Catriona Parratt, all from the University of Iowa, about gender theory, Japanese history, and sports has been of great help. I was also inspired by my discussions with Poshek Fu of the University of Illinois and by the distinguished works of Dr. Brownell and of Andrew Morris of California Polytechnic State University. I would like to acknowledge in particular Dr. Morris's collegiality. He read my manuscript patiently and offered generous support and valuable comments in detail. Prasenjit Duara of the National University of Singapore read the introduction and offered great commentary. John Crespi of Colgate University shared research materials, read my manuscript, and offered insightful comments. Eric Allina of the University of Ottawa led me to the online journal *Linglong* at the C.V. Starr East Asian Library, Columbia University, which enriched this book. I wish to thank Dorothy Ko of Barnard College for sharing scholarly materials with me and offering constant guidance and support. My colleagues in the Department of History at Ryerson University offered their unstinting support and encouragement.

I benefited from the comments of colleagues at the 15th Berkshire Conference on the History of Women in 2011, the Annual Conferences of the Association of Asian Studies in 2007 and 2011, the International Workshop on Modern Sports in Asia at the National University of Singapore in 2010, the Critical China Study Group at the University of Toronto, the Annual Conference of the American Association of Chinese Studies in 2006, and the Mid-Atlantic Regional Conference of the Association of Asian Studies in 2005. I wish to thank Charley Leary of the National University of Singapore and Cho Younghan of Hankuk University of Foreign Studies in South Korea, as well as Wu Yiching of the University of Toronto, for inviting me to the above-mentioned workshop and study group, respectively. The editorial evaluations of Tina Chen of the University of Manitoba and the other anonymous reviewer for UBC Press greatly improved the book manuscript.

I also received significant help during my numerous research trips to China from Niu Dayong of the Department of History at Beijing University, Lu Aiyun of Shanghai Athletic University, and Dong Xiaoping of Beijing Normal University, all of whom deserve my deepest appreciation. Thanks to Professor Niu's great efforts to accommodate my husband, Graham Russell Gao Hodges of Colgate University, as a Fulbright scholar in his department, my family stayed in Beijing during the 2006-7 academic year. Dr. Niu introduced me to Dai Longji, head of the Beijing University Library, who provided me with tremendous support in navigating the library. My daily trip there resulted not only in more materials to enrich and reshape my dissertation into a publishable manuscript but also in discovery of the topic of my second book project: a Hawaiian-born Chinese American Hollywood actress, Soo Yong (Yang Xiu). During my two trips to Shanghai, in 2006 and 2008, Professor Lu, a former student of Zhang Huilan, the "mother of women's modern physical education" in China, convened a meeting with several of Zhang's colleagues and patiently sat down herself to answer my long list of questions about Zhang. She showed me the lab, office, and apartment that Zhang had used for decades. Most importantly, Professor Lu enabled my access to Zhang's papers in the university archives, which are not open to the public. She continued to provide valuable information about Zhang's legacy. Dr. Dong guided me through the bureaucratic procedures at Shanghai Library, Beijing National Library, Beijing Athletic University Library, and the Second National Archive of China in Nanjing during my initial research trip in the summer of 2001. Liu Tong, a former classmate of mine at Beijing University and an editor at the China Book Company (Zhonghua shuji), happened to be on the same train to Shanghai and arranged with her relatives in Nanjing to provide me with much-appreciated accommodations. My friend Pan

Huaqiong, another former classmate and now a professor at Beijing University, helped me obtain sources from various libraries in Beijing while I was in North America.

I also thank the staff at the following libraries and archival institutions. Val Lem of the Library of Ryerson University provided generous help. Zeng Biao at Jiangxi Gannan Normal College and Shu Xiaoqing of Fujian Normal University kindly shared their research on Communist *tiyu* (physical education, sports, and physical culture) with me. Zheng Yuangao, a sports reporter for *Jiefang ribao (Liberation Daily)* in Shanghai, first introduced me to a one-page biography of Zhang Huilan that he contributed to *Shanghai tiyu jingcui (The Essence of Tiyu in Shanghai)*. As I traced Zhang's life in the United States, the librarians at Columbia University, the Massachusetts Institute of Technology, the University of Iowa, Mills College, and the University of Wisconsin helped me locate precious sources. Professor David Arkush also deserves special credit for helping me locate Zhang's dissertation at the University of Iowa. During my visit to Nankai University in Tianjin in December 2004, Zhang Hongguang provided important information on the work and life of Zhang Huilan and another pioneer female tiyu professional, Du Lunyuan (Zhang Hongguang's maternal great-aunt), at Tianjin Hebei Women's Normal College. I am grateful to Li Lili for sending me her unpublished memoir, intended only for friends and family, and for introducing me to her granddaughter in the United States. I wish to thank Pan Jie, an actress and another granddaughter of Li, for meeting with me and discussing her grandmother's life and career. Xiao Zhiwei of California State University at San Marcos kindly sent me the Li entry in his encyclopedia. Hur-Li Lee of the University of Wisconsin at Milwaukee purchased for me scholarly materials available only in Taiwan and invited me to introduce Li to the Chinese communities in Milwaukee. Nadine Kam of the *Honolulu Star Bulletin* published an article based on her interview with me about Li Lili during my first visit to Hawaii in 2007.

This book has been published with the help of a grant from the Canadian Federation for the Humanities and Social Sciences, through the Awards to Scholarly Publications Program, using funds provided by the Social Sciences and Humanities Research Council of Canada. A research grant and two travel grants from the Faculty of Arts of Ryerson University enabled me to conduct research in China from 2006 to 2007 and to travel to Singapore in 2010 and Hawaii in 2011 to present chapters of this book with international scholars. A special project grant from the same faculty contributed to the final production of this book. An Aydelotte Dissertation Fellowship from the Department of History, Dissertation Research Fellowships from the Center for Asian and

Pacific Studies, and a T. Anne Cleary International Dissertation Research Fellowship from the Graduate College, all at the University of Iowa, financed my research and a portion of the writing of my dissertation. The Pre-doctoral Fellowship from the Fisher Center for the Study of Women and Men at Hobart and William Smith Colleges helped me finish my dissertation.

I would like to extend warm feelings of gratitude toward Emily Andrew, acquisitions editor at UBC Press, for her patient shepherding of this book. I am also grateful to Megan Brand for handling my numerous requests and to Francis Chow for his expert copyediting.

My parents and my siblings have always shown love and support. Twenty-five years ago, they took turns bicycling sixty miles back and forth to deliver weekly supplies to my boarding school in a remote mountain area in Inner Mongolia. For a decade, they wondered patiently when I would ever finish my graduate education and get a job. I regret that my father, Gao Zhen, missed the good news of my tenure by a few months and will never see this book, but his love for life and his family even during his final months continues to inspire me. The blessings he sent through my mother over the telephone during his last few days offers some comfort. He said, "As father and daughter, we have no regrets toward each other." I thank my mother, Du Xiuhua, siblings Gao Yunfeng (高云凤), Gao Yunlong (高云龙), Gao Yunfei (高云飞), and Gao Yunpeng (高云鹏), and my sister-in-law Yu Shuhua (于淑华) for taking up the difficult tasks of caring for my ailing father and laying him to rest during my absence.

I first met my future husband Graham Hodges (郝吉思) in the summer of 2001 in the rare book room of the Shanghai Library. He introduced me to Li Lili by showing me her picture from a journal article. As a great life and intellectual partner, he has remained interested and supportive throughout the development of this book. He has tirelessly acquired valuable scholarly materials on my behalf, read every draft carefully, and offered much valued commentary. His loving encouragement, patience, and devotion to our family give me confidence that I can always count on him, which I consider the highest compliment to a spouse. Our twin sons, Graham Zhen Gao-Hodges (高然墨) and Russell Du Gao-Hodges (高然诗), are my constant inspiration.

Sporting Gender

Introduction

The 2008 Beijing Summer Olympics helped the Chinese people eliminate the nation's historical image as the "sick man of Asia." China's bravura performance in the games – its male and female athletes won more gold medals than any other nation and placed second only to the United States in total medals won – epitomized the nation's recent dramatic rise to global power.[1]

This soaring trajectory began during the 1930s, the era of national crisis *(guonan)* stemming from the Japanese invasions and the internecine conflict between the Nationalist and Communist Parties.[2] For those living under Nationalist rule, athletic competition in this period culminated in the participation of Chinese male and female athletes in the 1936 Berlin Olympics. Their participation grew out of calls for greater civil equality for women following the 1911 Revolution. Aligning their aspirations with Chinese nationalism, women called for gender equality in work, family, sexuality, education, and suffrage. Female sports competitions resulted from ambitions for women's education and the nation's hopes for a healthier citizenry. As the influential Chinese writer Lin Yutang observed in 1935, team sports had the potential to create a civic consciousness that he found so lacking in Chinese society.[3]

The Chinese delegation to the Berlin Olympics arrived in the German capital on 23 July 1936. The seventy-nine athletes, thirty-three observers, and twenty-four staff members were exhausted after a twenty-five-day sea voyage replete with rigorous training exercises, meetings, lectures, German-language lessons, and occasional stops en route to give exhibition performances to Chinese expatriates. Cheng Tianfang, the Chinese ambassador to Germany, Dr. Ritter V. Hart, the German International Olympic Committee member, and Shen Siliang, the Chinese delegation leader, made welcoming speeches. Three hundred local Chinese chanting "Long live the Republic of China!" saluted the athletes as they marched smartly out of the Berlin train station decorated with the ubiquitous Nazi regalia. The Chinese wore the same apparel they had donned for their official photograph with Chiang Kai-shek (Jiang Jieshi) and his wife before leaving Shanghai. The team's uniforms were a synthesis of Western fashion and Chinese nationalism. The men wore light-coloured Western suits emblazoned with the character for China on the front. The women wore white *qipao*, a formal dress style in Republican China produced under the "national goods" campaign *(guohuo yundong)* (see Figure 1). The women's attire reflected a self-conscious modern departure from the weak and bound-foot stereotype of the past. The *qipao* signified women's burden of maintaining a national essence; at the same time, the colour white, normally donned for mourning in China, took on a modern significance, indicating professionalism and metropolitan fashion: in short, the female Olympians were the pride of China. Indeed, displaying an independent spirit and the best of China at the games was deemed more important than expectations about winning. The Nationalist government had received ample military and other industrial aid from Germany in recent years, but the Chinese disliked the Nazis' insistence on racial supremacy. If Chinese athletes fared well in Berlin, their achievements would refute German racial propaganda. Learning from others was another important goal of the trip. After the Olympics, the observer delegation went on a fact-finding tour of European countries, visiting Hungary, Czechoslovakia, Sweden, and Denmark before returning to Italy to begin their passage home. Zhang Huilan (Hwei Lan Chang), a prominent female professor, administrator in physical education, and key government consultant on sports, recalled that, except for the Nazi propaganda, German training methods impressed the delegation. China's National Amateur Athletic Federation (CNAAF) showed the 1936 Olympics documentary bequeathed by German Agfa company at universities in Shanghai, Nanjing, and Hangzhou in 1937.[4]

The sizable delegation was a major upgrade from the 1932 Olympics in Los Angeles, when sprinter Liu Changchun was the sole athlete representing the 400 million people of China, a fact that made observers gasp. An important

1 "China's representatives at the coming Olympic Games leave for Berlin." ▶

Top right: "The athletes posing with Generalissimo Chiang Kai-shek after listening to his send-off speech." "The Generalissimo speaking." "Visiting Dr. Sun's Mausoleum."

Top left: "The delegates go on board the Conti Verdi ... crowds that sent them off with 'good luck' on their lips."

Bottom from left to right: "The girl track star Li Sen and her well wishers at the wharf." "Men and women Chinese boxing stars who will give exhibition matches in Berlin" (the third from right is Lu Lihua). "Mayor Wu (Tiecheng) of Greater Shanghai and Yang Hu, commander of the Wusong garrisons among the send-off party" (Li Sen is in the centre, with the mayor and the general on her right side).

Source: Liangyou huabao 118 (July 1936): 16.

大軍啓行

·我國世運健兒征西出發·

CHINA'S REPRESENTATIVES AT THE COMING OLYMPIC GAMES LEAVE FOR BERLIN

之總理陵形赴話後蔣調於我世會赴京前。時員右之為話出京合園影陵全後之長雲選手園參顧發手運謁加。後謁體操情訓影蔣士長訓謁前動

The athletes posing with Generalissimo Chiang Kai-shek after listening to his send-off speech. Right: The Generalissimo Speaking. Below: visiting Dr. Sun's Mausoleum.

園神之際技諸別，紙樂隊在政北派上來月選全泰，高吾，園場君。依雄歡碼軍府樂歡樓，在德廿手體也併尚民推催選上1行依務諾送樂歌並，這碼是温船五於世。為精族勝傑突情飛隊競特省頭日第船出六運

The delegates go on board the Conti Verdi. Above photos show the crowds that sent them off with "good luck" on their lips.

森赴李同學及同

The girl track star, Lee Sen and her well wishers at the wharf.

希其女將雛敬士字路送及務女女

Men and women Chinese boxing stars who will give exhibition matches in Berlin.

之女世運一選術手之男園器

Mayor Wu of Greater Shanghai and Yang Fu, Commander of the Wusung garrisons among the send-off party.

司與物獻會市中送等虎長之人

表 代 女 五 國 我 之 林 柏 在

2   The five female Chinese Olympic athletes arrive at Berlin train station.
From left: Zhai Lianyuan, Yang Xiuqiong, Li Sen, Liu Yuhua, and Fu Shuyun.
Source: Yang Xiuqiong, *Yang Xiuqiong zizhuan* (Hong Kong: Xinhua chubanshe,
1938), 30.

feature of the 1936 delegation was the inclusion of women. Swimmer Yang
Xiuqiong and sprinter Li Sen competed for Olympic glory, and Zhai Lianyuan,
Fu Shuyun, and Liu Yuhua participated in a "national skills" (martial arts)
performance (see Figure 2).[5] The nine female observers, including Zhang
Huilan, represented the emergence of women administrators and intellectuals
in physical education and sports; they also had the task of keeping tabs on
their youthful female athletes during the tour.[6] None of the Olympians of
1936 would have imagined that hot and cold wars would keep any large-scale
delegation from mainland China out of the Summer Olympics until 1984.[7]

Unfortunately, the Chinese female athletes, like their male compatriots,
fared badly in Berlin and failed to win a single medal. Back home, journalists
lamented that the athletes had "wasted 200,000 yuan of state money on a
goose egg" that lost face for China internationally. Criticism centred on Li
Sen and Yang Xiuqiong.[8] Critics derided Yang, arguing that her best swimming results, which had thrilled the Chinese people in the run-up to the

Olympics, compared poorly with other world athletes, and that she should have recognized this and not ventured to Berlin.[9] A dissenting voice in *Linglong*, a major women's magazine, defended the female athletes, stating that "it is a fact that the men did not make progress, but the relative progress made by the women cannot be denied." After all, it had been only twenty years since women had unbound their feet and begun participating in sports. Women's presence at the Olympics meant the liberation of women and strengthening of the Chinese nation.[10]

Competing internationally just six years after the first women's competitions in China's National Games, the female Olympians may be viewed, as Fan Hong has argued, as symbols of women's emancipation in China. Fan usefully identifies female athletes as "sportswomen," a term I will use in this book. In contrast to Fan's argument about emancipation, Andrew D. Morris has contended that their saga was part of a complicated and contradictory narrative that was often overwhelmed by nationalist demands. Morris concludes that Chinese women found scant liberation in the male-dominated Chinese media and the nation's Western-influenced *tiyu* (which can be roughly translated to encompass physical education, sports, and physical culture) world. I agree with Morris that women's experiences in tiyu were often complicated, but find much more evidence of emancipation than he acknowledges. Yu Chien-ming's recent book tilts against the idea of the nation as a guiding force in women's physical education; rather, she argues, such new forces as popular culture, film and print media, and competitive sports shaped physical culture.[11]

Morris, Fan, and Yu provide valuable insights. Fan and Yu argue that Chinese women used sports to shape their bodies, adopted sportswear and other modern clothing, and permed their hair. They travelled freely, attended school, and at times became famous, all signifiers of modernity and a perceived emancipation. Morris argues, however, that there were complicating factors. Sportswomen had to negotiate their freedoms with men, some of whom were duplicitous and predatory. Women faced limits on their sporting careers and found employment only in teaching. Many of their gains, as Yu contends, lay within the cultural realm rather than in politics and economics. In this book, I connect and expand on these arguments by showing that sportswomen could emancipate themselves in a complicated national society and improve nation building through their athletic accomplishments and personal styles. Above all, Chinese sportswomen faced challenges and created new, personal solutions as they pushed into new gendered arenas. These challenges and their responses occurred within the pressure cooker of a national crisis caused by internal conflicts and external attack by Japan.

Using the valuable findings of Morris, Yu, and Fan, I contend that certain aspects of this rise are beyond debate. The rise of women's sports was essential to nation building, at the centre of which lay the definition of its citizenry, involving gender, education, religion, ethnicity, and other qualifiers. Education, including women's education in tiyu, often with religious underpinnings, was critical to this effort. Gender has been particularly significant in the construction of the Chinese citizenry. Women's liberation and physical improvement were seen as keys to regaining Chinese self-respect and status among the world's nations. Prasenjit Duara argues that when various Chinese nationalists identified immutable, timeless essences as sources of the nation's identity, they pointed to women as the embodiment of the eternal Chinese virtues of self-sacrifice and loyalty, thereby treating women as national exemplars. When a woman's body and spirit became sites on which to rest the unchanging essence and moral purity of the Chinese nation, female gender ideology became particularly critical in nation building.[12] As scholars and officials in China, as elsewhere in the world, cast women in modern China as the embodiment of "the essential truths of a nation or civilization," reform efforts focused on uplifting and cultivating strong and healthy female bodies to signal modernity, progress, and the "civilized" status of a strong Chinese nation. Sports became the vehicle for achieving these seemingly clashing perceptions and goals, which were particularly acute during the uncertainty and turmoil of national crisis.[13]

Communists and Nationalists promoted female athleticism to counteract the image of China as a weak nation and to bolster its ability to resist the Japanese. Presenting China to the world as a progressive nation with civilized culture through their publications in English, liberal intellectuals such as Lin Yutang and journalist Tang Liangli highlighted women's "emancipation" and "the feminist movement in China," as exemplified by "the manner in which girls have taken to athletics."[14] Women's sports were key parts of a sporting culture in which Chinese athletes and their government sponsors embraced Western sports and created elite competitions that always supported the goals of the state.[15] At the same time, the meaning of those goals was contested. Evolving gender ideologies served as keys to defining a certain "version" of a nation, while Communists, Nationalists, liberal male intellectuals, and urban literate women with feminist mindsets each had their own vision of a strong, modern nation. All agreed that women's emancipation and national needs went hand in hand.

In this book, I strive to highlight the lives and times of individual athletes and sports administrators. This enables me to add colour and contour to their stories and to demonstrate the complexity of their interactions with state and

society. Using biography is, according to Susan Mann, a natural and historically significant method for writing Chinese history. Since the late Qing period
and the May Fourth Movement, Chinese women who made central contributions to the nation and its culture replaced traditional, virtuous women as
models and icons. Looking at women's lives and accentuating their achievements can contribute to our understanding of modern China, as Wang Zheng
and Danke Li have demonstrated. My methodology benefits from Wang's fine
recovery of women's lives during the Chinese enlightenment. Whereas Wang
depends largely on oral histories, I concentrate on primary sources from the
era, including archival materials, newspaper and magazine accounts, and
contemporary biographies and autobiographies. This enables me to recon-
struct the histories of women and their sports from the perspective of their
time. Furthermore, I have the benefit of writings by the sportswomen themselves, in the form of memoirs and academic studies or through interviews.
By drawing their emotions and voices closer to the surface, the writings
penned by those leading sportswomen allow us to discover their agency in
the complex dynamic of sports, gender, and nation building in the context of
national crisis.[16]

Instead of using biography as a historical recovery that maximizes knowledge of the quotidian lives of these sportswomen, this book uses their
life stories as windows into aspects of social and political negotiations over
the meaning of sports, gender, and nation during China's national crisis. I
have chosen athletes from basketball, track and field, and swimming because
these sports exemplified the connections between individual aspirations and
the goals of the nation. The athletic events I discuss are stages on which the
sportswomen and others reveal themselves and their times. Female athletes,
writers, and actresses were the first group of modern Chinese women who
entered public discourses through their fame and celebrity. While there is
abundant scholarship focusing on individual writers and actresses, female
athletes have been somewhat neglected. Morris, Fan, and Yu have collectively
identified many sportswomen but without exploring their lives.

Like their peers in writing and acting, individual female athletes rose to
fame, enabled by modern mass media, both print and visual. Joan Judge notes
how modern newspapers contributed to the creation of a "new citizenry"
and ensured national survival during the late Qing period. Catherine Yeh has
indicated the coincidental emergence of entertainment journalism.[17] Print
journalism had political purposes during the national crisis, as the Nationalist
government managed to insert tiyu as an essential context for modern media
to propagandize and mobilize the masses. When the Ministry of Education
called for newspapers and news agencies to start and maintain tiyu news

columns, "the various parties responded warmly, and the newspapers carried tiyu news among their already crowded columns."[18]

Major national newspapers such as *Shenbao (Shanghai Daily), Dagong bao (Impartial [Takung] Daily,* both the Tianjin and Shanghai versions), *Shibao (Eastern Times), Yishi bao (Social Welfare),* and *New China Daily* all followed the trend. The National Tiyu Academy persuaded the monthly journal *Teaching and Learning (Jiao yu xue)* to carry a special tiyu issue. Cinema studios were encouraged to make films on tiyu and national survival. Radio stations periodically broadcast tiyu common knowledge *(changshi)* and news. The Central Radio Station held a tiyu program on Saturdays. Chinese audiences of various radio stations fully enjoyed their lively reports of the 1936 Olympics.[19]

Leo Ou-Fan Lee describes how periodicals and cinema contributed to popular modernity beyond the scope of the nation-state. Morris notes how the emergence of tiyu in the press and mainstream periodicals provided "a means for modern sports fans to finally get to 'know' their dashing and distant athletic idols."[20] Frequently their athletic achievements, anecdotes of their private lives, and images of various poses circulated in serious national newspapers, tiyu periodicals, and various popular magazines and journals. With the image of female athletes offering inspiration and commercial attractions to the readers, even the semi-official and academically oriented *Qinfen tiyu yuebao (Diligent Tiyu Monthly),* the flagship journal of the dominant tiyu publishing house Qinfen shuju (Diligent Publishing House), used female athletes as cover girls. The popularity of such pictorials as *Liangyou huabao (Young Companion Pictorial)* and *Beiyang huabao (Peiyang [North Ocean] Pictorial News)* along with the growth of literacy among women in the Republican era accompanied the rise of female athletic stars.[21] When their images were printed next to those of famous actresses and their stories became intertwined in mass media, female athletes gained celebrity status and became household names. Their audiences included officials, other athletes, and male and female petty urbanites *(xiaoshimin),* who toiled in government offices, stores, and companies and studied at universities.[22]

As noted, by focusing on the experiences of famous female tiyu figures, I strive in this book to show the effect of sports on officials, athletes, and performers as well as on their audiences. Using varying perspectives, I demonstrate the broad influence of tiyu on Chinese culture. The impact of sports went beyond the media and athletic competitions themselves. Using newspapers, magazines, and biographical sources, I reveal the charged emotions of the spectators, the excitement of the athletes, and the contradictory impulses of government figures who applauded the female athletes while plotting to make them their concubines.

My approach to the political and institutional quality of women's tiyu in this era differs from that of Fan. While she sees women's emancipation as part of the struggle concluding in the 1949 Communist revolution, I concentrate, using the example of Zhang Huilan, on the creation of a women's sporting politics within the Nationalist government. Zhang's saga illustrates the rise of female sports administrators. Showing the connections between sports and politics does not mean that I eschew recent social histories of women in modern China. Rather, I strive to show how sports, politics, and social experiences intermingled.[23]

My work combines recent scholarly examinations of the quotidian aspects of modernity with the arrival of the Modern Girl. As Madeleine Yue Dong and others have shown, everyday activities such as the search for food and water, or popular attitudes about women's roles, highlight the process of modernity.[24] Sports events and heroines quickly became part of the routine quality of life, even as athletes rapidly broke each other's event records and as their fame rose and fell (Chapter 4). Chinese audiences admired their female sports stars as popular magazines mediated their reputations, and these stars' performances had an uncanny impact on their audiences. Visions of beautiful young women scantily dressed in sports uniforms dazzled male spectators and impressed female fans. The latter's enthusiasm blended into the arrival of the Modern Girl.[25]

The Modern Girl has fascinated scholars around the globe. Scholars of the Chinese version, called *modeng xiaojie/nülang,* have shown how ordinary women, influenced by cinematic images of film stars and advertising of personal products, embraced cosmetics, Western dress, and media interests. The editors of the recent anthology *The Modern Girl around the World: Consumption, Modernity and Globalization* have referred to the Modern Girl as a heuristic device that allows discovery of new arguments through fresh research. This book contributes to the ongoing discussion of the global flow of the dynamics between Modern Girl and New Woman. Perceptions of the Modern Girl in China were complicated by politics and social demands. Scholars have emphasized the radical culture of the Modern Girl, emergence of female-oriented literature and film, and the conservative retrenchment of the New Life Movement. In China the Modern Girl, which was powerfully attractive to the Chinese masses, especially young women, threatened, yet at the same time became integrated into, the aspirations of the nationalist movement. Leftist critics disparaged her. As I will show in this book, there was significant blurring of the boundaries between the Modern Girl and the New Woman. In part this was because Nationalists needed to find examples of modern women whose personae would uphold their views without discouraging young Chinese females. Leftists sought to rescue modernity from the shallow, commercialized "girl" of the early 1930s. Such attitudes affected the presentation and reception of sportswomen, even as the latter breached the boundaries between the naughty Modern Girl and the virtuous New Woman through their desires and agencies.[26]

Although it is recognized that physical education played an important role in the strengthening of female citizens and of the nation itself, none of the recent studies of the Modern Girl and the New Woman has highlighted the importance of sports to the emergence of the modern Chinese woman or to the creation of a healthy, vigorous body type to replace the sickly women of the "Mandarin Ducks and Butterflies School." This book will demonstrate the critical importance of the healthy, vigorous *(jianmei)* female body to the development of the nation.[27]

Numerous scholars have seized on the image of the Modern Girl as representing new, individual freedom to choose one's appearance and to be in step with modernizing feminism around the world. As the editors of *The Modern Girl around the World* explain, the term "girl" denoted "young women with the wherewithal and desire to define themselves in excess of conventional female roles and as transgressive of national, imperial, and racial boundaries." Scholars of China's *modeng xiaoje/nülang* may find that description too broad, but there is no doubt that the Modern Girl was politically and socially significant during the national crisis.[28]

Concomitant with my examination of the emergence of sports is an investigation of the meaning and effect of stardom and celebrity in China. There are no extant studies of fame among Chinese women in this era. Surely the athletes described in this book were products of what Leo Braudy called the "democratization of fame." They benefited from the creation of a fan culture within the burgeoning print and cinema industry in 1930s China. Athletes and film stars were often worshipped in common. In this book, I discuss how young female athletes handled their sudden, fleeting national notoriety in the 1930s.[29]

Talented, athletic women and female intellectuals were key figures in the emancipation of women in modern China. The Nationalist Party legalized such emancipation in the Civil Code of 1930, which gave women the right to choose their own husbands and equal rights of divorce. Women could be heads of households and, with certain restrictions, perform the same kinds of work and be paid the same wages as men. Overall, the law was a compromise between tradition and modernity, but it did affect self-supporting, independent women and inspired countless others to seek greater freedom.[30]

Under Chiang Kai-shek, however, the Nationalists were concerned that female freedoms ranged too far and constructed the New Woman as a key part of the New Life Movement. This gendered construct, as Sarah E. Stevens has argued, was meant to "symbolize the vision of a future strong nation [whose] character highlights the revolutionary qualities of the modern woman." The New Woman was strongly nationalistic and educated, and pursued love on the basis of free choice and social improvement rather than personal fulfillment or sexuality. As Hsiao-Pei Yen has noted, Chinese women recognized the conservative nature of the New Life Movement and strove to play an active role in moderating government attempts to control them.[31] In resisting government restriction of their freedom and pushing for freedom through athletics and personal style, sportswomen were feminists.

Much of the controversy surrounding the Modern Girl and the New Woman concerned fashion. I show in this book how tiyu entered the fields of fashion and mass media. These interstices are most apparent in China's burgeoning popular culture of magazines and films. Such periodicals and motion pictures encouraged viewers to follow the examples of female athletes by embracing tiyu to strengthen their bodies in preparation for war and national survival, while simultaneously promoting modern glamour. When women's tiyu was subtly transformed from a nationalist project to fashion, women were able to articulate their hopes through writing, clothing, and athletic achievement. Feminist attitudes often appeared in the women's weekly *Linglong*, which declared itself "the mouthpiece of women's circles, and the only weapon to launch attacks on men," and which steadily covered fashions, cinema, and sports for women. Such attitudes were not uncontested. Even *Linglong*, as will be seen in Chapter 2, had to compromise and redefine its purposes.

Understanding how tiyu and fashion mixed adds to the current debate over the Modern Girl and the New Woman. Most accounts rely on literary/ cinematic characters or on spotlighting single moments of otherwise anonymous women.[32] The characters I examine in this book were briefly famous as athletes, competing in a world that evokes ardent but fleeting enthusiasm. Athletes rarely address their personal lives in autobiographies, preferring to dwell on their achievements. Still, as historical sources autobiographies can be witnesses to an era. Materials on sportswomen abound in the sports, cultural, and news journalism of the crisis era. Sports journalism is a genre that records athletic feats but rarely provides insights into the performers. Newspaper accounts tend to highlight individual feats and scores while paying little attention to the individual's personality. I use photographs to illustrate athletic garb and non-sports clothing. Such images add to the dynamic emotions people feel about athletic achievement and, with words from government sources and journalism, can create national sensibilities about these female athletes.

Since fashion and glamour were linked to modern concepts of sexuality, the athletes' sexualities and family aspirations were often played out in the public media. Competing discourses of sexuality are keys to a narrative that created unexpected traps for young women. In imperial China, courtesans gained significant notoriety as "public women." A substantial literature developed around their lives and loves.[33] With such a legacy, it is not surprising that the sexuality of famous actresses and female writers and athletes who attained the status of national celebrities in Republican China underwent strict scrutiny and at times drew unwanted attention. Athletic careers require expansive, highly public displays of the human form, in addition to ubiquitous images in popular media. This phenomenon has received insufficient attention. Fan Hong has commented on how media popularity transformed sportswomen into "sports queens," into icons of desirable sexuality.[34] I go beyond Fan's valuable insights to broaden our understanding of such complex sexual dynamics as homosexuality, cross-dressing, forced concubinage, and state-sponsored moral purity, which characterized the new femininity as educated, healthy, prosperous women, by examining closely the apposite experiences of athletic administrators and the female athletes, whose hard, gleaming bodies so affected their audiences.

Some discussion of the origins and meaning of the term *tiyu* is necessary. As elsewhere, the rise of spectator and participant sports was associated with state formation and modernity. Earlier studies of Chinese sports have emphasized the massive impact of Western sports on Chinese society. Leaving aside the fact that such Western sports as basketball, baseball, and track had only recently emerged from earlier pre-industrial pastimes, I argue that sports in China (tiyu) has a strong Chinese component as well – and that at most, sports are a form of mediation between the Chinese people and the West. Scholars have interpreted *tiyu* in a variety of ways. Brownell and Morris puzzle over its meaning and an accurate English translation, since its meaning is too broad to be translated into "sports," "athletics," "physical education," or "physical fitness." After deliberation, Brownell uses "body culture" and Morris applies the term "physical culture" (a literal translation of the German term *Körperkultur*).[35] I find much value in the term "physical culture" and want to extend its use into fashion, film, government, and sexuality. I differ, however, with Brownell and Morris's understandings of tiyu as part of the Western-dominant linear narrative. Brownell suggests that "in Mandarin, the word *tiyu* came into use as a label for the new methods of physical education that Japan and the West brought to China in the late nineteenth century." Although she suggests that there was a genealogy by which the modern word *"tiyu"* came into existence, Brownell attributes it exclusively to Western- and Japanese-introduced events.[36]

Prasenjit Duara has informed my understanding of tiyu. According to Duara, when the linear representation of time and history underlying Western civilization (which replaces God with the nation as a united actor moving forward in time and "conquering uncharted territories") becomes hegemonic, "conceptions of time become tied to structures of power." Alternatively, Chinese civilization created its own representation of time by resorting to traditional history, which referred to "an earlier presumed existent ideal, or to a transcendent time of God" as "known certainty" in a cyclical structure. In so doing, Chinese nationalists and intellectuals created a timeless essence – in this case, womanhood – that became crucial in the construction of national identity and China's sovereignty over its own history.[37]

Tiyu involves not only Western sports and physical education but also ancient and folk forms of Chinese physical activities (such as martial arts, strategic chess, *qigong*, mountain climbing, boating), and military activities.[38] Tiyu gained a fixed meaning during the national crisis and became a firm pillar of nationalist goals. Events and movements affected concepts of tiyu. Since the late nineteenth century, the Chinese term for sport kept shifting – from *ticao*, to *yundong*, to *duanlian*, and so on, and eventually to *tiyu*. Japanese aggression added key dimensions; until then, the urban literate Chinese public had no definite opinion of tiyu. A key force of Western society, the Young Men's Christian Association (YMCA), introduced the unifying concept of "muscular Christianity," which linked the spiritual well-being of the individual with the national good. The Nationalist government's leaders and Nationalist intellectuals eventually indigenized the missionary-introduced "sports" curriculum into an official state agent for building discipline and stimulating the latent potential of the bodies of Chinese citizens as workers and soldiers during the crisis of war. Before the national crisis, although the curriculum of women's tiyu was relatively complete, emphasis was exclusively on health-oriented exercise and performance rather than on competitive games.[39] This intense moment in China's history promoted the growth of competitive sports for women, an arena from which athletic stars emerged.

Why does the national crisis serve as a proper context? From the Mukden Incident in 1931 until the close of the Second World War, the term "national crisis" and the sense of impending war penetrated official documents, intellectual speech and writings, newspapers, and magazines. As Hung Chang-tai notes, "war is not just about force and deconstruction; it is also about commitment, expectation, and construction."[40] An atmosphere of wartime tension dominated the development of tiyu as a means of acquiring national strength and reshaping gender order. The crisis required reinforcement and mobilization of human resources for war preparation domestically. The crisis of war intensified the efforts of Nationalists, Communists, and liberal intellectuals to strengthen the citizenry's bodies through tiyu and to build a strong, militant nation. As liberating and modernizing women had been central tenets of the Chinese national state since the revolution against the Qing Dynasty in 1911, creating a healthy, vigorous female citizenry augmented national goals and built confidence for the wartime efforts against the Japanese. Both the Nationalists and the Communists firmly desired a fit Chinese womanhood.[41]

The context of war is useful in decoding the dynamics involved in women's tiyu in the 1930s. I will concentrate on the period between 1931 and 1937, when elite athletic competitions were at their peak in China. The Mukden Incident is a reasonable starting point for the study of wartime culture and policies in Republican China, although to recover women's lives and careers, I make frequent references to slightly earlier times. At the other end, the Marco Polo Bridge Incident of 7 July 1937, in which the Japanese army attacked Wanping, a town near Beiping (the name for Beijing from 1927 to 1949), led to full-scale war between China and Japan. The subsequent loss of Shanghai, other big cities, and the major railroads plunged the entire nation into extreme distress. Along with so much else, women's tiyu came to a halt. Transportation restrictions caused the breakup of existing associations, and the periodic National Games were suspended. After 1937, a few games were organized among locals and students who migrated to Chongqing, Kunming, and Guizhou.[42] This book therefore highlights the 1930s, the "golden time" of women's sports in Republican China. The Second World War interrupted international sports competitions and affected Chinese women's tiyu, but again the need to examine life cycles will push my use of evidence beyond that point.

I want to be precise about what I mean by China during this period. During the national crisis, Republican China was both in formation and contested. The Nationalist Nanjing government consolidated its control of the east coast in 1927, but sizable if shifting regions in the interior remained under Communist control. Japanese imperialism in 1931 carved out a new puppet state, called Manchukuo, in the northeast. Most studies of China in this period focus on Shanghai and, to a lesser extent, Beiping and on Nanjing, the Nationalist capital. In this study, I extend my discussion of the influence of sports and nation building from Shanghai and Beiping to the Northeast

(Manchuria), to Hong Kong and Guangzhou (Canton) in the south, and to Chongqing and other cities in the west. I do so because athletes from these regions competed in national and international games, where they represented the Chinese state and its culture. I emphasize the areas primarily under Nationalist control because the modernizing influences of sports on women were far more visible in the regions that the Nationalist government directly controlled. Nationalism did not mean the same thing to all. China's citizenry all shared such goals as creating a stronger and healthier nation and repelling the Japanese invaders. The sportswomen discussed in this book often had their own versions of nationalism, one that demanded a stronger female public presence and recognition.[43]

No single approach can bring all these themes together, nor can a single method apply equally to the lives and social developments I describe and analyze in this book. At the same time, I have striven to address the common themes of the meaning of sports accomplishments, state control, media influence, fashion, and changes in gender and personal fates in each chapter. Accordingly, in Chapter 1, I spend much time examining the life and career of Zhang Huilan, a tiyu intellectual and educator. Zhang's example tells us much about the construction of tiyu culture and politics in women's colleges and about the interaction between Western missionaries and intellectuals and Chinese sportswomen. I then show how Zhang's intellectual work affected government and private sponsorship of competitive athletics. I compare her personal style with that of the Modern Girl.

The decade of the 1930s was a period when government policy meshed with popular enthusiasm for bodily fitness. Emphasis on personal health and hygiene supported the resistance against the Japanese and promoted a new vision of a fit Chinese citizenry in place of the unwanted image of a sickly nation. Chapter 2 is the least biographical chapter in the book. It looks at the rise of jianmei (robust/healthy beauty) as a force through examination of popular print press and demonstrates how Chinese women generally adopted an athletic style. The next few chapters are about sportswomen and their sports. Chapter 3 illustrates the rise of women's basketball during the national crisis by focusing on the basketball team of the Private Liangjiang Women's Tiyu Normal School (Sili liangjiang nüzi tiyu shifan zhuanke xuexiao), which was the signature project of the Shanghai physical educator and entrepreneur Lu Lihua. I look at how Lu realized her great ambitions for her team's athletic success. She often measured this by their prominence in international competition. I also examine the choices the players made about careers after college and how they constructed their identities as women in response to media pressure. Lu's players benefited by playing for an academic institution rather than seeking fame individually. I also study the gendering of basketball rules. Chapter 4 covers the lives and careers of track and field stars such as Li Sen and pioneers such as the "Harbin Four" and Qian Xingsu, who became "national heroines" in the early 1930s. I look at how athletic success brought them sudden fame, study the difficulties they experienced in maintaining their notoriety and athletic careers, and show how the Nationalist government used their examples to bolster its war effort. I also show how they faced key life decisions on love, marriage, and career based on their athletic identity. Chapter 5 illuminates the career of Yang Xiuqiong, the champion swimmer whose exploits captured the hearts and imagination of the Chinese people. While focusing on Yang's career, I trace the rise of swimming as a popular sport and examine the significance of Chinese female swimmers as performers and objects of adoration, and of their unique position as healthy and sensual women approved by the New Life Movement. This chapter analyzes the meaning of female competitive swimming and accompanying fame during a period in Chinese history when fitness and athletic prowess became intertwined with national political goals and individual ambition. Chapter 6 focuses on how the movie actress Li Lili's "athletic movie star" image served as a site where ideological values and political systems constructed and contested notions of nation and state during the national crisis. A concluding chapter considers the influence of these sportswomen on the later history of China.

1 Zhang Huilan (1898-1996): The "Mother of Women's Modern Physical Education"

In 1987, UNESCO awarded a medal of honour to Zhang Huilan (Hwei Lan Chang), the "mother of women's modern physical education" in China, for her service to world physical education (see Figure 3).[1] Zhang successfully carved out a career as a female tiyu professional in a world dominated by men, and survived momentous periods in Chinese history. She made the difficult transition from being a leading tiyu expert in Republican China to occupying an even more prominent position in the People's Republic.[2] As the first Chinese woman to earn a doctorate in physical education, from the University of Iowa (then known as the State University of Iowa) in 1944, Zhang was one of only a few women to serve in privileged administrative positions in both the private and public sectors of Chinese higher education and to be involved in central government missions (see Figure 4). Her story spans much of China's modern history, but her experience in Nationalist China is representative of the highly educated, socially conscious, newly emerging female tiyu professionals who strove to reform the Chinese citizenry during the national crisis.

Zhang's life and career during the national crisis developed through her trans-Pacific activities, which included serving in Chinese higher education and government and receiving advanced degrees and working in public health in the United States. Her case provides an international context to the gendered power dynamics in wartime trans-Pacific tiyu and public health. She worked closely with the leading global male figures in physical education (PE), public health, and social reforms, but within the male-dominated tiyu profession the status of female professionals underwent contradictory twists. At a time when China lacked the administrative organization of women's sports found in the United States and Europe, Zhang became the Chinese prototype of a professional woman who gained limited authority within the patriarchal political and professional administrations through state sponsorship and foreign education and assistance. She pushed beyond those limits. As a single woman who formed adult households with her former female

3   Shanghai Athletic University celebrates Zhang Huilan for receiving a medal of honour from UNESCO on 30 June 1987. Zhang is third from the right in the front row.
Source: Archives of Shanghai Athletic University

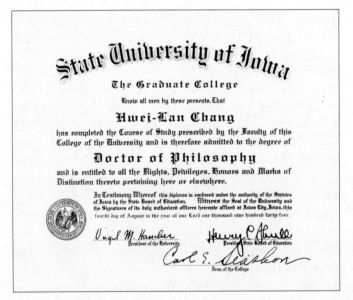

4   Zhang Huilan's Doctor of Philosophy diploma in Physical Education from the University of Iowa.
Source: Archives of Shanghai Athletic University.

students and colleagues, Zhang relied on female networks and flexible use of the patronage of male authority figures to sustain her career. She focused on legitimizing women's participation in competitive sports and promoting their presence in PE and public health through a combination of "scientific" data, domestically based maternal authority, and equal-rights rhetoric. Although militarism dominated in the wartime environment, Zhang aimed to instill a democratic ideology that could transform Chinese women's bodies from sickly to healthy. For her, as with other women in her field, tiyu became a means both of self-realization and of making a personal contribution to national salvation.[3]

Transnational Experiences around the National Crisis

Zhang Huilan was born into a teacher's family in Nanjing in 1898. Family tragedy scarred her early life. Her father, Zhang Chengze, died when she was young. A brother became an engineer and then died in early adulthood. Her mother, Zhang Bimin, sustained the family by working as a domestic for Presbyterian churches (see Figure 5).[4] Thanks to her family's association with the Western missionaries, Zhang was among the few girls attending school at the end of the Qing dynasty. After primary school, Zhang studied at a succession of YWCA missionary schools. YMCA/YWCA missionaries used an evangelical, muscular Christianity in an attempt to help China cure its weakness. The Y created community service organizations, including anti-opium and mass education movements, recreational activities, and public health campaigns, and also operated dormitories. Zhang's schools were part of this movement. From 1910 to 1916, she attended Friends High School in Nanjing. She credited her instructors there with teaching her kindness and generosity toward her students. She remained a member of Friends Church until 1949.[5] From 1916 to 1919, Zhang studied at Shanghai YWCA Tiyu Normal School (Shanghai Zhonghua Jidujiao Nüqingnianhui Quanguo Xiehui tiyu shifan xuexiao, abbreviated as "Nüqingnianhui tiyu shifan"), which had been established in August 1915. There she took classes in anatomy, physiology, biology, game theory, Chinese, and religion; learned to play basketball, tennis, softball, and cricket; engaged in track and field, martial arts, and gymnastics; and enjoyed European and American folk dancing. Professors from the Department of Law at Dongwu University (Dongwu daxue) and practising physicians taught her psychology and physiology. She interned at Xunguang Elementary School at North Sichuan Road, where she observed the development of children's tiyu under the tutelage of Chen Yingmei, vice president of the Shanghai YWCA Tiyu Normal School and China's first university-educated female physical educator. Chen was Zhang's principal

5   Zhang Huilan with her mother and niece.
Source: Archives of Shanghai Athletic University.

instructor. Zhang's studies, especially the emphasis on women's participation in competitive games, reflect the advances of liberal pedagogy since the 1911 Revolution and its much greater involvement in sports than previous scholars have argued. They also indicate early influences on the study of sports and scientific analysis that would reappear in Zhang's own work.[6]

After graduating from the Shanghai YWCA Tiyu Normal School, Zhang received a scholarship from Mills College in Oakland, California, and enrolled in its PE Department in August 1920. In 1921, she transferred to the PE Department at the University of Wisconsin at Madison, where she studied until 1923. She then returned to China but went back to Madison in 1925-26 to complete a Bachelor of Science degree, supported by a scholarship from the National Committee of the YWCA, New York.[7]

Zhang received financial assistance from missionary groups and possibly the American Boxer Redemption Program, a widely used scholarship for Chinese students. She was part of the new wave of Chinese female students journeying to the United States. Influenced by the May Fourth and New Cultural Movements and by American missionaries and feminism in the United States, such students were more iconoclastic, strove to break down gender barriers to professional employment, and justified their career aspirations on grounds of individual fulfillment, economic independence, and women's rights. They observed American women demanding suffrage, taking greater roles in public life, and working in professions previously reserved for men. Zhang's generation of Chinese students found liberation in choosing career over marriage; many never married. They were intensely nationalist and saw service to the nation as the meaning of life, despite nationalist tendencies to subordinate women's hopes to general goals.[8]

Whether Zhang chose to go the United States or American missionaries chose Mills and then Wisconsin for her, her destinations indicate a turning away from Japan as the preferred location for educating young Chinese women abroad. Zhang displayed considerable independence. At the beginning of the twentieth century, Chinese women studying in Japan generally accompanied fathers, husbands, or brothers. Later, poorer women funded by missionary groups became the typical Chinese female student in that country. Such women began their trip with little experience of coeducation but soon became integrated into mixed-gender settings. They did not reject men but sought them as allies and generally lived in essentially domestic female roles. Zhang Huilan, in contrast, lived alone until she found a female life-partner.[9]

After her initial studies in the United States, Zhang returned to Shanghai YWCA Tiyu Normal School to teach anatomy and folk dance.[10] For financial reasons, the school had merged in September 1924 with the PE Department of Ginling Women's College (Jinling nüzi wenli xueyuan), a comprehensive university founded in 1913 by the eight American women's-mission boards, including the Disciples, Episcopalians, Baptists, Methodists, and Presbyterians (North and South). In addition to the ubiquitous influence of the YWCA,

Ginling was the product of the Social Gospel and Student Volunteer Movements in the United States, which recruited many American female college graduates who felt stymied at home by offering them career tracks in China. Missionary schools in China rapidly became elite institutions. Joining a faculty composed of female scholars from China and the United States, many with doctorates from prestigious institutions, Zhang could observe and be influenced by the education and drive of such women. Female Protestant schools were renowned for instilling in Chinese girls a powerful ideology of service to the nation as well as the church. By combining educational and career networks for women, these schools taught girls that their future lay beyond the domestic sphere. Such lessons helped make real the notion of independent roles for women in occupations in service to the nation. Paradoxically, it matched the arguments of male physical education theorists who called for a separate women's tiyu and thereby divided physical education by sex based on national needs. At the same time, such separation amplified the influence, although not exclusively, of female intellectuals on Zhang's development.[11]

When Ginling Women's College initiated its four-year PE program in 1925, the program was originally designed to help students maintain and improve their health. Emily Case of Ginling and Norah Jervis, formerly of the Shanghai YWCA Tiyu Normal School, both Wellesley-trained PE majors, became leaders of the department. Basing much of their curriculum on the YWCA approach, the pair included biology, chemistry, Chinese, English, history, hygiene, music, ball games, gymnastics, and dance. Such courses were designed to foster greater physical activity among the students within a strong academic atmosphere, qualities the American faculty considered lacking in their Chinese students. Case and Jervis's control over the curriculum was brief, however.[12] Encouraged by the nationalist fervor inspired by the Northern Expedition led by Chiang Kai-shek in 1927, Chinese scholars took control over Christian schools across China. Despite misgivings among American missionaries, Dr. Wu Yifang replaced Mrs. Lawrence Thurston to become the first Chinese president of Ginling. Zhang replaced Case and became the first Chinese chair of the PE Department.[13] Wu's elevation and Zhang's promotion were important indicators of rising nationalism among Chinese women.

In a ceremony that masked the bitterness the American missionaries felt over their expulsion from power, Ginling honoured Thurston's contributions and celebrated Wu's inauguration on 3 November 1928. Principal speakers included Dr. W.S. New of St. John's University in Shanghai, Thurston herself, and the newlywed Madame Chiang Kai-shek (Song Meiling). After officially handing over the Seals of Office to Wu, Thurston offered a glowing affirmation of the transnational efforts of the school: "There is neither East or West ... when two strong men stand face to face, though they come from the ends of the earth." New's Orientalist response praised the accomplishments of Thurston in constructing Chinese womanhood: "You have built these mansions in the wilderness, so you have built up the mighty fortress of Christian character in the womanhood of China." Madame Chiang expounded on this theme by speaking of the responsibility that "education laid upon Chinese women. And the necessity of bearing that responsibility fully, if they would serve the nationalist cause in China and the cause of women throughout the world."[14] Speaking at the leading women's university in China, Madame Chiang's words affirmed the importance of women's education, nation building, and transnational exchanges. Their proximity at this event suggests that Zhang and Madame Chiang met. At the very least, the First Lady's words must have bolstered the professor's aspirations.

Wu and Zhang's accession to power occurred as the Nationalist government increased its emphasis on the importance of female athletes. In 1927, the government established a Ministry of Education (MOE), the first such official national body assigned to supervise tiyu. It held a national conference in 1928 to set the direction of tiyu instructions, which encouraged both sexes to become involved in tiyu activities in order to stimulate service to the nation. In April 1929, the government passed the Tiyu Law for Citizens (Guomin tiyu fa), which was revised and renewed in 1931 following the Mukden Incident. The law stated that "regardless of gender or age, the citizens of Republican China are obligated to receive proper tiyu training based on the results of a physical examination." It made women's participation in tiyu activities a legal requirement in the national interest. In addition, the law mandated athletic societies in every county and construction of public tiyu stadiums in every town, city, and region, a clause that naturally led to elite sports competitions. It required "scientific tiyu methods" to be applied in all sports activities and instruction.[15] Because much of this activity took place in schools, where the scientific method was paramount, Zhang Huilan's skills became all the more important. Xiaoping Cong reveals that PE courses ranked second only to Chinese-language curriculum in teachers' schools across the nation. Prospective teachers were required to take PE courses every term during their years of study.[16]

Zhang next took her talents to a larger venue. From 1928 to 1934, she was the only major female professor at the PE Department of the prestigious

National Central University in Nanjing, one of the two leading comprehensive universities in the country (the other was Beijing University), while continuing to teach at Ginling until 1930. Her American education and her national reputation in China won her a prominent position in the male-dominated elite university. Her monthly salary is an important yardstick of her value to the school. Since Chinese universities did not award tenure at that time, faculty members anxiously awaited the terms of their annual letters of reappointment. One of the very few female faculty members, Zhang was also among the highest-paid professors at the university, with a monthly salary of 260 yuan for a standard load of nine to twelve teaching hours each week. Her colleagues in the Faculty of Education included the famous painters Xu Beihong (1895-1953) and Pan Yuliang (1899-1977), the legendary prostitute-turned-artist who was trained in Paris, and musician Ma Sicong (1912-87) in the Department of Arts. Zhang was paid less than PE Department chair Wu Yunrui, who received 340 yuan, and Xu, who received 320 yuan; however, she was paid more than Pan and Ma, both of whom received 220 yuan, and other members of the PE Department, whose monthly salaries ranged from 40 to 190 yuan.[17]

As Zhang consolidated her position, she expanded her network by placing her students at tiyu schools around China. One such protégé was Du Longyuan (1897-ca. 1969). Du had studied with Zhang at the Shanghai YWCA Tiyu Normal School and Ginling Women's College, from which she graduated in 1931.[18] With Zhang's help, she started the PE Department at Hebei Tianjin Women's Normal School (Hebei Tianjin nüzi shifan xueyuan) in 1931 to expand women's tiyu beyond the two major metropolises of Beiping and Shanghai and to alleviate the "lack of tiyu leaders in North China." Du convinced Ginling Women's College and National Central University to loan Zhang for a semester to advise on structuring the curriculum. The two scholars devised a new pedagogy that included Chinese language, dance, music, art, English, general tiyu theory, tiyu history, physiology, and sports science, which combined the theories and practice of track and field, ball games, and martial arts. Hebei Tianjin Women's Normal School possessed good tiyu facilities; indeed, they were better than National Central's. By 1933, the school had built a gymnasium with a gallery for spectators, and later added a swimming pool (then a rarity in China), a small gym, a baseball field, tennis courts, and two more basketball courts. The school had exalted nationalist goals of instilling in its students "balanced development of physical, mental, and moral skills." It urged teachers to instruct on "morality, intelligence, and physique simultaneously, in order to develop generous and kind tiyu teachers and encourage talented tiyu cadres in society." Zhang's tenure at Hebei extended longer than initially planned. She worked there from 1934 to 1937, teaching anatomy and kinesiology. On her arrival, Du graciously ceded the position of department chair to her former teacher.[19]

Now that she was working at a research university, Zhang's reputation grew. She became a "significant figure" in tiyu circles, during the national crisis, as articles featuring her life and career appeared in popular tiyu periodicals such as *Qinfen tiyu yuebao (Diligent Tiyu Monthly)* and *Tiyu zhoubao (Tiyu Weekly)*.[20] Along with her prestigious teaching positions in higher education, her regular service in the tiyu committees of the Ministry of Education and her academic publications contributed to her rising profile. When the Nationalist government moved to centralize and standardize tiyu education, the MOE held the first national conference on tiyu in September 1932. Zhang served on its Research Committee for the Methods and Standards of Tiyu Examinations. While taking time out to visit the tomb of Sun Yat-sen, the committee drafted standards for tiyu schools across the country and urged investigation of whether or not the tiyu curriculum standards were being enforced equally at various levels of private and public schools. The committee authorized specialists to inspect school budgets, curricula, faculty and their salaries, and the lives of students.[21] Although Zhang and her fellow committee members set standards for a booming industry in tiyu education triggered by the Tiyu Law for Citizens, they regarded many of the new vocational tiyu schools as opportunistic and profiteering. The following year, the committee passed a proposal to set up a summer tiyu school directly under the ministry's supervision by 1934, in order to develop more tiyu leaders. The committee argued that the national tiyu authorities had paid insufficient attention to the new schools and that the latter's methods would harm the cause of Chinese tiyu and the ambitions of young men and women.[22]

Zhang also lent her reputation to competitive sports by serving on the boards of national and local games. In 1934, along with Qu Zhisheng and Zhao Wenzhao, she represented Hebei Province at the annual meeting of the North China Amateur Athletic Federation. They were informed that the China's National Amateur Athletic Federation (CNAAF) had decided in 1933 that athletes originally from Manchuria were allowed to represent the five Manchurian provinces and attend various domestic games, regardless of their current schools and locations. The North China federation accepted the Manchuria Amateur Athletic Federation's proposal to ensure that the territory that had been lost to the Japanese was not forgotten, a move that would influence the careers of a number of athletes described in this book.

Zhang's involvement lent a semi-official stamp of approval to women's competitive sports.[23]

Based on Zhang's prominent presence in PE and government tiyu missions, it was logical that she had joined the official Tiyu Observers' Group (Tiyu kaocha tuan) led by Dr. Yuan Dunli, which travelled with athletes to the 1936 Berlin Olympics to study tiyu in Europe. The presence of Zhang Huilan and the eight other female tiyu professionals indicated and ensured the firm place of women's tiyu on the state agenda. The agenda of the Tiyu Observers' Group (Kaocha tuan kaocha fangzheng dagang) listed the similarities and differences between men's and women's tiyu equipment in schools. As noted in the Introduction, Zhang and the other female observers were tasked with supervising the female athletes. During the difficult voyage, in which nearly everyone suffered from seasickness, the delegation held a series of meetings. Zhang reported on domestic women's tiyu at the eleventh meeting.[24]

In 1981, Zhang wrote a memoir of her experience in Berlin. She recalled that although female members were excluded from the serious *Internationales Sportstudentenlager* (International Tiyu Symposium), the head of the Chinese delegation, Hao Gengsheng, took the female observers to the "International Leisure Meeting" in Hamburg just before the games began. The meeting, which included art appreciation, ballroom dance, touring, and two "tea parties," was organized and presided over by Joseph Goebbels, Reich Propaganda Minister. After a cultural aide informed the Chinese that Germany was undergoing reconstruction from the First World War, Goebbels made a long speech about how the relationship between Germany and France had already improved and how peace was at hand. According to Zhang, the audience applauded him earnestly. On the eve of the Olympic opening ceremony, Zhang and her group received a major surprise: Chancellor Adolf Hitler was going to receive them. She recalled being rushed to the reception hall, where Hitler politely shook hands with all the representatives of various nations. Zhang and three men rendered a special performance of a variety of folk songs for the International Athletic Trainee Camp.[25] Another observer, Ms. Chen Yongsheng, published her recollections in 1938 and recalled that Hitler and Goebbels were very courteous, especially to the Chinese women; her observations suggest that at the time, the Chinese may have regarded the Nazi leadership as excessively exuberant rather than dangerous. Zhang's comments that the German leaders' activities were mere deceptions, however, even if her observations were made decades later, suggest that the Chinese women regarded Hitler warily. Her reactions alongside contemporary female voices presented later in this book indicate an uneasy feeling about Hitler even as the Chinese women celebrated their presence at the Berlin Games.[26]

When Zhang returned to China, the nation was in the midst of a deeper crisis, facing Japanese aggression that anticipated the later furious conflict in Europe. After the outbreak of full-scale war with Japan in 1937, she served briefly as chair of the PE Department of the newly formed United University (Lianhe daxue), which combined Hebei Tianjin Women's Normal School with Beijing Normal University and Beiyang University after those institutions moved to the interior of China. She then moved to Shanghai, where she served with the International Red Cross.[27] After the Japanese occupied Shanghai in 1938, Zhang left for the United States, where she spent almost a decade studying and working.

Zhang's ability to convince the Nationalist government to allow her to return to the United States for further study was remarkable. With China at war with Japan, the United States had become the primary destination for Chinese scholars and students who wished to study abroad. The Nationalist government had become far stricter about issuing foreign study permits. After July 1937, applicants had to major in military science, engineering, medicine, or other subjects related to military defence, which greatly limited the numbers of Chinese studying abroad. Tough currency restrictions curtailed scholarships and other financial aid. Students already abroad, including those using private funds, had to complete their degrees rapidly and return home immediately. In 1938, the Chinese government issued only fifty-nine permits.[28] Zhang's departure for the United States in the face of such severe restrictions indicates the high value that the Nationalist government placed on her career, especially as it tightened controls further in the coming years and increasingly sought to establish thought control over public and missionary schools and universities. Zhang had to negotiate such constraints in order to get a permit and funding for her study and research abroad. In America, as described later in this chapter, she used the skills she had learned in China to traverse bureaucratic mountains.

Setting the Theoretical and Scientific Framework for Girls' Competitive Sports

Zhang Huilan joined a new generation of male educators and administrators, most of whom were educated abroad and who devoted their careers to improving Chinese citizens' physical conditions. Her colleagues included Wang Zhengting, Wu Yunrui, Yuan Dunli, and Hao Gensheng. As Fan Hong points out, these educators established modern professional tiyu education, and wrote textbooks and critical texts about sports, elite competitions, and their biological effects. Andrew D. Morris has argued that female tiyu experts toiled in an atmosphere of male condescension,[29] an atmosphere that made Zhang's task all the more challenging. Her salary, as noted earlier, indicates that she successfully overcame such attitudes. Her effectiveness was also seen in her larger social influence. Zhang spurred the movement to permit girls to engage in competitive sports as part of the Chinese government's admission of sportswomen to the prestigious National Games. Women participated only in non-medal events throughout the 1920s, when women's sports were not regarded as being in the national interest. Morris observes that unruly male behaviour marred even those appearances: men disrupted the events in an attempt to keep sports a masculine preserve. Morris argues that such "loutish behavior" suggests that Fan's emancipation model of female athletics may be overstated.[30]

I argue that the combination of nation building and women's liberation during the national crisis made female competitions inevitable. It is clear that the careful and deliberate efforts of Zhang and other tiyu administrators built the scaffolding for full-scale female participation in competitive sports. Zhang exercised her influence by engaging in international "scientific" dialogues regarding these issues during the period of the national crisis.

Competing theories from Germany and the United States affected Chinese women's participation in strenuous athletic events and wartime tasks. Zhang noted that China became the battlefield for American and German philosophies of physical education, especially PE for women, as physical educators practised the theories of the countries where they had been trained.[31] There were close military ties between Chiang Kai-shek's Nanjing government and Nazi Germany, which the Chinese hoped would create a buffer against the imperialist designs of Japan.[32] Besides admiring the efficient German military state, many tiyu professionals in China highly regarded German sports and health programs. The 1936 Berlin Olympics are considered the most controversial world games ever, because Hitler used them to trumpet his ideology of Aryan supremacy. Despite some misgivings over Hitler's lumping of Chinese with other supposedly inferior non-Aryans, however, China sent an impressive and sizable delegation in its first big Olympic investment. The observers returned impressed with what they saw, and were particularly enthusiastic about the influence of sport and its ethics on German women. They reported that in Germany tiyu groups of young men and women engaged in all kinds of competitive games in addition to taking PE classes alongside standard curricula. They noted that "most of women's events were masculine *(nanxinghua),* and women were reported good at all the activities, such as horseback riding, shooting, swimming, rowing, hiking, driving, and cross-country racing." They detailed the demanding physical training that young German women underwent in such programs as the Youth Training Army and the Hitler Army, in order to become perfect citizens. Their official report included many photographs of various kinds of challenging gymnastic performances by European men and women.[33]

The appeal of German sports methods for women transcended official circles into mass media. To encourage Chinese women's participation, the popular women's weekly *Linglong*, whose impact I will discuss in Chapter 2, followed up the official Tiyu Observers' Group's reports on women in the German Youth Movement by reporting that six thousand camps were built for women aged seventeen to twenty-five. The women were obliged to work there for half a year as farmers, helping mothers with many children with domestic duties and contributing other public services. *Linglong* used German examples to justify women's citizenship based on their contributions and value in strengthening the wartime nation: "Modern war was a competition of national strength, which must involve the whole citizenry directly or indirectly, men or women, old or young, willing or not." *Linglong* attributed Germany's strength to its national devotion to tiyu activities for all women, including those who were old, pregnant, and sick. It called on all Chinese women to learn from the German "whole citizen's body strengthening movement." This was translated as *quanmin jianshen yundong*, which later became a familiar slogan in the People's Republic of China. Women were exhorted to develop *jianmei zhuyi* (robust beauty-ism) and to stop valuing sickly beauty. Photographs of German women's tiyu activities were scattered throughout the magazine.[34]

Since the Nationalist government had a strong if uneasy relationship with the German government and the Chinese public favoured many German sports methods, Zhang had to walk a fine line. Although she cited German women as legitimate examples of women's participation in competitive sports and strenuous physical activities, she rejected the government's concomitant militarism.[35] In her memoir, she noted: "In order to hide their criminal conspiracy to launch invasion, German fascists used the Olympics to run their propaganda machine to create the peace 'smoke' and cheat the world public view. They spent big money to run the games splendidly ... slogans insulting the Jews were carefully covered."[36] Zhang's recollections of the negative qualities of the Nazi Olympics, written six decades later, certainly reflected a historical condemnation of Hitler and his regime as well as personal tragedy caused by her suffering during the Cultural Revolution due to her participation in this trip. Her experience in Berlin taught Zhang the potential pitfalls of mass sports events and made her more determined that women's participation be designed to improve their health and self-esteem.

Through her education and contacts, Zhang found more inspiration in America. In the United States, the struggle over the scope of women's and girls' PE and athletic programs followed a gendered line. As a founding figure of modern PE, Charles H. McCloy (Mai Kele, 1886-1959) called on a new American PE system based on science, data, and experiments, replacing the old one influenced by European military practice, within the framework of modernity.[37] Making a point that deeply impressed Zhang, he argued persistently that competitive and vigorous sports must be integrated into women's PE in the same manner as for men's, in order to prepare women for the competitive modern world. His points collided directly with the belief of the majority of American female physical educators that vigorous and competitive sports were dangerous to women's health. Seeing McCloy's pioneering arguments as a threat to the status quo of a separate but less strenuous and competitive version of women's sports and PE and their authority within it, female physical educators particularly considered him an "outlaw." In response, in a paper presented to the National Association of Physical Education for Women in Colleges and Universities in 1930, McCloy urged female physical educators to do effective research. Such work would generate dialogue about competitive sports for women within a scientific framework and raise the status of PE in the general educational community.[38] It was especially courageous of Zhang to cross the gender line by adopting and developing McCloy's ideas for use in China.

When the gendered dynamics regarding competitive sports for women were transported from the United States to China, the process took racial twists. When McCloy exerted a cogent ideological influence over Chinese PE in the 1920s, he highlighted the importance of statistical analysis and synthesized Western ideals and Chinese sports traditions. In his early statistical research and writings, however, he argued that women were not biologically prepared for intensive training and should avoid violent physical competitions such as foot races and jumping.[39] Zhang may have influenced the later shift in McCloy's thinking, which I discuss below.

Zhang's views directly challenged those of the American female missionaries in China, who saw competitive sports as fundamentally masculine. Echoing the younger McCloy, Emily Case of Ginling Women's College felt strongly that Chinese girls were not fit for competitive sports and that women's PE was not the answer to the nation's needs.[40] Many of the Western faculty members shared Case's views, which conflicted directly with an emerging ideology espoused by Chinese faculty members. Twinning social Darwinism and modern PE thought, the Chinese faculty saw competitive sports and other rigorous activities as patriotic, the proper road to modernity, and the best means of dispelling the stereotype of China as the "sick man of Asia."[41]

Faculty disagreements about the role of women's tiyu surfaced at Ginling during the transfer of power to Chinese educators in 1927-28. Zhang was convinced that Chinese women's participation in competitive sports should work toward the national goal. While such a perception remained within a patriarchal paradigm, it did allow for greater female visibility. Zhang was well aware that the major obstacle to women's full participation in tiyu was the prejudice that a woman's body is born incomplete and weak. She would directly confront such attitudes, through her voice in scholarship regarding women's physical activities. Zhang resorted to the power of science to legitimize and expand women's participation in competitive tiyu activities. A significant proportion of her scholarly writing during the war addressed issues relevant to Chinese women.

As early as 1923, while a student at the University of Wisconsin, Zhang wrote an article for *The Chinese Student's Monthly,* published by the Chinese Students' Alliance in the United States. In this piece, Zhang argued that Chinese girls enjoyed sports as much as Western women. She believed that Chinese women's participation in the 1921 Far Eastern Games indicated that "the day is not far away that we Chinese girls will participate and capture the championship in the World Olympic Games for women. Then, and not until then, we will be able to convince the West that China is no longer a 'sick nation' – old and dying – but a hale and vigorous country full of youth and vitality."[42] Ignoring American female physical educators and McCloy's earlier objections to vigorous sports for women, especially Chinese women, Zhang confirmed and reshaped McCloy's later assertions. She exported data that she had collected in China and imported conclusions based on case studies of white females to justify the participation of Chinese girls in competitive sports. Zhang's transracial methods challenged the emphasis on the physical differences between the Chinese and people of other races expressed in Chinese official and public discourses. She recognized that available experimental data collected among white students implied that girls have lower motor capacity and less strength, endurance, and physical efficiency, but she refused to accept that the alleged physical differences could prove that boys' activities were physiologically harmful to girls. She argued that, rather than being biologically predetermined, women's weaker physiques were at least partly caused by existing athletic programs, which failed to offer sufficient physical training to strengthen their bodies. Rejecting concepts of women as an indistinguishable entity, Zhang justified women's full participation in athletic activities by inserting such specific analytic categories as individuality and age. She argued that individual girls with the right physical qualifications should be allowed to participate in vigorous events such as long-distance running and swimming.[43] In an article published in *Diligent Tiyu Monthly* in 1935, she discussed how individuality should be applied in the preparation of PE classes. Contrary to the general practice of mass exercise, she advocated that female students be divided by school year and by three or four skill levels. She recommended that instructors conduct frequent physical examinations in order to adequately judge individual students' capabilities.[44] She suggested that official sports rules be modified, because although the two sexes followed different patterns of growth, boys did not always grow faster than girls. For example, during middle-school age, "the difference in mean stature ... is less than one inch, or girls can be taller," so girls' volleyball nets should not be lower than those for boys in junior high.[45]

Zhang also directly confronted concerns about sports and women's reproductive health. Women's reproductive organs and menstruation frequently became the focus of debate regarding women's participation in competitive sports. Using anatomical facts, gynecological studies, and cinematographical demonstrations, McCloy had found that a healthy woman's reproductive organs would not be hurt by such vigorous physical activities as the high jump and broad jump. He believed that "[limiting girls' participation] as a rule, [was] based upon an erroneous notion of pelvic anatomy." Conscious of the gendered dynamic in the debate, McCloy blamed the misperception on "the conservatism of elderly persons who, especially when they are of the feminine sex, have themselves done little jumping." He challenged those who insisted that women should not jump to prove their arguments. The dispute became so tense that when McCloy first submitted his findings for publication, the editor of a professional journal in the United States "effectively suppressed [them] for three years." The article was finally published in Germany, and professionals in the United States had to wait for reprints in English.[46]

Zhang Huilan followed McCloy's conclusions and pushed the discussion by addressing whether menstruation would affect women's participation in competitive sports. This was a highly controversial subject. Frank Dikötter has demonstrated how Chinese gynecological treatises, self-help books on sexual hygiene, and outlines on obstetrics during this era all taught that the menstrual period was a pathological process demonstrating female weakness. Sports, in this view, could not be engaged during menstruation.[47]

In 1935, Zhang and co-author Sun Zhenghe, then an instructor in the PE Department of Ginling Women's College, published the textbook *Hehuan yundong (Gentle Exercise)*, which revised the "false" mainstream belief. They insisted that menstruation was a natural physiological phenomenon that accommodated lighter exercise.[48] In her American dissertation, Zhang's position became more radical. She claimed that "participation in interscholastic competition during menstruation was not detrimental to health, at least to Chinese girls, as long as the individual students' health was good." Aware of the lack of conclusive scientific evidence based on systematic or controlled data on that issue in the United States, Zhang cited examples of girls in China to change the views of American physical educators. She noted that despite the restrictive school policies regarding girls' participation in interscholastic competition, girls on athletic fields generally chose to disregard those regulations. Zhang urged serious "scientific" research before drawing conclusions on gender-related athletic issues.[49] Her arguments were highly radical for her time and even later. Her theory on the similarity between the physical growth of boys and girls before adulthood offered a scientific basis for the official policy in wartime China that encouraged competitive and military sports among young girls.

A Separate Women's Space and Network in Career and Life

Non-competitive gentle exercise served as the "scientific" base for American female physical educators in their effort to maintain women's PE as an exclusive sphere and thereby retain their professional authority. Despite advocating women's participation in competitive sports in the national interest and for female independence, Zhang did not neglect the topic of gentle activities for Chinese women. While many of her ideas found final expression in her dissertation, Zhang had long-term empirical exposure to new methods. In the United States, she witnessed the rapid growth of PE for women. Twenty states required PE for their students by 1921, and other states soon adopted similar laws. Female physical educators developed rapidly as a force and oversaw a tremendous surge in extracurricular athletics at the university level. American women developed a successful system of separate athletic contests, leagues, tournaments, and regulations created and governed by women.[50]

Gentle Exercise, which was published and widely advertised by the prestigious Qinfen shuju (Diligent Publishing House), expanded Zhang's intellectual status at a time when few textbooks on women's tiyu were available. In his foreword, Wu Yunrui, chair of the PE department at National Central

University, praised the authors for creating a much-needed textbook in their spare time. Wu noted that although the Ministry of Education had previously issued standards for secondary school tiyu curricula, there were no existing textbooks. He congratulated the authors for helping the MOE by filling the gap with such a textbook, which would be useful to PE teachers across China. The Wu family had a sizable investment in the book. Wu's father, Wu Jinghuan, translated some poetry in the frontispiece and a noted intellectual and Nationalist official, Wu Dingpei, prepared the book's illustrations. In their preface, co-authors Zhang Huilan and Sun Zhenghe acknowledged the influence of Western female educators by stating that the book was a collection of works from standard American and English women's PE sources. The book was intended to broaden the understanding of tiyu by going beyond track and field events and including gymnasium exercises, games, and rhythm activities for uplifting the physiques of China's citizenry.[51]

While teaching in Chinese universities, Zhang laboured tirelessly to establish curricula that included competitive sports such as track and field and basketball, as well as exercise-oriented gymnastics, dance, and other games. During her stint at the prestigious National Central University, the school allotted a tight budget to girls' PE. Out of devotion, Zhang used her own money to purchase blankets and mattresses from Shanghai to make floor exercises possible. She had to lobby the university administration extensively for a separate gym for girls to enable them to develop physiologically and psychologically.[52] Just as the development of correct posture made up a significant part of the women's PE curriculum advocated by American female physical educators,[53] *Gentle Exercise* highlighted the critical importance of cultivating correct posture. The authors contended that one-third of secondary school and college students had weak physiques and very bad posture, such as "gorilla-style" and "old Chinese teacher style." They emphasized the corrective power of the standard good postures, which they offered for students to follow, in terms of cultivating "calmness of body and mind" and inspiring respect from others.[54]

Zhang also pioneered in dance instruction. Dance, a newly introduced pedagogical tool, had contradictory meanings in Chinese popular culture. Dance performances by scantily clad young girls in the mushrooming worlds of song-and-dance troupes and commercial social dances, with dancing girls for hire in nightclubs, carried negative sexual meanings. Zhang had experienced earlier opposition to her ideas about incorporating dance in tiyu curricula. During her tenure at Ginling Women's College, Emily Case's disapproval of including dance in the PE curriculum had a strong racial overtone. She was concerned about the Chinese students' emotional instability and believed that "dancing is apt to be taught for its spectacular effect ... the program degenerates into a series of rehearsals for one exhibition after another." Despite Case's argument, the Third National Games at Wuchang in 1924 included well-received female folk dancing exhibitions.[55]

Zhang herself was not comfortable with social dancing. For example, during their trip to Berlin in 1936, she and other abstemious female observers returned to their hotel early to sleep, against the desires of their German hosts for late-night dancing.[56] Despite her personal reserve, Zhang maintained that dance was a legitimate and "clean" tiyu activity for female Chinese students. She constructed curricula and wrote textbooks emphasizing dance. She recalled in her 1983 memoirs how Chen Yingmei taught her to combine physical exercise into games and dance, and to observe the keys to physical movement. Chen used dance as a means of instruction and incorporated folk dances from Russia, Poland, Hungary, England, and Scotland into the curriculum.[57] Since Central lacked a piano needed for practising rhythmic dancing, Zhang offered one hundred yuan from her savings toward the purchase price of three hundred yuan. The piano never materialized because the man in charge of the school's finances disappeared with Zhang's money.[58]

Inspired by her American peers, Zhang Huilan argued for women's PE as a profession reserved exclusively for female physical educators. In her *Chinese Student's Monthly* article, Zhang contended that "a male teacher is not satisfactory, for the intimate relationship can not be established between the teachers and the students. Physical eduction teachers should have close touch with the students in order to fulfill their professional functions." She continued that young women needed female role models in order to overcome their parents' anxieties that physical education would do more harm than good. She called for rigorous training to produce qualified female physical educators. She raised the same arguments when attending the first national tiyu conference in 1932.[59]

In addition to writing, Zhang engaged in ample committee work at national tiyu conferences called by the Ministry of Education. During the first such conference in 1932, she devoted her efforts to the establishment of the program for women's tiyu. Her committee created tougher requirements for female tiyu teachers, concentrating on education and character.[60] She told reporters covering the meeting that women's tiyu "should be regulated within the women's physical and mental capacity, rather than using the standard set up by men's perspective or point of view ... the most suitable personnel to teach women's tiyu should be women, and men should not be used."[61]

Her experiences at Ginling influenced her beliefs. She joined a network of well-educated, professional female peers all associated with Ginling College.

Ginling prided itself on creating a familial world for Chinese students, faculty, and Western missionaries. Free from the constructs of their biological families and homes, Chinese women at Ginling could pursue individual goals and develop new identities within a nurturing institution, through the missionaries' promotion of both Confucian values and Chinese rejuvenation, sometimes through opposition to the missionaries themselves. Students and faculty felt a unique Ginling *qizhi* (school spirit). Many early Ginling graduates embraced school spirit over the traditional family and vowed never to marry.[62] Zhang first expanded women's influence in tiyu circles by maintaining close relationships with and offering constant support to her students, especially Ginling graduate Du Longyuan.

The Ginling spirit survived the ravages of war. The school suffered severely when its campus was transformed into a refugee camp during the Rape of Nanjing from 1937 to 1938.[63] Nevertheless, Ginling tried to maintain its "family" network during the full-scale war through correspondence and newsletters. In the fall of 1943, just before receiving her PhD, Zhang conducted a job interview in New York City with Dr. C.K. Chu of the Chinese National Institute of Health. She followed up by writing to report that she had contacted her former students to recruit new staff for the institute. To her disappointment, Chu did not bother to respond.[64] But Zhang persevered. When she later joined the Mass Education Movement (MEM) in Sichuan in 1945, she recommended several female professionals who had been affiliated with her Chinese universities for the movement's health project. The first was Lu Guizhen (Lu Gwei-djen, 1904-91), known as the assistant, lover, and second wife of the famous British scholar Joseph Needham (1900-95), who specialized in the history of science and technology in China. A Ginling graduate, Lu received her PhD in biochemistry from Cambridge University in 1940. She then went to the United States as a single woman and worked at various institutions and hospitals, including the Cancer Laboratory at the Columbia University Medical School, before returning to Europe and Needham. Zhang also recommended Mary Chen, a graduate of the Chemistry Department at Ginling who received her master's degree in nutrition and health education from Columbia University and then worked at the Shanghai YWCA Tiyu Normal School after serving at Ginling Women's College and National Central University. Another Ginling graduate, Lee Mei-chi, was studying home economics at Cornell University on a scholarship from the China Institute and expecting her PhD within approximately a year when Zhang recommended her. Zhang also invited Marjorie Wong to compile a diet suitable to China's financial state in times of peace and war. Wong, a home economics graduate of the University of Hawai'i, had taught at Hebei Tianjin Women's Normal School for a year and had received her master's degree in nutrition from Columbia University. She worked at Peking Union Medical College in Beiping as a dietician in the Chinese kitchen and taught nutrition to the nurses there for five years.[65]

Zhang carefully maintained good ties with Ginling and its president, Wu Yifang. In the early 1940s, Zhang wrote to Wu about her theories regarding the scientific basis of PE. She also sought funds from Wu. After she was pressured to leave the MEM in 1947, Ginling accepted her as a professor in its PE Department. The department was too small for a professor with Zhang's credentials; in other words, Zhang needed the job more than the job needed her. The job offer was, however, a gesture of care and favour from Ginling to its "daughter." In that context, Zhang pursued a joint position with Ginling and the newly organized Shanghai Coordinators Committee for Tuberculosis Control.[66]

In China, as elsewhere, getting ideas to the powerful is always necessary. Wu, a good friend of Madame Chiang, could, if she chose, transmit important recommendations from tiyu experts to the First Lady. Zhang herself had two opportunities to express her views to the most powerful woman in China: first when Madame Chiang presided over the ceremony transferring power in Ginling Women's College in 1928, and then in 1936, when the Generalissimo and his wife received the Chinese delegation bound for the 1936 Olympic Games.

The prospects for integrating Madame Chiang into Zhang's female professional network were dimmed, however, by the two women's conflicting definitions of nationalism. Superficially there were grounds for optimism. Both women had trained in the United States and were devoted to the importation of Western scientific knowledge of hygiene and its integration into the raw materials of Chinese nation building – the bodies of the Chinese masses to be tamed and disciplined. The goal was the development of modern "civilized" bodies of the wartime citizenry with "correct" spirits and ideologies. Both agreed on the need to change everyday living habits and traditional body theories, which were viewed as "backward" and "unscientific," into "civilized" and "scientific" behaviours and attitudes through the disciplining of body codes.[67]

The two women disagreed, however, over the "correct" political ideologies – the proper version of nationalism – to instill into the "uplifted" bodies, and this may have prevented a possible alliance between them. Since the Nationalist government prioritized military power and a centralized state, the New Life Movement sponsored by Madame Chiang invoked traditional Confucian hierarchical values coloured by German Nazism and militarism.[68] Madame Chiang's inspiration was more evident in the militarist wartime actions of Zhang's loyal former student Du Longyuan. Through Wu Yifang, Zhang learned that Du was running a women's school in her hometown in Jiangxi Province. Du was an ardent Nationalist who used her personally designed stationery to express her patriotism. It featured a national flag with a bright sun and a clear sky as the header, with militaristic characters radiating out from the centre: "Military First, Victory First" at the top, followed by "Nation First, the Country Second" in the middle, and "Gathering Will; Gathering Power" at the bottom. After the local government took over her school, Du was convinced that Madame Chiang would be sympathetic to her plight and wrote to Wu, asking for Madame Chiang's ears and intervention. There is no record that she succeeded.[69]

In contrast to Madame Chiang's party/state-centred militarist nationalism, Zhang adapted her theory to an alternative nationalism based on the classical "Three People's Principles," which Zhang claimed another Nationalist leader, Dai Jitao, regarded as "correct" ideology for tiyu.[70] Continuing the May Fourth Movement legacy of combining "science" and "democracy" and importing the spirit of PE from the United States, Zhang insisted that cultivating responsible individual citizens, educating civil society, and introducing democracy constituted the ultimate goal in modernizing Chinese citizens' living habits and uplifting their bodies. Simple and efficient hygienic principles "with profound scientific basis" had long been advocated in urban print as beneficial to tiyu oriented toward women's health. Zhang articulated hygienic principles as a political tool for enabling individual citizens to fulfill their rights and obligations in the fight against poverty, ignorance, superstition, poor sanitation, and inadequate government health services.[71] Despite the dominant position of the New Life Movement in official and popular discourses, Zhang never mentioned it in her writings. After she chose to work for the private MEM instead of the Chinese National Institute of Health, she wrote to C.K. Chu, the latter's leading official, in an attempt to clear up any misunderstanding or bad feeling. Her letter stated explicitly that "democratic procedure should be adopted in China."

The separate female network that sustained Zhang in her career extended to her private life and possibly her sexuality. She spent most of her private life in households formed with her female students and colleagues. When Zhang, Du Longyuan, and their former student and colleague Luo Aihua taught at Hebei Tianjin Women's Normal School, the three lived close together as good friends, along with Zhang's mother. Du and Luo never married either.[72] Later, Wang Rumin (1912-2008), Zhang's student from National Central University, became her lifetime partner. Wang was from a prosperous family in Wuxi, Jiangsu Province. After graduating from Central with a bachelor's degree in PE in 1935, she followed in Zhang's footsteps and taught at the Hebei Tianjin Women's Normal School. Although Wang did not accompany Zhang to America, she later joined her at the Sichuan MEM, Ginling Women's College, Eastern China Normal University (Huadong shifan daxue), and Shanghai Athletic University after 1949. Zhang and Wang shared an apartment near the campus of Shanghai Athletic University until Zhang's death in 1996. They lived an extremely frugal life, with Wang keeping accounts of expenses. In the 1980s, Zhang was seen using a blanket knitted from broken old yarn to cover her knees. The pair did their own cleaning and cooking and operated the coal stove by themselves. One friend recalled that Zhang and Wang divided a thousand-year-old (pickled) egg for a meal. Their living arrangements displeased Zhang's niece, Zhang Peiwen, who was more concerned about Wang's control of finances than anything else and eventually halted any financial sharing with her.[73]

Wang's constant presence raises questions about the nature of her relationship with Zhang. In her study of women in the Chinese Enlightenment of the 1920s and 1930s, Wang Zheng found that educated women often chose to remain single out of disgust and anger with male relatives and other men who took concubines or out of devotion to their careers. Unlike Zhang, however, none of the women Wang described had lifetime female companions.[74] Chinese intellectuals and artists began to conceive of same-sex relations *(tongxing ai)* in the late 1920s and 1930s, when intellectuals translated and circulated the writings and ideas of such Western sexologists as Magnus Hirschfeld, Havelock Ellis, Richard von Krafft-Ebing, and Edward Carpenter. Sigmund Freud's writings became known in China in this era. Male homosexuality was generally condemned at the time, although some liberal Chinese thinkers regarded it as a stymied form of heterosexuality. Discussion of female same-sex relations was rare in Republican China. Initial hints of change appeared in literature. May Fourth-era novelists incorporated lesbian love themes. Same-sex friendships and intimacy existed in Chinese schools and factories. The interpretation of Zhang's relationship with her student remains a matter of conjecture. There is fleeting evidence of a lesbian underground in 1930s Shanghai, but no indications that the tightly wrapped Zhang took part in it. What can be said is that the common life of Zhang and her partner was characteristic of many educated Chinese women.[75]

Scholars viewed the Second World War as a turning point in the formation of the homosexual subculture in the United States because the military
and the workplace provided new opportunities for young female soldiers
and working women to develop homosexual relationships. For independent
women, "the modern recognition of women's sexuality created new vulner-
abilities." The public scrutiny of homosexuality reflected social fears about
the institutional and political dangers posed by uncontrolled female sexuality.
Mainstream gender ideology in the postwar United States encouraged women
to return to the domestic sphere, and "women engaged in nontraditional
roles, whether economic, political, or sexual," were viewed as a threat. The
accusation of homosexuality was a powerful weapon that could be used to
destroy female authority.[76] In China, Zhang's marital status and family life
remained immune to the stigma attached to homosexuality and silent in
the historical record (even her interviewers did not put anything in writing)
due to China's specific social and historical context.

Zhang's personal behaviour was unlikely to attract criticism. Female tiyu
professionals in China emerged in a wartime atmosphere, where women were
welcomed onto production lines and even onto the battlefield, and masculine
women were encouraged. Women in public activities fell into the category
of gender-neutral warriors free of family obligation. This image provided
some space for working women and independent female authorities such as
Zhang. The fact that Zhang remained single made her a respectable career
woman who was devoted to society. On the other hand, the feminist movement in China was initiated by male intellectuals and later sponsored by
patriarchal state power. The patriarchs in control were comfortable with and
encouraged female networks in social causes. During Zhang's job interview
with C.K. Chu in 1943, Chu asked her to recruit her former students to work
for the National Institute of Health, although he failed to respond to her follow-
up letter recommending her female peers.[77] When Zhang was preparing to
leave the MEM in 1947, its leader, James Yen (Yan Yangchu, 1893-1990),
wrote to express his "sincere hope that Zhang would strengthen the health
program among women in Pi-shan, Sichuan."[78] Without the social context of
a moral panic over sexual and social deviance, Zhang's special household
arrangements with other single women escaped scrutiny and notice.
Xiansheng, a classical title for respectable male scholars, was applied to well-
educated professional women like Zhang and confirmed their sexless image.
The press and propaganda treated her as a worker rather than a woman.
Respect and sympathy for Zhang may explain the silence on her unusual
household in the literature.

Although the Chinese public was somewhat aware of homosexuality, the discussion was limited to gender crossing in terms of physiology and appearance. Traditional close female bonds involving physical intimacy as depicted in magazine photographs and endearment letters were well accepted as publicly expressed, legitimate sisterhood.[79] Yet the social consciousness of homosexuality was so new and limited in China that the formation of a strong subculture comparable to that in the United States was still far off.[80] Thus, the close relationships Zhang enjoyed with her students and colleagues were always accepted as legitimate and did not result in the persecution associated with homosexuality elsewhere.

How Distant was Zhang from the Modern Girl?

Although Zhang was around a decade older than most Modern Girls in China, she belonged to the same generation of those in United States and Japan. Her radical ideas on women's physical capacity to enjoy competitive sports that involved public body display, her unusual households, and her cultivation of a power network of single female professionals must have made her self-conscious about her relationship with the Modern Girl, who was perceived as oblivious to politics and national interest, indulgent in personal pleasure, and enjoying open sexuality. Like any academic, Zhang surely sought professional recognition for her accomplishments, but she did not pursue the media fame that athletes desired.

Zhang tried to distinguish herself from the personal styles of the Modern Girl through careful cultivation of her appearance. Two photographs taken at the first graduation ceremony of the PE Department at National Central University in 1932 show the thirty-four-year-old Zhang as the only female among five faculty members (nine in another photograph) and five male students (see Figures 6 and 7). She was fashionably dressed in a colourful *qipao* and black high-heeled leather shoes, but with her hands folded on her knees and her hair conservatively combed back, at a time when permed and bobbed hair were the contemporary fashions for young women. Although she appeared consciously respectable, her *qipao,* sporting a subdued floral pattern, lent an air of educated sophistication to her otherwise severely formal appearance. *Qipao*s required a tailor's skill and therefore some expenditure of cash, a factor that the thrifty Zhang would not have taken lightly. Since Song Qingling (Madame Sun Yat-sen) had made the *qipao* stand for an "anti-imperialist look," it had become standard dress for women of the May Fourth generation such as Zhang. Her high heels did not automatically reflect Western culture, as Chinese women had worn high heels with bound feet for

6 and 7   Faculty of the Department at Physical Education National Central University with the first class of five graduates. Note that Zhang Huilan is the only woman.
Source: Archives of Shanghai Athletic University.

centuries. It would also seem out of character for Zhang to wear high heels to identify with American flappers, the epitome of the Modern Girls, who used them to emphasize sexiness. Creating an air of authority might have been a reason, but overall Zhang's use of high heels had Chinese as well as Western connotations.[81]

Zhang was never a wife or a mother, but motherhood and marriage served as the persistent central theme in her calls for women's participation and authority in public health. Her proposal to tame the Modern Girl was inspired by her conflicts with some of her students, battles that were sometimes over clothing and appearance or about social class. To promote professionalism, Zhang demanded athletic clothing and shoes in her PE classes at National Central. Some wealthy female students who preferred their high heels and fancy *qipao*s, which were frequently associated with the Modern Girl, resisted. Some fifty girls signed a letter opposing Zhang's requirements. Zhang herself wore high heels, but not on the athletic court. Under the watchful eye of her male colleagues, she patiently explained her rationale and even offered to lend money to indigent students. Gradually the students accepted the new uniforms.[82] Confronted by the declarations of girls with "so-called modern ideas of independence" that maternal and child care were "an insult and absolutely extraneous," Zhang suggested that college should teach mothers and potential mothers to fulfill their maternal responsibilities. Apparently distancing herself from the students and adopting the tone of male author-ities, she argued that experience had shown that these so-called Modern Girls need more such training than the others.[83]

The social and political contexts in which Zhang emphasized women's public roles as mothers were fraught with the tensions between egalitarian gender ideology and the discriminatory burdens placed on women. On the one hand, the egalitarian gender system theoretically encouraged "sameness" between men and women in terms of participating in production and on the battlefield. On the other hand, concerns about domestic stability undermined the egalitarian claim by putting female sexuality under strict scrutiny. Women who were physically active in public were suspected of being prostitutes or sometimes of practising "sexual perversion." Zhang was aware that the state condemned immorality and employed state censorship relevant to tiyu. She adopted the role of a conservator of rather than a threat to traditional gender and class roles for her female network and for Chinese female citizens in general.

Concerns over motherhood had always been essential to male intellectuals and the state, both of whom addressed "the women's question" and "women's liberation." At a time when many health intellectuals in China argued that motherhood remained the best role for women, Zhang did not challenge the traditional family structure: a working father "under pressure and anxiety" and a stay-at-home mother. Instead, she tried to expand women's power and responsibility by broadening the functions of wartime homes. Zhang called on women to use principles of motherhood and wifehood to demand their authority and power over the bodies of other citizens – their children and husbands. She devised a concept of "family health care" that combined education, home economics, child welfare, and mental hygiene. Women played the central role. They were expected to contribute to the wholesomeness of their families by practising medicine broadly: curing the sick, preventing disease, and promoting health under a physician's supervision. Citing statistical data on the high childbirth death rate and infant mortality rate, Zhang tried to standardize child care. When she prepared to join the Mass Education Movement, she inquired which department of the college trained professionals to look after the emotional, mental, and physical development of the child from the period of birth to school age. She inquired whether there would be a Department of Home Economics and a Department of Child Welfare, or a combination of both. Zhang suggested detailed schedules for mothers to follow in taking care of their children at various stages, from pregnancy to school age.[84]

At the same time, emboldened and protected by her conservative use of conventional family and motherhood, Zhang raised issues notoriously associated with the Modern Girl. She advocated sports that required bare skin and mixed-gender social activities, and created dialogues on sexuality in the name of science. She argued that shoes were extremely important since good posture required that the weight of the body while standing be distributed evenly over both feet. While advocating gentle exercise for women, she promoted the radical and controversial new fashion that bared skin for the sake of tiyu and health. In contrast to moralist arguments that required women to cover up, Zhang urged women to bare their feet and avoid high heels (which, she preached, could lead to calluses, fallen arches, damaged foot nerves and internal organs) in tiyu activities. She even encouraged women to wear lighter clothing, with swimsuits being the optimal garb, presumably in physical exercise and for the sake of health.[85]

Despite facing moralist resistance to mixed-gender social events, including athletic activities, Zhang insisted on not only more competitive sports for women but also more space for women to play by advocating "co-recreation" (boys and girls playing together). She observed that although Chinese boys and girls occasionally engaged in tiyu events together, PE classes were separated beginning at the junior high school level. She suggested tennis, table tennis, badminton, folk dance, hiking, and ice skating (which she believed would not put undue pressure on girls or retard the learning of boys) as proper starting events for co-recreation. She recognized that open discussion of sex was highly sensitive and controversial, and admitted that she herself hesitated to discuss this topic in class, although she had conducted research on "Vinegar and Menstruation" at Mills College. She called on women, however, to raise their confidence and voices in the contradictory public discourse about what, when, and how to approach sex education. She encouraged female students to acquire knowledge about sex and challenged women to extend their maternal responsibility to the task of sex education, including reproductive hygiene, sexual function after adolescence, hormones, male and female sex characteristics, the male reproductive system, and the menstrual cycle.[86]

Zhang framed her pioneering arguments within the May Fourth and New Cultural dynamics of replacing the "feudal" and "backward" with modern thought sustained by the ever-powerful evidence of "science." She blamed old Chinese doctrine on "absolute segregation of men and women" for school authorities' opposition to co-recreation for the sake of the "moral standard" of the school. Similarly, she believed that contemporary silence on sex had deep roots in traditional Chinese culture. Zhang suggested that "progressive" scientific knowledge based on physiology, anatomy, and psychology could overcome the old beliefs and values. For example, she argued that since gender differences in physical capacities are physiologically negligible from the primary school to the junior high school level, girls would not necessarily be harmed by playing with boys. Zhang invoked new and rapidly shifting social dynamics during the war to justify the transition from "tradition" to "modernity." She observed that, due to tight interactions between China and the West, and migration of educational institutions and population from coastal cities to inland areas, social customs regarding gender relations had shifted closer to those in the West. The more visible Western influence led some pioneering boys and girls to call for reform in traditional social customs.[87]

Instead of advocating radical freedom in sexuality, Zhang, who was doubtless wary of being identified with the Modern Girl, was quick to frame her discussion within modern heterosexual marriage based on romance and love, despite her own possible connection with homosexuality. She claimed that "in order to have a normal sexual interest and happy married life and avoid aberration, adolescents need social contact with the opposite sex because their love objects are the opposite sex." Zhang cited various experimental studies to support her assertion, contending: "Certain physical activities used as 'co-recreation' enabled boys and girls to behave spontaneously, consequently contributing to their experience and adjustment, which would be a stabilizing foundation for solving new problems within marriage." Zhang cited statistical data to show that alumni of coeducational institutions had happier marriages and adult lives than those from gender-segregated colleges. Noting that ignorance about sex among Chinese youth led them "into whatever kind of married life by chance," Zhang introduced the concept of social hygiene defined by "physiology of sex, sex ethics in relation to marriage and the family, and the establishment and maintenance of a normal family life." Following eugenic and social Darwinist theory, she argued that marriage and sex education were serious social and political issues, since "heredity was significant in determining the physical, moral, and mental quality of the nation, and an individual can not improve the health of the next generation without proper selection of a mate."[88]

Following the May Fourth dialogue on women's chastity, enlightened professionals sought to modernize the discourse on sexuality and liberate women from the Confucian sexual order by keeping an open dialogue. Medical authorities sought to popularize "scientific" knowledge of human sexuality through the modern educational system and print industry. However, sex education, even as a scientific study, carried a deep stigma. For example, Zhang Jingsheng (1888-1970) was nicknamed "Dr. Sexology" and attacked as one of the three "intellectual demons" in Republican China for his pioneering work in sex education. Noted politicians ridiculed him, as did cultural figures, even including the writer Lu Xun, who himself launched a powerful attack on the traditional requirement of women's chastity through his noted essay "My View on Chastity."[89] Within this divisive context, Zhang Huilan strategically pushed the boundary of the taboo subject.

Manoeuvring in America among Powerful Male Patrons

In light of the complicated structure of patriarchal authority in her job and service, Zhang's position as a single professional woman was a delicate one. For professional women, marriage was a double-edged sword. Generally, these women saw marriage as a trap that denied any access to equality and freedom.[90] Other women, however, used marriage to powerful male figures as a means of making connections to boost their careers in a patriarchal power structure. Frequently, Zhang had to compete against those with marital connections for the limited resources available to women in life and career. The lives of Zhang Huilan and Gao Zi followed parallel tracks before Gao's marriage. Gao was Zhang's classmate at the Shanghai YWCA Tiyu Normal School. The two women were sent to the United States together in 1920. Gao was admitted to the PE Department at the University of Wisconsin, to which Zhang transferred in 1921. Both women returned to their alma mater in

Shanghai to teach in 1923 and 1926, respectively. Afterwards, Gao occupied the highest official positions among female tiyu professionals in China throughout the war, thanks to her status as the wife of Hao Gengsheng, the Tiyu dean/inspector *(duxue)* of the Ministry of Education, while Zhang continued to pursue professional training and became the best-educated woman in the field of tiyu. Hao and his good friend Wu Yunrui, the chair of the PE Department at National Central University, engineered Zhang's transfer from the prestigious Central to Hebei Tianjin Women's Normal School to enable Gao Zi to work at Central.[91]

Whereas scholars have studied women's valiant efforts in China's resistance against Japanese aggression, little is known about the work of Chinese women who travelled abroad during the conflict.[92] Zhang's education and career during the Second World War were greatly influenced by her powerful male mentors: Charles McCloy, Clair E. Turner (1890-1974), and James Yen. Through their leadership in professional institutions and regional and global organizations, prolific publications, and service in government missions, these men defined physical education, public health, and rural mass education as serious transnational "scientific" professions during and immediately after the war.[93] Their patronage propelled Zhang to the front lines of these fields and facilitated her trans-Pacific identity and activities. By focusing on women in China in her academic writings in the United States, Zhang added new gender and racial dimensions to the transnational dialogues in these emerging fields. By working with these prominent Americans and with Yen, one of the most progressive minds of his generation, Zhang benefited from their scientific but liberal approaches.

Zhang returned to Mills College from 1938 to 1940 and earned her MA in physical education. From 1940 to August 1944, she studied with McCloy at the University of Iowa, where, at the age of forty-six, she became the first Chinese woman to receive a PhD in PE. McCloy directed her dissertation, "A Colligation of Facts and Principles Basic to Sound Curriculum Construction for Physical Education in China." The cooperation between the two had begun with McCloy's own trans-Pacific career: he had taught Zhang as a missionary teacher at the Shanghai YWCA Tiyu Normal School almost three decades earlier. Soon after his arrival in China in 1913 as secretary of the PE Department of the National Council of the YMCA, McCloy moved into other positions of power. He helped to lay the foundation of modern PE in China and bridged Chinese sports to the international stage through numerous articles and books on PE published in Chinese (in which he was fluent) and through service in the CNAAF and Far Eastern Athletic Association. He returned to the United States in 1927, earned a doctoral degree at Columbia

University's Teachers College in 1932, became a professor at the State University of Iowa (later the University of Iowa) in 1930, and developed into a world figure in PE. Even when he was physically absent from China, McCloy worked as a channel for trans-Pacific communication by training students such as Zhang Huilan and publishing articles in the weekly newspaper *Detroit Saturday Night* to enlighten readers about the nature of the Chinese people and their culture.[94]

McCloy's impact on Zhang was considerable. His advice and contacts meshed with her understanding of the urgent need to uplift women in poverty-stricken and war-torn China. Zhang expanded her work into public health, a field in which McCloy had vast experience as well as contacts (he served as the chief expert consultant to the US War Department, advising on fitness programs for the navy, air force, and army military hospitals and academies from 1941 to 1945).[95]

McCloy provided tangible support and connections for Zhang. He arranged for a two-year scholarship from the State Department that enabled Zhang to spend one year (1940-41) at the Department of Biology and Public Health at the Massachusetts Institute of Technology (MIT), where she obtained a certificate in public health. There she encountered one of the founders of public health, Clair E. Turner, who directed her thesis, "The Development of a Program of Hygiene for the National Teachers' College for Women, China." On her graduation from Iowa in 1944, Zhang continued her training in public health at summer schools at MIT and at the University of California at Berkeley (Turner had just taken up a new appointment as the first professor in public health at the latter). Turner had developed an interest in China and Asia in earlier years. He took a world tour during his 1935 furlough, lecturing at Calcutta University, the University of the Philippines, the University of Hawai'i, and the National Central University in China, where Zhang had taught. He served as a consultant to the Chinese National Ministry of Health and Education in 1936, touring the interior of China at the invitation of the government and participating in the national health education conference. At the end of the Second World War, he showed strong interest in China's postwar health education program by making connections with government officials. He served as the chairman of the Health Section of the World Federation of Education Associations from 1927 to 1940.[96]

To sustain her career, Zhang depended on the patronage and goodwill of powerful male figures in her fields, such as McCloy, Turner, and Yen. Their trans-Pacific activities and interests provided the necessary channels and connections for her transnational academic writings and professional activities. Within the patriarchal power structure, the sponsorship of dominant figures gave her crucial access to resources; for example, the scholarships they arranged were her special lifeline during her long sojourn in the United States from 1937 to 1946, during which she had no steady income. At the same time, Zhang had to face the downside of association with these patriarchs: forceful wills making decisions for her. Her resistance was mostly subtle; she manoeuvred around the patriarchal power structure itself, although at times direct confrontations were unavoidable.

Zhang's relationship with Clair Turner and Chinese government officials was hazardous. She respected and feared Turner, who was only eight years her senior. In addition to making arrangements for her health studies during summer school sessions, Turner helped Zhang gain access to and deal with China's bureaucracy, which tended to neglect professional women like her. He arranged that job interview for her with C.K. Chu in 1943 in New York City. Chu, however, failed to respond to Zhang's follow-up letter or to make arrangements for the scholarship that he had promised for her training in Boston. At the same time, Zhang's application for a scholarship from the US State Department was rejected on the grounds that, since the Chinese government (Chu's agent) was going to hire her, China was responsible for her training expenses.[97] Left high and dry, Zhang sought help from Turner, who managed to secure for her a five-month scholarship of $150 per month from the American Bureau for Medical Aid to China (ABMAC). Although the funding was not from the Chinese government, Chu's indirect approval was still required. Responding well to white male authority but not to Zhang, Chu granted his approval of the ABMAC scholarship and finally, in September, sent Zhang a letter through Turner, offering her a job as a technical expert with the Department of Health Education at the National Institute of Health.[98]

In August 1944, when Zhang went to the ABMAC office in New York City to discuss her possible job appointment within Chu's institute, she happened to see James Yen, whose office was on the same floor. In contrast to Chu's bureaucratic arrogance, Yen immediately invited Zhang to join the Mass Education Movement in Sichuan. At the same time, the ABMAC scholarship was reduced to three months at $120 per month without explanation. Zhang stopped pursuing the scholarship, declined Chu's job offer, and joined the MEM in October.[99]

Her work with Yen was significant in the expansion of public health in China. Yen had initiated the Rural Reconstruction Movement in China using American connections made during his missionary years and his education at Yale and Princeton Universities, and he became a global figure during the national crisis. In 1923, he had founded the National Association of the Mass Education Movement (MEM) to support mass literacy campaigns throughout

China and to construct a pilot project of comprehensive rural reform in Ding County, Hebei (North China). At the same time, Yen established the American Cooperating Committee for fundraising. In 1933, the MEM took control of the county government. Later, it established experimental centres in Hengshan, Hunan Province (Central China), and Xin-tu, Sichuan Province (West China), through collaboration with the provincial governments, in order to make sure the basic principles and methods of the MEM were applicable over different regions. In 1940, the MEM established the National College of Rural Reconstruction to train rural reconstruction professionals. During the Second World War, Yen returned to the United States and organized the American-Chinese Cooperation Committee (later the American-Chinese Committee of the MEM) to secure American support. Intending to integrate rural villagers into the nation-state through citizenship education based on "science" and "democracy," the MEM developed health care programs with various approaches to teach villagers how to live a "civilized" and "hygienic" life.[100]

Zhang conducted public health fieldwork in various places in the United States under the sponsorship of the MEM. Yen directed her fieldwork report, "Health Education in the Public Health Program."[101] Their relationship was often personal. After Yen met Zhang in August 1944 and invited her to join the MEM, he immediately wrote his wife about it. Mrs. Yen had taught Zhang at the Shanghai YWCA Tiyu Normal School, and when Zhang was at Mills College in 1940, she had written to Mrs. Yen to inquire about the possibility of joining the MEM.[102]

Once employed at the MEM, Zhang used gifts to cultivate Mrs. Yen. Considering the significance of physical appearance to Zhang's identity, it was not coincidental that the gifts and chats centred on clothing and personal grooming. As soon as Zhang joined the MEM in October 1944, she bought four pairs of stockings for Mrs. Yen as gifts. To keep the relationship both personal and formal, Yen reimbursed Zhang for three pairs and kept one as a gift.[103] There were further exchanges of a Schaeffer pencil, a purple hankie, and some dress fabric, "which did not wrinkle easily and is worth lots of use," between Zhang and Tang Chiyi, Yen's secretary at MEM headquarters in New York City. Zhang told Tang and Yen's other secretary, Hong (who was replaced by Tang), how she took up the important domestic skill of sewing to fit in with the MEM spirit. After Zhang told Hong that she had learned to make cloth "frog" buttons, Hong joked that she could learn the skill from Zhang and set up a business to become rich instead of sitting and typing. Soon, Zhang told Tang that she was taking up the more challenging task of making dresses, even with a pair of scissors only three inches long while her sewing kit was packed and awaiting passage to China. Tang responded that she was going to depend on the newly available professional tailors in China. The two women exchanged sympathies over tooth and nose ailments, and the shock of watching their hair turn grey.[104] When the relationship between the MEM and Zhang deteriorated in 1947, the change was reflected in the women's friendship as well. Zhang and Tang stopped calling each other by their first names, instead using the formal "Ms. Tang" and "Dr. Zhang."[105]

Zhang employed more direct means to negotiate her way among male sponsors and supervisors. When disagreements occurred, she was not afraid to stick to her position, using subtle negotiation but not shrinking from direct confrontation. At the same time, she learned to use the male power structure to her advantage. Zhang declined the position at the Department of Health Education, for which Turner had arranged her interview with C.K. Chu, in order to accept Yen's invitation to join the MEM. Turner's patronage then turned into pressure, which Zhang dealt with by making use of Yen's patriarchal power as head of the MEM.[106] Zhang intimated, and Yen agreed, that the interview between Zhang and C.K. Chu did not lead to any "legal" obligation to Chu and that Zhang had only a "moral" obligation to Turner due to "his consistent kindness and interest" in her. Turner thought otherwise, however, and insisted that Zhang needed Chu's approval before she could join the MEM. Turner adopted different strategies in dealing with Yen and Zhang. Considering Yen as the major challenger to his patriarchal authority but an equal, Turner negotiated with him professionally during his special trip to New York City to meet with Yen in person. He suggested that it was Yen who was obliged to deal with Chu and the government directly, and to secure a different scholarship for Zhang. Yen was upset by the confrontation and blamed Zhang for putting herself and him in an "embarrassing position." While asking for Yen's forgiveness, Zhang justified her action with nationalism. She maintained that she had not embarrassed herself because her transfer was "prompted by a much bigger issue": to serve the nation in the best way. In the end, Turner and Yen reached a gentlemen's agreement that "neither should interfere with Zhang but leave the final decision entirely to her."[107]

Turner, however, exerted forceful pressure on Zhang behind Yen's back. When he saw Zhang in Cambridge, Massachusetts, the following day, he ignored his agreement with Yen and insisted that Zhang seek "approval" from Chu by writing a letter under his immediate supervision. Zhang finally rebelled and refused to do so. Rather, she suggested that Turner, Yen, and she discuss a courteous letter to Chu regarding her "choice." Although Turner agreed, Zhang sought to ensure Yen's support by asking to meet with him alone before all three met. "I could feel what was deep in Prof. Turner's heart throughout our conversation. He may suggest [that I] have it [what Zhang sensed in Turner's mind] put in the letter to Dr. Chu. I shall tell you what it is when I come to New York in October." We can only guess what Zhang feared in Turner's heart, but meeting with Yen privately before dealing with Turner was an important tool that she used to confirm her alliance with Yen. They had planned to meet before Yen saw Turner in Washington for the first time, but the plan was upset by Turner's unexpected visit to Yen in New York. Surprised by Turner's pressure on Zhang and approving of the way Zhang handled her "old professor," Yen assured Zhang that they would "talk over things first by ourselves" before seeing Turner again.[108]

The cooperation between Zhang and Yen was soon disturbed by an imbalance of power between the government and private organizations, as represented by Chu and Yen, respectively. After Zhang's move to the MEM was finalized, she wrote to Chu, wishing no misunderstanding and embarrassment. Zhang flattered Chu's patriarchal pride by saying that his "broad mind," which she observed through their short interview, "would guarantee their future co-operative effort in China's health fields."[109] Charles Hayford suggests that "rural reconstruction as a movement remained largely without political backbone; they seemed to feel that decent, educated, selfless men and women could spontaneously band together to produce reform."[110] As shown below, the relationship between Zhang and the MEM had changed subtly due to pressure from Chu. Tang Chiyi mailed the "Terms of Fellowship Grant of the American-Chinese Committee of the Mass Education Movement" from New York on 9 June 1947, for Zhang's signature. The document stated that fellows trained on MEM scholarships were obliged to serve full time for at least two years or more according to the amount of the scholarship, in order to avoid being required to return the full amount. Just as she had firmly refused Turner's request to write Chu under his supervision, Zhang abruptly refused to sign the document. She returned it unsigned "because it in any way whatsoever does not apply to my case."[111]

Zhang's frustration as a single professional woman was endless. Toward the end of the Second World War, she was ready to sail back to China but because of informal discrimination against women in public spaces, few boats were accessible to them and she had to wait almost half a year for a passage. In March 1945, the Executive Offices of the Committee on Wartime Planning for Chinese Students in the United States of the China Institute in America announced that advance arrangement was necessary for personnel who needed to return promptly for the anti-Japan and reconstruction causes.[112] James Yen pleaded with the State Department and the Chinese Embassy in Washington, DC, that Zhang was a badly needed MEM staff member who deserved priority passage.[113] In June, Zhang applied with the War Shipping Administration to sail on 30 November 1945. After waiting at Yale University for two-and-a-half months, she was notified that her passage was scheduled for 1 March 1946. She then travelled to San Francisco, ready to begin her journey at any date, but had to wait for three more months, with all her luggage packed, before finally getting her ticket on 29 May. Her journey was delayed one last time before she finally departed in June. The impatient Zhang checked continually with the shipping line reservation clerk; because of her persistence, he stamped "urgent" on her application many times.[114]

Zhang emphasized to Yen that seeking a priority berth as a professional was "a legitimate procedure." She complained to him: "Yes, the passages for women are few, but there are women going, not necessarily all of them were connected with the government officially." She observed that the few slots for women were occupied by "the daughters or daughters-in-law of the 'big shots,'" and cited the examples of the "daughter-in law of Mr. Sun," who attended Mills College when Zhang was there and had married "only a year ago," and a daughter of the first mayor of Tianjin (Zhang had met the mayor at a dinner party in that city in 1937).[115] Zhang also complained that the boats were crowded with government workers. Although she did not challenge the gender discrimination policy of the Wartime Shipping Administration directly, her complaints of the unequal treatment of government workers and private employees implied an injustice. The Chinese government bureaucracy was male-dominated, and professional women without marital connections had limited access. Zhang showed her frustration with the powerlessness of the MEM by urging the organization to contact the Chinese Embassy rather than the Wartime Shipping Administration because the latter "knows nothing about the MEM" and only followed the advice of the embassy in granting passage to Chinese people. She advised stiffly: "I think the staff of the MEM should have at least (the) equal privilege if not more to get passage."[116]

On returning to China in 1946, Zhang worked briefly at the MEM's College of Rural Reconstruction in Xiemachang, Baxian, Sichuan. C.K. Chu visited her in Baxian in March 1947, and Zhang wrote soon after that "for certain reasons, I felt I must leave." In October that same year, she left rural Sichuan for the joint appointments in Shanghai and Nanjing.

Throughout Zhang's trans-Pacific life and career around the time of the national crisis, she developed and exercised her professional authority through intertwined strategies. Her primary focus was on improving the power and health of Chinese women. Crossing gender and racial lines, she synthesized conflicting arguments regarding women's physical activities and gender roles to maximize Chinese women's space within the context of the national crisis.

Zhang combined the rhetoric of equal rights for women and of female gender difference to promote women's space and status in the tiyu profession and the field of public health. She emphasized both their professional efforts and intellectual work and the social power of personal and social motherhood. Zhang was the product of the rhetoric of gender equality in newly emerging professions based on academic training in science or social science, and took equal opportunity for women as one of her professional goals. The entry of educated women into a sexually integrated public workplace was crucial to the modern transformation of Chinese culture.[117]

Looking at Zhang's life and career provides a new perspective on Christina Gilmartin's well-known description of female activists. Gilmartin used the example of Communist women engaging in a "complex dynamic of agency and compliance." Zhang was part of the system as a professor and government consultant, but at the same time she carefully, inexorably pushed her own beliefs, founded on scientific observation, to create a respected women's space within the tiyu world.[118]

Joining the New Order

After the Communist takeover of China in 1949, Zhang Huilan, like many other Chinese intellectuals, had to decide whether to flee or to join the new government. There was some danger in choosing the latter, because her previous career had been so closely identified with the Nationalist government. However, her liberal nationalism and alienation from the militaristic party state made her choice easier. The People's Republic of China determined that Zhang would be of great value in creating its new society. She took part in the preparatory meeting of the National Sports Commission in 1949, as one of the very few key tiyu participants who were holdovers from the "old China." The meeting was studded with major figures. Vice Chairman of the State and Chairman of the People's Revolutionary Military Committee Zhu De; Liao Chengzhi (son of the Nationalist leader Liang Zhongkai and He Xiaoning, who had headed the Nationalist Party's women's organization), chairman of the National Committee of Youth Association; Feng Wenbin, the general secretary of the Chinese Communist Youth League; and leaders of tiyu in the early years of the People's Republic all made speeches advocating that all workers in the tiyu field unite to contribute to the new democratic tiyu for national citizens. Representatives from the Northeast region, Northwest region, East China, Central China, Beijing, and People's Liberation Army spoke. Representing East China, Zhang, according to the state mouthpiece, the *People's Daily*, proclaimed:

We can see the glorious victory, great achievements and unification of tiyu workers in Beijing under the leadership of Chairman Mao and the people's government. We should learn from them ... The meeting was to ... set the new direction and tasks of tiyu and solved the basic problems we have been facing. This is a glorious and epic-making page in Chinese tiyu history. We will firmly support the directions of Vice Chairman Zhu and the report of comrade Feng Wenbin, we will try our best to pass the message to all the tiyu workers in East China, and will use real actions to guarantee the principle and task of new tiyu can be enforced.[119]

As part of the new government, Zhang Huilan and Wu Yunrui served on the Preparation Committee as representatives from Nanjing. Wu served by virtue of his position as professor and chair of the PE Department of Nanjing University and Zhang joined as professor and chair of the PE Department of Ginling Women's College.[120]

Following the meeting, Zhang became the first dean of East China Normal University in Shanghai as well as a professor in the university's Department of Anatomy. Three years later, in 1952, she became the first dean, and the founder of the Athletic Science Department (with emphasis on anatomy), at Shanghai Athletic University, which was formed through a merger of the PE departments of Nanjing University, East China Normal University, and Ginling Women's College. Zhang devoted herself to what must have seemed her dream job. From the 1950s to the 1970s, she served as the associate minister of the National Sports Commission, the associate director of the Chinese Olympic Committee, a representative to the Second and Third People's Congresses, a member of the fifth Political Consultative Congress, an executive committee member of the National Women's Federation, and the consultant to the Shanghai Branch of Jiusan xueshe (September 3 Society). In the 1950s, she was selected as one of the "National Advanced Workers." She donated her personal savings of 20,000 yuan to Shanghai Athletic University to set up a scholarship for research.[121] On 1 November 2012, the university unveiled a statue of Zhang at its sixtieth anniversary celebration, which demonstrates the continued relevance of her legacy (see Figure 8).

Zhang maintained her personal life with Wang Rumin. During the Maoist years, when romance and sexuality were silenced, homosexuality dropped from public consciousness. Even during the Cultural Revolution, when Zhang's education, skills, wisdom, and length of service were burdens rather than currency and Zhang and Wang were treated harshly in general, their shared household was viewed as an innocent sisterhood immune from harsh

8 Zhang Huilan's statue unveiled at the sixtieth anniversay of Shanghai Athletic University in 2012. Standing is Lu Aiyun, Zhang's former student, professor and chief librarian of the university.

scrutiny. Survival of their relationship during this treacherous time suggests that it was closer to the monastic than to the sensual.

In summary, as the best-educated woman in the field of tiyu during the national crisis, Zhang expanded professionalism in the fields of sports, hygiene, and public health. She epitomized the situation of female tiyu professionals like her. Her career demonstrated the importance of education for ambitious women. She interacted with powerful leading male figures on both sides of the Pacific Ocean. She displayed agility in dealing with slippery politics and patriarchal males. Faced with the dilemma of being a single professional woman, Zhang maintained and exercised her professional authority while negotiating with male patrons and cultivating female support networks, both of which involved complex power dynamics. Focusing on expanding women's space, she sophisticatedly used the strategy of extending women's maternal roles. She helped liberate women's bodies by using the authority of science to counter the stereotype of "being born weak." Likewise, she argued for gender equality based on "sameness," uniqueness of womanhood, and the May Fourth view of family, stressing love and enlightened wifehood for the sake of the nation. All of these served as crucial loci for efforts of the Nationalist government and urban literate feminists to deal with the contradictions involved in redefining Chinese gender through tiyu.

Central to the life and career of a powerful professional woman such as Zhang Huilan, whose authority was based on advanced training in science, were the mixed meanings of sexuality. Zhang legitimized the public display of girls' bodies with bare skin in competitive sports through scientific data. She took the radical position of advocating gender-integrated tiyu activities, but with the conservative rationale of cultivating a "happy" heterosexual marriage. She tried to preserve women's physical education as an exclusive profession for female physical educators by questioning the propriety of mixed-gender student and teacher dynamics. Consistent with the conservative government position of preserving traditional family structure in an unstable time, Zhang highlighted the importance of motherhood and wifehood in extending women's social roles in reforming and uplifting citizen's bodies. In attacking the college-educated Modern Girls who allegedly indulged in personal pleasure and abandoned obligations to their families and the nation, Zhang, who herself was about one or two decades older than the global New Woman or Modern Girl, sounded distant and asexual. Her network of high-profile unmarried, highly educated, career-oriented transnational professional women reinforced this gender- and sexually neutral image. At the same time, throughout her life she formed households with ambiguous sexual dimensions with her former students and colleagues. The complexity of her personal life did not diminish the importance of her strong enthusiasm for women's competitive sports, which lent intellectual weight to a rapidly developing social phenomenon. That development is the topic of the next chapter.

2 Nationalist and Feminist Discourses on *Jianmei* (Robust Healthy Beauty)

In Chapter 1, I examined how Zhang Huilan's scholarship furthered the acceptance of Chinese women's tiyu and competitive sports. While Zhang and her colleagues created an intellectual basis for competitive sports, government policies of the late 1920s combined with popular enthusiasm propelled sports events into the national spotlight. China's burgeoning print media were quick to take notice. Soon, popular journalism expansively covered women's sports and competitive events. Print journalism was a powerful force in recognizing athletes with unique talents and gifts and making them visible. Star making did not mean creating an elite class. Newspaper and magazine coverage of spectacular athletic feats in competitions sponsored by the Nationalist government augmented and strengthened the connections that ordinary Chinese felt with famous sportswomen. Female athletes became celebrities, still linked to their public as symbols of the freedom of economic mobility. As Leo Braudy has argued in his classic study *The Frenzy of Renown,* celebrity was part of the "democratization of fame" that accelerated with technological innovations in printing in the nineteenth and early twentieth centuries. Celebrity became a modernized version of fame.[1] Human notoriety increasingly became focused on accomplishments in public spaces, few of which were more visible than at athletic stadiums, in swimming pools, at beaches, and on basketball courts. Spectators wanted to know more about the athletes they admired, in part to confirm their loyalties through comprehension of the athletes' better personal qualities. Motivated by historical interest in gossip and concerns about what human characteristics lay behind athletic feats, spectators devoured news about the personal lives of their heroes. Women's gender only heightened the need for more personal knowledge. Although most articles were simply about athletic achievements, others added personal details or created sympathetic characters through nicknames and anecdotes. Athletes composed autobiographies or allowed others to describe their lives. By publicizing their own histories, athletes then made their bodies and reputations even more available for public consumption, so that others might emulate their accomplishments. In so doing, athletes working with or studied by popular magazines supported the nationalist and feminist agenda of *jianmei* women's bodies.

Jianmei can be translated as "fit or robust/healthy (beauty)," a quality that can be gained only through exercise. In this chapter, I show how feminist and nationalist dimensions subtly intertwined the personal ambitions of athletes in the translation of the modern Western categories of jianmei and tiyu into China during the national crisis. I examine popular journalism as a powerful force in creating desire for a jianmei body culture in China. Inevitably, coverage of competitive sports and the encouragement of jianmei culture mixed with fashion and gossip, producing a fan culture and pushing competitive sports and tiyu further into the public consciousness.

Numerous general and sports-oriented magazines chronicled the lives and achievements of sportswomen, but I will focus on articles and images in *Linglong*, a weekly women's magazine published in Shanghai from 1931 to 1937, to show the various interactions between public morals *(fenghua)* and the new fashion concept of jianmei. The interaction between state-regulated female body codes in the New Life Movement and jianmei (cultivated through tiyu), backed by a populist feminist agenda, affected popular culture in contradictory ways. On the one hand, the plain, makeup-free style in jianmei exemplified moral women's austerity. Conversely, the bare legs and feet of jianmei female bodies were often viewed as harmful to public morals *(you shang fenghua)*. Within these contradictions, as jianmei and tiyu became prevalent in fashion and the mass media, Chinese women gained an enabling female space through complex interactions with the nationalist agenda.

Linglong was part of the explosion of women's reading materials in late-1920s China. Magazines published adulatory articles about fashion, movie stars from Hollywood and China, modern womanhood, and sports. Chen Zhenling, the editor, was a woman. Leo Ou-Fan Lee has persuasively argued that *Linglong* was instrumental in creating a women's market for film.[2] I argue that it also generated national excitement about fitness and having a jianmei body, one that impelled women to emulate famous stars from the worlds of sports and film, especially American styles. Sometimes those worlds intertwined, making for an even more powerful message about being both jianmei and modern. As Sarah Frederick has argued about Japanese women's magazines during this period, such periodicals represented changes in modernity, including urbanization, consumer capitalism, Westernization, and transformation of gender roles.[3] I would add that the development of competitive sports went hand in hand with ordinary women's desires to emulate their favourite athletes in their fitness and their modernity. Although *Linglong* was not the only magazine to cover sports events, its extensive coverage made it notable in commercial media.

My argument engages that of Prasenjit Duara, who states that although "different women's groups and publications loosely affiliated with the Nationalist Party expressed radical and feminist points of view ... the dominant political tendency represented the view of a modern patriarchy." He suggests that "women's passivity and their being spoken for represented the political meaning of their gender."[4] In response, I argue that women, especially those who were educated and urban, fashioned active roles for themselves within a limited space through nuanced and complex negotiations with the dominant but self-contradictory wartime patriarchal nationalist forces. In *Linglong,* editorials by Chen Zhenling and contributions by other urbane, educated women offered an alternative voice that has been generally neglected by scholars who focus on state or institutional forces.

One of the ways in which women did this was through discussion of jianmei. European life reformers popularized and publicized ideas of the healthy and beautiful body in the cinema and the popular press through photographs, drawings, anatomical models, textual descriptions, and exercise guides.[5] Similarly, jianmei entered Chinese popular culture through highly successful pictorial magazines published by the Commercial Press and Liangyou Publishing House. Liangyou's flagship journal, *Liangyou huabao (Young Companion Pictorial,* 1926-45), which ushered in a phase of pictorial journalism, reflected this urban taste for the "modern" life.[6] With the growth of literacy among women in the Republican era, women's publications emerged as an integral part of the rising popular press. As noted in the Introduction, according to *Linglong's* "Survey of Women's Magazines and Journals across the Nation" in June 1933, there were twenty-three women's periodicals of various kinds across major cities in China.[7]

Among popular women's periodicals, *Linglong* distinguished itself as the standard for promoting jianmei and tiyu for women. In 1931, it initiated a column to advocate tiyu and advance health through tiyu photographs and articles. Readers were asked to provide relevant materials. In 1932, an editorial stated that "our magazine particularly carries tiyu news, especially about women."[8] By 1933, the magazine was urging its readers to recommend it "as the only mouthpiece for all sisters, paying special attention to women's jianmei," to friends and relatives so that all could rid themselves of their sickly appearance.[9] The name *Linglong* (literally, "chiselled") is from the expression *xiaoqiao linglong,* used to describe objects or people as small-sized but elegant. According to a middle-school student athlete, Lan Diqing, "today I see the little and lovely copy of *Linglong*, of which I have heard for a long time. Its elegant look and rich contents show the good future of women in our nation and explain why society views the magazine so highly."[10] True to its name, the magazine was pocket-sized, ranging in length from thirty to eighty pages. Its contents varied from love, sex, marriage, fashion, makeup, tiyu, and entertainment to interior decorating, popular psychology, new careers, war, and politics, taking the form of articles, advice columns, and commercial advertisements as well as illustrations and photographs. The Sanhe (Three [Heaven, Earth, and Human]-Harmony) Publishing House in Shanghai published *Linglong*. Sanhe also ran Ping-Pong houses and sold medicines to cure women's diseases (all advertised in *Linglong*).[11] When the first issue of the magazine appeared on 18 March 1931, it was inexpensively priced at seven-hundredths of an ounce of foreign silver, or twenty-one copper coins.[12] It was available nationwide, in cities as disparate as Chengdu, Hankou, Jinan, Quanzhou, Kaifeng, Hangzhou, Mei County in Sichuan, Tianjin, Nanjing, Yunnan, Shanghai, Hangzhou, Ningbo, and Changsha, and even overseas in Sumatra.[13]

Linglong's audience replicated that of the Modern Girl. As Madeleine Yue Dong has observed, the Modern Girl look was a necessity for women who worked as teachers, clerks, secretaries, saleswomen, and typists in government institutions, schools, companies, and stores. Employers demanded the Modern Girl look from job applicants. A jianmei figure amplified fashionable attire, permed hair, and makeup.[14]

Linglong became a multivocal space for women. Educated urban young women such as students, teachers, and other professionals were fans, but workers, housewives, and labourers also conversed through advice columns about new and old social situations faced by women. *Linglong* called for contributions about "housewives, arranging the home, sewing, cooking, education, practical issues, and teachers, workers, and farmers' lives and marriages."[15] It also included the voices of men, especially those of its chief photography editor, Lin Zemin, and its founder, Lin Zecang, who were concerned with women's issues.

Echoing the state ideology of patriotism of the 1930s, *Linglong* repeatedly called on women to make sacrifices for the nation, educate themselves in politics, and develop courage, power, and bodies as tough as men's. In 1937, on the eve of Japan's invasion of northern China, *Linglong*'s editor urged feminists to prioritize nationalist concerns because women's liberation had to be sought through national liberation. The editor contended that "the urgent task for women today is to unite and fight for the national liberation movement because all citizens, male or female, should struggle in such a national crisis.[16] At the same time, although the term "feminism" *(nüquan zhuyi [zhe])* never appeared in the magazine, *Linglong,* in proclaiming itself on almost every front cover to be "the mouthpiece of women's circles, and the only weapon to launch attacks on men," exemplified a feminist agenda.[17] The very contradiction between patriotic nationalism and feminism demonstrated the complex interaction between these discourses. While articulating women's special interests, rights, and identities, *Linglong* embraced nationalist rhetoric that sought both to empower women and to endorse gender equality, hence justifying and legitimizing women's expanded space.

For the editors of *Linglong,* the Western category jianmei and advocacy of a strong physique for women were at the core of the magazine's feminist agenda. The caption to a photograph of a row of strong Western women aiming rifles reads: "Women's rights/power in the modern world are well developed *(jinshi nüquan fada)*." The magazine claimed that women surpassed men in various fields, but regretted that women's natural physique was weaker. To counteract their "natural" deficiency, it claimed, women globally should pay close attention to jianmei and tiyu.[18]

Consistent with the concept of jianmei as Western, *Linglong* presented its feminist agenda behind jianmei in a global context by importing news and stories about women around the world, particularly the West. The value of the stories is not in their historical authenticity but in what they can tell us about the attitudes and sensibilities of the editors and readers. *Linglong* expressed deep worry about the international trend of the "women going home movement" and concern that "the good wife, wise mother" ideal would negatively affect the Nationalist government. Using the rhetoric of linear historical progress, *Linglong* identified that trend with "feudal China," and purported that the progressive and modern state in China that had liberated the Chinese version of Henrik Ibsen's famous heroine Nora would not return her to darkness. They opposed the Labour Meeting of the League of Nations that banned women from heavy manual labour, arguing that no limitations should be placed on women's proven physical capacities. The editors pointed out that in the United States the seemingly gender-neutral clause that companies should lay off one member of married couples first actually targeted married women.[19]

Linglong made direct political statements. It condemned the "dictatorship in Europe" for "pushing the wheel of history back to the darkness." It argued that gender discrimination was the basic principle of Nazi Germany. Although the Chinese press sometimes praised German women for being as masculine as men, especially in terms of physical training, it was said that masculine women and effeminate men were hated in Germany. *Linglong* declared that

Germany's Three K – *Kinder, Küche, Kirche* (Children, Kitchen, Church) – movement was outmoded and an "insult and challenge to women in the world."[20] *Linglong's* radical criticism of the West, especially the Nazis, focused on women's equal rights and opportunities in the workplace. The cosmopolitan outlook of *Linglong* may also be seen in its bilingual covers, which offered an English title, *Lin Loon Ladies' Magazine.* Although *Linglong* did not explicitly declare itself to be a feminist magazine, we can infer its feminism from its acknowledgment of women as an oppressed group, provision of a public forum to address women's issues, advocacy of women's equality, especially in physical and economic aspects, and engagement with international feminist movements. How it expressed that feminism was constrained, however, by the social and, most especially, the political context of the national crisis.

Jianmei Cultivated through Tiyu as Western and Modern

When jianmei emerged as a significant women's urban fashion aesthetic during China's national crisis, it was closely associated with tiyu. For women, tiyu, or the cultivation of muscular strength, was a necessary tool for cultivating a jianmei body. But what exactly was jianmei? In 1933, *Linglong* declared that "this journal pays special attention to jianmei," and started a "Beauty Advisor Column" *(meirong guwen lan)* as the primary forum for the debate on jianmei. Writers and editors contributed articles and responded to readers' comments.[21]

Jianmei cultivated through tiyu was presented as international (that is, Western) and modern through examples of Western women. It was argued that since their specialized schools and magazines actively advocated physical activities and health, Western women enjoyed exercise, paid close attention to their weight and posture, and were usually very jianmei. Chinese magazines featured photographs of white women in miniskirts, swimsuits, or gym shirts and shorts, ice skating, jumping over gymnastics horses, standing on their heads, and dancing, to show that "Western women have gained jianmei physiques through athletic exercise." The camera angles frequently accentuated strong, bare legs and fashionable high-heeled sandals. The caption of a photograph of a scantily clad woman with powerful legs and wearing high heels read: "It is not about new clothes; she is just showing you her jianmei legs." This combination of a jianmei physique and high heels indicates the frequent blurring of what was considered modern.[22] Magazines used paintings and photographs of nude Western women with "healthy curves" to persuade Chinese women to shift their attention away from pretty faces and toward robust physiques. Western advertisements and films also accentuated the sensuality, presumed wealth, and civilized personality of women in high heels.[23]

The primal energy evoked by the "natural" athletic body became a significant theme. *Linglong* borrowed images from European sources. European life reformers worshipped unspoiled nature, the antithesis of the contrivance of modernity: sun and water became symbols of cleanliness, strength, beauty, and sexual innocence. Fit and beautiful nude bodies framed in these elements were elevated to a spiritual principle and constituted part of the pure, reverential contemplation of nature.[24] Photographic portrayals of "Sun Bathing" and a "Primal Fit and Healthy Life" *(yuanshi de jianmei shenghuo)* depicted nude white women sunbathing on the beach, lying on grass in front of a pond, or playing in water in various athletic poses.[25] On the other hand, *Linglong* also made the connection between the "natural" body and the body revered by European fascist movements, reporting that Benito Mussolini had ordered women to pay attention to jianmei and had commanded artists to depict women's jianmei curves because "a weak mother cannot give birth to strong children."[26]

Images of glamorous Hollywood stars reinforced jianmei as a fashionable Western aesthetic. *Linglong* quoted Greta Garbo in 1936 as saying: "Jianmei is our lifeline and supply of food and clothing ... The proper sports for me are golf and bicycling."[27] In addition to beautiful faces and artistic talents, jianmei physiques appeared to be indispensable for success in Hollywood. In the pursuit of a sturdy figure, sport replaced dieting. In one cartoon, *Linglong* showed Jean Harlow, Marlene Dietrich, Joan Blondell, Janet Gaynor, and Joan Crawford as representatives of modern feminine beauty. While the editors admired Dietrich for her "lively and mysterious style," Blondell for her "lively gestures to artists' taste," Gaynor for her gentleness, and Crawford for her distinctive sensual beauty, they lauded Harlow as "exemplifying jianmei for modern women." Blondell, who is the central figure of the cartoon, replete with wide shoulders and long legs, was depicted as "a famous artist's ideal girl." *Linglong* editors interpreted her as the anonymous global standard (ideal or exemplary, rather than average) beauty that combined the above assets (see Figure 9). Over the years, *Linglong* showed numerous Hollywood actresses as "Jianmei Stars" performing various activities. Riding was a popular sport, and many photographs showed actresses jumping fences on horseback. Starlet Claire Dodd cut a striking pose in riding attire: boots, loose masculine pants, and a wide belt. Other images were more improbable, showing actresses clad in tight tank tops and shorts or miniskirts but wearing high-heeled sandals while dancing, hitting tennis balls, bowling, lifting free weights, doing gymnastics, posing with basketballs, or, most tellingly, learning to sprint from world-class male runners. Even demure actresses with slender figures were described as robust athletes. Jianmei was thus applied widely.[28]

Life reformers who accepted eugenics in Weimar racial science and medicine viewed physical beauty as an indicator of a healthy constitution. A healthy and beautiful body was characterized by the harmonious and purposeful interactions of its constituent parts. Ideal health and beauty were promoted as the "science of the normal" that could be manipulated, managed, and disciplined through specific measurements.[29] Accordingly, *Linglong* frequently presented absolute (not average) "international" standards of jianmei in terms of exact measurements. In 1932, it reported that although the Venus de Milo of Greek antiquity had stood as the norm for jianmei for hundreds of years, (Western) aesthetics experts had now elected a more beautiful American woman to replace her. The Venus's measurements were 5 feet, 5.5 inches tall, 120 pounds, with 34.5-inch chest, 5.43-inch wrists, 26-inch waist, 36.5-inch hips, 21.5-inch thighs, 13.4-inch calves, and 8-inch ankles.[30] In 1934, *Linglong* reported that an International Beauty Institute (Guoji meirong yuan) had invited representatives from various nations to meet every March to adjudicate an annual beauty norm. The institute set the measurements for a woman's "international standard beauty" for 1935 to be 5 feet, 7 inches tall, 130 pounds, 35-inch chest, 35-inch hips, blond, and physically fit. The American actress Mae West met these standards.[31] In March 1935, *Linglong* reported that the institute met in New York for the Twelfth Beauty Examining Conference, and decided that Miss 1936 should be of "small and lilting figure *[liuxian xing]* without heavy makeup" to incorporate naturalness into modern beauty. In addition, "the hair was to be at least two inches long, the wave of hair should not be too thin, and the neck should be revealed." A twenty-three-year-old dancer who weighed 100 pounds and was around 5 feet tall with natural brown hair was considered a candidate.[32] While unequivocally Western, the standards for jianmei on the pages of *Linglong* were also fickle and often contradictory.

Translating Jianmei: Discourses of Chinese Modernity

From such sources, one could easily envision *Linglong* as a Western-style magazine, yet its concerns were about Chinese women. When *Linglong* "translated" and popularized Western, modern categories of jianmei and tiyu among urban literate women in China, the editors faced an interesting twist of racial dynamics. The weekly publication viewed Chinese women as lacking jianmei qualities and lagging behind Western standards of jianmei. To change this, it encouraged fashionable Chinese women to relate to the images of Western women and match "international" (Western) standards. Corresponding to the self-Orientalism in state discourse that viewed the Chinese as physically weak and sick, *Linglong* argued that the women of the "sick man

9   "The poses of the international standard beauties." The centre figure on the left is called "a famous artist's ideal girl."
Source: Linglong 5, 168 (8 May 1935): 98-99.

of Asia" were, essentially, even weaker. It viewed Chinese women's "genetically weaker physiques" as a significant hindrance to gaining equality with Chinese men and the cause of their inferiority to Western women.

After reporting the standard measurements required for entrants to the beauty contests, *Linglong* begged: "Reader sisters, please examine your own weight, height, chest, hips, and waist to see whether they fit the standards of this year or next year."[33] Fitting the frame of beauty without racial adjustment confirmed the inadequacy of Chinese women. "Our nation's women can be *jian* [fit] but not *mei* [attractive], or *mei* but not *jian*. We do not have the type of *jian* and *mei* woman." The chief editor, Chen Zhenling, raised the only dissenting voice in an answer to a nineteen-year-old girl's question regarding standard weight. "The International Beauty Institute sets standards annually, but they do not apply to our nation at all because the standards do not make allowances for differences in race and regions." Yet the editor followed the pattern and set rough standards for women of the Chinese nation: 5 feet tall and 130 pounds. Gradually, though, precise standards dissolved into the rather vaguer "wide chest," "large and erect breasts," "high nipples," "ample behind," "slender waist," "even-proportioned figure," and "strong legs."[34]

Although the failures of Chinese female athletes in international games confirmed the inadequacy of Chinese women, *Linglong* promoted Chinese athletes as models and bridges toward the adoption of Western categories of jianmei.[35] Their images, in competition and in standard and fashionable athletic poses, were ubiquitous in the magazine. Under the caption "Jianmei Gestures," female athletes were shown at track events and throwing and jumping in field events and in ball games.[36] Dancing was considered one significant tiyu activity that linked jianmei with fashion. From 1932, dancers began to wear short dresses, sleeveless shirts, and gym shorts to show their jianmei legs and arms.[37] Other photographs emphasize robust legs. The reader sees, for example, groups of "robust athletes" in shorts and sneakers, crouching to reveal their sturdy figures and highlight their legs. Five thick-legged girls from Southeast Tiyu School, who posed with their left arms tucked behind them and their right arms up, elbows out, with their hands tucked behind their heads, were labelled as "the strongest" in the Second Shanghai Middle School Games. In a photograph captioned "The Healthy Legs of Students from Southeast," the camera focused on the legs of a row of girls lying on their stomachs while turning their heads back toward the camera. In the same caption, it was explained that "developing jianmei legs needs daily exercise."[38]

Jianmei athletes brought athletic elements into contemporary fashion poses. Under the caption "*xiong* [grand or masculine] among Women," the national sprint star Qian Xingsu, whom I will discuss in Chapter 4, appeared with fashionable bobbed hair and a *qipao* (a modern dress popular in the Republican era) behind bamboo stalks. Other "jianmei athletes" wore *qipao* with numbers on them, just like athletic sweaters, or matched their Western coats with numbered sweaters. School athletic teams in fashionable dresses deployed themselves around sporting equipment such as gym bars and basketball hoops under the label "jianmei girls." Athletic outfits were promoted as chic. Such combinations indicated that athletes were combining the formal dress of *qipao* with their team's identity, thereby elevating the status of their sport and demonstrating professional pride in their accomplishments.[39]

Such stylistic confusion appeared elsewhere. The circulation of new images of Chinese female athletes with bobbed hair, T-shirts, and gym shorts in popular magazines promoted the aesthetic concept of jianmei as an alternative to current urban fashion norms of slender beauty in high heels and fancy *qipao* and with permed hair. Setting regional stereotypes against each other, *Linglong* called "female compatriots" from the northern province of Shandong – with their tanned skin, tall figures, and strong bodies – "a female army of amazons" and admirable representatives of the jianmei ideal. Shanghai-style Modern Girls were called on to learn from Shandong girls, by removing their high heels and makeup and dashing to the athletic fields.[40] Despite the outstanding performance of Shanghai teams in various games, "the pale Modern Girls" and *mingyuan* (young bourgeois ladies of note) from Shanghai were viewed as mere "Lin Daiyu-style sickly beauty." Lin was a depressed and tubercular heroine in the eighteenth-century novel *Honglou meng (Story of the Stone)*, whose beauty was based on her sickly weakness.[41]

Linglong presented the shift to jianmei from the traditional "Lin Daiyu-style sickly beauty" as a "scientific" linear progression. According to editor Chen Zhenling, human views of beauty evolved with time through education. Due to the restriction of Confucian morals *(lijiao)*, bound feet, and the absence of female exercise, the depressed, sick, thin-faced Lin Daiyu became the model followed by women and appreciated by men. With time and change, new expectations for women, and the advocacy of publications, jianmei was the new look. Round-faced women were now considered attractive.[42]

In this formulation, weak women in high heels appeared not modern but backward and shameful. An advertisement for *Baofeijiao*, a medicine for respiratory diseases, depicted the dangers faced by those in high heels, even though, as noted, female intellectuals sometimes wore high heels. A slender woman in a short, tight skirt, fitted medium-length coat, and high heels, wearing a scarf over her permed hair, held a handkerchief to her mouth while walking in heavy rain. A hole in the ground before her warned: "Beware of falling into the trap of tuberculosis *(feilao)*." A strong physique was now considered the basis for a strong will, noble character, foresight, and the great hopes of modern men and women. Physical training on athletic fields and mental training were taken as essential requirements for New Women.[43] Writer Zhu Yaoxian viewed the "tanned jianmei women jumping and running on the grass-covered athletic fields, something never before seen," as evidence of progress. "Their determined, enduring, and brave spirits are admired by their weaker sisters and surprised men." Echoing Chen Zhenling, one woman argued that beauty had progressed. Modern women were more beautiful than those in the past because of "progress in clothing," lively facial expressions influenced by Western films, and, most important, "tender figures with even-proportioned muscles" gained through tiyu.[44]

Soon *Linglong* was presenting jianmei as the "general desire of modern women." By 1936, Chen presented a reader's letter "regarding the key to jianmei" as "a general concern of girls."[45] *Linglong's* readers responded enthusiastically and participated actively in the redefinition and reconstruction of Western jianmei and tiyu for Chinese women. An editorial in *Linglong* drew attention from a woman's face to her figure by declaring that "makeup is deceptive and temporary, but jianmei is self-cultivated and will last until old age if you persist" and that "jianmei is not about being big or fat or using makeup, but having a fit physique, healthy skin colour and lively gestures."[46]

Readers, both male and female, and the editors discussed the jianmei of specific parts of the female body. Most attention was drawn to women's breasts and legs, which had never before been considered an important aspect of Chinese feminine beauty. Whereas male readers framed the discussion around hygiene centred on women's weaker physique and reproductive organs, women were mainly concerned with the aesthetic dimension.[47] Editorials and articles offered "must-know" secrets to achieving jianmei, such as exercise, being worry-free, getting enough sleep and good nutrition, proper medicine, surgery, and books. Western women were cited as models for following these rules. Writers criticized Chinese females for being lazy about hygiene, but argued that "fortunately they are beginning to pay attention to the benefits of swimming."[48]

Tiyu and jianmei entered into the sensibilities of ordinary urban literate young women who were attracted to modern fashion. These qualities were promulgated as necessary qualities for modern national womanhood, as indicated by the captions to photographs published in *Linglong*.[49] Here, ordinary women appeared in stadiums wearing T-shirts, shorts, and sneakers, carrying tennis and badminton rackets. Lines of girls in shorts and T-shirts, lying face down on the ground and holding their legs with their hands, represented pioneering Modern Girls who practised bare-handed gymnastics.[50] Even fashions such as permed hair, fancy and tight-fitting *qipao*, and high heels, which were identified with the Lin Daiyu sickly style, began to be associated with such sports as swinging, roller skating, and miniature golf.[51] Women were sorted into categories according to various standards, such as noble, cute, motherly, funny, mysterious, masculine, family-oriented, weak, or playful, but there was always a tiyu-related category, characterized as "active, open and agile." Plain, short, and lightweight clothing, more or less following men's styles, was recommended. Long dresses and "French-style high heels" were discouraged for fear of "hurting the natural and relaxed beauty" of the tiyu style.[52]

As jianmei, promoted by popular magazines such as *Linglong,* became an integral part of urban femininity, it also penetrated various artistic fields of

modern popular culture, including photography and cinema. Jianmei justified the depiction of naked female bodies on artistic grounds, which it deemed
free from moral sanction. Nonetheless, it seems that Chinese models were
not readily available for such poses. In the series of nude photographs published in *Linglong*, the same model of a slight and unbalanced figure with
a large lower belly and small breasts was used again and again; however,
the photographers portrayed her in imitation of Western themes of bodily
expression and to experiment with a distinctive image of Chinese or "Oriental" physical beauty. Evoking an atmosphere of biblical paradise, the
model stood, smiling toward the camera, in front of a willow tree in a lush
garden. In "Regret," the model knelt on a piece of stone topped by a large
cross, with her head bowed in front. The breasts were emphasized by specific
positioning of the hips, hands, and arms. In other photographs, such as
"Oriental Body Beauty," "Chinese Body Beauty," or "Tranquil Beauty," the
same model was shown presenting traditional Chinese musical instruments
in various gestures.[53] Although these images had little to do with jianmei, the
popularity of jianmei ideals had altered readers' expectations to such an extent
that they appeared less risqué than trite.

Athletic jianmei emerged as an integral element of Chinese domestic cinema and female stardom.[54] I will discuss this extensively in Chapter 6, and a
few examples will suffice for now. As physical fitness became an essential
requirement for female beauty rather than a threat to femininity, even the
demure Chinese "Movie Queen" Hu Die (Butterfly Wu, 1908-89) was photographed playing tennis. In contrast, the new trend of physical fitness among
actresses shook the confidence of 1920s popular actress Ruan Lingyu (Lily
Yuen, 1910-35), noted as she was for her weak beauty, and contributed to her
depression and suicide.[55] Jianmei and athletic activities became such popular
clichés for depicting Chinese movie actresses that the magazine commented
with sarcasm: "Female movie stars took athletic activities as the fashion for
the year before last; writing was the fashion last year, and what about this
year?"[56] In its movies column, *Linglong* introduced and commented on international and domestic films and actors as well as cinema gossip. Approximately one-third of each issue contained colour illustrations of Hollywood
movie stars who exemplified jianmei physiques, as well as domestic jianmei
stars and even fashion poses of ordinary readers.

What are the implications for constructing femininity out of this growing
visibility of women's bodies in public spaces? Leo Ou-Fan Lee points out the
necessity of interpreting mass print culture and cinema through not only the
institutional but also the social context. He argues that nation as a "community" and "modernity" are both "idea and imaginary, both essence and surface."

Focusing on the pictorial magazine *Young Companion Pictorial,* Lee demonstrates that the images and styles in popular newspapers, novels, and periodicals contributed to the rise of a contour of collective sensibilities and significations in the "public sphere," and conjured up a collective visionary imaginary of modernity. They "do not necessarily enter into the deepest of thought" and go beyond the ideological confines of government policy.[57]

Lee also suggests that the publicly displayed "modern" women's body, either in fancy dress or nude, played crucial roles in shaping imagined modernity in the public arena of urban society. Resisting the facile accusation of "male gaze and lust, hence leading to objectification and commodification of the female body," Lee ponders:

> But what if some (even large numbers) of the readers were women? And what if pages of nudes were placed in the journal together with pictures of Chinese and world leaders, athletes and Hollywood movie stars? ... I would argue that the display of the female body had become part of a new public discourse related to modernity in everyday life.[58]

Building on Lee's argument, I wonder what the difference might be if the editors and contributors of the journal were women? Would the display of the robust female body be part of a female-to-female feminist discourse? Nearly all of the writers from *Linglong* cited in this chapter were female.[59] The answer is evident in the following episode. There was a rumour in 1935 that eleven young men, led by a certain Ouyang Hai, launched a campaign to select "Miss Guangzhou" by focusing on jianmei thighs: "Thick, big, firm, smooth, and well-proportioned."[60] *Linglong's* female writers quickly condemned it: "Beauty selection manipulated by men focuses on sensuality *[rougan]* and legs for their pleasure. That is the biggest shame for women, and we are absolutely against it." Criticizing the Miss Guangzhou competition as the "thigh beauty" *(datui meiren)* selection, the female writer called on Chinese and foreign sponsors of Miss Shanghai to use as judging criteria morality, talent, and jianmei.[61] Female editors had to tread a thin line when it came to presenting images of healthy athletes, who appear innocent and almost desexualized. Furthermore, they reiterated that the ideal woman was an all-around citizen, exemplary not only in jianmei physique but also in morality and talent.

In sum, in translating an imported ideal of jianmei into a sign of Chinese female modernity, *Linglong* played a significant role in the history of modern journalism and Chinese modernity. In so doing, it naturally created more public awareness and enthusiasm for sports and elite athletic competitions.

Jianmei and the State

The reception of jianmei took a downward turn with the advent of the New Life Movement (NLM) in 1934, which was in part a response to the national crisis caused by Japanese aggression. The Nationalist government sought to impose dress codes and limit prostitution, and in so doing exert ultimate control over women's bodies. The desire for healthy female bodies did not diminish, but women wearing leg-baring sports attire were deemed harmful to public morals. Herein lies a fundamental contradiction in the discourse of jianmei in the 1930s and an opportunity to see how women responded to political change.[62]

A deeper contradiction lies with the very conditions of China's desire for modernity. In order to appear modern, China needed to retain a degree of Western cosmopolitanism; in order to assert its unique identity, China tried to identify national essences in spirit, morality, and culture. Women's bodies served as the site for the clash of these two impulses. On the one hand, the Nationalist state wanted to show progress by abolishing "feudal" and "backward" restrictions on women's bodies. On the other hand, it attacked the liberation of women's bodies from state control as Westernization harmful to the traditional morality and spirit advocated in the NLM.[63]

In theory, tiyu remained a desirable national undertaking. The 1929 Tiyu Law for Citizens, which was carried over to the 1930s, addressed the need to fight against traditional attitudes that would hamper a successful tiyu program for women. Article 4 stated "All customs that hinder the regular physical growth of young men and young women should be strictly prohibited by the counties, municipalities, villages, and hamlets; and their programs should be fixed by the Ministry of Education and the Training Commissioner's Department."[64] Although this clause was primarily directed at the prevalent rural customs of breast binding and footbinding, it became public policy in other ways.[65]

The Nationalist government's viewpoint on jianmei during the New Life Movement became overwhelmingly negative; jianmei was lumped with revealing "Western" dress and even prostitution. The attire of Modern Girls as evinced by calendar models and movie stars – heavy makeup, permed hair, fancy clothes, and high heels – was labelled as "bizarre dress" *(qizhuang yifu)* that was harmful to morals and therefore banned. In June 1936, the Nationalist government deemed it illegal for women to wear extravagant clothes and permed hair. Chiang Kai-shek instructed officers on the streets to enforce the law by accompanying violators to their homes to change their clothes, and by jailing and fining those who resisted. As a result, fewer modern, fashionable women were seen in public. When the actress Huang Jing arrived by boat in Chongqing in a Western dress that revealed part of her breasts, soldiers stopped her at the pier and told her to go back to the boat to change. Since her luggage had already been sent to the hotel, she had to borrow clothes from a servant before being allowed to land.[66] The Nationalist government went as far as launching a "hair-tying movement," promoting the traditional *ji* (a bun on the back of the head). On 21 January 1935, the Nanchang Military Headquarters ruled that soldiers could not marry women without a *ji*. A clause was added to the NLM rules, discouraging women from wearing their hair loose, bobbed, or permed. Not all of these rules were uniformly applied or were generally effective. As we shall see in Chapter 5, the noted swimmer Yang Xiuqiong, who was promoted as the poster girl of the NLM, either ignored or defied these directives in her widely publicized physical presentations.

Local authorities responded to the central state's directives in various ways. The municipal authority of Hangzhou and one governor, Huang Shaohong, banned permed hair as the first step in enforcing the NLM, because women in their territories travelled to Shanghai and spent large amounts of money on permanent waves. The leaders of Shanghai women's circles asserted that the *ji* was preferable to haircutting in terms of cost, time, and even natural beauty. The Shanghai Girls' Middle School, the private Peiming Girls' Middle School, and women's groups in Jinan, Daxia, and Fudan Universities proposed the organization of an Alliance of Female Students for Long Hair (Nüxuesheng xufa da tongmeng) to dissuade students from cutting their hair. The Educational Bureau of Guangdong drafted strict dress codes banning female students from permanent waves, makeup, high heels, or jewellery such as diamond rings or bracelets.[67] Young men in various cities (particularly Hangzhou, Nanjing, and Tianjin) voluntarily organized "modern fashion destruction troupes" *(Modeng pohuai tuan)* with strong fascist overtones to violently enforce the state bans in public spaces.[68]

Women involved in the jianmei movement attempted to soften the New Life Movement's attacks on modern girls.[69] They agreed with certain aspects of the NLM's argument. Many urban women and men were disenchanted with what they perceived as excessive Westernization in young women. As early as 1931, some literate urban women attempted to legitimize an alternative image of "new women" based on tiyu and jianmei, as opposed to the Modern Girls identified with heavy makeup and fancy clothes. Gradually, jianmei and "bizarre dress" became opposite sides of a dichotomy in the New Life Movement. Female educator Cao Xiulin, a Wuben Women's School (Wuben nüxiao) graduate and teacher at Huifen Women's School in Shanghai, advocated disciplining the disgraceful and superficial fake New Women – whose "modern" beauty was marked by attractive clothes, foreign creams, or powders – by creating authentic ones through tiyu and jianmei. As noted in Chaper 1, Zhang Huilan, generally an advocate for emancipating women's bodies through sports, had argued against high heels, but only because they hindered exercise. She used high heels herself in formal portraits. While Modern Girls were labelled as "flower vases" and "playthings," a writer in *Linglong* suggested using "Girl of This Age" or "Girl of Today" for the "real New/Modern Woman" who had a clever brain, the ambition to fight for great causes, and, most important, a jianmei physique.[70]

Akin to the German life reform movement, the New Life Movement considered fancy appearances as foreign and corrupt, associated with gender mixing in entertainment venues and with the decline of women's purity and morals, while it viewed clean, simple, and practical clothing as indigenous, culturally authentic, moral, and identified with motherhood in a domestic sphere. Tiyu was prescribed as treatment of this fancy appearance. *Linglong* reported that "different nations hold different views on women's jianmei and status. Some respect women's dignity *[renge]*, while others take women as playthings and women's dress styles are influenced consequently."[71]

It is ambiguous, however, how far *Linglong* raised voices in opposition to those who wanted to close down the choices available to women about how they looked and what national style they represented. One contributor described how Germany had lost its original national character and united spirit after its women's clothing styles became fancy and colourful as a result of "bad influences" from southern Europe. It was said that German women abandoned exotic and fancy clothes in favour of hygienic and artistic clothing when they decided to pursue motherhood. Furthermore, *Linglong* criticized Japanese women for their lewd, excessive use of face powder, while it admired the German Nazi party's banning of women with makeup from its political meetings.[72] An editorial explicitly condemned female "bizarre dress" in China for being influenced by evil, extravagant Western customs.[73] Indulgence in social life, fancy clothes, and hedonism were criticized as the wrong direction for Chinese women, who had only recently gained freedom after the May Fourth Movement had advocated wholesale Westernization.[74] In this way, the anti-fashion proposal in *Linglong* was a veiled argument for the superiority of Chinese culture and morality. This claim rings hollow, however, because both the terms and standards of judgment were Western.

Of the various means of abolishing women's "bizarre dress," the most commonly used was to identify it with prostitution.[75] It is in this area that the state's attempted control over women's bodies reached extreme proportions. Zhou Quanchu, the Shanghai Provincial Police Bureau chief, ordered prostitutes who were adorned with fashionable clothes and modern makeup to wear a badge shaped like a peach flower in order to distinguish them from ladies and female students from good families. The strategy was also used in Hankou, Nanjing, Changsa, and Guangdong. Prostitutes resisted having to wear the badges by hiding them inside their clothes or underneath large scarves, so the authorities established follow-up policies. The Public Safety Department in Hankou proposed to the city government that specific areas be reserved for prostitutes, who were at the time living throughout the city. Gradually, permed hair and high heels, a combination often used by athletes, replaced the peach-flower badge as a legal signifier of prostitution. Shanxi Province ordered prostitutes to wear high heels and permed hair or be punished as illegal secret prostitutes. On 1 May 1935, prostitutes in Taiyuan were ordered to start wearing the badges, permed hair, and high heels.[76] High heels and permed hair, the fashionable attire of urban Modern Girls, became unequivocally associated with degraded womanhood.

Patriotic, pure, and moral womanhood cultivated by tiyu and jianmei cut a visual contrast with decadent figures in the pleasure quarters. In a photograph series titled "South and North Poles," fancy-looking prostitutes posed near a door. Female members of a Chinese hiking team *(Zhonghua buxing tuan)* with short hair, plain T-shirts, and *qipao* were presented as positive contrast. The team was said to have walked for two years and to be planning to walk for eight more, investigating the situations of citizens across the nation.[77] Since mothers and wives fulfilled their patriotic obligations by raising their families, women in pleasure quarters could be reformed into patriotic citizens by serving in combat or helping mothers and wives with household work. The precondition was training their will and dignity through tiyu and military drills.[78]

In Nanjing, the capital, singers were similarly trained as part of the New Life Movement, and were organized into first-aid teams to prepare for war. In 1934, after someone cut the fashionable clothes of a Modern Girl as she crossed Taiping Road, popular singers in the Qinhuai area (a traditional pleasure quarter) were frightened into wearing the plain clothes of "national products" and little or no jewellery. The singers, to reinforce their new image of "cherishing youth, having a sense of shame, and fostering the New Life Movement," reduced their time for socializing and exercised every morning by riding bikes and doing breathing exercises.[79] A female correspondent to *Linglong* founded the School for Women of the Pleasure Quarters (Jiaofang nüzi minzhong xueshe), which charged only one yuan for registration. Tiyu was a significant part of the curriculum, along with general academic education, proper morals for women *(fudao),* and domestic training.[80]

But urban literate women were not satisfied with the anti-prostitution drive of the Nationalist government. Some opposed the authorities' association of "bizarre appearance" with prostitutes and the plain jianmei style with "women of good family." The Women's Progressive Association *(Funü xiejin hui)* of Taiyuan asked the city to rescind the order that prostitutes wear high heels and permed hair. They feared that glamour would become the privilege of prostitutes and that women of "good families" supporting the New Life Movement would lose control in the domestic power balance, jeopardizing family and social stability.[81] Concerned with the dignity of prostitutes as women and with their potential virtues, as exemplified by historical legendary prostitutes whose stories centred on courage and patriotism, some women writers for *Linglong* called on "the gentlemen in authority" to be "generous, tolerant, and more careful about their attitude." They called on social forces, including education rather than state power, to persuade women to adopt a jianmei plain style.[82]

There was resistance to such severe opinions. One 1936 editorial in *Linglong* advocated the decoupling of women's hairstyle and morality, hence returning the agency of self-fashioning to the women, prostitutes included. This editorial argued that hairstyles as mere decoration should not be controlled or manipulated by men. "Perming, cutting, or keeping their hair long are women's personal freedoms, and have nothing to do with so-called moral questions." "Do they not know that the officially sanctioned *ji*-chignons can be as costly and sensuous [as permed hair]? So, the women problem will never be solved until women themselves are involved." Some women called for a ban on the sensuous styles of the chignons; progressive women were to cut their hair in the interests of gender equality, modernization, and civilization.[83] The plain jianmei style fit perfectly with the image of the virtuous and patriotic New Woman and therefore had broad appeal during a period of national crisis.

State and journalistic discourses on dress and anxiety regarding modernity took the most radical form in a concerted attack on the exposure of female skin in public. By order of Mayor Yuan Liang, the Beiping Social and Public Safety Bureau made it illegal to reveal female legs and feet unless performing manual labour. *Qipao* hemlines were required to be within 1 inch of the top of the foot, the sleeves down to the elbow, the collar 1.5 inches high, and the side splits no more than 3 inches above the knee. Short tops were to cover the belt loops and be worn with skirts. Knitted short tops without buttons were banned. Trousers had to be worn with tops that were loose around the waist and that covered 3 inches of the seat. The shortest pants had to extend 4 inches below the knee. Walking on the street in pajamas, slippers, or bare feet was banned. The latter injunction indicates the still-prevalent erotic quality of bare feet. Display of bare feet in art was historically considered pornographic in China. Female government employees, teachers, and students, and female dependents of male government employees, were ordered to begin following the law within half a month, and other women within one month. Policemen on duty were responsible for enforcing the law and violators were to be detained and punished. The order was printed and distributed to households by the Public Safety Bureau. To enforce the rules of the New Life Movement, the local government of Xi County in Anhui Province punished men with bare arms and women showing their chests with one day of manual labour.[84]

Besides regulating the length and shape of women's clothing, the authorities instituted a series of gender segregation measures to counter the liberalizing threats brought about by the display of women's bare skin. The Guangdong Political Research Association *(Zhengzhi yanjiu hui)* banned men and women, including those from official families, from swimming, walking, travelling, eating, and living together outside the home. Theatres were not to show movies performed by both men and women (actors would play the roles of the opposite gender). In order to ban coeducation, Beiping mayor Yuan Liang ordered the Social and Public Safety Bureaus to recruit and help contractors build women's dormitories in various districts.[85]

The official fear of exposed female skin in public was symptomatic of a larger anxiety about the visibility of women on city streets and in new urban professions. This attitude was widespread among the urban population, as evidenced by an essay in *Linglong* by a male contributor who contended that the massive numbers of women seeking economic opportunities in cities were transformed into "abnormal 'Modern Girls' who abandoned family, chastity, friendship, and honesty – enjoying pleasure without restriction." In support of his argument, the writer paraphrased an article with a similar tone from the Japanese newspaper *Yomiuri Shimbun,* called "Chinese Modern Women and Women's Education." The journalist's solution was "to return to ancient ideas and respect traditions, banning men and women from walking together, and women from revealing their legs or feet."[86]

The Nationalist state, however, had to maintain a delicate balance in order to discipline and exert control over women's bodies. On the one hand, it sought to liberate women from traditional restrictions and to bring them up as healthy citizens. On the other hand, it invented a spiritual "national essence" to curb the liberating trend brought about by the new fashions in the media and public culture. Within this context, bare skin was no longer an expression of the desirable jianmei style associated with tiyu but was instead construed as the most bizarre of all appearances. The campaign against bare skin in public represented the most draconian measure of the Nationalist state's attempt to control women's bodies.

Resistance from Urban Writers

Official discourse did not remain unchallenged. Although a 1934 editorial in *Linglong* called on youth to obey the official ban on bare skin and mixed-gender social activities, female authors in *Linglong,* who viewed these bans as "hostile," "insulting," and "hysterical," and with "anger" and "shame,"[87] defended bare-skin fashions and jianmei in their own discourses of civilization. The New Life Movement promoted Confucian morals as a Chinese national essence and rejected jianmei bare skin as an example of Western material civilization; however, the flip side of timeless "national essence" is stagnation and backwardness. *Linglong's* defenders of bare skin played up this underside: "It seems that every barbarian nation has, or had, a tendency to regulate women's appearance and segregate genders to enforce morality." Using a liberal progressive logic, they attacked the New Life Movement ban as "going against the trend of history" and asked rhetorically: "Should China keep pace with the currents of the time or return to the ancient barbaric convention of locking women at home?" During the opening ceremony of the Eighteenth North China Games in Tianjin on the morning of the national day in 1934, Madame Yu Xuezhong (governor of Hebei Province), who had bound feet, was invited to cut the ribbon. People joked that "maybe female athletes with bare chests and legs betrayed the New Life Movement. Madame Yu ... with her bound feet ... may fit the New Life Movement better!"[88]

One powerful critique of the official obsession with bare skin took the form of advocacy for female livelihood. "In order to relieve the national crisis, the NLM should shift attention to economic development and national defence," wrote one contributor. Under the pseudonym "A Rural Woman in Shanxi Province," the author called attention to rural poverty – the root cause that deprived girls of clothing. "We fifteen- or sixteen-year-old girls in the countryside work in the cold fields with bare feet and legs because we do not have money to buy trousers and shoes. But the officials and moral defenders in urban social and public safety bureaus ignore our needs and only focus on abolishing bare legs and feet." The writer's correlation of poverty with bare feet contradicted Mao Zedong's arguments to European theorists that bare feet were healthier than women's shoes.[89]

Others resisted by deploying the authority of science. In 1934, for example, the Beiping Women's Association (Funü hui) argued that bare feet and legs should not be banned because, according to medical science, it was hygienic to reveal the legs and feet during the hot summer, allowing the sun to kill germs and reduce disease.[90] Several *Linglong* authors echoed this argument by stating that women whose legs were covered with long trousers tended to become emaciated. Such views were distinctly modern and reversed older prohibitions on the display of bare feet.[91]

Chinese attitudes toward nudity may not have coincided with Western views. Whereas the naked body, and especially the Western classical male nude body, took on numerous meanings according to who was promoting it in early twentieth-century Europe, its promoters in *Linglong* narrated the rise and fall of Roman and Greek history in terms of the appreciation of the beauty and strength of the male body, and stated that the Greek legacy of appreciating the innocent beauty of the body was reborn in the modern arts.[92] Nudism and the North American and European nudist movement *(luoti shenghuo yundong)* (discussed at length in *Linglong*) were, moreover, regarded as entirely natural and associated with freedom from sexual connotations. *Linglong* believed that the movement originated in Germany, where, it said, because of the popularity of naturalism, the human body and sexual liaisons between men and women were not viewed as "shameful" or "mysterious." Under the heading "Glimpses of German Nudist Life," the editors of *Linglong* introduced a series of photographs featuring individuals, couples, families, and groups of various ages and gender, with outdoor athletic activities as the most common theme. Large nude women were shown in various poses, climbing cliffs and sitting or standing in the mountains.[93]

Linglong described the nudist movement as universal and enduring. The nudist organization in the Finnish capital, for example, was commended for its strict regulations. Only those who were strong and free of disease were qualified, and members were required to take an oath in order to join. Males and females supervised each other to make sure that no one fell into romantic relationships; non-family members were not allowed to kiss.[94] The nudist movement in the United States, in turn, appeared institutionalized, commercial, and fashionable. According to a newspaper article, a hundred nudists gathered in a seven-hundred-acre "nudist yard" in San Diego to exhibit the pleasure of bareness to visitors. Its "nudist queen," a beautiful twenty-two-year-old girl, announced that she would travel to New York to carry on her "natural life" there. Her harmonious and loving family life (five of her ten siblings were believers in nudism) was emphasized to highlight the moral correctness of her actions.[95] Nudism, it was concluded, reduced the mystery of the human body and improved morals and happiness.[96] Besides progressive trends from the West, defenders of naturalism also called attention to "primitive" minorities who, like innocent children, were construed as effortless practitioners of naturalism with physical strength and beauty. Naturalists cited Oswald Spengler's *The Decline of the West* as evidence that natural human bodies, particularly from "primitive" societies, were healthy, authentic, and moral. Such humans had well-developed muscles and shiny skin from exercise in the sun, cold water, and air.[97] Similarly, women of Tibet, Hainan Island, and the Yao ethnic group in China were admired for enjoying bare-skinned customs, strong physiques, positive gender roles, and free romantic relations in their simple and natural lives.[98] The counter-discourse of urban writers regarding the official ban on nudity contrasted civilization and barbarism.

In conclusion, when journalists transformed and promoted the Western modern concept of jianmei as fashion among urban Chinese women during the national crisis, its meanings shifted constantly within various contexts: as modern tiyu, as morally threatening bare skin, and as progressive naturalism. Articles in the popular magazine *Linglong* demonstrated that China participated in the global media (news and trends from Europe travelled quickly) and that Chinese modernity was constructed from Western ideas and motifs, in a discursive field dominated by the West. Jianmei, like Chinese modernity, was the result of cultural translation. Yet resourceful editors and readers found a space to critique both the West, in the form of Nazism, and the Nationalist state, in the form of the New Life Movement. In its coverage of sports and elite competitions, *Linglong,* in association with other magazines, strengthened jianmei and sports in China. In this, we see the "feminism" of *Linglong* and the jianmei discourse it helped to popularize. How this new thinking played out on the basketball courts, track and field arenas, and swimming pools of the nation are the topics of the next three chapters.

In the first two chapters, I demonstrated the transnational spread of women's tiyu and jianmei through Zhang Huilan's career and expansive coverage in the media. I now move on to specific sports to discuss their adoption in China, the development of competitive sports, and the lives of the top female athletes.

3 The Basketball Team of the Private Liangjiang Women's Tiyu Normal School

Arthur Daley, chief sports correspondent for the *New York Times*, wrote in 1939 about the male teams in a sport the Chinese had commonly regarded as masculine since YMCA missionaries introduced it to the nation in 1895:

> Somehow or other one cannot imagine foreigners playing basketball. Hence it was a distinct surprise to this writer in 1936 to watch two Chinese teams' scrimmage at the Olympic village outside of Berlin. One quintet used the fast break and the other employed a slow, deliberate style of play. They were not bad, either, although there was nothing of the slick ball handling and long shots we are accustomed to see. And the ironic touch of the entire Olympic basketball tournament was that China was eliminated in the first round by – of all nations – Japan.[1]

After the distinguished career of Yao Ming as the first Chinese international basketball superstar, that sport is now firmly viewed as male power competition.[2]

Women, however, were the first internationally famous Chinese basketball players. Although the Nationalist government selected two men's basketball teams to represent China in the 1936 Berlin Olympic Games, the women's basketball team of the Private Liangjiang Women's Tiyu Normal School (Sili liangjiang nüzi tiyu shifan zhuanke xuexiao), abbreviated as "Liangjiang Tiyu School," based in Shanghai was the best-known basketball team in Asia during the 1930s. The team's leader was Lu Lihua (1900-97), the founder and president of the school. In her study *Women in the Chinese Enlightenment,* Wang Zheng demonstrates Lu's important role in the formation of modern Chinese womanhood by examining her experience with the school. Wang's interviews with Lu and subsequent commentary tell us much about the philosophical dimensions of a life spent in tiyu, but offer little beyond cursory notice of her extraordinary success as a female promoter of women's basketball.[3]

As demonstrated in Chapter 1, the 1930s saw the emergence of politically adept, sophisticated female sports administrators such as Zhang Huilan. Lu's achievements foreshadowed those of modern university athletic directors with limited official affiliation with the state. Lu epitomized the indigenous cosmopolitan women who devoted their lives to tiyu education for patriotic and practical reasons. This chapter explores how, through her guidance in the treacherous, competitive political and commercial environment of Shanghai, the basketball team became Liangjiang's brand name, and shows how Lu's entrepreneurial efforts popularized women's basketball. The rise of the team made basketball one of the most significant sports that demonstrated the collective physical competitiveness of China's female citizenry during the national crisis. The team's success evoked national pride and spirited audience response. Lu's shrewd use of mass media, her creative networking with male political, cultural, and educational figures, and her ambitious travel plans indicate her remarkable effectiveness.[4]

Yu Chien-ming has generally described the world of female ball players in Shanghai, but has not discussed individual careers or important contests. With the life of Liangjiang's progenitor, Lu Lihua, as the starting point, this chapter goes beyond Yu's pioneering work and addresses how the Liangjiang team was a powerful vehicle for female physical educators and athletes who hoped to construct successful modern careers during the wartime emergency.[5]

Born in 1900, Lu was the daughter of a grocer and his illiterate, bound-foot farmer wife in Qingpu, a village outside Shanghai. She rebelled early by refusing to have her feet bound. Despite her humble background, the young Lu was influenced by the rapidly growing modern print media. She eagerly read *Shenbao (Shanghai Daily)*, to which her father subscribed. After graduation from a nearby private school, Lu studied at the Chinese Women's Gymnastics School *(Zhongguo nüzi ticao xuexiao)* in Shanghai. Inspired by the May Fourth Movement, she became devoted to physical education and industrial enterprises and founded Liangjiang with her own money in 1922.[6] Three years later, she organized the Liangjiang basketball team, a year after the Third National Games allowed women to demonstrate their basketball skills in non-medal exhibitions. She dissolved the team in 1937 when Liangjiang left Shanghai, and reorganized it in Chongqing in 1940 after full-scale war broke out.[7] During its twelve years of existence, the team maintained its stability and continuity as an institution, emerged as the leader in domestic women's basketball, and gained international fame despite rapid player turnover. Lu recruited outstanding basketball players from middle schools beginning in 1929. Most were teenage girls, ranging in age from seventeen to nineteen. Her first stars were Shao Jinying and Tu Yunsheng, who were then joined by

Xi Jun, Yang Ren, Zhuang Shuyu, Wang Lan, Long Jingxiong, Xiang Dawei, and Li Yinjun.[8] The next full cohorts came in 1932 and 1933. The second group of significant players, including Chen Baixue, Chen Rongming, Chen Jucai, Pan Meng, Yang Sen, Shi Ruixia, Chen Qiying, Xiao Zengqiong, Zheng Hongying, and Zou Shande, were active until 1936. The players were divided into teams A (Liangliang) and B (Jiangjiang).[9]

Liangjiang's players graduated from the school and became tiyu teachers, entering the world delineated by Zhang Huilan and other members of the Ministry of Education. Lu agreed with such goals: "Since the goal of tiyu schools is to bring up tiyu teachers, the team members dispersed to various locations to teach in middle schools or colleges upon graduation." By 1933, from the first group of Liangjiang players, Zhuang, Shao, and Wang had returned to Jimei and Yude schools in Fujian; Tu had returned to Guang'an, Sichuan; Xi had gone to Qingdao; and Yang, Xiang, and Long had gone to Changsha, Hunan.[10] In 1936, from the second group of players, Pan began teaching at a middle school in Hunan, while Chen Jucai became the director of the Chinese Education Committee in the Philippines.[11] Teaching tiyu was the best occupational choice for Liangjiang's graduating players because there was no other professional demand for their athletic abilities. Once they took jobs in the tiyu profession, however, the players lost their amateur status, which was essential in order to play in competitive games.[12] The Association for [Chinese] Women's Basketball in Shanghai *(Shanghai Zhonghua nüzi lanqiu hui)* regulations stated that "all the school teams and other amateur teams in Shanghai recognized by this association can become members ... Due to the amateur nature of this association, players who are not qualified for the amateur status cannot compete in games."[13] The association actively investigated and answered queries about the amateur status of players. In tournaments, opponents scrutinized each other's amateur status. Snooping occasionally paid dividends: Liangjiang lost its eligibility for the 1930 Shanghai Municipal Games after an opponent discovered that player Xi Jun had been a physical educator.[14]

Making statements that modern sports administrators are only beginning to address, Lu, as just noted, strove to ensure that the school's athletes graduated and found work in tiyu schools. The experiences of these Liangjiang athletes and their subsequent placement as teachers and administrators made them important forerunners of contemporary sports educators. Lu cited the student-teacher relationship between her first and second groups of players to demonstrate the continuity of the team. She argued that "our graduates popularize what they have learned. The newcomers they send us are evidence of the success of Liangjiang. Chen Rongming and other representatives of

Sichuan in the Fifth National Games are all students of Tu Yunsheng. Yang Sen, Pan Meng, and Chen Baixue are students of Shao Jinying."[15] *Qinfen tiyu yuebao (Diligent Tiyu Monthly)* echoed Lu by commenting that, after making great contributions to the team, the players "entered adulthood to advocate women's tiyu." News reporters in Shanghai, home of the Liangjiang team, noticed the rapid turnover of players but were impressed with the team's continued success. They were convinced that Liangjiang's success lay in its ability to "coordinate players' agility." Observing that the team maintained its lofty status even as promising newcomers replaced graduating members between 1932 and 1933, the media were confident that the third major shift of players in 1936 would not affect the team's tradition of success.[16]

Liangjiang's Triumphs in Local and National Games

As Susan K. Cahn has demonstrated, American women's basketball emerged from regional recreation leagues rather than from collegiate athletics, because female college administrators viewed basketball as fundamentally unfeminine and dangerous.[17] In contrast, Liangjiang Tiyu School served as the cradle for women's basketball in China. Liangjiang's basketball team led the wave of popular enthusiasm for basketball. Aided by government directives mandating women's participation in sports and by newly formed associations, women's basketball rapidly grew in popularity in the 1920s. Initiated by Chongde Girls' Secondary School and supported by the semi-official China's National Amateur Athletic Federation (CNAAF), the Association for [Chinese] Women's Basketball in Shanghai was formed in 1929. The Association ensured nationalism and purity in all aspects of the players' performances. In 1933, it regulated that "the balls used in games should be national goods ... [and to guarantee hygiene] the players should use their own towels in the shower after games."[18] Journalists applauded basketball players for their team spirit. The women's magazine *Linglong* commented that the "ball game depends on both collective spirit and individual skills. With excellent athletic skills and spirit, teams from coastal cities usually won the domestic tournaments."[19]

The rise of the Liangjiang basketball team grew out of the school's desire to transform its image from an institution developing skilled, fashionable dancers to one cultivating strong female citizens with military courage, as desired by the Nationalist government. The media soon paid attention. From 1927 to 1929, popular magazines frequently featured photographs of Liangjiang students performing different dances in feminine dress, often the equivalent of programs of commercial song and dance troupes or of collective calisthenics.[20] In the 1930s, mainstream periodicals, including *Funü Xinshenghuo yuekan (Women's New Life Monthly)* and even those oriented toward housewives showed Liangjiang students performing martial arts (national skills) with or without weapons, Western-style boxing, military drills, Girl Scout tasks, emergent medical care, high jump, and boating under the caption "Jianmei new women," sometimes as cover girls.[21] Lu Lihua's strong nationalist attitudes appeared on the *Guoshu zhoukan (National Skills Weekly)* based in the capital, Nanjing. After moving to Sichuan and Yunnan in 1937-38, Lu wrote a report to discuss the national goods campaign there.[22]

Individual Liangjiang students inspired Chinese women during the war. After the Mukden Incident in 1931, newspapers circulated the story of Yao Ruifang, who led a team from the Youth Hot Blood Group to Support [Manchurian Resistance General] Ma Zhanshan from Jiangsu and Shanghai Area *(Suhu qingnian yuan Ma rexue tuan)* in combat. A serious-looking Yao was depicted in a photograph wearing the same uniform as male soldiers in the background and displaying a black armband mourning the loss of Manchuria. In a story praising her as the model for Chinese women, Yao stated: "Since every citizen is responsible for the rise and fall of the nation, how can women let men be solely responsible?" Two other Liangjiang students followed in her footsteps.[23]

The Liangjiang basketball team led the transition of women's basketball from a health- and exercise-oriented game into a competitive sport by initiating inter-city games. In 1930, the team launched the first such competition in Chinese women's basketball by braving the brutal winter to tour two major northern metropolises, Tianjin and Beiping. Liangjiang won every game in three days of intensive exhibitions in Tianjin.[24] *Beiyang huabao (Peiyang Pictorial News)* reported that the athletic circle of Beiping "was alarmed" by the prospect of such a formidable opponent. As expected, Liangjiang won all five games in Beiping against the American School, Qinghua University, and Beiping Women's University, as well as secondary schools Ziqiang, and Xingxing.[25]

Male academic leaders hailed the overwhelming victories of the Liangjiang basketball team. The president of Nankai University, Zhang Boling, who was a trustee of Liangjiang, donated a banner with the characters *chang ti dun yi* (advocating tiyu and promoting friendship) at the closing ceremony of the team's visit to Tianjin. In his speech, Zhang warmly applauded Liangjiang's unprecedented adventure within the nationalist framework: "The excellent skills and benevolent and chivalrous spirit of the Liangjiang Basketball Team should serve as the model of our nation. I hope our city, inspired by the friendship games, will strive to advocate women's tiyu."[26] As Lu rightly observed, the trip "changed the whole atmosphere of women's basketball by making the society shift its close attention to it and embrace it warmly."[27] It firmly established the team's national fame. Zhang Boling's enthusiasm for the team indicates Lu's ability to form an alliance with a well-connected man. Her work at a gender-specific college was acceptable as long as she remained within the school's geographic limits; as she eagerly attempted to take her team on the road to play before mixed audiences, her actions became controversial. For the time being, Zhang Boling was an important ally who could shield her from criticism and enable her to expand her team's (and her own) horizons. Such "gender in motion" needed male protection, or at least approval.[28]

Lu built on these successes to expand her influence and the team's reputation to South China. In a rare foray into government work, she was hired in the summer of 1933 by the Education Bureau of Guangdong Province to teach in its summer training seminars. Under her guidance, celebrities in the tiyu circles of Guangdong and Fujian Provinces invited the team for exhibition games in brutal summer heat.[29] To confirm the team's rising status, Tiyu zhoubao *(Tiyu Weekly)* paid close attention to who greeted the team.[30] Liangjiang won five out of six games played in Xiamen, but was unexpectedly defeated by Chen Baixue's alma mater, Jimei, because of carelessness, fatigue, and the absence of top players. Nevertheless, Liangjiang's victory over Xiamen's all-star team proved the team's ultimate competitiveness. Liangjiang lent three members to the short-handed Zhongnan team of Hong Kong to satisfy the audience, and won overwhelmingly. It defeated a Portuguese team easily and then vanquished Meifang, the Hong Kong champion, in a fiercely fought game. In Guangzhou, Liangjiang handily defeated two local teams. With each victory, the team's fame grew.[31]

News of Liangjiang's triumphs extended the team's influence into the nation-building efforts of the interior regions. Provinces in the remote northwest, including Gansu, Qinghai, Ningxia, Shanxi, Suiyuan (part of today's Inner Mongolia), Mongolia, and Xinjiang, competed in the Seven-Province Games on 5 September 1933. The provincial governments planned to use basketball games "to encourage interest in tiyu among the general masses in the Northwest and to strengthen the nation and citizenry." Lacking tiyu experts, especially for women, the games hired teachers from Liangjiang to direct and serve as referees.[32] In addition to integrating the border region, Liangjiang launched a tour in late 1934, playing against basketball teams along the train route from Nanjing to Shanghai, including Nanjing, Suzhou, Wuxi, and Zhenjiang. The team won all thirteen games. In December 1936, Liangjiang played exhibitions in Central China, including Hankou and Anqing.[33]

Meanwhile, the Liangjiang basketball team played a central role in the National Games, aiding in the successful integration of women's competitive muscle in the nationalist cause. When women's basketball competition started in Shanghai in the 1920s, very few teams participated. In the Fourth National Games in Hangzhou from 1 to 11 April 1930, when women were allowed to compete in basketball for the first time, participants were mainly from the coastal areas. Fifteen five-member basketball teams from Shanghai, Jiangsu, and Guangdong, as well as two teams from Beiping, competed.[34] During the next three to five years, Liangjiang's pioneering regional tours shifted the landscape of women's basketball in China by triggering strong and rapid interest among women, including some in the hinterland. The new trend ensured that more teams across China and Southeast Asia qualified for the Fifth and Sixth National Games. The Fifth National Games in the Central Stadium of Nanjing from 10 to 20 October 1933 saw twelve more provinces (Hong Kong and Fujian in South China; Sichuan in Southwest China; Anhui, Jiangxi, Hunan, and Hubei in Central China; Hebei, Henan, Shandong, and Suiyuan in North China; and Harbin in Manchuria) and Nanjing itself send women's basketball teams.[35] In the Sixth National Games in the newly con-structed Jiangwan Stadium of Shanghai from 10 to 22 October 1935, sixteen women's basketball teams from fifteen provinces competed, with teams from Zhejiang, Qingdao, and Malaysian Chinese replacing squads from Guang-dong, Harbin, Hong Kong, Suiyuan, and Anhui that had competed in the Fifth National Games.[36] The well-attended National Games laid a solid foun-dation for women's basketball in China.

The Liangjiang basketball team contributed to the success of Chinese women's basketball by raising the general quality of play in the National Games. Liangjiang players were key members of the Shanghai women's basketball team, which won championships in the Fifth and Sixth National Games. (A Beijing team won the championship in the Fourth National Games.) Lu captained the Shanghai team at the Fourth, Fifth, and Sixth National Games. Fierce competition between the Shanghai and Guangdong teams during the Fourth National Games dominated the cover of *Linglong*.[37] The wife of Zhejiang Civilian Bureau *(Minzheng ting)* head Zhu Liuxian donated a silver cup for the team's championship in the Fifth National Games.[38] In another acknowledgment of Liangjiang's achievements, *Diligent Tiyu Monthly* featured a prominent photograph of the champion team. Lu was granted the honour of contributing an article to accompany the photo-graph. She began the piece by exclaiming "Satisfied! Satisfied!" to express her enormous pride in her team, and concluded by firmly framing the team's leadership role in building a stronger nation. "Rather than an ultimate goal, the tournament is only a useful tool to advocate tiyu for strengthening the nation and making its citizens healthy," she claimed.[39]

Since perception of national strength required competition against other nations, Lu's ambition was for the Liangjiang team to compete against foreigners. The first signs of this were observed in YWCA basketball games and the Multi-national Basketball Games *(Wanguo lanqiu yundong hui)* in Shanghai. Since its establishment in 1929, the YWCA Basketball Association had held basketball games periodically. The Liangjiang team competed against two other Chinese teams, Dongguang and Peicheng, and two Western teams in the YWCA basketball games in early 1931. The Western YWCA team ousted Liangjiang from the tournament. *Shenbao* commented that the former "overshadowed a lethargic, disinterested Liangjiang squad." Coming back from this defeat, Liangjiang won three consecutive championships from 1932 to 1934 and secured the nickname "the undefeatable troop." When the CNAAF initiated the first Multi-national Basketball Games in Shanghai in 1930, its Preparation Committee selected the best players from Liangjiang, Qiangnan, and Liuxing to join the Chinese team. Dominated by Liangjiang players, the team won four consecutive tournaments from 1933 to 1937, defeating American, British, Japanese, French, and Dutch teams and demonstrating that Chinese women could compete successfully against Westerners.[40]

Since national pride was at stake, competition in the Shanghai international games was tense. *Shenbao* took a strongly nationalist tone as it closely followed Liangjiang's performances. Criticism of officiating was one example of this. Disputes between Chinese and Western teams were common and players frequently challenged the judgment of Western referees, a subject I will discuss in more detail later. In the 1930 YWCA games, two frustrated Chinese teams left in protest against the Western referees, whom they believed to be biased.[41] Lu believed that Liangjiang lost a game in the 1933 games because a referee refused to penalize the Western team for rule violations. Liangjiang filed a formal complaint with the games' authority, requesting the Western referee's removal.[42] In the 1935 games, China's women's team easily defeated the Western teams, mainly the Green Team, which had defeated Liangjiang the previous year. *Shenbao* commented, with strong racial overtones: "Chinese fans were all smiles, while the frustrated blondes sighed."[43]

Having handily dispatched local expatriate teams, Lu and her team nurtured larger international ambitions. Andrew D. Morris has discussed the formation of "a greater China" through tiyu communities between China and the Chinese communities in Southeast Asia by focusing on men's sports.[44] The Liangjiang basketball team fuelled national pride through pioneering transnational competitions in East and Southeast Asia. Its overwhelming victories in 1931 in Japan and Korea solidified the team's reputation. That May, the team, consisting of Shao Jinying, Long Jingxiong, and six others and captained by Lu Lihua, visited Nagasaki, Tokyo, Osaka, and Nagoya for "friendship" competitions – the first-ever Chinese women's overseas athletic encounters. The team won nine games and lost three. Its reputation growing, it received a telegram from the Korean Athletic Association inviting it for a short visit to Korea. The team arrived in Pyongyang on 22 May and won every game in front of huge crowds before returning to China by way of Dalian in Manchuria. Lu considered this trip "an unprecedented creative action in the history of Chinese women's basketball." She believed that the team "won glory for the nation" not only by winning overwhelming victories on the court but also by insisting successfully that the Chinese national flag be raised and the Chinese national anthem be played along with the Japanese flag and anthem.[45] The significance of Liangjiang's victorious trip overcame the failures that sprinter Sun Guiyun, who had risen to prominence during the Fourth National Games in 1930, suffered in the Far Eastern Games in Tokyo in the same year.

Such international events, which by now were becoming routine, indicate how female athletes were in the vanguard of women's travel and shifting gender roles. Various contributors to the volume *Gender in Motion* note the slow, halting changes in women's travel and work outside the home during this period. By contrast, Lu and her team, along with athletes chosen by the Nationalist government to represent China in international competitions, travelled regularly around the nation and to foreign destinations, making travel arrangements and operating independently, without much apparent male supervision. The team's excellent reputation ensured these cosmopolitan travellers a ready welcome from Chinese and international sponsors of games and tournaments.[46] An editorial piece titled "The Feminist Movement in China" in the *People's Tribune,* a Shanghai-based English periodical edited by the influential journalist Tang Liangli, mentioned in particular Liangjiang's YWCA championships and its victorious tour of Southeast Asia, which I will discuss below. The editorial praised Lu and Liangjiang for helping "turn back the pages of history," in an "extraordinary reversal of the national conception of women's role in life and society."[47]

The players had already shown degrees of cosmopolitanism. Most came to Shanghai from other provinces. The majority of Liangjiang players were from the coastal provinces of Fujian and Guangdong, "the hometown of overseas Chinese," whose residents tended to have Southeast Asian family connections and many relatives who were sojourners or permanent migrants to the Americas.[48] For example, Chen Baixue of Jimei, Fujian, was the niece of a famous "patriotic" expatriate, Chen Jiageng. Shi Ruixia and Chen Jucai from Fujian returned from Java and the Philippines, respectively, to study at

Liangjiang in 1932. Chen Rongtang of Fujian, who had just begun studying at Dongya Women's Tiyu Vocational School (Dongya nüzi tiyu zhangke xuexiao), spoke Mandarin, Fujian dialect, and Malayan, since she had spent time in Malaysia, where her father conducted business. Huang Shuhua was from Weipu, Fujian; Yang Sen and Pan Meng were both from Chaozhou, Guangdong. Women's colleges such as Liangjiang played an important role in creating national identities and freeing Chinese women from domestic constraints. The significance of team spirit should not be overlooked either. In her study of women in motion from rural Shandong Province, Ellen R. Judd has argued for the importance of kinship networks. Earlier, I noted the frequent turnover of players at Liangjiang. During the years that they played together, however, the Liangjiang team fostered a kind of kinship and created its own community in a large urban setting.[49]

Following Liangjiang's overseas tour in 1931, its success in East Asia and the transnational background of its players prompted more overseas invitations. Other schools joined Liangjiang on Southeast Asian trips.[50] In January 1935, the tiyu association of Chinese in Manila telegraphed to invite Liangjiang to its annual ball games. Undoubtedly, Lu hoped to capitalize on regional loyalties in the team's trips to Southeast Asia. Like other women's basketball teams, Liangjiang team members declared that they should accept the invitation immediately, because they wanted to popularize the tiyu spirit of Chinese citizens among overseas Chinese women. Connections between Liangjiang Tiyu School and the Chinese communities in Southeast Asia had been established by recruiting students there and sending back graduates. Lu, who happened to be planning a trip to investigate education there, claimed that a second purpose of the trip was to examine the careers of Liangjiang alumnae in the region.[51] From 2 February to 23 May, she led the team's visit to sixteen cities in the American Philippines, Dutch Indonesia, British Malaya, and French Vietnam, including Bandung, Malacca, Kuala Lumpur, Singapore, and Saigon. During the two-and-a-half-month tour, Liangjiang won thirty-two out of thirty-eight games.[52] The trip concluded with Lu Lihua's proud declaration:

As the only competent women's basketball team in China with solid skills, brave spirit, and rich experience, Liangjiang's fame rings around the Far East. Wherever the team went, the overseas Chinese celebrities and foreigners welcomed us warmly by arranging tours of schools, institutions, and famous sites and showering us with banquets and shiny and beautiful gifts such as silver shields, *ding*, cups, mirrors, kettles, and banners ... Liangjiang even beat

上 海 兩 江 女 體 師 範 京 征 選 京 滬 沿 錦 及 南 洋 歷 球 隊

10 "The Shanghai Liangliang basketball team that tours along the train route from Nanjing to Shanghai and Southeast Asia."
Source: Qinfen tiyu yuebao 2, 5 (10 February 1935): 316.

the American-Philippine team three times, and a French team in Vietnam. Locals swarmed to watch each game and praised Liangjiang's excellence.

The media confirmed that overseas Chinese were exuberant, at times even emotional, at every victory (see Figure 10).[53]

Money was the lifeline of the team, but prospective budgets were unusually lean and Lu and her team had to raise money to finance their travels. Lu ran a tight ship during regional trips. To reduce costs during the tour of South China, the team moved from Xinya Hotel in Guangzhou to the dormitory of Lingnan University, where Lu was teaching summer seminars.[54] Lu cited the team's ability to overcome the "enormous financial cost" as part of their achievements in the tour to East Asia.[55]

Although the Nationalist government did not select the privately sponsored Liangjiang basketball team to compete in the 1936 Berlin Olympics, the team was the first from China to plan to compete on the world stage, before China's initial competition in the 1932 Olympics. Even as she acclaimed the team's pioneer status in launching the East Asian trip, Lu Lihua lamented: "Although our overwhelming triumph stunned the public there, the popularity of women's basketball in Tokyo, Nagasaki, and Seoul impressed us. How could we be content when we are compared with the international women's basketball?"[56] The Japanese bombing of Shanghai on 28 January 1932 destroyed Liangjiang's new campus and killed Lu's second husband, Gu Zhenglai. Rather than dash her global dreams, however, the Japanese attacks strengthened her ambitions for a tour of the West by her team.[57]

Less than ten days after the Japanese attack, on 7 February, Lu and the Liangjiang basketball team issued a formal declaration of their intent to tour Europe and America in response to the national crisis: "Foreign invasions are pressing daily, and the national crisis is urgent *(waiwu riji, guonan fangyin)*. When the whole country rallies iron and blood to resist the strong enemy, our team plans a trip to the West at this life-and-death moment of our nation." Lu was very likely inspired by "King of Beijing Opera" Mei Lanfang's successful tour of the United States in 1930. Believing that civic and official diplomacy should be employed simultaneously, the declaration unveiled an idealist goal of "cultivating affections among citizens, especially female citizens, of various nations, to promote world peace" and to avert the impending war crisis.[58]

Two days later, Lu released a detailed plan for the proposed tour. The delegation would include nine players, the director, a secretary responsible for interpretation and public relations, and one coach. The trip's purpose was to select all-around players to show the best of China. Selection criteria included strong physique and ambition, excellence in basketball skills and academics, and a morality sufficient to represent the national spirit. To emphasize that selection of the players was an absolute "scientific" procedure, a Dr. Niu Huisheng of the Bone Hospital of Shanghai was hired to examine the physiques of candidates. The team planned to circle the world, departing from Shanghai in March, stopping in the Philippines, San Francisco, Chicago, New York City, Boston, London, and Marseilles and other European cities, then heading back to the South Pacific Islands before returning to Shanghai in September. During the four-month trip, the team would spend one month in the United States and its territories, two months in Europe, and one month in the South Pacific Islands.[59]

Although Lu presented the team's budget as bare bones, funding the trip remained the primary difficulty. The China Travel Agency drafted a minimum budget of 54,000 yuan. The cheapest fare for each individual was 2,500 yuan, and the total for the team was 30,000 yuan. Room and board for each individual was 2,000 yuan, for a total of 24,000 yuan. Fully aware of the international currency market, the travel agency predicted that the totals could be slightly lower if the price of gold dropped. The Chinese National YWCA chief of staff, Zheng Shujing, planned to arrange for the team to stay at local YWCAs, considered the most economic and hygienic places suitable for women's lodgings. The preparation committee proposed to contact the Chicago Exhibition to coordinate Liangjiang's trip with it, in order to highlight the trip as the action of a national enterprise.[60]

Lu's male supporters called on society to contribute to the team's expenses. In the name of the Shanghai municipal government, Pan Gongzhan approved a Bureau of Education request that Liangjiang be permitted to raise funds from the public to rebuild its bombed campus.[61] Shen Siliang, the chief of staff of the CNAAF, argued that Liangjiang's glorious history contributed to nation building by reversing the stereotype of Chinese citizens engaging only in empty talk. He encouraged people to change their customary negative attitudes and "roll up their sleeves" to offer substantial donations to make the proposed world trip possible. Presenting the relationship between the team and the public as give-and-take, Shen gave assurances that "Liangjiang will not disappoint the citizens."[62] Instead of attracting donations, however, the sizable budget sparked controversy. The overwhelming view was that Liangjiang's planned trip was not worth the proposed 54,000 yuan despite its lofty nationalist goal. Rather, it was suggested that the sum could be used to build gymnasiums or purchases planes and steel helmets badly needed for national defence. Some defended Liangjiang by asking: "Without their proposed trip, who would raise the money to build gymnasiums or buy planes and helmets? At least Liangjiang had a strong will and determination." Others doubted that Liangjiang would ever raise such a large amount of money.[63]

The controversy grew. The proposed trip to the West became a media-driven drama. The Preparation Committee proposed periodic press conferences for international and domestic media to give progress reports on preparations for the trip. Initially, as Shen Siliang noted, "newspapers unanimously supported Liangjiang's proposed trip." Major journals and newspapers, including *Shenbao, Tiyu Weekly,* and *Zhongguo kangjian yuebao (China Health Monthly)*, which was run by the general secretary of the Executive Yuan Chu Minyi, carried the full texts of the declaration and plan.[64] Newspapers and magazines gave details of the proposed trip and proclaimed its significance: "While winning games would certainly be glorious, losing would 'demonstrate the active struggling spirit of the daughters of grand China during the national crisis.'" Articles stated that the trip "deserved moral and spiritual support from across the nation," thereby linking Lu's plans with hopes for the nation in a time of crisis.[65]

Just as Zhang Huilan needed powerful male patrons to sustain her career, Lu was fully aware that the support of powerful male figures from various circles was essential to the success of a trip initiated by a private institution and led by a woman.[66] Four days after Liangjiang's declaration, Shen Siliang issued a public statement on 11 February extending his support and confirming the lofty mission of the proposed trip: "When our nation is in deep crisis and the whole world is second-guessing its ability to survive, their trip would be able to offer some new excitement to change foreigners' view of our nation. Their admirable and well-intended ambition is not far different from bravely confronting the enemies in battlefields." Ma Xiangbo (1840-1939), the founder of Zhendan, later Fudan, University, a prominent figure in education and one of Liangjiang's first trustees, echoed the idea that the basketball team's trip would be a new means of strengthening the nation during the national crisis.[67] Inspired by Shen and Ma, male supporters warmly embraced the plan and formed the Preparation Committee for the Liangjiang basketball team's world tour. Shanghai mayor Wu Tiecheng served as the chairman, Ma as the honorary chairman, Zhang Boling as the honorary vice chairman, and Wang Zhengting, Chu Minyi, and Shen as committee members. Zhu Shaoping, head of the Global Students Association, was entrusted with most tour arrangements. Shen accepted the responsibility of arranging competitive exhibitions. Reactions from America were promising. Responding to Shen's inquiry, the New York Amateur Athletic Union telegraphed, welcoming Liangjiang's visit. It asked about the Liangjiang basketball team's plans so that it could invite various teams in the United States to compete against the Chinese female ball players. *Tiyu Weekly* enthusiastically predicted that since the Preparation Committee "are responsible for everything, the trip should materialize soon."[68]

To improve their skills against foreign teams and build public confidence, the team invited Western women's teams in Shanghai to play exhibition games. Tao Bing, the chief of the Tiyu Staff at the YMCA, scheduled such games in February and March at a local YMCA basketball court. The Preparation Committee invited key leaders to watch the games. Unfortunately, however, Liangjiang lost three of its four games at this critical moment.[69] The defeats had a devastating impact. To observers, Liangjiang's defeats demonstrated that the team lacked sufficient athletic skills to compete successfully on the tour, a fact that spoke louder than various opinions in newspapers. When Liangjiang sought official approval from the Shanghai municipal government on 7 March 1933, the government decided that "the trip should be delayed because its timing during the national crisis is not right." The rapid collapse of official support highlights the fragility of women's forays into male-dominated venues. Had Lu's team been successful, support for their ambitions might have continued. Given the team's earlier successes against

Western teams, however, it appears that male officials rushed to judgment as Liangjiang suffered defeat on the court.[70]

After the trip fell through, the honeymoon was over; the relationship between the Liangjiang team and the media turned sour. Calling the plan "merely a dream," an article in *Tiyu Weekly* criticized Liangjiang's publicity as "arrogant," "bragging," "empty words," and "fancy declarations." It viewed Liangjiang's seeking of approval from the Shanghai municipal government at the last minute as "a wily move" to use government discouragement as an excuse, because Liangjiang was too embarrassed to withdraw from its own bloated ambition.[71] Tianjin's *Dagong bao (Impartial [Takung] Daily)* pointed out that Liangjiang had intended to cultivate affection among nations through the trip as its response to the national crisis, but Japan had launched brutal aggression after Liangjiang's trip to East Asia.[72] Eventually, *Tiyu Weekly* chose to forget the acrimony over the proposed world tour and said that the trip had been "halted by national crisis."[73] These attacks made a lasting impact on Lu. She never mentioned the trip again, neither in her review of the Liangjiang basketball team's glorious history after its triumph in the Fifth National Games nor in her interview with Wang Zheng in the early 1990s.[74]

Lu then turned to other ventures. Just as its bombed campus rose from the ruins, Liangjiang recovered from the traumatic month-long drama by undertaking regional and overseas tours, and remained a dominant figure in Chinese women's basketball. Tiyu periodicals frequently acknowledged the "iron team's" prominent status and glorious history. In early 1936, *Diligent Tiyu Monthly* noted that, "due to its great domestic and international reputation, Liangjiang occupies the most glorious page in Chinese women's basketball history.[75]

The team's extensive travels helped expand the players' horizons. Lu made it a point to present her teenaged players as sophisticated travellers. In widely circulated photographs after the Southeast Asian tour in 1935, the smiling players wearing light-coloured *qipao*s posed before an ocean liner in the Shanghai harbour. Such images, as noted in the Introduction, conveyed unmistakable messages that the team was cosmopolitan and highly professional. They enhanced the impression that the young women were experienced travellers whose presence in the public arena and on long voyages was unremarkable, even routine.[76]

Media and Market within the Discourse of Popular Modernity

The pioneering activities of the Liangjiang basketball team were not only political but also economic and cultural. Articles on women's basketball appeared next to stories about new elevators, telephones, tall buildings, cars, suits, Western food, and Western hygienic products for coping with menstrual flow.[77] Lu Lihua had to run the basketball team of the Liangjiang Tiyu School as a business and deal with the challenges and opportunities of the modern market. Led by Liangjiang, women's basketball became the first commercialized and audience-oriented sport, and the school's team had a significant impact on Chinese crowds. Chapter 2 noted the development of sports and fitness journalism. As the rise of the Liangjiang team was being celebrated as a series of media events, women's basketball games were becoming integrated into popular culture. Riding a surge of nationalism, the team marshalled print media, cinema, music, radio, and sports to publicize its history and achievements.

Lu emphasized the school's modest origins to highlight its success. According to her, when Liangjiang first opened with seventeen students at a rental property at Dengnaotuo Road in Hongkou District, "the primitive conditions were too pitiful to describe." With the help of the head of the Education Bureau of Shanghai County, Li Songtang, and the head of public stadiums, Wang Zhuangfei, Liangjiang borrowed a public stadium in 1925 for the basketball team to use. In 1927, Liangjiang rented rooms in Western-style garden houses opposite the White Cloud Daoist Temple on Fangxie Road. After the basketball team's famed tour of North China, Liangjiang no longer stayed under others' roofs but moved into its own newly constructed building at Daji Road in Ximen in the fall of 1930.[78] On New Year's Day 1931, the school proudly celebrated its tenth anniversary at the new downtown campus. *Shenbao* offered a detailed account of the attending celebrities and the new building. Among the six hundred guests were Pan Gongzhan (the head of the Social Bureau), Ma Xiangbo, and Chu Minyi. The auditorium was filled with banners and inscriptions from state ministers, provincial chairmen, the Shanghai mayor, the commander of the Shanghai Regional Police, and other officials. Famous educators such as Huang Yanpei, Shen Enfu, and Jiang Hengyuan, and noted journalist Ge Gongzhen, bestowed mirrors, silver frames, and trophies on Liangjiang. Nankai University president Zhang Boling and Foreign Minister Wang Zhengting telegraphed their congratulations. In the hallways of the main building hung autographed photographs of Chiang Kai-shek and Military Minister He Yingqin. In the exhibition room were enlarged photographs of the basketball team and Lu. The school was open for public tours for days and received about four hundred visitors.[79]

Considering the highly acclaimed campus "too small and noisy, and life in Shanghai too luxurious for students to focus on their work," the pragmatic Lu made a smart business move. Within a year, she had rented out the campus and bought ten mu (Chinese acres) at the picturesque Xiangyin Road in the suburb of Jiangwan, with convenient access to transportation. However, after the school renovated the ten Western-style houses there and prepared to start the new term on 15 February 1932, it suffered catastrophic losses from the Japanese bombing of Shanghai on 28 January. Lu felt that "material damage was limited, but the spiritual damage was extreme," and it was partially the need for spiritual recovery that led to the proposal for a world tour. After the trip was cancelled, and with Liangjiang suffering overwhelmingly negative media coverage, Lu sought to revive the institution by rebuilding and expanding the campus. In all its student recruitment advertisements, Liangjiang emphasized how it had survived the bombing and illustrated its expanded equipment and facilities with photographs. It promised to open the campus to the public and hoped that the new facilities would "not disappoint the high expectations of society."[80] Since a swimming pool was considered a symbol of modernity due to the advanced technology and expense involved, Liangjiang held a grand opening ceremony for its swimming pool in 1934, attended by Shanghai's mayor. Reports of the ceremony and photographs of the pool were featured in both professional journals such as *Da Shanghai jiaoyu (Education in Grand Shanghai)* and popular magazines such as *Libai liu (Saturday)*. In 1936, a special series on Liangjiang School in *Zhongguo xuesheng (Students of China)* featured photographs of the school's gate, swimming pool, faculty and student dorms, administration building, basketball court, and stadium.[81] The *People's Tribune* editorial on the feminist movement in China described how Liangjiang's campus was equipped with tennis and basketball courts, a running track, a gymnasium, and a swimming pool, arguing that such facilities enabled the Chinese girl to stride as freely as her Western sisters.[82]

Lu and her team fended off rumours, severe competition, and jealousy in order to survive the treacherous business environment in a complicated metropolis, especially when the media was constantly scrutinizing expenses associated with the Liangjiang team's frequent trips. Lu had to resort to the media and to legal actions in order to explain both herself and Liangjiang. For example, after a certain Liu Xiufang spread a rumour that Liangjiang was charged with wrongdoing by the Ministry of Education, Lu sued him for slander. After the case was settled, both sides issued a joint announcement in *Shenbao*, with Liu admitting fault and Lu forgiving him.[83] Like the proposed trip, these battles illustrate all the contradictory dynamics involved in a female-run pioneering private educational enterprise.

Zhang Huilan's male patrons in the United States helped her secure precious financial resources necessary for boosting her career without stirring sex-related rumours. In contrast, although the Liangjiang basketball team's nationalist rhetoric attracted numerous powerful male backers, their support was limited mainly to glorious words rather than substantial financial assistance. Lu's manly style and worldly wisdom helped her gain support from influential male figures,[84] but in an interview with Wang Zheng, she complained of a "lost reputation" and hinted at gossip accusing her of improper sexual relations. Gossip was a common and effective way of attacking an independent, strong woman who pursued a career outside the home and who networked with male celebrities in various circles. The background of some of her supporters made the matter more complex. For example, Shanghai mayor Wu Tiecheng, one of Lu's major backers, was involved in the murky world of the underground opium business.[85]

Although the Liangjiang team cooperated with other women's basketball teams during the international games in Shanghai in the first half of the 1930s, conflicts continued in the competitive world of women's private tiyu schools. In an incident that foreshadowed future battles among universities for star athletic recruits, for example, Liangjiang was involved in a highly publicized dispute about enrolling basketball players in 1932. After some athletes transferred from Shanghai Jiangnan Tiyu School (Shanghai jiangnan tiyu xuexiao) to Liangjiang, Jiangnan criticized the players in the popular newspaper *Shibao*. The players published a response the following day and threatened to sue Jiangnan. The harsh public exchanges facilitated by mass media created a sensation in the tiyu world. *Tiyu Weekly* charged that "the leaders of these two schools are not running their schools for the sake of tiyu. Otherwise, why do they yell at each other in newspapers just for a few athletes? The quality of a school is not determined by human flesh used as advertisements! It is senseless for schools to use these few students that way."[86] The periodical's comments crystallized the similar dilemmas of many universities in the United States that have pursued glory in athletic success to the present day.

The Liangjiang team's unprecedented profile, raised by the planned world tour, led to other publicized disputes within the community of female basketball players in Shanghai. For example, on 11 February 1932, *Tiyu Weekly* reported that Lu personally invited three well-known players, Dongnan Women's Tiyu Vocational School (Dongnan nüzi tiyu zhuanke xuexiao) students Pan Yueying, Wang Zhixin, and Lu Xueqin, who had played with Liangjiang team members on the Chinese national team in various international games in Shanghai, to join the world tour. The three sought approval from their parents and from Dongnan president Ms. Yu Ziyu and academic dean Ms. Qin Xingshi. Yu and Qin were convinced that the trip related to *guoti* (national dignity), would win glory for the nation, and would herald a new era in Chinese women's basketball, and granted their full support.[87] For some reason, Lu immediately stated to the media that an invitation had never been extended and that the staffing would stick to the principles laid out in the team's formal declaration, which seemed to suggest that the three Dongnan players were not qualified.[88]

Insulted, Pan Yueying published a public letter to Lu in Shanghai newspapers, including *Shenbao,* on 16 February, detailing how Lu had actually extended the invitation that she was now publicly denying. Asserting her willingness to contribute to national causes, Pan focused her attack on the already controversial huge budget for the world tour and the facilities on the Liangjiang campus, which had just been destroyed by the Japanese bombing. She stated that, after finding that Liangjiang did not even have a gymnasium and "great athletes have to use an open field of several yards and broken buildings in danger of collapse, I changed my mind and decided not to participate." Challenging its significance for national defence, Pan attacked the proposed trip as pure vanity. She urged Lu to cancel the trip and use the funds already raised to expand Liangjiang's facilities. She concluded, "Madame Lu could use the share of funds for my trip in building your school."[89] The letter drew immediate attention to school facilities. "Short Flute," a satirical column in *Tiyu Weekly* asked: "Pan's public letter has revealed that Liangjiang is not what we thought – its equipment is so simple and plain. What about facilities in Dongnan, which are still unknown to outsiders? Did others manipulate Pan's letter? If not, Lu should take Pan's letter seriously."[90] Lu did not respond but someone else did on her behalf, defending the nationalist mission of the proposed trip.[91]

Why would controversies over the proposed budget lead to attacks on Liangjiang's facilities? For private institutions such as Liangjiang and Dongnan, built entirely by female tiyu teachers, their facilities were measures of modernity, credibility, and the success of women's tiyu schools, and were frequently featured in the schools' advertisements in mainstream media designed to recruit students. The Liangjiang basketball team's increasing prominence was also reflected in the three-stage development of the school's campuses,[92] whose facilities demonstrated the team's financial well-being and its much-envied clout with powerful male patrons.

Liangjiang's reliance on inexpensive ticket sales to raise funds made the team vulnerable to public disorder.[93] For example, when the team played against Beiping Women's University and Xingxing School during its North China tour in 1930, tickets were sold for only 0.2 yuan and the low price drew many spectators. In addition, mixed-gender games turned into spectacles,

◁ 影合前賽比隊球江兩與隊球大女平北 ▷
○攝廑維宗○   （報本期上載情詳）
Group photo of the basket ball team of the Girls' College of the Peiping
University and that of the Liang Kiang Girls' Academy.

11 "Group photo of the basketball team of the Girls' College of Beiping University and that of the Liangjiang Girls' Academy." Note the male audience in the background.
Source: Beiyang huabao, 19 November 1930.

with perceptions of scandal and indecency attracting large crowds. For Liangjiang's weekend matches with the two Beiping schools at the YMCA court, the YMCA set up wooden platforms in three layers around the court, which soon became packed with spectators, "without spare room for an extra pair of feet." Before the games began, the Liangjiang and Beiping Women's University teams posed for photographs, one of which, taken by Zong Weigeng, an employee of Lianhua Studio and photographer of many movie stars, showed a background of paying spectators, most of them male, sitting on the platform and wearing Western hats (see Figure 11).[94]

Despite their superficial sophistication, the unruly and overcrowded audience interrupted the games frequently as spectators were pushed onto the basketball court. After tickets to Liangjiang's match with Beiping Women's University sold out, crowds gathered outside the gates, broke past the guards, and pushed inside. When the newcomers tried to squeeze onto the severely overcrowded platforms, the platforms collapsed and "a weird scene appeared when human bodies and basketballs rolled all over the court." On the last day of the competition, the YMCA set up a wooden fence outside the stadium. Undeterred, the crowd knocked down the fence and invaded the court, stopping the game. The organizers had to beg large, strong male basketball players from Beiping Normal University and Minguo University, who had played there an hour earlier, to try to restore order by yelling and pushing the audience back. The field house was filled with screaming and spectators' hard-soled shoes damaged the court.[95]

The audience swarmed to the games played in Tianjin despite very cold weather. Some local citizens who missed games there followed the team to Beiping. Such dangers did not deter Lu and other promoters. Embracing the enthusiasm of Tianjin spectators, Liangjiang returned to that city for two friendship games against Tianjin Women's Normal University and the Little Lamb Team organized by Liangjiang alumni.[96]

Lu Lihua ably negotiated these spectator behaviour problems by portraying the games as entertainment. When Liangjiang was invited to Qingpu County to play against two local men's Red and Blue Teams in late 1934 and early 1935, welcoming banners flew across town and all entertainment businesses closed during the games. Since everyone wanted to see the famous Liangjiang players, the audience was unprecedented: between three and four thousand people from the city and nearby villages and towns watched the first game at the public stadium, and more than five thousand attended the second.[97] The widely publicized albeit unsuccessful plan to tour Europe and America actually boosted Liangjiang's fame. During the team's 1933 South China tour, more than seven hundred men and women crowded into a fully lit basketball court in a remote location on a hot July evening to watch Liangjiang's first game against Guangdong Women's Normal School.[98]

Unruly audiences and perceived commercialism caused administrators of American women's colleges to be concerned about women's basketball.[99] In contrast, ever keen to increase the fame and popularity of her players, Lu welcomed the enthusiastic and sometimes unruly fans as evidence of progress, however contradictory, in women's basketball. According to her, when basketball was first introduced in China,

> disorderly clothing, stiff movements, unfamiliarity with rules, and low spirit of the very few teams marked the extremely shallow and premature status of Chinese women's basketball. When the players did not understand the essence

of the game, how could they gain sympathy from the society and have "fans" like today? When athletes performed beautifully with high spirits, the audiences were inspired and excited.[100]

Lu's nonchalance about the crowds notwithstanding, the spectators' behaviour is worth considering. Haun Saussy has described Chinese history since 1900 as the "Age of the Crowds," citing the Boxer Rebellion, the May Fourth demonstrations, the Cultural Revolution of 1966-76, and the Tiananmen Square demonstrations of 1976 and 1989 as evocative examples. Certainly, crowd behaviour at Liangjiang's basketball games was not as significant as at those major events, lacking even the overt nationalism apparent in the riots over a basketball tournament between Chinese and Russian players in Harbin in 1926. Yet the largely male audience expressed, however inchoately, the anxieties and fascinations that young Chinese men felt over Lu's basketball team. Seeing sparsely dressed, talented young women playing a men's game surely pushed the audiences, however unwillingly and uncannily, into sudden shocks of modernity. When referee Dong Shouyi used Mandarin to ask the audience to retreat five yards from the court line, spectators whispered to one another, wondering where this out-of-province referee came from.[101] Lu, ever the strategist, was willing to expose her players to possible danger for the sake of the sport and of publicity for her school. The unruly crowds, doubtless composed of students and *xiaoshimin* (lower-middle-class/petty urbanites), found themselves in a new environment that caused them to become uproarious.[102]

Although the media highlighted these contradictions involving the Liangjiang basketball team, they proved to be an ally, however fickle, to the female players. The team's commercialized public performances were closely integrated with the media, and their influence extended to cinema and radio. For example, Liangjiang students performed in the hit films *Jianmei yundong (Exercise for Robust/Healthy Beauty)* and *Tiyu huanghou (Queen of Sports)* in 1934.[103] Wu Kaisheng, a famous lawyer, former consul to Switzerland, and head of the Chinese Office in Geneva, and Lin Kanghou, a noted gentleman in Shanghai social life, made periodic speeches on the Yamei (Asian-American) radio station seeking support among ordinary citizens for Liangjiang's proposed world tour.[104] Besides video and audio coverage, the press, especially through pictorials, was most important in propelling the Liangjiang players to popular stardom.

A shrewd businesswoman with great talent in modern media relations, Lu consciously engaged the most powerful members of the press as part of her business dealings. She maintained good relations with the media through

○ 攝璋錫王 ○　　最近抵津之上海兩江女子籃球隊

The Liang Kiang Basket Ball Team, Shanghai, now arrived in Tientsin for matches.

12 "The Liangjiang Basketball Team, Shanghai, now arrived in Tianjin for matches." Note their uniforms and the male coach, Qian Yiqin.
Source: Beiyang huabao, 12 May 1931.

exchanges of gifts, such as a scroll given by Liangjiang to the magazine *Tongji xunkan (Tongji Ten-Daily).*[105] Lu skillfully publicized the team's competitions in inter-city, national, and international games and proposed tours. For example, before the team departed for its initial trip to Beiping and Tianjin in 1930, she invited journalists to a banquet and press conference, where she announced the team's upcoming tour of East Asia and declared that the trip to the north was in preparation for it.[106] Her ploy worked and the most influential media organizations across the nation publicized both tours extensively. As soon as the team arrived in Tianjin in 1930, *Peiyang Pictorial News* and other popular journals such as *Hong meigui (Red Roses)* published group photographs of the Liangjiang team adorned with the greetings of the women's basketball teams of Tianjin Women's Normal University and Beiping University (see Figure 12).[107] Back home in Shanghai, *Shenbao* hailed the team's victory repeatedly and *Liangyou huabao (Young Companion Pictorial)* featured photographs of the competitions.[108] After the Liangjiang team returned to Shanghai, Lu, whom the media now called "Captain," did not forget to send the media a note for the host institutes in Beiping and Tianjin, thanking them for their hospitality and highlighting the enormous success of the trip.[109]

The official newspaper *Zhongyang ribao (Central Daily)*, *Shenbao*, *Young Companion Pictorial*, *Diligent Tiyu Monthly*, and *Students of China* all covered the team's tours of East and Southeast Asia in 1931 and 1935. *Shenbao* reporter Huang Jiping accompanied the team on the East Asia trip, and the newspaper featured his observations of those countries and games.[110] The press began scrutinizing the performance of individual players to determine their value to the team. For example, when the China women's team easily defeated the Western teams, mainly the Green Team, in the 1935 Multi-national Basketball Games, *Diligent Tiyu Monthly* reported that Chen Jucai had made two good shots in the first minute and that Chen Rongming had performed well; after the first round, realizing that the Western teams were not worthy opponents, the Chinese team replaced the two strong Chens with Wan Shunxiang and Chen Rongtang.[111] In addition, the famous Kuihua Photoshop and China News Agency took standard portraits of the whole team or individual players or of action shots on the court. Those photographs circulated in popular journals, including *Dongfang zazhi (Eastern Miscellany)*, *Libai liu*, and *Linglong*.[112]

Challenging Gendered Rules on the Basketball Court

There is more to the story than Liangjiang's on-court successes and Lu's off-court manoeuvring. The Liangjiang team played a central role in making and redefining basketball as a game. The very way the team played basketball tells much about gendered rules for Chinese sports in this era. Basketball employed systematic gendered rules. Devised by Senda Berenson of Smith College in the 1890s, specific regulations for women's basketball in the United States lasted until 1972, when a legal challenge of their restriction on equal opportunity in sports and education for women led to the enactment of Title IX of the Education Amendments of 1972.[113] Even as Lu and her team were boosting the popularity of women's basketball during China's national crisis, they had to negotiate the gendered rules that were often applied locally and that weakened women's basketball's otherwise modern impact. As a female sports administrator in a milieu dominated by men, Lu fared well and linked her efforts to nationalist drives to develop a wartime female citizenry. In a spectator sport, gendered rules complicated the construction of proper womanhood through its interactions with the media, the audience, and other players.

During Liangjiang's golden years, from 1930 to 1936, rules for women's and men's basketball were constantly being negotiated. Whereas female scholars and administrators in the United States insisted on using women's rules in a gender-segregated environment to maintain their power and authority,[114] in China, pushed by female tiyu authorities such as Zhang Huilan, competitive sports for women and "co-recreation" in the name of national needs and gender equality became popular. However, male tiyu scholars and administrators who had been educated abroad struggled to maintain a gendered order during the wartime uncertainty. As the only sport with systematic gendered rules, basketball allowed male sportsmen to maintain control; by drafting and interpreting rules formally and academically, they insisted on a female version of the game. Led by the Liangjiang team, however, female athletes who were encouraged to be strong and fit in the national interest contributed to the shaping and defining of the game through their flexible practices on the courts. The popular media facilitated the controversies and negotiations.

Basketball was ill defined and lacked universal rules when it was first played in China. Early on, a game similar to basketball, called "commander ball" (*siling qiu*) was popular on school campuses.[115] Women's courts were originally divided into three zones, with three players from each team fixed in each zone. After 1921, Chinese officials adopted the half-court rule, with six players for each side.[116] To prepare for the upcoming Fifth National Games, the CNAAF published *Zuixin nanzi lanqiu guize, 1932-3 (New Rules for Men's Basketball)* and *Zuixin nüzi lanqiu guize, 1932-3 (New Rules for Women's Basketball)* in 1932. Up to 1938, the noted Diligent Publishing House published the gendered rules edited, reviewed, and approved annually by the CNAAF. The manuals were inexpensive and widely circulated; for example, the 1933-34 and 1934-35 versions sold for only 0.2 yuan. Newspapers, magazines, and pamphlets repeatedly advertised the rule manuals and highlighted major changes.[117]

The new men's basketball rules were designed to increase competitiveness, speed, and power and to help make the games exciting and watchable. The rules for women's basketball were designed to restrict physical movements and protect their perceived proper femininity as counterpoints to the strengths and personalities of individual players. Facing the reality that actual practice in women's basketball commonly fell outside the official rules, however, the new regulations were an attempt at compromise: they accommodated female players' hopes for more freedom and excitement in order to convince women to abide by gendered rules. The CNAAF acknowledged: "It is the fact that various women's teams have adopted men's rules, for which we do not see any other reasons except freer movements ... The recent new rules should solve the above contradictions."[118]

Gradually, new rules for women allowed more court space, which increased speed in movement, passing, and dribbling.[119] Concerned with maintaining proper femininity and ladylike styles, however, controversial regulations regarding defence were imposed. The regulations permitted more freedom of movement but tried to restrict players' aggressiveness in skills and attitudes. The 1932-33 and 1933-34 rules abolished bans against vertical movements and use of both arms by defenders "as long as players do not touch their opponents." To avoid breaking the taboo of physically running into one another, defenders were allowed to use only a single arm in the corner of the court.[120] The 1933-34 rules recognized that "in theory, basketball is a game without body contact. In reality, when players run fast in a limited area, it is absolutely impossible to completely avoid contact. Inadvertent touches should not be penalized. If a player accidentally touches the ball in the opponent's hands or the body of opponents and leaves immediately, she should not be penalized either."[121] The 1934-35 rules added that "intending to intimidate the opponent holding the ball in various ways, including waving hands in front of her eyes, is a violation. Unintentionally touching the hands or arms of the opponent holding the ball does not violate the rules." Such clarifications suggest that women's teams in China played as physically as they were allowed.[122]

The new rules were enthusiastically embraced by the popular media as a framework for facilitating "basketball's evolution toward perfection,"[123] but they did not necessarily make the games less confusing or controversial. In 1933, noted male tiyu scholar and administrator Wu Bangwei recognized that the game was evolving despite the existing official rules: "Sports rules change annually, but we do not have the highest authority to coordinate and announce the new rules. Consequently, different regions adopt different versions of rules, which always leads to disputes in competitions and obstructs popularization of tiyu."[124]

Male scholars strove to define the game. Declaring that the new basketball rules were more complex than they had realized and that most people did not understand them thoroughly, the Research Branch of the Association of Basketball Referees in the Tianjin Tiyu Association met on 28 March 1933 to "scientifically research" the regulations, and subsequently published its results under the general title of "Required Knowledge for Basketball Athletes and Referees."[125] In response, a certain Zhou Jiaqi published an article discussing the real meaning of rules by citing the original English text.[126] While the games were in transition, more translated and edited books entered the market as "necessary tools for coaches, players, and spectators." As early as 1926, a certain Wang Huaiqi authored *Zuixin nüzi lanqiu youxi* (*Latest Women's*

Basketball Games). In 1934, Song Junfu, a professor in the PE Department of Northeast University, published *Nüzi lanqiu xunlian fa (Methods of Coaching Women's Basketball)* with Diligent Publishing House. Qinfen's advertisement for the 1.4-yuan volume claimed:

> Since women's physiology is different from men's, it is natural that the methods of coaching women's basketball are different. This book offers practical, complete, and detailed directions in the basic movements, offence and defence, and alternation of strategies in women's basketball. The noted tiyu expert Gao Zi performed the one hundred movements. The book discusses the differences between the rules of men's and women's basketball at the end.[127]

Complying with the official basketball rules and male tiyu scholars and administrators, all domestic official women's basketball competitions employed women's rules. The Chinese authorities strongly resisted the trend of adopting men's rules in formal international basketball games for women by banning participation by Chinese female players. For example, China at first refused to send a women's team to the Far Eastern Games (FEG) in 1930 when the organizers proposed to use men's rules; the China women's team competed only after the organizers shifted back to women's rules.[128] To align with the Olympics, the FEG eventually adopted men's rules for women's basketball as an exhibition event. The Sixth National Games followed the rules of the recent FEG in preparation for the 1936 Olympics, with women's basketball as an exception. The National Games maintained their previous decision to include women's basketball with Spaulding or American rules as a formal competitive event. To avoid confusion, the Games' authorities took pains to let participants know which rules to use.[129] Confusion over the gendered rules probably ruled out consideration of the Liangjiang basketball team for the 1936 Olympics.

In practice, led by Liangjiang, women used both sets of rules flexibly. Rules were often negotiated on the spot. To facilitate matters, Liangjiang hired male coaches to train strong players familiar with both men's and women's rules. Contrary to American female physical educators' objection to male coaches for female players due to fears of sexual exploitation,[130] Liangjiang's male coaches were warmly embraced as the legitimate authorities to help female basketball players fulfill their obligations as wartime examples of fitness and to advocate for female players in the male world of the sport. Liangjiang hired a professional coach for its basketball team after 1929, after being urged by someone writing under the pen name Female Warrior (Nüxia) in *Shenbao* to avoid wasting talents on the team.[131] Alumna Shao Jinying was the only female coach. After Liangjiang lost to Western teams in the 1930 YWCA basketball games because of the team's unfamiliarity with men's rules, the Shanghai Basketball Committee hired Qian Yiqin, a noted male physical educator and author of many textbooks, to coach the China women's team, which was dominated by Liangjiang players, in preparation for the Multi-national Basketball Games in 1931.[132]

Liangjiang also hired male administrators. As part of the school's recovery from the 1932 Japanese bombing and the controversial plan for a world trip, Hu Zhengqu (William) was hired to coach and do general teaching. A detailed biography in *Diligent Tiyu Monthly* stated:

> Hu is the second son of the rich businessman Hu Changqi [who lives] in Canada, whose family is originally from Enping, Guangdong. He attended McGill University for two years and learned Chinese with Dr. Jiang Kanghu, the head of the Chinese College of McGill University. After winning glory for McGill and overseas Chinese in various athletic games, Hu was respected as an "all-around athlete" by Canadians and praised by Americans as a rare talent, particularly good at basketball, hockey, baseball, and American football. Admired by his team members, Hu always served as the captain.[133]

In 1935, Liangjiang also hired a male graduate of Dongya, Jiang Gaodi from Shandong, who had played basketball in national games.[134]

Despite the half-court rules in domestic games, Liangjiang's female players battled hard around the midcourt line, as photographs in the official *Quanyun hui teji (Special Collections on the National Games)* and *Young Companion Pictorial* show; the latter commented that "heroines are different from the past."[135] Accustomed to the women's rules in formal competition, Liangjiang performed better under these rules in the international games in Shanghai. In the Multi-national Basketball Games in 1935, the China women's team easily defeated the Western team known as the Green Team, the squad that had defeated Liangjiang in the YWCA tournament the previous year, and *Diligent Tiyu Monthly* attributed the victory to both Liangjiang's surprising progress and the half-court rule.[136] Following the international trend, however, the YWCA basketball games shifted to men's rules in 1935 and Chinese teams, including Liangjiang, stumbled and lost the tournament. When the YWCA games shifted back to women's rules in 1936, very few Chinese teams returned.[137]

Strict observation of the rules dipped during Liangjiang's numerous exhibition tours, as both sets of rules were used flexibly.[138] Out of ten games in

Japan, only one used women's rules and one combined both. Liangjiang lost four times due to travel fatigue and unfamiliarity with outdoor competition. The team won all its games in Korea using both sets of rules. Out of thirty-eight games during its two-and-a-half-month tour of Southeast Asia, seven employed women's rules, and Liangjiang won thirty-two games.[139] Led and influenced by Liangjiang, other women's teams alternated between both sets of rules as well.[140]

The inconsistency between the official line maintaining gender division through separate rules during an unstable period and the flexible practice of female players led to heated debate in the discourses of women's special physiology, psychology, and morality. At the core of the ultimately inconclusive and contradictory debate was whether basketball was too strenuous for women, with both sides citing the power of science, as Zhang Huilan did. In 1932, *Tiyu Weekly* deemed a submitted essay titled "The Black and White [Women's] Team [in Tianjin] and Menstruation" "unpublishable and silly," but conceded that the essay did have a point in calling for the basketball community to follow the rules closely because they were "based on careful research in physiology, techniques, and interest." In contrast to Zhang Huilan's argument that menstruation was a natural biological process, the journal used it to illustrate the vulnerability of women's bodies.[141]

Contrary to Zhang Huilan's emphasis on the similarity of physical development of young girls and boys, *Tiyu Weekly* invoked the innocence and vulnerability of young girls to stress the damage to women who played by men's rules. In April 1934, at the newly built Kailuan basketball field in Tianjin, the Black and White team played exhibition games against ten elementary schools using men's rules according to the FEG standards. *Tiyu Weekly* noted that "the strenuousness of the competition was unprecedented." It argued that it was "genuinely regretful" that those in charge of school tiyu, who are "supposed to be experts in education theories, age, and physiology," allowed young girls to "blindly follow the trend" by competing in strenuous activities harmful even to the health of adult women. It went on to ask: "Who would be responsible for the long-term physical damage of the girls?"[142]

Female writers and periodicals oriented toward female readers disagreed. As early as 1929, the "Sports Column" *(tiyu jie)* of *Young Companion Pictorial* stated: "Basketball is an elegant sport that is neither too strenuous nor too gentle, and beneficial to the whole body."[143] Female writer Zhou Wenjuan argued that it was not the rules but the strength and skills of the opponents that determined the degree of competitiveness and strenuousness of the games. Assuming that male players were stronger and more skilled, "men's rules do not necessarily make the games more strenuous, but men's games using women's rules would be just as competitive." Complaining that women's rules were too clumsy and restrictive, she encouraged women to play with men's rules to make the performance more "lively, smooth, and graceful."[144]

Using American and Japanese basketball authorities as the ultimate arbiters, both sides introduced their own research or experiences to back up their arguments without acknowledging the contradictions swirling around the rules in the international basketball community. *Shenbao* reported that the Japanese YWCA shifted from men's to women's rules in its twenty-fifth anniversary year and actively enforced the transition in early 1931. The article quoted the Japanese YWCA's chief of staff as saying that men's rules had proved too strenuous for women's bodies and that the new rules would help popularize basketball among women.[145] In 1933, *Tiyu Weekly* carried an article translated from English that argued that "basketball involving free running is most suitable for men but too strenuous for children, girls, and women." The article even warned men to play four-session rather than two-session games, in order to avoid physical harm by using more intervals.[146]

Those who supported women's use of men's rules paid special attention to an article titled "Is Basketball Too Strenuous?" published in the American *Athletic Journal* and authored by Everett Bean, a basketball coach at Indiana University. *Tiyu Weekly* first published it in a translation by Sun Yiwei of Qinghua University at the end of 1932.[147] Oddly, it also carried another translation of the same article by a prolific author with the pen name Jianmei (robust/healthy beauty) in 1933. Both translators highlighted the "scientific" power of detailed statistics and attached charts with data collected at a seminar on basketball skills in Indiana University for players who participate in the Big Ten games. They concluded that it was a myth that basketball was too strenuous for women, noting that frequent timeouts were allowed for rest and recuperation.[148]

Both camps soon began to ask how the Western "science" underlying basketball rules should be applied locally. In contrast to Zhang Huilan's argument that body-related scientific data could be applied across races, advocates of separate rules cited racial differences in physical abilities. After the YWCA basketball games in Shanghai adopted men's rules in 1934, male writer Wen Haiyu argued: "Basketball has developed for a long time in the United States, and American women with much stronger physiques have experienced a long evolution in adopting men's rules. Since Chinese women's basketball has only had ten years of history, using men's rules would overwhelm their stamina [which was] inferior to men [and Western women]." He insisted that Chinese women should stick to women's rules suitable to their physiques to "avoid heart and lung diseases."[149] Shao Jinying echoed the view that Chinese women's bodies were "weaker and more fragile" due to "restraint in the inner chamber by the old customs and values." Instead of advocating separate rules, she argued for examining individuals' physical conditions as the key to maximizing the benefit of basketball to women. She urged the expansion of women's leadership in popularizing women's basketball beyond Shanghai into the hinterland, "since male directors are not familiar with the specific physiques and physiology of women."[150]

Others criticized blind worship and rigid copying of Western "science" in China's modernization, in the introduction of machines, and in regulation of women's bodies, and called for flexible rules for Chinese women's basketball. According to an article in *Tiyu Weekly:*

> The methods of basketball became "scientific," and consequently static and rigid ... The most laughable thing is that some people believe that only the methods newly learned from the United States are scientific and modern. They claim that "Without America, without Springfield [where most leading male tiyu educators and administrators were trained] there is no basketball." When they always follow others, they have lost the ability to create and invent.[151]

The author cited the successive defeats of the Shanghai Zhenru basketball team, composed mainly of Jinan University players, during their invitational trip to the Philippines in the spring of 1931 as an example of how the "scientific methods were laughed at as 'outdated.'" In 1934, another article, in *Diligent Tiyu Monthly,* echoed this ridicule by stating that "their techniques were fifteen years old and the Filipino critics laughed loudly." In the same article, Liangjiang's victories in Japan and Korea in 1931 were cited as examples demonstrating "the leap forward of China's basketball."[152]

Some resorted to referring to women's "special nature or character" to argue that men's rules were designed for "rational" men while women's rules were for "emotional" women, and were designed either for their protection or for the dignity of the games. The media frequently cited reports of female athletes crying in public as evidence of their emotional nature and lack of self-control, whereas male athletes were rarely covered that way. Although travelling was an integral part of the success and image of the Liangjiang team, the media sometimes reported on team members' inability to endure its hardships. The Tianjin *Dagong bao* reported that when the boat reached rough waters in the middle of the team's tour of North China in 1930, all eight members became seasick and could not eat for days; the players reportedly

cried hard and bemoaned the trip.[153] *Shenbao* reported that the games originally scheduled in Liaoning were cancelled due to the illness of two players and
the brutal cold weather.[154] Newspapers frequently mentioned how female ball
players cried after losing a game, as in the 1934 coverage of the Third National
Games and of the FEG by *Dagong bao* and *Shenbao,* respectively.[155]

Wen Haiyu argued that women with weak nerves lacked self-control and
the ability to make sound judgments. According to him, when women played
by men's rules, which allowed running with the ball, they violated the rules
50 percent of the time. Women's competitive natures led them to try too
hard to win and to neglect their own physical well-being. More grabbing and
jumping, allowed in men's rules, would easily cause harm to their skin and
tendons. Women's playing under men's rules made refereeing impossible
and raised fears that women would get hurt and become afraid of basketball,
possibly giving up the game completely.[156]

Male journalists chimed in with criticism of women's styles of play. When
the women's basketball team of Daxia University lost games in Nanjing in
1933, the reporter for the school journal criticized the strict refereeing style
of female physical educator Yang Xiaorang of National Central University.
The reporter believed that "since women cannot adequately control their
movements because of their weaker bodies, referees should be flexible and
forgiving, rather than frequently penalizing them for unintentional violations."
Labelling Yang's style as rigidly sticking to rules and theories and lacking
flexibility in practice, the reporter questioned her qualification as a referee
with "noble and saintly heart."[157] Another reporter commented that women's
particular competitive natures were beyond tiyu and had nothing to do with
the shortcomings of men's rules.[158]

Confusing gendered regulations and the practice of employing men's rules
were attacked as sources of shame and scandal. Exemplifying the complex
twists of the competitive circle of women's basketball, whereas the media
credited Liangjiang for progressive leadership in women's basketball, it heaped
blame, ridicule, and criticism for using men's rules on other women's teams,
especially the troubled Black and White women's team in Tianjin. *Tiyu Weekly*
listed the latter as the "most evident example" of a women's team scandalously
using men's rules, noting that "influenced by Liangjiang women's basketball
team, women's basketball in Tianjin has made some progress in techniques
and skills"; however, forgetting the basics and ignoring women's rules, their
development was "abnormal" *(jixing).* When the team went to Beiping to
compete, "the games had to be cancelled, because it [the team] did not know
the women's rules."[159] After frequent contradictions and bad publicity involving the Black and White women's and men's teams, a reader of *Tiyu Weekly*

applauded their efforts and progress after hiring foreign coaches, and advised the teams to "watch out for their arrogance, to avoid offending people and inspiring bad publicity; cultivate team unity and be immune to outside rumors and gossips; and improve organization and leadership." This reader pointed out in particular that "it is not only inglorious, but against the essence of athletics for a women's team to adopt men's rules."[160]

The Liangjiang basketball team complicated the issue further by competing against men's teams under men's rules. In 1930, it played against teams such as Tongzi, Transportation University, and Shanghai journalists.[161] After the opening ceremony of the "Games of the Construction Division of Zhejiang Province" in Hangzhou in 1933, Shanghai journalists and the head of the division organized a team to play against the Dongnan and Liangjiang teams.[162] In late 1934 and early 1935, the tiyu association of the business circle in Shanghai's Qingpu County invited Liangjiang to compete against its men's Red and Blue Teams, since they did not yet have a women's basketball team. Liangjiang lost to the Red Team and beat the Blue Team.[163] According to Lu Lihua, during Liangjiang's tour of Southeast Asia in 1935, "when competing against local men's teams, men's rules were used for five times out of twelve games and the competition was so tense. Liangjiang only suffered small setbacks (five defeats) caused by a loss of stamina. Most of the twenty-eight games against women used men's rules and Liangjiang won all the games."[164]

Competitions between men and women were controversial. As early as 1930, the CNAAF announced publicly that the China Basketball Court would not allow any mixed-gender games: "Since the physical structure and strength of men and women are totally different, it is absolutely impossible for them to compete in strenuous basketball games. Women's physiology and the true meaning of advocating tiyu would not permit it."[165] While the CNAAF's position based on concern over physiology was not respected in practice, the media escalated the attacks to the domain of morality. The Tianjin *Dagong bao* viewed the rise of mixed-gender swimming and basketball in Shanghai as disturbing and "abnormal": "As a strenuous sport with limited space, there are many chances for physical contact, falling, and sliding, which would lead to ill-meant cheers from audience and athletes." The paper advised tiyu circles to be "careful about following new trends for vanity, and spreading bad influence to the general society, especially young students."[166] It appeared, however, that young students did not share these concerns. As early as 1928, a young male student observed that since all youth enjoyed being close to and impressing the opposite sex, co-ed sports would help encourage the development of skills and interest. His classmates always rushed to play ball games during the ten-minute break because female students participated.[167]

Despite official disapproval, mixed-gender basketball games had spread to Beiping from Shanghai by 1932. An article titled "A Scene of Fleshy Combat between Men and Women" in the Beiping *Chenbao (Morning News)* denounced the practice. It argued that due to differences in physical strength, mixing genders in such a competitive game led to confusion of rules, injured women, and obstacles in the development of men's skills. In addition, the article suggested that mixed-gender games were not about serious skills and competition but rather about vulgar and immoral entertainment and amusement for the audience. It described male athletes who made fun of female athletes like hungry tigers teasing a lamb. Whether intentional or not, the article argued, those physical movements led to mixed-flesh combat that hurt the dignity and self-respect of female players and did not fit with tradition.[168]

Between the New Women and Modern Girls

In addition to defining basketball's rules, the emerging stars among Liangjiang players began consciously redefining wartime womanhood. As mentioned, Lu and her players recognized the power of publishing. In an article about issues in publishing, Lu wrote that writing, publishing, and reading together constituted an integral whole.[169] Both Lu and her most noted player, Shao Jinying, advocated the cultivation of a new female wartime citizenry through tiyu. In 1933, Lu voiced her opinion on how to improve women's tiyu and urgent programs in public health and hygiene, particularly in Shanghai. She published an article in *Tiyu Weekly* titled "The Tiyu Urgently Needed for Chinese Women." It claimed that "in order to make women in our country all have strong and complete physiques, they have to go through certain degree of training in tiyu. It is urgent to advocate tiyu for women now." Later, she voiced her concern over the danger to young girls in the pursuit of a curvy, slim body.[170] In a 1934 article in *Diligent Tiyu Monthly*, Shao wrote that "popularizing tiyu among women is just as important as bringing up specialized athletes for competing fields. Both girl students and women in society should use public stadiums common in big cities to exercise in spare time and improve their health."[171]

The Liangjiang basketball team was ever keen to promote a new image of modern Chinese women. Since the May Fourth Movement began to address the "women problem," there had been various definitions of the "New Woman" in cinema, literature, and political writings. Now the Liangjiang basketball team emerged as one of the first groups of celebrities to declare its members representatives of the New Woman. The goal of a number of its trips, especially the international ones, was clearly stated as presenting the New Women of China. What kind of New Women did these athletes represent?

Liangjiang's version of the New Woman was distinctly liberated. Lu proclaimed that the "liberated New Women" of her team would show the world through the proposed world tour that they could compete against their global counterparts on the athletic field and overcome the prejudice that Chinese women "remained in the inner chamber with bound feet." The team intended to reinforce the image of the New Woman by learning the essence of international sports for the benefit of Chinese citizens, especially women whose bodies had been sickened by restrictive traditions.[172] Although the tour did not materialize, one team member never forgot its mission. Chen Baixue proudly took every opportunity to introduce the New Woman image and to break stereotypes. On the boat to Southeast Asia, she corrected an American passenger's perception of child brides in China by informing him of the actual marital age of modern Chinese women, and she highlighted her team's adventure to reinforce her point. She wrote that it was important to "at least let them know Chinese women are not as they imagined," and noted that he listened with respect.[173]

The "Short Flute" column in *Tiyu Weekly* was convinced of the feminist aspect of Liangjiang's proposed tour: to represent the New Women of a grand China as a whole. Considering economic independence as a significant dimension of the image, the column argued in favour of raising money for the tour as a women's cause and asked all Shanghai women to contribute.[174] The journal announced that Yan Shuhe, the head of the Shanghai Women's Bank, would assume responsibility for financing the trip. Unfortunately, the bank ended up only donating an upstairs office, for the Preparation Committee, in its building on prestigious Nanjing Road. This was announced as the initial support from domestic women's circles,[175] but in fact it was the only material support the team received for the planned tour.

At the same time, the New Woman represented by Liangjiang was firmly political and patriotic. Both the team and the public were convinced that Liangjiang could fulfill its nationalist obligation only by presenting the image of the New Woman. Using tiyu within the framework of social Darwinism, Lu hoped that the New Women of Liangjiang would help convince the world that "the post-[1911] revolutionary Chinese nation was rising in the Orient," and that China would be able to shed its shameful image as the "sick man of Asia" and prevent foreigners from seeing it as vulnerable to invasion. Shanghai mayor Wu Tiecheng echoed the sentiment that the proposed world tour's significant mission was "to show the spirit of New Women *(xin funü)* in our nation and to demonstrate the revival of the Chinese nation."[176] The feminist and nationalist sentiment of the trip was also acknowledged by Chen Zhenling's editorial in *Linglong*.[177]

As the liberating and nationalist rhetoric of Liangjiang's New Woman image coalesced, at its centre was a masculine warrior. Significantly, the media described the performance of female players using classic military combat terms. As the team's fame grew, newspapers and magazines conferred on the players' militaristic, masculine nicknames. During Liangjiang's 1933 trip to the south, the media scrutinized the players minutely. Besides providing detailed biographical information and a team photograph, *Tiyu Weekly* described the performance of every single Liangjiang player and used nicknames for all of them after interviewing the team's male staff – despite poor communication due to dialect differences. Only the small and lively Pan Meng was given a feminine nickname: "Little Bird." Short, agile, and lively Yang Sen was called "Tuxingsun" (a legendary spirit passing through the earth without leaving a trace) for her ability to pass and shoot skillfully with a single hand. Short and slim Chen Baixue was called "Little Zhang Fei" (a bad-tempered legendary general in the Three Kingdoms) for her bravery and aggressiveness. Huang Shuhua was praised for being equally brave and aggressive. Chen Jucai was called "Da jiangjun" (Grand General), since she was not eager to claim credit for herself despite her outstanding skills.[178]

As the rules for women's basketball were being made and remade and the discussion on whether basketball was too strenuous for women continued, the popular media praised the Liangjiang basketball players for their masculine strength and manly style and attributed their victories or defeats to body size. The skill displayed by Chen Rongming in the team's tour to South China was described as "just as good as men's."[179] In both the Fifth and Sixth National Games, the champion Shanghai team, composed mainly of Liangjiang players, was praised for having "played in a manly style and being much more competent" than its opponents.[180] Lu Lihua considered the fact that "the teams from Beiping [led by former sprint champion Sun Guiyun], Fujian, and Guangdong were especially brave and blunt with manly style" to be evidence of progress in women's basketball in China.[181] The players' physiques were viewed as key to whether they could play in a manly style and win games. According to *Tiyu Weekly*, Liangjiang prevailed in tense competitions against the top Hong Kong team, Meifang, during its 1933 tour because of the grand physiques of Liangjiang players, who demonstrated manly strength and competed in men's style, dominating the petite Meifang players. A commentator noted: "The only difference was that the half-court system was used."[182] After defeating a Western team many times in the YWCA basketball games in Shanghai, Liangjiang lost unexpectedly in the last round in 1931. *Shenbao* commented that the only reason for this loss was that the Western players were "too tall" and could grab the ball more easily, comments that indicated the reporter's belief that Chinese players were not biologically equipped to compete against Western teams.[183]

Although the image of the New Woman represented by Liangjiang players centred on physical capacities, the players' bodies and appearances played a key role in debates about gender, fashion, and clothing. The team photographs frequently found in the media offered fans who could not attend the games a chance to "meet" the players and provide straightforward visual representation of the New Women and see for themselves what a New Woman looked like. Typically, the players posed neatly in single file or in a human tower, sporting bobbed hair and unique uniforms of long-sleeved jerseys, short-cut shorts, and white caps. Their appearance – combining such "Modern Girl" features as bobbed hair with skin-revealing uniforms – was so influential that other teams labelled the adoption of such a look as "Liangjiang-ization" *(Liangjiang hua)*.[184] In contrast, Lu Lihua stood in front, wearing high heels, a Western dress, and a suit jacket – clearly distinguished from the uniformly dressed players. As with Zhang Huilan, authority more than sensuality was the reason for wearing high heels.[185] Aside from their bobbed hair, which was perhaps a nod to the team's adoring fans among the female petty urbanites, the unique dress of the players in the photographs was not accidental. Lu viewed clothing as a mark of the organization, discipline, and professionalism of a basketball team, and cited it as an essential element in measuring the quality of a team, next only to skills and spirit. One section in Liangjiang's widely circulated plan for the world tour focused on clothing. Responding to the national goods campaign in China, it stated that "the team's uniform will be made of best quality, national-goods fabrics and must be of plain but grand style, in order to demonstrate patriotic spirit." Competition uniforms included short shirts made of white silk carrying the team's name and the number of the player, black shorts with white stripes, and white sneakers. The plain black-and-white uniforms were to demonstrate jianmei. Players' everyday outfits consisted of short shirts with skirts to display the elegance and health of Chinese female students. Formal *qipaos* were reserved for important social occasions and were intended to display traditional oriental art.[186]

Consistent with the masculine-warrior image of the New Woman, female basketball players who adopted men's clothing were accepted and even encouraged. *Shenbao* praised Liangjiang player Chen Rongming as being "without any feminine style at all."[187] In a popular volume profiling noted female athletes, Chen Rongming and Chen Jucai appeared with very short hair, suits, and ties in their formal portraits.[188] When the stout, tall Chen Juchai cross-dressed as a young man during the National Games, she was banned from the women's dorm by guards who refused to believe that she was indeed a woman.[189] Xi Jun, whose grand style audiences believed was not much different from men's, usually played in long pants and a white hat with rolled-up rims.[190]

Liangjiang's promotion of a masculine-warrior New Woman to represent Chinese women sometimes drew criticism. When its relationship with Chinese masculinity grew, subtle tensions emerged. While some celebrities and members of the media confirmed both the nationalist and feminist meanings of Liangjiang's proposed world tour, they also saw the New Woman as competing with men. Ma Xiangbo stated that the trip would demonstrate that the strong and independent team was an example for men. Articles in *Tiyu Weekly* agreed that the trip was not only "related to national dignity *(guoti)*, but also would open a new era for Chinese women's tiyu and lay the foundation for women's self-sufficiency and their ability to keep up with men."[191] After an American team defeated the China men's team to win the much-advertised Ninth Multi-national Basketball Games in 1934, the audience shifted its enthusiasm to the women's team. The China women's team, again dominated by Liangjiang players, defeated American and British teams and won the tournament. *Shibao* ran a news piece titled "Chinese Women Take Revenge for Chinese Men" (Zhonghua nü'er guo wei xumei tuqi). *Diligent Tiyu Monthly* credited the Liangjiang girls who "saved face for the men's team."[192]

The public, however, harboured ambiguous attitudes toward the "confused" gender order within the nationalist cause. Observing that the China women's team, dominated by Liangjiang players, had outperformed the China men's team in the international games in Shanghai, some male writers published humorous pieces in popular tiyu magazines to express their subtle discomfort. A fictional piece, "Wild Tiyu History," read:

There is laughter coming from the women's dorm nicknamed the Forbidden City near whose gate are parked four cars ... with red flags embroidered with the characters "Women's Basketball Team of Shanma University" on the top. The cars moved with the roaring engine. Naturally, male cheerleaders occupied the first car, the female basketball team took the two cars in the middle, and safety guard led by Wang Xingsan sat in the last car. The cheerleaders sang triumphant songs all the way with great style, but the female "generals" are still not satisfied. One slender player even planned to order the cheerleaders to carry her in. Concerned about maintaining her modesty, she marched the field slowly under her own power.[193]

Some charged that the gender and ages of team members were inadequate credentials for representing China. One article in *Tiyu Weekly* suggested that the team "lacked talent with deep knowledge of Europe and America to fulfill its diplomatic obligations. Since all the team members were younger than twenty years of age, foreign countries might find use of such young girls to represent China as laughable." The writer attributed Liangjiang's fundraising difficulties to the qualification of the team for its proposed nationalist mission,[194] a point of view shared by many. Rich overseas businessmen funded men's basketball teams and the formation of the "greater China sports community" across Southeast Asia as early as 1929, and Manchuria's warlord funded male sprinter Liu Changchun's trip to the 1932 Los Angeles Olympics. None of these donors stepped up to provide the Liangjiang basketball team the chance to demonstrate the competitive skills and muscles of the New Women of China.[195] The only exception was Hu Wenhu's contribution toward the team's expenses during its Southeast Asia tour, but only after Lu successfully facilitated the participation of overseas Chinese athletes from that region in the Sixth National Games, including arranging for Liangjiang students to greet those athletes from Malaya. The media called it a "smart business move."[196]

Gender ambiguity opened the Liangjiang New Women to attack as over-liberated, superficial Modern Girls *(modeng nülang)* who indulged in sexual and material pleasures. Conscious of the fluid boundaries between the New Woman and the Modern Girl, Lu and her team consciously distanced themselves from the latter. Lu promoted the patriotic New Woman as an antidote to a flabby and sickly citizenry stemming from "over indulgence in banquets and other pleasures," habits commonly associated with Modern Girls.[197] Players were encouraged to adopt masculine styles consistent with nationalist goals and to suppress feminine personal styles identified with Modern Girls. One female writer warned that women basketball players who used their feminine charms at such serious occasions as basketball games would only lose their dignity and reinforce stereotypes of women as men's comic playthings who could only be the objects of their sexual desires. She suggested that players adopt a serious and calm attitude to make the games professional and formal.[198] However, when individual players entered popular discourse by rising to stardom before the public's gaze, a mixture of fashion, sex, vulgarity, and romance appeared in the commercialized relationship.

13 "The Liangjiang Basketball Team touring in Japan." *From left:* Xiang Dawei, Yang Ren, Zhuang Shuyu, Long Jiongxiong, Wang Lan, Tu Yunsheng, and the captain, Shao Jinying.
Source: Beiyang huabao, 12 May 1931.

14 He Lili, a cover girl of *Young Companion Pictorial,* demonstrates basketball, along with swimming, as highly fashionable.
Source: Liangyou huabao 106 (June 1935).

The Liangjiang team and the sport of basketball were sometimes viewed as femininely romantic and fashionable. *Peiyang Pictorial News* featured a photograph of the team taken in Japan with a romantic poem as the caption: "The carpet-like fragrant grass and the colorful evening clouds make people drunk. The Liangjiang team members happily lined up to lie on the grass" (see Figure 13).[199] *Young Companion Pictorial* featured He Lili, a fashionable cover girl, dressed in a swimsuit while demonstrating basketball techniques in a swimming pool known for its sensual and romantic atmosphere (see Figure 14).[200] Movie stars took up basketball as high fashion. Actress Hu Jia organized a basketball team for the cinematic circle in order to remedy unhealthy appearances among actresses. The "athletic movie star" Li Lili, the subject of Chapter 6, donned a uniform with the number 10 emblazoned on the back, and played the forward position on the court of Daxia University as a Southern Ocean Business School (Nanyang gaodeng shangye zhuanke xuexiao) basketball team member while students circled the court.[201]

Sensuality predominated among spectators of women's basketball.[202] Basketball was introduced as a "civilized" modern game acceptable to the well-behaved audiences of modern movie theatres, but the behaviour of the unruly spectators was comparable to that of crowds at traditional noisy opera theatres. The media blamed the discrepancy between expectations and reality on the audience's sexually charged desire to gaze at the bodies of female players. After reporting the chaotic incidents in Beiping in 1930 (described earlier), the *Peiyang Pictorial News* reporter commented: "It was embarrassing that the audience does not know or follow rules ... Since the majority only came to see women playing with balls, unpleasant rumors and gossip flew around." The pictorial tried to preserve the respectability of the team by carrying, on the same page, photographs of Zhang Xueliang and Chiang Kai-shek in front of a crowd of officials after paying their respects at Sun Yat-sen's tomb.[203]

The sexual undertones of the chaotic spectatorship of women's basketball extended beyond the court. As mentioned, during the three-and-a-half days of the North China basketball tournament in Beiping in February 1931, the spectators' overcrowded platform collapsed from the weight of the audience. Fans also frequently stopped games by pushing onto the court. Finding no room on the platform, one male student decided to stand on a little cart belonging to a staff member. When confronted, he shouted, "I spent 0.2 yuan on the ticket. How can you stop me from watching?" – to which the staff member replied, "Your 0.2 yuan did not buy my cart. Therefore, you are not allowed to climb in it." While one game was in progress, an old woman in the audience suddenly screamed at an old man next to her, accusing him of pushing his body against her on purpose. The audience cheered loudly that "a woman that old still complained of sexual harassment." Throughout women's competitions, the audience would shout, "Legs!" To protest such disorder, Tianjin men's and women's basketball teams withdrew from the tournament.[204]

Managing women's basketball teams with players whose personae were commercialized and sexualized could be a sensitive and dangerous task, as demonstrated by a tragic incident involving the Black and White teams in Tianjin. After the noted male player He Buyun joined the team in 1929 and captained it to national fame, jealous teammates began to persecute him. It was his relations with female team members that eventually led to his death, however. Prior to the opening ceremony for the newly constructed Anli Company basketball court, some female players changed their clothing in an office. Concerned about such a lack of modesty, and acting as the captain, He tried to stop them, which led to an explosive confrontation. Manipulated by his opponents, the team used this as an excuse to drop him from its roster. Anger and frustration aggravated what had previously appeared to be minor heart or mental conditions, and He was hospitalized at the French Hospital in Beiping. After glimpsing for only a few seconds the first issue of *Athletic Weekly of the Black and White Teams,* whose coverage of the confrontation had sexual overtones, he went into shock and died in June 1933 at the age of twenty-three. The Tianjin Competitive and Progressive *(jingjin)* Association memorialized him but drew no connection between his sudden demise and athletic competition.[205]

The media paid close attention to the appearance of female basketball players, but, contrary to Lu's views, contended that attention to clothing would hurt the seriousness and professionalism of the Liangjiang team and its nationalist goals. Even the article in *Tiyu Weekly* that defended Liangjiang's proposed world tour believed that Liangjiang had "made a mistake in mentioning trivial details relevant to the beauty of clothing." Although socialization would be essential, the purpose of the trip "was to demonstrate national spirit, observing tiyu in Europe and America, not to exhibit Oriental arts."[206] It seemed that the writer had reason to be concerned for Liangjiang. For example, Lu Lihua was proud of her team's black shorts, which she considered evidence of professionalism and discipline – essential spirit for the New Woman.[207] *Peiyang Pictorial News* noted, however, that during their stint in Beiping the Liangjiang players entered the court wearing black shorts under bloomers; when they removed the bloomers in order to compete in shorts, the audience cheered along. "Because of Liangjiang, there is a saying popular in Beiping now, 'Watching women compete in basketball –

worshipping under black shorts.'"[208] Sensual gossip spread about the "pink legs" of Liangjiang students revealed by the black shorts.[209] The media quickly noted the discrepancy between the "insufficient athletic skills and fashionable uniforms of Suiyuan team from the remote area, which was beaten by the Guangdong team" in the Fifth National Games.[210]

Female basketball players who wore fancy clothing and makeup were attacked as unserious Modern Girls who indulged in pleasure and vanity, and betrayed the true meaning of tiyu. In 1932, *Tiyu Weekly* reported that "the few basketball teams at Nankai Girls' Secondary School could benefit from modesty and hard practice. Unfortunately, they pay exclusive attention to clothing. The basketball players are not concerned with cost as long as the clothing looks modern and mirrors the style of rich ladies. That is really a tragedy in women's tiyu."[211] One writer criticized female basketball players for giving priority to appearance and neglecting domestic duties and skills: "As soon as they rise in the morning, ball players Yin and Mei put on clothing specially made for ball games, painted on red rouge and dark eyebrows, and carelessly organized their bedding."[212] Both male and female writers condemned female basketball players who appeared on court with shiny clothing, dazzling bracelets, heavily powdered faces, painted thin eyebrows, permed hair in the fashion of the "Modern Girl and foxy spirits," and adornments suitable only for beauty pageants or fashion shows. A female writer was concerned that the contradictory appearance could "backfire by leading to so much mean criticism, sometimes involving attacks on individual morality and characters." She suggested that athletic clothing should be light, comfortable, and convenient, and that athletes should understand that cleanliness is beauty.[213]

Attention to female players' bodies naturally extended to interest in their romantic lives and marital status. Susan K. Cahn demonstrates how suspicion of homosexuality among muscular female track stars in the United States forced athletes to highlight their femininity and engage in heterosexual romances.[214] It is hard to judge whether the cross-dressing and masculine styles of some Liangjiang players reflected their homosexuality or simply reflected a desire to cultivate a serious and professional demeanour as a defence against the gaze of male fans. Regardless, there was never a hint of such suspicion in the media. Without the necessity to prove her heterosexuality, Chen Rongming consciously cultivated a nunnish image of devotion to her career as a woman who shunned romance and marriage. According to Lu Lihua, most of her students never married, and she herself lived as a single person most of her life despite three brief marriages, an experience common to many career women in Republican China.[215] The media reported, however, that "Miss Lu Lihua is quite good looking" and pursued her marriage, family life, and even widowhood with interest. Like Zhang Huilan, Lu used the themes of romance, marriage, and a happy family life to foster the popularity of tiyu among housewives and to advocate for gender equality and an end to gender segregation in socialization. As early as 1927, she published two articles titled "The Equal Opportunities between Men and Women" and "The True Meaning of Open Socialization" in the pioneering magazine *Xing zazhi (Magazine of Sexuality)*. In 1937, she wrote on the relationship between women's tiyu, healthy housewives, and perfectly happy families in the midst of national crisis.[216]

Instead, the spotlight shone on those players engaged in heterosexual relationships. Gossip columns hailed Liangjiang's most prominent player, Shao Jinying, as the ultimate Modern Girl. Since Shao was successful as a physical educator and basketball coach and in her marriage to a top tiyu administrator and professor, Liu Xuesong,[217] the media tirelessly sought sensational evidence in her early romantic life and career. After she graduated from Liangjiang in 1932, *Linglong* featured a photograph of Shao sitting on a metal fence covered by flowers, as a jianmei woman. Evidently lacking a traditionally pretty face and slender figure, she was admired for her physical strength.[218] Before marrying Liu, Shao was involved with Gao Zhaolie, a Fudan University graduate and fellow Xiamen resident. To work with Gao, Shao abruptly broke her teaching contract with her alma mater and joined Jiangnan Tiyu Normal School. There were public disputes and threats of lawsuits between the two schools before Shen Siliang and other top tiyu figures stepped in to mediate the quarrel, enabling both Shao and Gao to work for Liangjiang instead. The mix of love affair and disloyalty, essential ingredients in the making of a Modern Girl, caused a stir in the media. Reporters followed Shao and Gao closely as the couple led the Liangjiang teams tour of the South in 1933 and then vacationed in Tianjin during the winter break. Unconcerned, the couple proudly shared the details of their private lives. *Peiyang Pictorial News* carried prominent photographs, with captions describing them as an engaged couple. The engagement was cancelled suddenly in late spring 1934, after Shao switched her love interest to Liu Xuesong, the tiyu inspector/supervisor of Zhijiang University in Nanjing. The media portrayed this twist in Shao's romantic life as characteristic of a Modern Girl and associated it with the unpredictable and fast-moving machine age. Newspapers used the exaggerated phrases and titles commonly found in "Mandarin Ducks and Butterflies" romantic novels to describe the shock and confusion of the public at such a frightening and unpredictable shift in love affairs. *Tiyu pinglun (Tiyu Review)* and *Diligent Tiyu Monthly* commented that "the speed of love between Liu and Shao is faster than an express train."[219] It was not accidental that the humorous piece "Wild Tiyu History" used cars with roaring engines to symbolize dominant female basketball players residing in the political centre, the "Forbidden City," as hints about the problems of the confused gender order. References to fast modern transportation were frequently employed to suggest the Modern Girl's indulgence in material pleasures and disloyalty. Unlike cinematic actresses, who were often bothered by such coverage, Shao exhibited self-assurance and control of her romances. She and Liu married, and she adopted her husband's name. *Diligent Tiyu Monthly* reported that their marriage was harmonious, and the former basketball star gave birth to a son in July 1935.[220]

The intensive tours and media coverage of Liangjiang players contributed to a renegotiation of the legitimate social space for women. While flexibly using basketball's rules, the team played an active role in defining basketball as a sport for women. Their co-ed games and socialization contributed to the end of gender segregation in society. During the National Games and Far Eastern Games, or inter-city and overseas friendship games, the organizers usually held banquets after the matches, to which they invited both male and female players.[221] As powerful and confident athletes, the latter enjoyed relatively more freedom in romance and sexuality than ordinary women. What, then, was the significance of the Liangjiang basketball team's breaking of the gendered rules? Complementary to Zhang Huilan's ideas, their actions extended the gendered boundaries for women, symbolically broke down gender segregation in society, and redefined women's legitimate space during the national crisis.

The history of the Liangjiang basketball team reveals much about the emerging importance of sports in 1930s China. Led by the entrepreneurial Lu Lihua, the school made women's basketball a national sensation and stimulated much discussion about the role of women and sports in Chinese society. Much of the interest focused on Lu's controversial plans and on her energetic espousal of her school, its players, and their successes and failures. Her actions combined her individual ambitions with service to the nation-state. At the same time, she could not fulfill her dreams because her government connections and support were unstable at best. Lacking genuine government investment and recognition, Lu and her school had to manoeuvre on their own. Defeats on the basketball court became organizational disasters. Fame and victory were insufficient tools for building long-term success.

The players, who as students naturally transitioned between matriculation and graduation, drifted into the background of the Liangjiang story. Their career paths reveal a developing network of physical education jobs after their graduation. Without a Chinese women's professional basketball league, still a dream today, or government support for outstanding players to participate in international competitions, Liangjiang's players had nowhere to go to continue competing. They were a powerless elite, enjoying brief moments of fame but unable to wield clear political power. Many of them became tiyu teachers, a career that was a natural extension of their playing days and that contributed to the overall strength of Chinese women.[222] Although teaching meant fading into anonymity, their lives still had meaning within tiyu.

Following the end of the War of Resistance against Japan (Second Sino-Japanese War, 1937-45), Lu organized a co-ed secondary school intended to revive Liangjiang. She encountered difficult wrangling with the Nationalist Party. In 1950, a year after the Communist Party took power in mainland China, officials from the Municipal Bureau of Education in Shanghai visited the Private Liangjiang Women's Tiyu Normal School. They informed Lu Lihua, the school's principal, that the government was seizing the school and that a former student, the wife of party official and noted historian Zhou Gucheng, would be placed in charge. After being forced out, Lu had nothing left. She was assigned to work first in the Fifth Woolen Sweater Factory and then as an employee of the Shanghai Historical Society until her retirement at the age of sixty-two. Her tiny apartment was searched for documents during the Cultural Revolution. Lu was rehabilitated in 1980 and became a member of the Shanghai People's Political Consultative Conference. She viewed her past life without bitterness and saw herself as a person of dignity and pride. Her understanding of her life, recorded by Wang Zheng, provides a model for comprehending the lives and meaning of the other sportswomen encountered in this book.[223]

4 The Evanescent Glory of the Track Queens

Of all modern sports, Chinese nationalists considered track competition to be the ultimate test of human power and speed. Track events served as the perfect metaphor for social Darwinist competition among modern nations. Success at track meets was critical if China wished to compete globally. Journalists insisted that China's eventual participation in the Olympics should focus on track and field, "since they are the main events and interest of international games."[1] A strong showing by Chinese women at these events would demonstrate the renewed strength of a once-threatened nation.

These political and cultural expectations placed heavy burdens on successful female track and field competitors, who became known as track queens or even as "Queens of Sports." As I will show in this chapter, multi-talented female track stars rapidly rose to fame but then faced obstacles to making a living while preserving their amateur status. They devised various strategies, including accepting the patronage of politically influential men, making connections with popular male athletes, constructing non-threatening public personae that emphasized traditional virtues such as filial piety and self-sacrifice, highlighting rural origins, and adopting the philosophies of the New Life Movement (NLM). Once the track queens chose to abandon their amateur status, they became university students and subsequently teachers, or immersed themselves in marriage. Despite these moves toward respectability, they had to cope with an ambiguous sexual persona. Their uniforms, which necessarily exposed large portions of their bodies, accentuated their sexuality. The track queens were therefore vulnerable to sexual predators and scandalous rumours, and practised celibacy to fend off both.

Becoming Track Queens

Sun Guiyun (dates unknown) was the first track queen. After women were first allowed to take part in track and field events during the Fourth National Games in 1930, Sun, who competed for the No. 1 Girls' Secondary School of the Special District of Eastern Province (formerly the Congde Girls' Secondary School; abbreviated as Dongte No. 1 Girls' Secondary School) in Harbin,

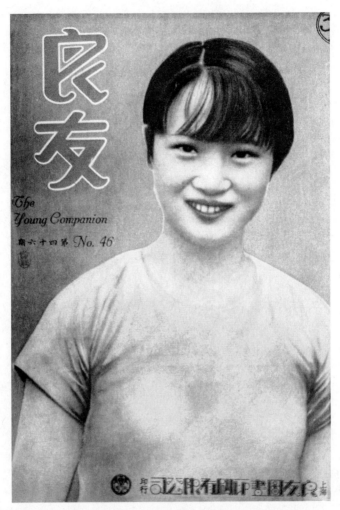

15   Sun Guiyun on the cover of *Young Companion Pictorial* as
the first "Queen of Sports."
Source: Liangyou huabao 46 (April 1930).

Manchuria, became the first female athletic superstar.[2] Women competed in
track events, shot put, high and long jump, and softball throwing. Sun earned
the moniker "flying general" after her overwhelming triumph in every track
event. She broke national records in the 50- and 100-metre dashes, and ran
the anchor leg for the Harbin team that set the national record in the
200-metre relay.[3] Swimmers did not take part in the games, so Sun had no
rival as a celebrity. *Beiyang huabao (Peiyang Pictorial News)* published numerous photographs of her, standing by the trophies and her team. Shortly

after, Liang Desuo, the noted photographer and editor of *Liangyou huabao (Young Companion Pictorial)*, photographed her for the cover of the magazine, essential real estate for new celebrities (see Figure 15). The caption celebrated her as the "victorious national *tiyu jia*" (tiyu expert), a title hitherto reserved for male tiyu professionals, and Sun thereby joined the ranks of noted movie actresses and wealthy women. Furthermore, the magazine gave her equal coverage with elite men, placing her image next to a photograph of the president of Fengyong University (Fengyong daxue) reading the magazine.[4] The noted public relations expert Huang Jingwan published biographies of Sun in *Wenhua (Essences of Literature)* and *Funü zazhi (Women's Magazine).*[5]

Sun's triumph was short-lived as fame derives only from today's success. Qian Xingsu (1915-68), of Dongya Women's Tiyu Vocational School in Shanghai dethroned her at the Fifth National Games in 1933 by winning the overall women's championship. After the achievements of Sun and her peers convinced the Nationalist government and the public of women's physical capacity, the distances of track events were lengthened for the 1933 Games. Qian set national records in the 100- and 200-metre dashes and in the newly added 80-metre low hurdles, anchored the Shanghai team's victory in the 400-metre relay, and broke a national record and won a silver medal in the long jump.[6] Quickly linking her achievements with their political agenda, the Executive Yuan of the Nationalist government created a special banner for her with five characters, 全国新纪录 *quanguo xin jilu* (new national records).[7]

Her talent in the long jump ignited Qian's celebrity. She placed second in this event in the First Secondary School Games in Shanghai in 1930 but repeatedly set new national records in all three Shanghai Municipal Games preceding the Fifth National Games. In unofficial high jumps, she became the first Chinese woman to leap above five metres and her ability earned her the nickname of "the flea." As early as 1931, during the Second Shanghai Municipal Games, *Young Companion Pictorial* featured Qian's photograph, introducing her as the national record holder in the long jump and prominently noting her record (see Figure 16). *Tiyu xinsheng (New Voice in Tiyu)* captured her jump style in an action photograph.[8] During the Fifth National Games in 1933, however, Qian's unprecedented multiple talents inadvertently caused problems. By competing in five events, she violated the rules of the games and avoided being penalized only by arguing that the relay was a group event.[9] Unfortunately, the 200-metre dash and the long jump were scheduled for the same time. Journalists had predicted that Qian would definitely be victorious in the long jump, and in her first three tries she broke the national record. After setting a new national record in the 200-metre dash, however,

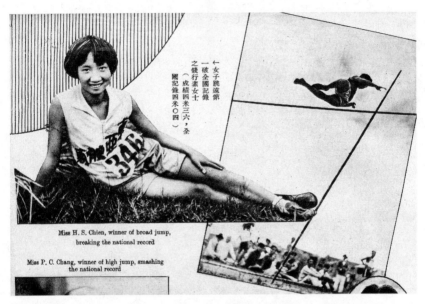

Miss H. S. Chien, winner of broad jump,
breaking the national record

Miss P. C. Chang, winner of high jump, smashing
the national record

16 "Miss Qian Xingsu, winner of broad jump, breaking the national record."
Source: Liangyou huabao 63 (November 1931): 25.

she returned to the long jump too exhausted to break the record set by Guangdong athlete Li Yuanfen. *Xinwen bao (News)* commented regretfully that "Qian won the 200-metre, but gave way to Li Yuanfen in the long jump."[10]

Qian first showed her talent in track events at the Multi-national Games *(Wanguo yundong hui)* in Shanghai in 1931, where she placed a surprising second behind her Western opponent in the 200-metre dash and delivered a major victory for China by taking first place in the 400-metre relay along with her schoolmates. She took third and fourth place in the 50- and 100-metre dashes, respectively, the following year.[11] In the Sixth National Games in 1935, Qian still broke her own record in the 80-metre hurdles, finished second in the 100- and 200-metre dashes, and took fifth place in javelin after becoming exhausted in the 200-metre dash. The press remained enamoured of the charming Qian and promoted her, along with new track stars Li Sen, Jiao Yulian, and Peng Aipu, as "the four Shanghai dashers." Photographs of the quartet, arms around each other's shoulders, appeared frequently in the popular tiyu journals.[12]

Artist Ye Qianyu's special journal on the Fifth National Games praised Qian's multiple talents lavishly. On the same page that showed male athletes participating in all-around competitions, a photograph featured Qian engaging in archery, with the caption "She is really an unbelievable girl capable of various athletic events ... by breaking three national records, Qian won glory for Shanghai."[13] A photograph of Qian flying over the hurdles read: "This girl is really smart, thorough at all eighteen categories of weapons [a cliché for multi-talented imperial military officials]. No wonder everyone praises her."[14] *Qinfen tiyu yuebao (Diligent Tiyu Monthly)* echoed: "She is not only good at track and field events, but also excels at academic courses, ball games, dance, national skills, swimming, and music." The journal recognized, however, that multiple skills were associated with limited career choices for female athletes, noting: "Because Qian studies in a normal school and will work as a physical educator under our national context, she has to balance various skills." The journal argued for her specialization, in the national interest, writing that in order for Qian to "enter the world stage, make the blondes follow after her, and win glory for the nation," her coaches had to carefully direct her toward a specialized focus.[15]

Tiyu periodicals and other journals acknowledged Qian as the new track queen. *Diligent Tiyu Monthly* and *Rensheng xunkan (Life Ten-Daily)* put her on their covers. The former featured portraits and very short biographies of two outstanding athletes *(yundong jia)* and two notable tiyu scholars/administrators *(tiyu jia)* in each issue; it honoured Qian in December 1934.[16] The magazine *Qianqiu (Varieties)* bestowed on Sun and Qian the title "Model Lady: the Queen of Sports" in 1931 and 1933, respectively.[17]

The third and most illustrious track queen was Li Sen (1914 [1917?]-1948) of Dongnan Women's Tiyu Vocational School in Shanghai, who emerged at the Sixth National Games in 1935. She had an earlier brush with fame when she represented Hunan Province at the Fourth National Games in 1930, but her poor performance dashed any hope of immediate celebrity.[18] This time, however, she won three gold medals in the 50-, 100-, and 200-metre dash, set new national records in the 50- and 200-metre dash, and took second place in the long jump.[19] Inspired by the hit film *Tiyu huanghou (Queen of Sports)*, the media returned its gaze to the track queens. *Young Companion Pictorial* published Li's autobiography. The pictorial's series of "Celebrity Memoirs" in 1934 and 1935 included the warlord general Feng Yuxiang, administrative expert Gan Naiguang, politician Chen Gongbo, journalist Ge Gongzhen, public relations expert Huang Jingwan, and the Chinese American actress Anna May Wong (Huang Liushuang).[20] Right after the Sixth National Games, the magazine's October 1935 issue included Li Sen's "My Tiyu Life" as one of the two representatives from tiyu circles in the series (see Figure 17).[21] With enthusiasm customarily shown to movie stars, fans

17 Li Sen's autobiographical essay.
Source: Liangyou huabao 110 (October 1935): 17.

besieged the new track queen for autographs at the games. Overwhelmed and tired, Li slipped away.[22]

In June 1935, Li had competed in the Third Multi-national Track and Field Games in Shanghai, which featured teams from China, the United States,

Japan, Russia, England, and Germany. China won both the men's and women's championships, Russia took second place, and the United States placed third. *Young Companion Pictorial* commented that "the performance of men was only so-so, but women set three new records." Coverage featured a photograph of Li receiving medals at the top of the platform, with an American girl to her right in second place and Qian Xingsu to her left in third place.[23] Along with fifty-six male and eight female track and field athletes, Li participated in games against Westerners in June 1936 in Shanghai, which served as both a rehearsal and a selection process for the 1936 Olympics, and won the 100-metre dash.[24]

Li's achievements convinced the Chinese government to select her to represent the nation at the Berlin Olympics in 1936. This was the first time that Chinese women took part in the Olympic Games since the nation had become a member of the International Olympic Committee in 1922. Li faced great obstacles. In an article titled "An Examination of Chinese Participants to the 11th Olympics" in *Diligent Tiyu Monthly*, a writer, presumably male, using the pen name "the Reporter," stated that it was a tough task to select even a small number of representatives "from the malnourished Chinese track and field circle. As far as their skills are concerned, none of Chinese athletes deserves the trip to Berlin." He suggested sending only four to seven of them to Berlin, in order to "save public money for developing tiyu in other ways." No female athletes were included on his list.[25]

In Berlin, thirty-six competitors in the 100-metre qualifying dash were divided into six groups. After Li finished fourth – 8 metres and 1.1 seconds behind the winner, Poland's champion from the previous Olympics – she was eliminated from the next round of competition.[26] In its special issue on the 1936 Olympics, *Shidai manhua (Modern Sketch/Epoch Cartoons)*, the leading satirical magazine in China, ridiculed her defeat and that of China's male track and field Olympians with a group photograph captioned, "China's modern youth in 1936: the Chinese track and field team in the 1936 Olympics and their trophy" – the "goose egg" marked with the characters for "special prize for China; Made in Germany" (see Figure 18). Li tried to be upbeat, offering an interview regarding her experience and defeat in Berlin on her arrival in Shanghai harbour with other athletes.[27] Although she did not win any points or medals, Li first appeared on the international platform as the face of China's "New Woman."

Track queens were the offspring of the marriage between government policies and mass media. Neither parent was reliable and female track and field athletes faced the greatest uncertainty of any of the sportswomen discussed in this book. Their careers were brief. Financial reward was non-existent, and

一九三六年中國現代青年的動態

第十一屆世界運動大會我國田徑標錦隊及所得之錦標合影

18 A "goose egg" for Li Sen and her team after their defeat in the 1936
Berlin Olympics.
Source: Shidai manhua 29 (20 August 1936).

they had to forsake their athletic careers to survive. The government that
largely sponsored the competitions in which they excelled offered little support. The media made the track queens famous and then quickly abandoned
them or questioned their respectability.

Indeed, female track skills had only recently gained respect. Until the late
1920s, due to lack of playing fields and equipment and to its very physically
demanding nature, track and field was neither popular nor well developed
in China.[28] As indicated in Chapter 1, Zhang Huilan pushed a new understanding of the competitive potential of women's bodies. Inclusive state
policies and expansion of schoolgirls' tiyu during the national crisis stimulated
the growth of women's participation in track and field competitions. After
the enactment of the Tiyu Law for Citizens in 1929 and its revised version in
1931, women's sports became more common in schools. Female students
from government-run or monitored tiyu institutions participated in women's
competitive games. Besides producing female PE teachers, the higher-level
tiyu institutions transformed informal student games into highly organized
collegiate athletic programs under the control of paid administrators and

professional coaches. Female athletes from these schools competed in inter-collegiate, local, and national games and in international competitions, setting new records at various levels. The struggle against Japan gave a new nationalist meaning to track and field events, previously regarded as masculine, as suitable competitions for women. By the mid-1930s, women's track and field, which required fewer facilities and permitted a greater number of participants than individual games, became popular in most tournaments. Women's performances in the three National Games in the early 1930s inspired journalists to coin the term "track queens" to honour their accomplishments.

In Chapter 2, I noted the rise of a new journalism that combined sports coverage, fashion, and the goal of a jianmei body. Prestigious, widely circulated, women-oriented popular magazines such as *Young Companion Pictorial* based in Shanghai and *Peiyang Pictorial News* based in Tianjin nurtured female track and field stardom. The popular press and cinema promoted track and field athletes much like movie stars or fashion models, and a fan culture soon emerged, the impact of which extended beyond sports. Images of young female sprinters displaying their muscular legs and torsos in high-cut shorts and tight T-shirts entered popular fashion and public consciousness. Such fame was fleeting, however. The hit film *Queen of Sports* depicted the fate of track queens who rose and fell at dramatic speed as the "Queens of Sports," a nickname that recognized their overall prominence among female athletes.

Learning from a Japanese Star

The personae of China's track queens had multiple origins and reveal the complex nature of Chinese sportswomen's personalities. In the late 1920s, as with other modern sports brought in from the West, European and American track and field athletes dominated the coverage in the mass media. In 1927, *Young Companion Pictorial* carried a photograph of the champion French women in T-shirts and high-cut shorts displaying their overtaxed bodies and sweaty faces at the finish line of a track event at the International Women's Games in Sweden.[29] More lighthearted were later images, such as those in the 1930s of an American sprint coach instructing a scantily clad American actress crouching playfully at the starting line, which replaced the older images of blonde women competing seriously in track and field events.[30]

By the close of the 1920s, the most significant model was from Japan, a nation with which China was experiencing rising military tensions. In general, Chinese intellectuals and officials regarded Japan as a country that had improved its racial physique, even though its people were "originally inferior to the Chinese." Tiyu training had enabled the Japanese to compete with Europeans and Americans.[31] Kinue Hitomi (1907-31) was proof of Asian women's physical assets. She held Japan's national records in fifteen track and field events, the sole exception being the high jump. Her performance in the long jump at Japan's national games in Osaka in 1928 propelled Japan into the world record books. She participated in several international competitions as early as age fourteen, and in 1928 became the only Japanese woman to compete in the Amsterdam Olympic Games, winning silver in the 800-metre race. She set world records in Amsterdam in the 50-, 200-, and 400-metre dashes and in the triple jump. Hitomi worked as a reporter for the *Osaka Daily News* before her premature death from pneumonia at the age of twenty-four following an exhausting competitive and promotional schedule.[32]

Chinese nationalists viewed Hitomi as an inspiration for Chinese female track athletes. She was popular in China, and her image was ubiquitous in the Chinese media. In 1928, the popular women's magazine *Jindai funü (Contemporary Women)* featured a photograph of her disembarking at Shanghai en route to Japan after the Amsterdam Olympics.[33] When a journalist for *Tiyu zhoubao (Tiyu Weekly)* travelled to Japan, he took pains to visit her and received an autographed photograph. After her death, the journalist detailed Hitomi's achievements and mourned her with deep affection: "In the afternoon of August 2, the world's great and beautiful star ... passed away with a smile on her face. Not only Japan, but also the world, mourned over the tremendous loss to the tiyu field." His sentiment was echoed by other journals, such as *Nü xuesheng (Female Students)* and *Tiyu xinsheng (New Voice of Tiyu)*. Even after the Mukden Incident, interest in Hitomi remained strong in China. Shanghai's Diligent Publishing House published her book *Nü yundong yuan linzhen zhiqian (Female Athletes before Competition)* in 1931, two months after her death. Throughout the early 1930s, the publishing house continued to advertise the inexpensive book in its flagship journal *Diligent Tiyu Monthly*, highlighting the fact that Hitomi "wrote the book based on her own experience." The Chinese media respected her as the "the number-one legend in the world history of women's sports" and admired her contribution to creating "a positive image of Japanese women on the world stage" by "going to Europe and America to compete" and "inspiring a strong physique among Japanese women."[34]

Hitomi's death sparked debate in Japan and China over whether women should participate in strenuous track and field events. On the same page that carried an advertisement for her book, writers cited surveys and statistics of female Japanese athletes to dissuade women from participating in athletic activities at a young age and/or during menstruation.[35] Nevertheless, despite her tragic premature death, Hitomi's accomplishments set the standard for Chinese athletes.

The Track Queens during the National Crisis

Japanese aggression in Manchuria called for new Chinese heroines to replace Hitomi. Despite their admiration for the Japanese star, the track queens had to find homegrown sponsors for their ambitions and unite their personal dreams with the hopes of the nation. Although the Japanese distanced themselves from other Asians, they tried to "civilize" and incorporate the various Asian ethnicities into a single nationality by using the rhetoric of true egalitarianism. This approach differentiated Japan's racial principles from the German Nazi theory of pure blood. The Japanese pan-Asian project presented Manchukuo, a puppet state founded in 1932, a year after Japanese invasion, as a "national space" that was connected to "redemptive societies" (religious organizations with universal beliefs) and pan-Asianist ideologists in Japan.[36] Besides alleging a common culture between Japan and Manchukuo, the Japanese sought to enter Manchurian athletes in international competitions to bolster their claims that the puppet state of Manchukuo was an independent nation, albeit under Japanese supervision.

In the struggle over Manchuria, the warlord Zhang Xueliang sponsored male track and field stars from the region to represent Chinese masculinity. As early as 1923, the *Manchuria Daily News* reported that "the sports promoted by the local Chinese Young Men's Association under the auspices of the Taitun Jihpao in the recreation ground of West Park turned out to be a great success." Those athletic activities were called the "grand social event between the local Chinese and Japanese."[37] China, Manchukuo, and Japan all tried to use the Manchurian track and field team to gain recognition of their "nation states" internationally. The Nationalist government claimed the identity of these athletes as proof of its civilized status and as a ticket to "the forest of nations" *(minzu zhilin)*.

Manchurian male track and field stars such as Liu Changchun and Fu Baolu were hailed as lasting national examples. Fu, a pole jumper (whose mother was Russian), became the only Chinese athlete to compete in the finals in his sport at the Berlin Olympics under the Chinese banner.[38] Liu emerged as the "track king" and even "King of Sports" throughout Republican China by becoming China's first Olympian – indeed the only athlete to represent China at the 1932 Los Angeles Olympics – and also participated in the 1936 Berlin Olympics.[39] The widely circulated *Tiyu Weekly* published the "Diaries of Liu Changchun," which he wrote during the Los Angeles Games, and

"Reflections on Participating in the [1936] Olympics."[40] Liu represented Manchuria under Japanese occupation at all the domestic games that he attended.[41] He remained in the nation's memory as the track king until Liu Xiang won China's first gold medal in men's track and field (in the 110-metre hurdles) at the 2004 Olympics in Athens.

Sun Guiyun rose to prominence alongside Liu Changchun. After outstanding performances in the regional games in Manchuria organized by Zhang Xueliang, they led the Manchurian women's and men's track and field teams to triumph at the Fourth National Games in 1930 and became the most popular athletes in China. *Peiyang Pictorial News* showed the two stars from Manchuria as good friends and equals,[42] while the host city, Hangzhou, dedicated "Guiyun Bridge" and "Changchun Road" near the Provincial Stadium in recognition of their achievements.[43] Their experiences soon diverged, however. After her defeat at the Ninth Far Eastern Games (FEG) in Tokyo in June 1931, Sun made brief comebacks as a track star at some regional games. In the Fifteenth North China Games in Jinan, Shandong, in 1931, she won two championships, broke the national record in the 200-metre dash, and won the highest total score in track and field. Liu's performance declined, but he still won championships and continued to represent China internationally after Sun had disappeared from track competitions.[44]

Zhang Xueliang's influence proved beneficial for Sun Guiyun. He supported Sun's matches against Hitomi, which were rare for Chinese female athletes. In 1928, he organized the United Games of Three Northeast Provinces, in which Sun and her teammates participated as guests and set new records.[45] The following year, he sponsored the Fourteenth North China Games in Shenyang (Mukden) at Northeast University's new stadium, the largest in the nation and newly built at a cost of over 20,000 yuan, and again Sun won several championships.[46] That same year, she had her first chance to compete against Japanese athletes in the German-Japanese-Chinese Athletic Games at Shenyang, Manchuria, organized by Zhang. In an early example of her competitive strength, Sun ranked third in the 60- and 100-metre dashes, and *Peiyang Pictorial News* proudly carried a photograph of her to mark her achievements.[47]

After Sun's overwhelming victory at the Fourth National Games, *Tiyu Weekly* praised her for inspiring women's track and field, expressed satisfaction with "our heroine's performance," and challenged her to "catch up with the Japanese superstar Kinue Hitomi soon."[48] It was not long before Sun and her teammates had their chance to face top Japanese athletes. In June, just two months after the Fourth National Games, the Harbin women's track and field team led by Sun travelled to Tokyo to compete in the Far Eastern Games. As Sun and one of her teammates stood on the boat's gangplank in their formal outfits waving to the crowd, the famous journalist Ge Gongzhen of *Shenbao*, Republican China's largest newspaper, captured the moment in a photograph that circulated widely in the media.[49]

Unfortunately, Sun and her teammates fared poorly in Hitomi's home country, partly due to the psychological pressure of national expectations but mostly because the Japanese superstar was simply better. Sun participated in the 100- and 200-metre dashes and the 400-metre relay, which were generally longer than her previous track events. Burdened with her new fame and high expectations from her compatriots, she was so nervous that she made three false starts in the 100 metres and was disqualified. She stated that the failure "constituted an enormous blow to my spirit." Frustrated and disheartened and "not expecting to perform well," she failed to appear for the 200-metre race.[50] Sun's failure in Japan puzzled even the noted writer Lu Xun, who had studied in Japan as a young man. "Sun Guiyun was a good runner. Somehow, once she arrived in Japan, she could not run anymore, as if crippled."[51]

Despite their setbacks, Zhang Xueliang received the Chinese team warmly when they returned via Shenyang. The *Peiyang Pictorial News* carried a photograph of the six female athletes, taken by the Dongbei (Northeast) Photography Agency, with Sun Guiyun in the middle. In the same issue, a short piece focusing on her failure in Japan stated that "Sun seemed very embarrassed, said that she failed the public and extended her apology."[52]

Qian Xingsu also benefited from association with a powerful male figure: Liu Changchun, nicknamed "Legendary Sprinting Master." A week before the opening of the Fifth National Games, Shanghai's *Shishi xinbao (New Newspaper of Current Affairs)* published a special issue devoted to the games. Under the title "Saipao jie zhi quanwei: nan Qian bei Liu xiangying pimei" ("Authorities in Tracks: Southern Qian and Northern Liu Complementary and Reflecting Excellence") in large bold print, the article was filled with admiring words and high expectations for her.[53] Sun and her team were sent to the Ninth Far Eastern Games to uphold the nation's honour. In contrast, overshadowed by the new female superstar – swimmer Yang Xiuqiong – Qian's Shanghai track and field team was not granted the same chance to compete in the Tenth Far Eastern Games in Manila in 1934. *Linglong,* the Shanghai-based women's magazine with a strong feminist tone, noted their absence. It had had high expectations for "the ideal track team" headed by Qian. Disappointed, it featured a photograph of the Fifth National Games champion, the Shanghai women's track and field team, in sweaters and gym shorts, headed by a man in a suit and carrying a cane. Its editorial pointed out: "It is a pity that women's track and field will not participate in the FEG."[54] Right after the Sixth National Games, the October 1935 issue of *Young Companion Pictorial* included only Liu Changchun and Shanghai's Li Sen as representatives from tiyu circles in its series of celebrity autobiographies. Next to Liu Changchun's saga of "Twelve Years on the Athletic Field" was Li Sen's "My Tiyu Life."[55]

Despite setbacks in several events, the prominence of female Manchurian athletes in track and field prompted prominent male nationalists to use them as symbols of precious national resources in need of patriarchal protection. The Nationalists contended that female suffering and sacrifice should be understood within the context of state politics. Anti-Japanese propaganda included images of the suffering bodies of Manchurian women as symbols of Japan's brutal humiliation of Chinese masculinity. Conflating female suffering with the nation's plight, Nationalist messages pushed Manchurian women's competitive feats to the foreground. Portraying Manchuria as Chinese was crucial to disproving Japan's claim that it represented Asia. To support its claims, the Chinese government sought top Chinese athletes and a Chinese agent who could preside at international sports meetings. The Nationalist state also used athletes as symbols to stress China's sovereignty over Manchuria. In September 1933, the Northeastern Provinces Games were held for "athletes-in-exile" *(liuwang xuanshou)* from Manchuria living in Beiping. Refugee athletes fired the audience's emotions when they marched at the end of the procession at the Fifth National Games, a scene later echoed in the film *Queen of Sports.*[56]

The Limits of Stardom

Despite the track queens' accomplishments, their fame was short-lived, in contrast to their male counterparts. Making a living was the key problem: female track stars had limited employment opportunities. Because national sports regulations excluded tiyu teachers from amateur competition, athletes needed to find jobs that would earn them money while protecting their amateur status. Government practices and beliefs exacerbated the track queens' anxieties over status and employment. In order to compete in the tiyu teacher job market, female athletes in Republican China could not afford to specialize in a single sport. Instead, they strove to develop themselves into all-around athletes with multiple talents.[57] Consequently, they reached the full potential of their physical capacities during the brief shining moment of their athletic careers.

Male stars received government jobs that preserved their amateur status. On returning from the 1932 Los Angeles Olympics, Liu Changchun took a job in the municipal government of Beiping while training hard in the dash "to wash the shame for the nation in the future."[58] In February 1935, he began working in the Ministry of Communications for a monthly salary of 120 Yuan even as he trained at the National Central University stadium. He even lived at the headquarters of Lizhi she (励志社), a fascism-coloured youth organization affiliated with the Nationalist Party, before moving to his own place. By 1936 he had transferred to the Ministry of Foreign Affairs. In contrast, Sun Guiyun's career did not last long after her defeat in Japan. Her hometown of Harbin was occupied, and she fell into difficult circumstances but attracted none of the assistance that Liu received.[59]

Teaching tiyu was the only feasible career for female athletes, but taking a job in physical education disqualified them from further competition. The track queens were keenly aware of this difficulty. In her autobiographical article, Li Sen expressed her strong desire to compete in the 1936 Olympics before "serving society" and relieving her family's difficult financial situation by becoming a physical educator on graduation.[60] Since teaching positions were rare, Li considered a job offer from Hunan warlord He Jian a rare opportunity to create a great career combining Western sports with national skills (martial arts). She happily accepted his offer, although, as explained later, that decision nearly became disastrous.

Qian Xingsu became a teacher. On her graduation from Dongya in 1936, the Zhirenyong Girls' Secondary and Elementary School hired her to supervise its students' daily exercise, while she still held the record in the 80-metre low hurdles.[61] Over the next decade, she taught at girls' secondary schools in Shanghai, including Wuben, Mingde, Qixiu, Datong University, Jinan University, and Dongya, until 1949. In 1950, she began teaching at Fudan University and coached the track and field teams of various Shanghai colleges and universities. According to Ge Min, the author of a brief biography of Qian published in 1990, "she was well-liked by her colleagues because she was modest, sincere, and kind to people." Li Sen had a similar experience. After the start of full-scale war with Japan, she worked briefly at the Hunan Martial Arts Institute for a monthly salary of 90 yuan, then transferred to Chengdu, Sichuan, to teach tiyu. Her records in the 50- and 200-metre dashes stood until 1949.[62]

Like several of her colleagues, Sun Guiyun pursued higher education. As early as 1931, there were rumours that she would quit tiyu in order to focus on her academic work. Preparing for the entrance exam to the prestigious

Qinghua University, she skipped the Seventeenth North China Games in Qingdao in 1933.[63] The following year, she enrolled as a freshman in the college of liberal arts at Daxia University and then transferred to Shanghai University (Hujiang daxue) in Shanghai, schools that de-emphasized athletics. Instead of using her fame to promote women's sports on campus, Daxia University abolished athletic tournaments and withdrew from various competitions to concentrate on PE. Sun was active in basketball initially but lack of practice diminished her speed.[64] Similarly, a few months before the Mukden Incident in 1931, Sun's teammate Wu Meixian joined the summer school of Nankai University in Tianjin, which recruited her to its first co-ed class with a view to strengthening its athletic program.[65] At any rate, Wu ended her sports career after transferring to Fudan University in Shanghai, where "she did not run well any longer."[66]

Both Sun and Wu soon left their celebrity behind in favour of marriage and family. On 23 April 1936, Sun married Hu Zhenxia, an employee of the Xinya Hotel. The media covered the event and carried wedding photographs of the happy bride dressed in a Western-style wedding gown and carrying flowers.[67] Intending to transfer from Fudan to Shandong University, Wu went to Qingdao in 1935 and stayed with the head of the Bureau of Social Affairs, Chu Tiesheng; she was soon engaged to Chu's colleague Tu Shaozhen and they were married in Qingdao Municipal Hall on 12 January 1936. The reports of Sun's and Wu's weddings referred to them as "former female athletes" and observed repeatedly that they were gaining weight and had abandoned athletics.[68] Similarly, Li Sen married an air force officer, Wang Longde, from Shaanxi Province in 1938 at Chengdu. The couple had a daughter named Wang Lingling and a son named Wang Naibing. Li died from complications of childbirth in 1942.[69]

The national media showed little sympathy for the plight of the track queens unless national interest appeared to be threatened. As Sun's running career faded, *Young Companion Pictorial* reduced the size of her portrait drastically even as it celebrated with large photographs two other female athletes who set new national records at the Tianjin Municipal Games.[70] Sun was expected to win the 80-metre hurdles at the Fifteenth North China Games, but Shandong athlete Zhang Suhui beat her by one second. The crowd applauded Zhang loudly and reporters rushed to take her photograph.[71] As the newcomers began breaking national records and mounting serious challenges to the reigning track queens, journalists celebrated the rapid turnover of female track stars in language suggesting the national interest. *Diligent Tiyu Monthly*, which had always given Qian favourable and extensive coverage, featured Li Sen, along with another female athlete, as its cover girls in 1935 and carried highly flattering personal stories:

> During a time period when women's tiyu lags behind, emerging dash talents such as Miss Li suddenly took the lead by beating the national record holder Qian in three events in the international games in Shanghai and set new records ... In the upcoming National Games, Li will replace Sun Guiyun, who rose in the Fourth National Games in Hangzhou, and Qian Xingsu who starred in the Fifth National Games in Nanjing.[72]

Only the magazine *Libai liu (Saturday)* cast a nostalgic glance at the past represented by the former track queens.[73]

After the Mukden Incident hindered the Manchurian female athletes' further participation in competition, the media mourned their absence as a symbol of the nation's suffering. Responding to the challenge of "saving the nation through tiyu," the Sixteenth North China Games were held in Kaifeng, Henan, from 10 to 13 October 1932. New heroines from Shandong took over the championships in track and field. *Tiyu Weekly* "regrets and is sad that the heroines and other talents from Liaoning are not heard of any more. How much we lost as the result of Japanese occupation of Manchuria."[74] Through such reportage, celebrity and politics were intertwined in the brief careers of the track stars.

Taming and Controlling Masculine Images

Female track and field stars, more than women in any other sport, had to contend with societal anxieties about excessive masculinity. In the United States in the 1930s, as Susan K. Cahn has observed, the masculine reputation of track and field caused American middle-class white women to abandon the sport, opening up room for otherwise segregated black women to achieve national and international excellence.[75] The high visibility of blacks in American track and field posed problems for the Chinese, however. Racist attitudes in Republican China meant that very few blacks served as role models for Chinese women. Although an editorial in *Linglong* noted that all people of colour in the world were happy for "the great natural physique and surprising power" demonstrated by black athletes in the Olympics,[76] there was little desire to emulate them. Not until the 1936 Berlin Olympics did the Chinese media, frustrated with the defeat of Chinese athletes, alarmed by Nazi racism and Japan's imperialist ambitions, and inspired by Jesse Owens's overwhelming triumph, briefly embrace African American athletes as models. The front cover of the leading cartoon magazine, *Modern Sketch*, devoted to the 1936 Olympics featured a drawing of a muscular black woman scantily clad in a banana skirt with the caption "Victory of Coloured People in the Olympics." Probably inspired by the popularity in Europe of the American chanteuse Josephine Baker, who specialized in nearly nude performances, the image is an almost unique example of Chinese portraiture of black Americans.[77]

In contrast to the American media, which shunned the "masculine moments" of female track and field stars,[78] the Chinese media carried visual and textual materials that emphasized the gritty nature of competitive track and field and applauded the women's spirit of struggle and sacrifice. Magazine photographs featured the runners' sweaty faces and twisted bodies leaping over the hurdles or straining at the finish line, celebrated explosive moments of power and speed, and emphasized the passion of the runners. Capturing athletes in action emerged as a special subfield in photography. Images of Sun Guiyun at the finish line of fiercely competitive races, taken by the owner of the noted Wang Kai Photography Studio, appeared in various magazines, including *Keda zazhi (Kodak Magazine)*.[79] *Linglong*'s cover featured photographs of Qian Xingsu flying over the hurdles and breaking the record in 200-metre race at the Fifth National Games.[80] After Li Sen won glory for China by besting her white opponents in the Third Multi-nation Track and Field Games in Shanghai in 1935, *Young Companion Pictorial* prominently portrayed her charging over the finish line in the 100-metre dash; another photograph showed her, with hair streaming wildly, smashing the national record in the 50-metre dash during the Sixth National Games. Journals presented the two track queens Qian and Li receiving awards together, and described their fierce competition at the finish line. Qian was noted for her beautiful running style and powerful charge.[81] Top pictorials showed the movements of track stars preparing to run, "digging in their heels" or "putting some earth on their heels" as they positioned themselves for a powerful start.[82]

Echoing the experiences of Liangjiang basketball players, nicknames given to the track queens often had masculine connotations. Muscular female track stars exacerbated the anxieties nationalists felt about maintaining hierarchical gender standards during wartime. For example, the media picked up the subtle shift in gender dynamics when a cartoon showed Qian, with her giant jianmei figure in a T-shirt and high-cut shorts at the centre, followed by a tiny male journalist begging, "Miss Qian, can I take a picture with you?"[83] The unconventional gender order could be quickly associated with Modern Girls' being out of control. Modern modes of transportation were familiar metaphors used to depict Modern Girls; for example, Sun Guiyun was described as an "express train," an ambiguous nickname that combined nation building with machine-age speed, confusion, and disloyalty. At the Fourth National Games, the audience chanted Sun's "express train" moniker. When her track career faded after the Mukden Incident, journalists invoked the name "express boat" to exaggerate her involvement in swimming. In 1931, for example, *Young Companion Pictorial* reported that "Sun practices swimming daily with great progress ... the 'express train' could evolve into an 'express boat.'"[84]

In order to help the track queens serve nationalist goals, athletes, their advisers, and the media used various strategies to combat perceptions of excessive masculinity, thereby adding a gendered understanding to nationalism. One means of easing anxieties about "masculine" female athletes was to employ male coaches. Just as male coaches channelled the Private Liangjiang Women's Tiyu Normal School basketball team to the nationalist cause, they maintained patriarchal control over the track queens. Among the track stars, only Sun and her teammates, all of whom became famous before the Mukden Incident, had a female coach, Huang Shufang, a graduate of Liangjiang and the first female tiyu teacher in Harbin. After the Mukden Incident, Huang taught at Liangjiang, from which she resigned in 1935; she moved to Hankou to get married, thus ending her coaching career.[85] Male coaches subsequently took over and supervised taxing training schemes for the female track stars in the name of the national interest.[86] Dong Chengkang, who had gained experience competing in the Seventh Far Eastern Games, coached Qian. Recognizing her agility and energy, he devised a training schedule to help her realize her full potential. Since the athletic field of Dongya and Nanshi Public Stadium lacked sufficient tracks, Qian and her teammates rose before dawn daily, regardless of the weather, and ran about three *li* (1.5 kilometres) to the China Baseball Court, which had hosted the Eighth Far Eastern Games, at Tianwentai Road (today's Hefei Road). Dong had Qian compete against male students in order to improve her skills and determination, a test she enjoyed. A Mr. Wen first coached Li Sen in Dongnan. After he resigned for health reasons, Guo Xiaofen stepped in. The athletes and the public appreciated the male coaches' professionalism and formality. Li wrote for *Young Companion Pictorial* that "without good coaches who knew the correct training methods" in her hometown, Hunan, she had been "fooling around" before her "formal training" began with the male coaches at Dongya. She continued: "I did not even know how to start the race with the tip of my toe before Mr. Guo taught me. I attribute my current achievements [at the Sixth National Games] to Mr. Guo's direction." Similarly, *Diligent Tiyu Monthly* attributed the achievements of Qian's "slim body" to her efforts and those of the coach.[87]

Men were also perceived as proper governors of track queens' emotions. Journalists' perceptions of women's "special emotional nature," similar to those used to justify gender segregation in basketball, mandated male mentors who could offer rational guidance. The media observed that female track stars were especially emotionally vulnerable in defeat or during disputes. For example, Sun was tearful during her team's disputes with the Guangdong team over the 400-metre relay championship at the Fourth National Games, and *Peiyang Pictorial News* reported that "the heroines who lost in the Fifteenth North China Games in Jinan, Shandong, in 1931, including Sun Guiyun and Wu Meixian and Xiao Meizhen from Beiping, cried in public."[88] Days after Wu Meixian entered Nankai University in September 1931, she lost the 50-metre dash due to a late start and was disqualified in the 100-metre dash for a false start in Hebei Province's selection meet in Tianjin, organized by Zhang Boling for the Fifth National Games – and consequently lost the chance to compete in those games. *Zhonghua huabao (China Pictorial)* reported that "the nationally famous athlete cried loudly in public." The Tianjin audience felt such sympathy for her that organizers invited her to compete in the 100-metre dash, a gesture that comforted the spectators.[89]

Coaches were not the only male authorities over female track and field stars' athletic skills and emotions; male academics and journalists pronounced on their performances and career choices as well. For example, after Sun's defeat in Tokyo, the academic journal *Henan jiaoyu (Education in Henan)* published an article discussing how she positioned herself to start in competitions.[90] A man also influenced Qian's career choice. From 1927 to 1930, Qian studied at Jiading Middle School in Jiangsu Province, where she excelled in both academics and athletics. On graduation, she faced the dilemma of choosing between a career as a schoolteacher and pursuing her interest in physical activities. Qian took the entrance exams to both Huangdu Normal School and the ancillary teachers' program (equivalent to high school) at Dongya Women's Tiyu Vocational School. Finally, her old principal, Chen Fengzhang, steered her to an athletic career. Chen argued that she had the patriotic obligation to help strengthen citizens' bodies, the race, and the nation at a time when China was being insulted as the "sick man of Asia" and invaded by imperialist powers. Convinced by these lofty nationalist goals, Qian entered Dongya. After finishing the teachers' program, her excellent academic and athletic achievements guaranteed her acceptance to Dongya's undergraduate program in 1933.[91] Following Qian's major triumph at the Fifth National Games, Sun Hebin, a professor at Dongya, stated: "Miss Qian's posture and speed at the finish line were perfect, but she started late in the 100- and 200-metre dashes, and 80-metre hurdles. If she can improve her starting times, she could do better." This sentiment was echoed by a male writer in *Diligent Tiyu Monthly:* "Her hurdling skills are absolutely correct and beautiful."[92] Male journalists also offered detailed explanations of how the third track queen, Li Sen, won fierce competitions against capable opponents at the Sixth National Games.[93]

Media and track athletes softened their masculine images by highlighting traditional feminine virtues. One requisite characteristic was a genial personality. Chen Rongming, a Liangjiang basketball player and a champion in track and field events at the National Games, recognized that "a good athlete needs good temperament and cultivation [which she suggested were customary female virtues]. Otherwise, you would leave a bad impression on people who would say that you do not have athletic morality/sportsmanship, which could lead to ultimate failure on the athletic field."[94] A second virtue fit more closely with Confucian ideals of femininity. The teenaged female track stars used modesty protectively to ensure their popularity. As they made the transformation from country girls into metropolitan celebrities, Li Sen and Chen Rongming remained humble about their achievements. Li wrote: "I won a few championships at the Sixth National Games this time. From my personal point of view, I was really lucky ... In every competition I have participated so far, I always thought that I would not have any chance to win."[95] Male journalists dutifully reinforced this perception. A *Shibao (Eastern Times)* reporter noted Li's "calm silence and serious look" when he exclaimed, "Congratulations! Congratulations!" to her after her major victories, and reported that Li blushed when she read Mayor Wu Tiecheng's flattering comments on her skill in the long jump.[96] When the editors of *Diligent Tiyu Monthly* asked Chen Rongming to write an article, she was surprised and expressed concern over whether she deserved the honour due to her "childishness." She wrote: "As a girl only in my teens, my experience and skills are far from mature ... I dare not to say that I have perfect experience, but just enough to deal with everyday competition."[97] The girlish innocence and humble style of the female celebrities, which corresponded well with the authority and maturity of their male mentors, was reflected on the cinematic screen, as will be discussed in Chapter 6.

Despite the extraordinary individual achievements of female track and field stars, the media argued that collective spirit, rather than personal achievement, should be celebrated. This attitude further dampened personal celebrity. It was not a coincidence that the track stars' competitive spirit was most clearly displayed in the only collective track event at various national games: the 400-metre relay. Sun Guiyun was especially praised for picking up her running shoes to compete again. Her struggles and tears for the collective honour were considered "heroic."[98] Such thoughts also appeared in cinema. The popular film *Queen of Sports* was about "true tiyu spirit" based on egalitarianism rather than on the outstanding track star as "athletic queen." In his writings, director Sun Yu repeatedly de-emphasized the individual winners in track and field, and hoped to popularize tiyu events with the film. Commenting on Sun Guiyun's curtailed competition in Tokyo, the film sent an unambiguous message that track queens should possess the honourable spirit of "good start and good end" for the sake of the collectives they represented, whether a school, the city, or the nation.[99] When the film became a hit across China, some tiyu professors offered theoretical support for curbing women's competitive spirit in track and field. Zhu Shifang, a professor at Chinese Women's Tiyu Normal School in Shanghai, insisted that individual outstanding performances and tournaments should be de-emphasized in order to avoid hurt feelings and to safeguard women's weak bodies, vulnerable minds, and lack of judgment. She argued: "Since women are more jealous and competitive than men in nature, improper encouragement of individual competition would hurt their health." She advocated an emphasis on collective sports rather than individual competition when scores were publicized.[100]

To ensure a consistent collective spirit, team spirit provided peer support for the track queens as they negotiated the uncertainties of celebrity. After Sun Guiyun, Wu Meixian, Wang Yuan, and Liu Jingzhen/Xiao Shuling of the Harbin track and field team won the overall championship and Wu won the long jump in the Fourth National Games, they were promoted as "four tigresses" or as the "Harbin Four."[101] At Dongya, Qian formed a team with her classmates Zhang Pingxian, Liu Jingfang, Sheng Bi, and Lu Jing, all outstanding track and field figures in Shanghai. They became known as the "Five Tigresses of Dongya" after winning for their school in the First Secondary School Games in Shanghai in 1930.[102]

Li Sen created her own female support group. Having first left home as a young girl who then had to find her way in the confusing metropolis, Li formed a caring sisterhood with other girls from her hometown of Hunan. First, she followed two Hunan students, Chen Shufang and Peng Aipu, who would perform well in the National Games, to Liangjiang Tiyu School. While waiting for classes after officially registering, Li was visited by another Hunan girl, who was studying at Dongnan Women's Tiyu Vocational School. Convinced by the latter that the two could be good, caring friends, and considering such bonds to be more important than a school's athletic program, Li decided to transfer to Dongnan. As a result, she not only forfeited the tuition and fees she had already paid to Liangjiang but also had to go through complex procedures to retrieve her luggage from Liangjiang.[103] When the entertainment media reported the incident under the title "Lu Lihua held Li Sen hostage," it escalated into another much-publicized drama involving Liangjiang's competition for talented student athletes.[104]

Filial piety was also considered an important quality among female track stars. Inspiration came from a familiar Japanese source. A reporter for *Tiyu Weekly* extolled Japanese icon Kinue Hitomi, whose "personality was extremely gentle and she had a strong sense of responsibility and was extremely filial to her parents." Li Sen was celebrated for similar qualities. She wrote for *Young Companion Pictorial* that after middle school, she "begged" her mother to "allow" her to go to Shanghai to attend a tiyu school. Worried that she was too young for an unfamiliar city, her mother suggested that she wait until after high school. Li agreed because "I did not dare to disobey my mother." She combined modesty and filial piety as she recalled that "I dared not ask my mother to go to Shanghai for the Sixth National Games although I wished to, because I was not fully confident in my performance. Otherwise, we could have had a happy gathering." Such qualities were expected of illustrious female athletes.[105]

The track queens were also expected to demonstrate a spirit of self-sacrifice and the ability to endure physical hardship, which were necessary qualities to justify the rigorous training program administered by their male coaches. These qualities contributed to the acknowledgment of women's physical strength in the heated debate among Chinese female tiyu academics over whether competitive track and field events were too strenuous for Chinese women. Broadening the discussion to an international level, Zhang Huilan addressed the issue. She recognized that physical educators in many nations tended to limit girls' participation in certain athletic activities that were assumed to be harmful to their health. Citing the American model, Zhang noted that her research revealed that only one institution out of five colleges and universities and two high schools in the Bay Area of California taught track and field events. They viewed track and field as too competitive, too masculine, and too injurious to the developing heart and pelvic organs of girls, and of little recreational value. She pointed out, however, that the fact that more girls participated in track and field events in Germany proved that it was safe for Chinese women to do so as well.[106] In contrast, the claim of Zhu Shifang that there should be a gentle female version of exercise-oriented track and field was ignored.[107]

Overcoming physical adversity was a key ingredient for fame. After Wu failed in the Hebei Province selection process for the Fifth National Games, *Peiyang Pictorial News* showed sympathy by highlighting in a photograph her endurance while under a doctor's care for a leg injury.[108] In another example, while Qian Xingsu fulfilled her nationalist duty by joining the movement originated and dominated by women's basketball teams to expand China's influence to the Chinese community in Southeast Asia, it was her professionalism and endurance of physical injury that deeply impressed the locals. After her fame as the new track queen reached Singapore and Malaya, the noted "patriotic overseas Chinese" Chen Jiageng and Hu Wenhu convinced their basketball and volleyball associations to invite Qian, in the winter of 1934, to lead an athletic team to the region. Qian led the ten-member "Nanyou Tuan" (Touring South Delegate of Dongya), consisting of members of the school's women's track and field, basketball, and volleyball teams, on a journey from Shanghai to Southeast Asia. The delegation travelled through Hong Kong, Saigon, Singapore, Penang, Kuala Lumpur, and other places for two months, from 26 January to 26 March 1935. Excessive practice during the trip aggravated her old foot injuries, which worsened after she fell on her way to the hospital while avoiding a car driven by an American woman. Nevertheless, Qian performed with her injuries to satisfy the enthusiastic Chinese communities, and despite her poor showing at the meets, her spirit was deeply admired. The Chinese business communities, led by Chen and Hu, celebrated the delegation with banquets, and authorities in Singapore published a set of twelve postcards to memorialize the group's activities.[109]

Heralding Rural Origins

Nationalist rhetoric celebrated the rural backgrounds of the track queens. Biographies and autobiographies emphasized their humble roots. Qian Xingsu was born into a labourer's family in Jiwang Temple Town of Jiading, Jiangsu Province, where life was "frugal and plain." Her mother, Chen Fumei from Zhenru Town of Shanghai, spun cloth and sustained her family diligently and industriously. Her father, Qian Ansheng, was a carpenter with a hobby in martial arts. Qian credited her parents with directly instilling in her such virtues as being physically active, working hard, and being diligent.[110]

Chen Rongming was from a small village in Guang'an County, Sichuan. Chen and Li Sen both had a "very unfortunate family background" – their fathers died young and their mothers had to struggle financially. Li was five months old when her father died of tuberculosis as a college freshman. Her mother was a student at Hengyang No. 6 Normal School (later No. 6 Secondary School of Hunan Province). After she graduated, the school rewarded her mother's hard work and excellent performance and showed sympathy by hiring her as the dean of students. Li wrote: "My mother and I are life to each other and we depend on the earnings of my mother's blood and sweat." From 1928 to 1934, Li studied at her mother's school. Based on her outstanding academic and athletic abilities and her difficult family situation, the school waived her tuition.[111] On the other hand, Chen Rongming, whose mother raised her and her older sister alone, was almost forced to leave school because of her family's financial difficulties. Fortunately, she managed to borrow money from relatives to "leave my hometown and follow the running Yangtze River to Shanghai to enter Liangjiang."[112]

Academic commentators emphasized such humble backgrounds, arguing that the success of track queens stemmed from their origins in the vast countryside. Sun Hebin believed that the powerful physiques of the Harbin Four derived from their childhood in the mountains. As typical women from coastal and central China, Qian and Li were physically slim and short and had gentle temperaments. According to Sun Hebin, their outstanding performances were due to diligent practice ensured by their humble backgrounds, as well as to correct running techniques.[113] Athletes themselves confirmed this observation. For example, Chen claimed that her humble background helped her focus on her career in track and field. She traced her athletic career back to "running and jumping games in a paradisiacal creek with sand banks" in her early childhood, when she knew little about such Western sports as "track and field, tennis, basketball, or volleyball."[114]

References to one's rural background called attention to a vexing issue for female track stars from the countryside: whether or not they would be corrupted by exposure to Shanghai, the model of Chinese modernity. The metropolis became an ultimate destination for most track stars. Chen acknowledged the "magic social power" of Shanghai and acknowledged that "the modern city and capital of Chinese culture" ultimately shaped her into a tiyu celebrity.[115] At the same time, the metropolis was perceived as treacherous and filled with traps for these young women. The Shanghai-based *Tiyu Weekly* warned Sun Guiyun and Liu Changchun against coming to "the sin city" in order to preserve their athletic careers. Even the athletes' school choices came under scrutiny. Sun left Beiping for Shanghai to take the entrance exam for Dongnan Women's Tiyu Vocational School, which was accused of waiving her tuition in 1933. This caused consternation among purists in China. *Tiyu Weekly* commented: "If that was true, the future of Chinese athletes is pitiful and the future of China is not bright."[116] Even Li Sen concluded that her loss due to switching from Liangjiang to Dongnan was a rude first lesson that she had to learn in the complex city.[117] In the film *Queen of Sports*, the rural/urban dynamics were reflected in how the innocent and pure would-be "queen of sports," fresh from the countryside, rejected her Western-educated suitor, who mixed English words awkwardly in his speech.

Humble origins could be political assets. Their physical prowess and popularity made track queens attractive to the New Life Movement (NLM),[118] which had as one of its integral goals the building of citizens' physiques and encouragement of the national spirit through tiyu. To promote women's tiyu, the hinterland province of Jiangxi held the first women's games in its new public stadium. The audience was composed strictly of female students. Invited by a Mr. Cheng, who headed the Provincial Education Division, Qian Xingsu led fourteen athletes from Dongya to the games as role models from modern, metropolitan Shanghai. Consistent with the NLM's spirit of discipline and militarism, after the opening ceremony "they performed collective gymnastics in neat white shirts and black skirts, and circled the stadium three times while martial music played." The team had its photograph taken before the tomb of a local general. It had a chance to display individual excellence when it was invited by the Division of Education of Anhui to demonstrate track and field skills at Anqing, the provincial capital at the time. Reporting Qian's records in the 50- and 80-metre hurdles, *Diligent Tiyu Monthly* applauded her team for "contributing to the development of women's tiyu in those two hinterland provinces." *Shenbao* echoed: "[In ancient times,] Confucius toured the various nations to spread *dao* (the way), Qian ran in and out of the motherland to teach and demonstrate." To compare a slender young track queen to the Confucius was innovative, if not presumptuous![119] Li Sen's ascent to the international stage took on a strong militarist tone as well. When the Olympic delegation gathered in Shanghai to receive intensive training before leaving for Berlin, municipal authorities received Li, who, dressed in a light-coloured *qipao*, posed with Mayor Wu Tiecheng and uniformed police chief Yang Hu (see Figure 1).[120]

Qian was able to extend her interest in Chinese medicine to exploration of alternative perspectives on health.[121] She and Li lent their names to campaigns promoting the general health of the citizenry. In 1935, the two track queens cut the ribbon at the opening ceremony of the Fourteenth Exhibit of Hygiene and Exercise in Shanghai.[122] In the middle of the war, Li published a public letter in *Xiandai nongmin (Modern Farmers)* imploring opium addicts to quit for the sake of a stronger and healthier nation.[123]

The Danger of Glamour and Fame

Despite their achievements and service to the nation, the track queens, as women, were vulnerable to public censure. Because they were defined by their appearance and perceived sexuality and were regarded as icons of popular modernity, they were inevitably attacked as Modern Girls. Their fame attracted unwanted rumours. Images of their body types helped defuse such criticisms. Whereas in the United States female track and field stars were stereotyped as threatening, manly creatures with homosexual tendencies,[124] racial dynamics as well as smaller physical size combined to soften the masculine images of Chinese track queens. Although magazines often cited the petite body size of Chinese female athletes as evidence of the "natural" physical inferiority of Chinese women, the track queens' slim figures helped them appear feminine and non-threatening. While large body size and a masculine style were considered advantages for female basketball players, slim figures *(jiaoxiao linglong)* were favoured for the track queens,[125] whose feminine glamour the public embraced.

Initially the track queens' fashion sensibilities attracted positive notice. Noted journalists depicted them favourably as lovely, modern fashion stars by detailing their clothing. *Peiyang Pictorial News* reported that during the Fifteenth North China Games, "the audience was all attracted to the colourfully dressed little birds in the heated sun. The female athletes from Harbin opened a new era for the nation by wearing shorts and vests." Sun Guiyun and Wang Yuan fascinated the media with such modern "summer fashions" as Mandarin collars, flowery gowns, and wide-brimmed straw hats of various styles.[126] Ye Qianyu's special journal reported that Sun and Guan Liuzhu of the Shanghai volleyball team were among the ten *modeng nülang* (Modern Girls) selected by the journalists.[127] In August 1936, while Li Sen and the swimmer Yang Xiuqiong were being ridiculed by *Modern Sketch* for their defeat in Berlin, *Young Companion Pictorial* featured the bride Sun Guiyun as its cover girl for the second time (see Figure 19). Four years later, China's first "queen of sports" was remembered as a glamorous fashion star with heavy makeup, fake eyelashes, fairy-style head decoration, and silk gown. Li was equally noted for her *modeng* style. She was dazzling in light-coloured pants with fashionable masculine suspenders, which were rarely seen even among actresses, in both the photograph accompanying her autobiography in *Young Companion Pictorial* and the one in the edition of *Modern Sketch* ridiculing her defeat.[128]

At the same time, there were signs that commercialization was creeping into the appealing image of the track queens. Besides political leaders, well-known private companies granted Sun Guiyun and Liu Changchun numerous awards after their victories in the Fourth National Games. The China Enamel Factory gave her an enamel frame, the Anli Company, a valuable fountain pen set (Wing On), two bolts of Sanyou fabric, and three dozen handkerchiefs.[129] Hitching their products to the fame of the track queens was not limited to domestic business. The "patriotic overseas Chinese" businessman Hu Wenhu served as one of the six honorary trustees of the China's National

19   Sun Guiyun in her bridal outfit, on the cover of *Young Companion Pictorial,* as a glamorous fashion star.
Source: Liangyou huabao 119 (August 1936).

Amateur Athletic Federation (CNAAF) and sponsored the Southeast Asian trip of Qian Xingsu and her team. His company frequently advertised its Tiger Balm ointment *(wanjin you)* in popular journals in Republican China – surely Qian's much-publicized trip helped raise the brand's profile. Even the *Shibao* reporter quoted Li as saying, "*Shibao* is my favourite because its news is the most up-to-date."[130]

When female track and field stars appeared frequently in advertisements with a strong nationalist twist, their images merged with nationalism. In *Diligent Tiyu Monthly,* a drawing of a robust woman with bobbed hair in a loose short-sleeved shirt running with a javelin pole occupied the centre of an advertisement for the Great China *(dahua)* Athletic Equipment Company. The text read: "Tiyu can save the nation, but if we use foreign goods, benefits flow outside. Let's hope all Chinese athletes use national goods; then, Republican China can be a rich nation with a strong citizenry." Despite the patriotic appeal, the woman's bobbed hair was borrowed from fashions popularized by Western film stars.[131] Other images showed Chinese women competing against their Western counterparts. An advertisement promoting *Young Companion Pictorial* captured Chinese and Western women with twisted faces and straining bodies charging toward a finish line, with the Chinese women slightly ahead. Large characters in the middle read: "*Jiezu xiandeng* [Fast Feet Reach First] ... There are only 500 opportunities among ten thousand readers."[132]

Fashion and glamour reporting naturally led to stories of sexuality and romance, which could turn vulgar and treacherous. More scandalous and sensational than the crowd at the Liangjiang basketball game (see Chapter 3), the masses in Kaifeng swarmed to the site of the Sixteenth North China Games to peek at the bare legs of the track and field athletes training for the competition. The authorities had to call in the local martial arts group, Big Knife Association, to restrain and disperse the dangerously unruly crowd.[133] There was a subtle sexual dimension to the dynamics of the bodies of the track queens and the lenses of photography journalists, who were predominantly male. Ye Qianyu's journal included a photograph of the slender Qian Xingsu being photographed by a circle of male reporters.[134]

After presenting Sun Guiyun and Wang Yuan as fashion models on the athletic field, *Peiyang Pictorial News* commented that they "appear like modern versions of [the legendary female warrior] Mu Guiying. Therefore, so many modern men fall for them."[135] Soon, sensational reports of Sun's new interest in swimming vied with "the shocking news of Sun's engagement."[136] Until 1935, the movie magazine *Diansheng (Cinematic Tone)* was still reporting Sun's triangular love story as entertainment news alongside stories about movie stars.[137] Other stories were more directly personal. The gossip journal *Yule (Entertainment)* confused Qian's name with someone else's, causing a rumour that she had divorced even though she had not yet married. In a sensational tone, the journal, under the title "The Private Life of an Athlete," discussed her "physiological changes" (i.e., menstruation) as the factor that made her appear emaciated and affected her athletic performance.[138] One overly intrusive male *Shibao* reporter tried to enter Li Sen's dorm room, a private and sensitive place where male visitors were prohibited, in order to interview her. He waited in front of the building and noted her red pants as soon as she appeared.[139] Other stories were standard gossip fodder. *Diligent Tiyu Monthly* circulated a rumour that track and field athletes selected for the 1936 Olympics were forced to cancel their last round of practice because they went dancing every night during their stay in Shanghai.[140] *Cinematic Tone* reported the twists and turns in Li's hunt for love and a job after the Olympics.[141]

Most such activities were reported as natural in the lives of attractive young people, but a more sinister problem arose. With Chinese track queens being portrayed as "public flowers" akin to actresses and even prostitutes, rumours surfaced that some track stars had become concubines of powerful male figures. These rumours reflected a public view of female track and field stars as public women not suitable for marriage. Most perniciously, lacking the protection of an institution such as the Private Liangjiang Women's Tiyu Normal School, with its worldly matriarch, Lu Lihua, who watched over her basketball players, track stars attracted unwanted sexual advances from powerful men. Those who rose to stardom could not escape various forms of patriarchal dominance or even physical violence and sexual harassment.

The first victim was Wang Yuan. Libellous media rumours convinced the public that she had married or become the concubine of "the traitor" Bao Guancheng, Manchukuo's ambassador to Japan, and had joined the tiyu group of Manchukuo. In her comments on this scandal, Fan Hong notes that Wang Yuan had "sullied the honor of the woman athlete,"[142] but other research indicates that Wang had been the victim of vicious gossip. Before the rumour was proven false, however, newspapers across the nation all condemned Wang's behaviour as harming women's chastity and morality, and as insulting to the whole tiyu circle and to national dignity *(you ai zhenjie, you shang fenghua, you ru guoti)*. These grave accusations of collaborating with the Japanese caused such damage that even Wang's long-term good friend and teammate Wu Meixian turned against her, to the point that both women even threatened each other with lawsuits. Wang tried to dispel the rumour by meeting with reporters at the Beiping train station after taking an express train from Tianjin for a vacation, emphasizing that she had "been living in Tianjin and never returned to her hometown in Manchuria." Journalists focused on her appearance instead and commented that Wang, adorned with loose bobbed hair, a signifier of Western modernity, appeared "very jianmei in a black leather coat." After Wang refuted the rumours of concubinage, *Young Companion Pictorial* tried to help her retrieve her reputation by featuring her along with the famous writer Lao She as the "figures worth noting" in 1933.[143] Despite Wang's recovery of her reputation, the incident further demonstrated the personal cost to athletes of maintaining national pride during wartime.

As noted earlier in this chapter, after the 1936 Olympics, Li Sen attracted the unwanted attention of the warlord He Jian of Hunan (who had executed Mao Zedong's first wife, Yang Kaihui, in his suppression of the Communist movement). He sent his staff to meet Li in Shanghai, offering her a job as the tiyu teacher at Hunan National Skill Bureau and one hundred silver dollars for travel expenses. After the noted Olympian accepted the job and met He for the first time in early 1937, she was unnerved by his rude, lustful gaze and repeated questions about whether she had enough money to spend, rather than anything relevant to tiyu. Li's concern over He's "evil intentions" was confirmed by a friend, who warned Li about He, using the example of a student from the Female Teacher Training Class in the National Skill Bureau who had committed suicide out of shame after being seduced by He. Clenching her teeth, Li said, "I am not a weak person who is easily bullied. Despite his powerful position, I do not think He dares to touch a single hair of mine." She endured until late fall, when He lured Li to his home to rape her. Shaken, the tearful Li was convinced by her friend that He would assassinate her unless she left quietly. She escaped to Sichuan within the week, and the friend, following her instructions, mailed the following unsigned note to He: "Morality and benevolence fill your mouth, but only immoral and treacherous ideas are in your mind; if you do not repent, you will bring destruction to yourself."[144]

Male reporters and academics threatened by the sudden stardom of the track queens were quick to cast blame on such traits of Modern Girls as vanity and indulgence in material and sexual pleasures. Even female author Zhong Qi, who adopted a strong feminist position in defending Wang Yuan's freedom in love and marriage, attributed her troubles to vanity. Zhong began an article by saying: "Having enjoyed the spotlight in the National Games in 1930, Wang Yuan became a celebrity. As her name filled the newspapers again, the concubinage incident was just used as another hoax to create attention."[145] On other rare occasions when questions were asked about the dramatic rise and fall of the track queens, blame was cast not on the discriminatory social and institutional structure but on Modern Girl vanity associated with the athletes' sudden fame. Noting the absence of the Harbin Four from the Fifth National Games, and hoping that the newer female track stars would not decline as fast, Sun Hebin pointed out that "the ages of most world record setters are

close to their 30s, as exemplified by Chinese [male] athlete Hao Chunde."
Sun concluded that the rapid fall of the Harbin Four demonstrated that

> the most advanced thing about women is their vanity. Since the society tends
> to root for women particularly ... It is not surprising that Sun Guiyun and Qian
> Xingsu have been praised and admired everywhere. Those young women
> without independent wills only enjoy the praise and forget about diligent
> practice or practice for show and without any real progress.[146]

A male writer for *Tiyu Weekly* reinforced Sun's explanation of the fate of the
Harbin Four by citing the dispute between Wang Yuan and Wu Meixian over
the concubinage incident, of which he admitted he knew few details, as evidence of their "lack of spiritual cultivation." He observed that since "the four
athletes were transformed into four stars from the North China Games in
Liaoning to the Far Eastern Games in Tokyo, their clothing, makeup, behaviour, and way of talk have gradually been modernized *(modenghua)*."[147]
Another male writer in the journal extended blame to "the majority of the
modernized Chinese female citizens." He suggested that it did not matter
even when the incident turned out to be all rumour, because "even it [the
rumour] was true, it would not be surprising ... Since indulgence in material
pleasure became epidemic among modern Chinese women ... regardless of
being athletes or not."[148]

Since the Modern Girl accusations of the track queens were more treacherous, the athletes were unable to enjoy their love life unmolested. In self-
defence the track queens cultivated a girlish, asexual persona devoted to the
patriotic cause. They sought ways to portray themselves as women who ab-
stained from romance and pleasure, under the strict guidance and protection
of male family members, and devoted themselves to athletic training and
academic schooling for nationalist goals.

Female track and field stars in the United States highlighted their feminine
attractiveness and heterosexual romances to counter allegations of homosexuality.[149] Influential tiyu scholars such as Zhang Huilan used romantic love
and marriage to justify co-recreation. Even Zhu Shifang, who advocated a
less strenuous version of female track and field, recognized and encouraged
heterosexual dynamics, stating: "Better to have the opposite sex to be present
during competition in order to offer encouragement and trigger strong interest."[150] However, discouraged from seeking romantic love and marriage within
the charged atmosphere of their sport, Chinese track and field heroines tried
to portray themselves as "devoted nuns," although some of them ultimately
chose marriage and family instead of an athletic career. One model for such

a choice came from America. In an article titled "Female Athletes Will Not Marry" in *Linglong*, Mildred (Babe) Didrikson (1911-57), a white working-class American track star who won gold medals in the javelin and hurdles and a silver in the high jump in the 1932 Olympics, was praised for both her impressive athletic skills and her strong will and determination not to marry early. She was quoted as saying that "marriage is like a decathlon – dish washing, house cleaning, laundry, general cleaning, cooking, child care, shopping, menu planning, making beds, and mending socks."[151] There was no mention of the rumoured lesbian behaviour and her "masculine" physical appearance, "independence, bold wit, and athletic virtuosity," which had caused enormous controversy in America.[152] Coinciding with the disappointment and anxiety over heterosexual love that filled the pages of contemporary women's magazines, the article commented that a woman's professional promise would be negatively affected if she married at the peak of her career: "Modern women always buried their lifelong hopes [for a career and independence] because they continually sought romantic love. For ordinary people, marriage is the tomb of love; for athletes, marriage is the tomb of athletic career."[153]

A male writer in *Linglong* defined love as "the beautiful flower of life and blood, evoking wide sympathy and the most determined struggles." Individual romantic love was called small, narrow, meaningless, shameful, and dangerous, able to corrode even strong wills during a national emergency. Young men and women were called on to focus their attention not on individuals but on their families and their country in order to achieve a grand nationalistic love. The passion one would experience in romantic love should instead be used to fight for the nation. The logic was that until territory was recovered and national humiliation cleansed, people would not lead settled lives – without a strong nation, there could be no home, no security, and no love. Grand love for the nation would eventually cross the boundaries of national territories, and lead to the realization of a world of "great unity *[datong shijie]* free of oppression and war."[154] The reproductive function of women and motherhood in service to the nation became the elements of womanhood used to justify competitive women's tiyu events. As the mothers of citizens and the centres of their families, women were expected to practise masculine tiyu activities and become fit, strong, and brave in order to bring up masculine citizens for the nation.[155]

The romantic lives of the most popular male and female stars at the Fourth National Games were cast in gendered tones. In a statement published in *Linglong*, Sun Guiyun was careful to please readers by emphasizing that she was not interested in romantic love but instead was devoted to the cause of track and field. Sun humbly noted that the statement was not an article, but "a report to friends on my recent situation":

> Recently, I am working particularly hard on track and field, for my honour, and to fulfill the expectations of you, my friends. Someone is saying that I am very interested in studying love. This is not true, and there is none of this kind of business whatsoever. Maybe people made up surprising news because they love me so much. I am not a potted plant [without feeling], and maybe I will love someday, but now it is not the time for a romantic life. I hope in the future there will be no more of these questions disturbing my work, which I am devoted to.[156]

A romantic relationship between Liu Changchun and "national skills" expert Yue Xiuyun from the Qingdao Shaode School was disrupted by Yue's disapproving father. Although Liu gained sympathy when "he left for Beiping regretfully" after Yue dared not see him again, a *Linglong* article emphasized that her father had scolded Yue because "their relationship was sparking sensual gossip."[157]

Other female track and field athletes shared Sun's sentiment of shunning romance and marriage while pursuing advancement in their athletic careers. Chen Rongming emphasized the conflict between athletic ambition and marriage, writing: "My efforts and progress in athletics unexpectedly called attention to some boring people who started to propose marriage. I angrily scolded them, asking why people were so evil and said that I was determined to develop and grow into a bigger world."[158] There was no media report about Qian Xingsu's romance because of the protection offered by her girlish image and "good-girl" reputation. Multiple sources noted her short and slender figure, mild temperament, and girlishness. Compared with Sun Guiyun and Wang Yuan, who were portrayed as fashion leaders, Qian was frequently described as appearing "totally innocent, with a little girl's hair style, in flowery socks and cloth [rather than leather] shoes." Instead of dressing herself in Modern Girl fashions, Qian sought to present herself as an urban innocent.[159]

Avoiding the fast life in Shanghai was essential to a good reputation. Aware of the importance of maintaining a country-girl image to sustain their roles as the queens of sports, the track stars distanced themselves from the "pleasure and unhealthy indulgence" associated with the "sinful metropolitan centre." Li Sen wrote for *Young Companion Pictorial*:

> I am not interested in the colourful life outside campus and am still a layman for various kinds of Shanghai-style urban life ... I absolutely have no idea what

parks in Shanghai look like, because I have never entered one. I have only watched movies three times, twice invited by a classmate and once on campus after a studio used the campus to shoot the film. I entered a dance hall only once, as a girl scout trying to raise money. After a glance, I was so scared that I ran out immediately. The air inside the dance hall was so bad. Probably people will laugh at me as a country bumpkin.[160]

Family offered another layer of protection to legitimize the public display of the track queens' bodies. The photograph that accompanied the report of Sun Guiyun's new interest in swimming showed her in a swimsuit; it was actually a group photograph of Sun, her elder brother, Guiji, who was then studying at the College of Russian Literature and Law in Beiping, and her younger brother, Guiyu, a student at No. 3 Harbin Secondary School, taken during the Harbin Water Games. The brothers wore swim trunks but were shirtless, which was daring even among men, yet they provided family guardianship by shielding Sun's body. Their presence helped make her swimsuit respectable and less sensual. Sun strove to transform her image from a sprinter to the middle-class and feminine persona of a swimmer.[161] For her part, along with her filial piety, Li Sen highlighted her mother's distant but powerful watchfulness, crediting her mother's instructions with instilling in her discipline and immunity to Shanghai's sinful pleasures. "'In such a colourful and noisy place as Shanghai, young people like you have to be very careful. Dance halls, cinemas, and all the other entertainment places can degenerate youngsters.' I keep her words deep in my heart to avoid making her worried."[162]

Devotion to athletic practice, a bookworm image, and commitment to nationalist goals helped track queens counter sexually charged journalism. Only desexualized devotion was suitable for lofty nationalist goals. The male journalist who argued that it was Modern Girl-style vanity that led to the speedy fall of the Harbin Four offered his remedy. He called on the women to "consider the loss of their hometown, work hard together, make good use of their youth, and recover their honour."[163] After apologizing to the nation for her failure in Tokyo, Sun Guiyun assured the public of her determination. "I will practise hard in the future. I am planning to attend the second public athletic meet in the first stadium to practise along with Russian women this Sunday, in order to make progress."[164] While reporting her resistance to the sinful pleasures of Shanghai, Li Sen demonstrated how she spent all her time and energy on the athletic field. "I have been in Shanghai for a year, hiding in my school for most of the time like a hermit to deal with the heavy school work. I get up at 5:30 every morning to practise and hardly have any free time except weekends."[165]

Young Companion Pictorial reported that Sun was pursuing swimming and academics as proof of her respectability.[166] The Harbin Four were noted for their constant pursuit of higher education, and Qian was reported to be sophisticated in academic learning and especially "well cultivated in litera- ture." When asked by a reporter during the Sixth National Games whether she liked to read novels, Qian responded that the serious writer Lu Xun was her favourite. Consistent with her ambition to study in Japan, she mentioned that she had even read Lu's recent work, which had been published there. The reporter tried to engage Qian in a discussion of Henrik Ibsen's *A Doll's House*. This famous play had been translated and staged in China after Lu Xun published his famous essay "What Happened after Nora Left Home" in *New Youth*, the flagship magazine of the New Culture Movement, in 1918. Lu Xun's essay highlighted the significance of economic independence in women's pursuit of equality. Modestly, Qian did not offer any comments. The reporter praised her excellent Mandarin despite her humble background and concluded: "This innocent little girl is still very young. Work hard, our soldier!"[167] Similarly, the media reported Li Sen's ability in crafting essays, her good handwriting, and even the fact that she had pretended to be a news reporter.[168]

A Subtle Feminist Agenda

Feminist circles in China were aware of the dynamics of sovereignty, civiliza- tion, and competitive bodies. They were also anxious about Chinese women's participation in the struggle for China's status as an independent nation-state. Before Liu Changchun's debut in the 1932 Olympic Games, one *Linglong* article stated that "all the civilized nations of the world are preparing eagerly and enthusiastically. The bronze nerves and iron bones of male and female athletes are the backbone and creator of strong nations." The article pointed out that tiyu was an index of a certain country's national strength and the degree to which it was civilized. Physical competence, rather than so-called spiritual civilization, would earn China the authority to survive as a nation- state in a competitive world.[169]

Women's magazines warmly celebrated Li Sen for winning the chance to compete in the 1936 Olympics. Besides publicizing a "list of competent athletes who will compete in the 1936 Olympics," *Young Companion Pictorial* featured a photograph showing the tiny Li standing with the larger male track and field athletes. *Diligent Tiyu Monthly* placed Li on its cover. Wearing a dressy suit with athletic details, she was shown receiving flowers from well-wishers and a banner from her alma mater just before the delegation left Shanghai harbour for Berlin (see Figure 1).[170] Cartoons illustrated the dynamics between athletes and female spectators. At the Sixth National Games, a cartoon showed Qian ahead in a race and a woman in the crowd yelling, "I am so delighted!"[171]

Women's magazines subtly reinterpreted the collective spirit demanded of the track queens and distilled it into a new life philosophy for female citizens. Under the title "Glimpses of the First National Games [under the Nanjing Government]," the first page of the 1930 issue of *Young Companion Pictorial* that had Sun Guiyun on its cover prominently showed Sun in action on the track. The accompanying editorial stated:

> A brave and sacrificing spirit is the essence of tiyu. It is righteous to sacrifice individualism for the public interest. It is authentic courage for one not to be afraid when losing or arrogant when winning. With the above two spirits, one can achieve big. We know in the field of life, there are permanent tournaments waiting to be won.[172]

A photograph showed female students crouched at the starting line before a co-ed audience at the First Shanghai Middle School Games in 1931. The caption editorialized:

> In racing, some reached the finish line very soon, some pretty late, and others never did. As long as one tries her best to finish, at no. 1 or 10, she remains similarly respectable in our eyes. The same is true in society; the result is more important than the process. Regardless of the speed of achievements, society grants all respect, except those who give up in the middle because of poor endurance and will. Running slowly is not shameful, but the shameful thing is to lose the courage to finish and give up half way.[173]

Athletes had their own understanding of the alternative meanings of championships: personal fulfillment and ambitions. In their otherwise modest autobiographies, Li Sen and Chen Rongming were not shy about expressing their determination, persistence, hard work, and great ambition; however, their stated goals were subtly transferred to personal "interest and progress" in a "bigger world." Chen declared: "I will not be arrogant about my triumph and ashamed of my failures; instead I will look forward to the future." She hoped that her "frank" thoughts "could encourage girl readers to start to liberate their own bodies from the prisons of slim waists and pale arms and help them to a new path." *Young Companion Pictorial* carried scenes from the Sixth National Games showing girls flying over the hurdles; reporters commented that "in women's low hurdles, everyone struggles to go faster, in order to jump and gain instant fame."[174]

Young, ambitious women opted to pursue track and field as a career, as idealized in the film *Queen of Sports*. Despite difficulty in finding jobs, some track queens made conscious efforts to help others pursue the dream. Qian funded a Xingsu Scholarship at Dongya Women's Tiyu Vocational School to promote women's tiyu. Along with a Tianqi Scholarship set up by Shanghai celebrity Hou Tianqi, it made available forty scholarships for poor middle-school graduates at the school.[175]

The most radical feminist voice emerged in the heated debate regarding the relationship between the sexuality of the track queens and the national plight. In the gendered treatment of the sexual exploitation of female track and field stars as demonstrated by the swirling rumours about Wang Yuan's concubinage, female writers offered rare defences of the right of track stars to be individuals free of obligations to the national interest. Zhong Qi objected to the overwhelming newspaper coverage condemning Wang. She argued that Wang's free choice in love and romance as an independent woman of "the new time" should be respected, even if she really became a concubine. Zhong went further, questioning why "all the blame of concubinage fell on women for their self delinquency? What about men's seduction through money and power, and even rape?" Detaching nationalist meaning from the female body, Zhong boldly declared that "it was absurd to blame Wang for marrying a Manchukuo official and more so to argue against her being a concubine of a Manchukuo official." She continued that since the government had failed in its responsibility for maintaining the security of the territory and allowed Manchuria to be seized, "Wang's rumoured marriage should be just as natural as marriage between Chinese and foreigners." She concluded that, rather than argue that Wang should become a concubine, "what I am arguing is the fairness to allow people the choices for survival without the oppression from certain [nationalist and sexist] opinions or ideas." She pointed out that "public criticism over Wang's rumoured concubinage" was as backward as praising a so-called chaste woman who committed suicide after the death of her fiancé, with banners, plaques, and a grand funeral by local gentlemen. Both incidents reflected that "the core of Chinese customs and culture are still 'three obediences and four virtues,' despite some newly imported Western stimulants and popular jargon on the progressive evolution of human society."[176]

In summary, female track and field stars faced numerous obstacles once their athletic achievements made them famous. There were pressures to recognize them collectively rather than individually. Their presence in the public sphere and in the media made political figures and academics nervous. Powerful men lusted after them. Within China, their public imagery was often sexualized. Female track stars had to downplay their urges to be Modern Girls and to accept the transient quality of their fame and the inequities of policies that preserved amateur status for men but pushed women into premature retirement from athletics. They had to seek protection by following past standards of behaviour. For the fortunate, the developing world of tiyu education provided succor and employment; nevertheless, although tiyu teaching or marriage provided sanctuary, female track stars had to abandon dreams of greater fame. Such dreams would come to fruition in another kind of athlete, as we shall see in the next chapter.

Despite their vulnerability, the track queens appeared more powerful and visible than all contemporary female athletes. They managed to compete on national and international stages in the name of national interest. Their images were ubiquitous in print and cinema. They made the display of a powerful and strong female body acceptable and legitimate within the context of the national crisis. Although China's track queens quickly left the athletic field for teaching jobs or marriage, their explosive demonstration of physical capacity laid the foundation for a redefinition of women's abilities and gendered roles in the wartime environment, and despite their transient fame, they profoundly influenced China's fashion, popular culture, and modernity.

5 "Miss China" Yang Xiuqiong (1918-82): A Female Olympic Swimmer

In 1934, *Liangyou huabao (Young Companion Pictorial)*, the most influential and popular women's magazine in the 1930s, tried to quantify a "standard womanhood" to inspire Chinese women during the national crisis. Their methodology was consistent with the "scientism" that had dominated the Republican era since the May Fourth Movement, in which numerical data were used to prove scientific points. As noted earlier, Zhang Huilan employed statistics to undergird her "scientific" findings on female participation in competitive sports, and popular magazines used specific measurements of various parts of the body to define "standard beauty." *Young Companion Pictorial* cited various qualities of ten individual women as essential ingredients comprising the "standard womanhood," which was visually presented as a perfect circle composed of the images of those women (see Figure 20). The caption specified "Yang Xiuqiong's swimming skill, Ding Ling's talent in literature, [the daughter of senior Nationalist Party member Hu Hanmin] Hu Mulan's filial piety, [the aviatrix] Lin Pengxia's adventuring spirit, [senior Nationalist Party member] He Xiangning's artistic skill, Madame Chiang's [Song Meiling] virtuous assistance to her husband, Song's mother's longevity and fortune, Mrs. Silas Aaron Hardoon's wealth, [the "Movie Queen"] Hu Die's fame, and Zheng Lixia's dancing skill." Not surprisingly, they selected the richest, most powerful, and influential women in China with strong nationalist backgrounds. As the sole athlete, Yang's face occupied the top of the circle, a testament to her extraordinary representation as "standard womanhood."[1]

Acclaimed as "Miss China" and the "Mermaid," Yang Xiuqiong captivated the Chinese public from her first victories in swimming competitions in Hong Kong in 1930 until her disappointing performance for China in the 1936 Berlin Olympics. During these years, she thrilled her fans by winning championship after championship. Andrew Morris and Hsiao-pei Yen have ably introduced the magnitude of Yang's fame as the most widely known athlete in China.[2] In this chapter, I extend their historical reconstruction of Yang by uncovering her conflicted position in the dynamics between the New Women

20 "Standard Womanhood."
Source: Liangyou huabao 99 (1 December 1934): 22.

and Modern Girls within both official and popular discourses during the national crisis. As a typical, simultaneous representative of each, Yang's dramatic rise and fall showcased the contradictions among national needs, cultivation of proper femininity, and the sexuality of the publicly displayed female body. By emphasizing the narrative of the most popular athlete, I examine the reality and the imaginary of a famous and attractive young woman during treacherous times.

I emphasize how her intelligence, her poise, and her supportive family enabled her to build her own identity. Using contemporary magazines and her own writings, I demonstrate the intricacies of Yang's career in word and image. Pictures of Yang were ubiquitous in the media in the 1930s. The dozens of photographs and drawings of Yang indicate male gazing, may also be considered representative tools of *jianmei* (robust/healthy beauty) and the fashionable modern womanhood, and show her own agency through her choices of adornment. Yang inspired much affection and popular goodwill, especially among the petty urbanites *(xiaoshimin)* who thrilled to her ac-complishments and among sports enthusiasts. Her fame and grace, while attributed to her skills, enabled fellow Chinese to continue identifying with her. Yang gained additional popularity by making many personal appearances on behalf of the New Life Movement (NLM), at the openings of swimming pools and railroad terminals and in charity competitions. Rhetorical skills were but one of several tools that she possessed. She expressed herself ably in journalism and autobiographical writings. Another plus was her family, which worked as a team. She invariably performed with her sister and younger brother, and sometimes with her father. Her parents were constantly present and, one can safely conjecture, served as guardians.[3]

Yang's education and family partially shielded her from unwanted pursuers. Fan Hong noted that successful swimmers often came from the educated middle classes.[4] Yang's family background went beyond that. Fully aware of the sexual vulnerability of their attractive young daughter, her prosperous family defined Yang's career as a family cause and offered guidance and pro-tection during her moments of fame. Yang was proud of her family's back-ground, which she described as "educated and scholarly for generations" *(shidai shuxiang)*. She was born in Dakeng, a dairy village in the hinterlands of Hong Kong. The family of her father, Yang Wanxing (also known as Zhunan), was from Yangwu Village of Dongguan, Guangdong, and immi-grated to Hong Kong when he was very young. The family of her mother, Long Lizhen, was from Bao'an, Guangdong, but Long was born and raised in Hong Kong. Yang Xiuqiong's father was seven years older than her mother when they made an arranged marriage. Yang later stated that her parents were harmonious and that the family was happy. Her parents moved to Dakeng, where her father's older brother operated a large milk factory. As the second daughter, Yang was raised as a boy along with her younger brother until she was four or five years old. When she was older, her mother taught her practical domestic skills, including cooking, bookkeeping, ironing, and cleaning, in order to prepare her for marriage.[5]

Popular media such as *Linglong* referred to the Yangs as the "swimming family." Swimming was the passion and occupation of choice for the entire family. Yang's father was the swim coach of the Nanhua (South China) Athletic Association, and his children were his talented students, a teaching method little used in Chinese or Western societies until many decades later.[6]

Soaring into Fame as the "Mermaid" and "Miss China"

Yang Xiuqiong cultivated fame through triumphs at official athletic games and overwhelming coverage in the popular media. To become Miss China, a title commonly found in beauty pageants, she used her superior athletic skills to demonstrate national strength and helped define feminine fashion and glamour in China's popular modernity. She showed learning, wisdom, and intelligence in her writings. Taken together, these qualities blurred the boundaries between the New Woman and Modern Girl.

Yang first gained public notice as the "water spirit" in 1930 at the age of twelve, when she won the 50- and 100-metre freestyle championships in the swimming competition of Hong Kong and took first place in the Third Water Games of Guangzhou.[7] She gained national fame and earned the nickname of "Mermaid" after the government added the female 50- and 100-metre freestyle, 100-metre backstroke, 200-metre breaststroke, and 200-metre relay events to the Fifth National Games in 1933. Winning all four individual titles and swimming as a member of the champion 200-metre relay team from Hong Kong, Yang was the brightest star of the games.[8]

The Nationalist government selected her to compete in the Tenth Far Eastern Games (FEG), held in Manila in May 1934 – the last such event before tensions leading up to the Second World War put a stop to them. Yang proudly related how she and three other women and nine men, mostly from Hong Kong and Guangdong, took an American postal boat to Manila, where she won three championships and the overall individual competition. Had she not been disqualified in the 200-metre race for not touching the wall, she would have won all her events. The media featured her triumphs in its review of the games, praised her for "winning glory for the nation," and called her trophies invaluable, noting that every time she won, Republican China's national anthem was played and its flag was raised to the rafters. Having travelled to Manila in a second-class cabin, Yang returned in first class, a treat that she modestly considered not as a personal favour but as a tribute to her country. Her triumphs, the first in Chinese women's overseas athletic competitions, more than matched the victories of the men's soccer and basketball teams over their Japanese opponents, and she was proclaimed as Miss China after the games.[9] The domestic media reported that, inspired by her fame, Australia planned to invite Yang to perform in that country.[10]

After her return to China, Yang's success in national competitions continued. In the Sixth National Games in 1935, she took second place in the 50-metre freestyle after Guangdong's Liu Guizhen, who also finished second in the 100-metre freestyle and third in the backstroke. Yang won the 100-metre freestyle and backstroke events, breaking the Far Eastern Games records, but lost in the 200-metre breaststroke, which allowed the Guangdong team to beat their Hong Kong counterparts and win the championship. Yang was disappointed in her performance but regarded it as a good lesson: she had started too quickly and lost energy. The media, however, viewed her loss seriously and blamed it on her high living. A series of photographs recorded how Yang and Liu looked before, during, and after the competition, with Yang's expressions ranging from proud to sad. The caption to Liu's photograph introduced her as the one who beat the queen.[11] Nevertheless, Yang survived such criticism and went on to further acclaim, displaying her skills in the Water Recreation Games in Hong Kong in 1935.[12]

The Chinese public expected Miss China to conquer the world beyond Asia. The caption to a photograph introducing a top Western swimmer noted that the "female water spirit of Europe could be a good match for her counterpart in Asia, Yang Xiuqiong."[13] As the 1936 Berlin Olympics approached, the Chinese Olympic Committee invited Yang to join the delegation after she broke national records in several competitions in Hong Kong.[14]

There were warnings about Yang's competiveness against world-class female swimmers. "The Reporter," a writer who cast doubt on track queen Li Sen's participation in the Olympics (see Chapter 4), similarly noted that Yang's best records in the 100-, 200-, and 400-metre freestyle competitions in the Far Eastern Games were well short of even the slowest times of the Japanese swimmers, who were absent from the games. The editorialists urged Yang not to go to Berlin, lest the Chinese people be embarrassed by what they feared would be a poor performance.[15] The warnings were apt. Yang failed to place in the 100- and 400-metre freestyle events, even though her times were Chinese records. She accepted her failure, noting that although her swimming styles were the same as those of the best world athletes, she did not breathe as well, which led to fatigue. She felt that she had peaked at the Sixth National Games and that future progress would now be incremental.[16]

Yang remained popular for the next decade. After the Marco Polo Bridge Incident in 1937, she took part in the National Games in the wartime capital of Chongqing, and won eight championships.[17] An article in *China at War,* a monthly published in English from 1939 to 1945 by the China Information Committee in Chongqing and distributed to overseas readers by the Chinese News Service in New York, described her as the nation's most popular female athlete. In a twist on her nickname, the writer called her the "Beauty Fish," a term suggesting unfamiliarity with the English translation of the Chinese word *meirenyu.* Yang continued to participate in swimming events and volunteered as an instructor for the Shanghai YWCA's new swimming class for women in 1947. Some entertainment magazines even speculated that she would become the captain of a boat.[18]

Although editorialists prayed that Yang's beauty would not overshadow her athletic accomplishments, there is no doubt that her loveliness and the sexy nature of the sport created a media frenzy. As Susan K. Cahn has argued in the American context, although both swimmers and track athletes relied on strength, speed, and technique, media commentators and their public saw the two sports as distinctly different. The media described swimmers as ideal figures of American womanhood. There was little danger to a woman's femininity and potential motherhood in swimming. Contemporary observers distinguished between track, with its ugly, muscle-bunching effects, and the attractive, muscle-stretching qualities of swimming. Swimming enhanced the feminine physique by keeping a woman's figure soft and rounded as she developed a larger chest and supple, long legs. Cahn's observations fit the Chinese setting well.[19]

Yang became a media darling in the 1930s. Press coverage paid as much attention to her physical appearance and beauty as to her athletic skills. Only a few photographs showed her in action,[20] partly because of photographers' inability to shoot high-quality images in the water. During the Fifth National Games, a reporter from Nanjing described her as "elegant and with noble temperament, bright eyes, straightforward personality. Her robust figure wears jade-coloured clothing, looking like a female Greek soldier. She talks gently with very endearing, southern tones."[21] *Linglong* repeatedly noted her slender figure and beautiful face, and called her the "standard beauty" on water, matching the "standard beauty" on land, actress Xu Lai. The media reported that Yang was greatly admired by Xu and other movie stars.[22] However exaggerated, such descriptions indicate Yang's notoriety.

Most photos featured her in swimsuits. The most prestigious popular magazines, *Young Companion Pictorial* and *Linglong,* featured the scantily clad swimmer on their covers (see Figure 21). She was portrayed with straight hair bobbed at her ears, posing with confidence and a smile. *Young Companion Pictorial* featured her in swimsuits of various styles three more times from

21   Yang Xiuqiong as the
cover girl of *Young Companion
Pictorial.*
Source: Liangyou huabao 77
(June 1933): cover.

22   *Right:* Yang Xiuqiong in a
daring two-piece swimsuit during
the Sixth National Games in 1935.
Left: Other heroes and heroines
of the Games.
Source: Liangyou huabao 110
(October 1935): 8.

1930 to 1936, showing her competing in the Guangzhou games as well as sitting in leisurely fashion on a diving board with Hong Kong swimmer Mo Shenlan as water dripped from her feet. The most notable image from the Sixth National Games showed her with permed hair and wearing a two-piece swimsuit, which was quite daring for her time (see Figure 22). Women's swimsuits were undergoing a slow evolution. Most women wore one-piece wool suits that became matted, heavy, and often smelly when wet. Serious competitors such as Yang tried silk fabric, which could shave precious seconds off event times but had the disadvantage of becoming transparent when wet. Whereas other young women revealed more skin, Yang may have compromised by using a wool two-piece suit. At the very least, she showed an advanced sense of modernity. As Lin Yutang commented: "From bound feet to one-piece bathing suit[s] is indeed a far cry, and these changes, superficial as they seem, are nevertheless profound. For life is made up of such superficialities, and by altering them, we alter the whole outlook of life."[23]

As interest in Yang intensified, ubiquitous images of her gradually showed a variety of high-fashion and glamorous outfits. After she won the local water games in 1930, *Jindai funü (Contemporary Women)*, a popular magazine published in Shanghai, portrayed a very young, serious-faced Yang posing by her trophies dressed in a loose-fitting, full-length *qipao.* Such dresses, as noted in Chapter 2, had ambiguous connotations, either signifying high status or providing scandalous examples of Modern Girl excess. Yang's images tilted increasingly toward the latter.[24] As her photographs on magazine covers accentuated her appearance outside the context of swimming, she appeared in heavy makeup and displayed permed, shoulder-length hair. As the champion of the women's programs in the Seventh Guangdong Water Games in 1934, Yang was shown in a tight dress and sandals with butterfly-shaped decorations, standing in front of a swimming pool, a purse hanging on her left arm.[25] One journal called her expected trip to Shanghai for the Sixth National Games "the pink news." The Entertainment News column of *Diansheng (Cinematic Tone)* noted that her clothing and jewellery – a white gold ring on her middle finger – were too splendid for a student who was not yet engaged. During the games, Yang posed with her mother at the Shanghai Swimming Pool, wearing a very fashionable equestrian outfit adopted from a man's suit (see Figure 23).[26] Afterwards, a smiling, confident Yang appeared in *Linglong* once in fancy Western dress with a low neckline. The caption emphasized her exotic quality: "This is a lady grown up in a foreign land. Some say that she is like a Mermaid. Do you think she looks like one? (see Figure 24). Other images showed her accentuating a suit jacket or bracelets, or holding her trophy with her hair blowing wildly in the wind."[27] As the Chinese delegation

池泳游市海上於攝視母同時台運全屆六

23   Yang Xiuqiong and her mother posing at the Shanghai
Swimming Pool during the Sixth National Games. Note Yang's
highly fashionable outfit.
Source: Yang Xiuqiong, *Yang Xiuqiong zizhuan* (Hong Kong: Xinhua
chubanshe, 1938), between 26 and 27.

headed for Berlin for the Olympics, *Linglong* published a special issue on
swimming, with a photograph of actress Li Lili churning through the water
on its front cover. The back cover featured Yang attired in formal Western
dress, a wide-rimmed hat, and fluffy white gloves while sitting in a domestic
setting (see Figure 25).[28] Yang's attire befitted her role as model for the female

24 "'Mermaid' from a 'foreign land'?"
Source: Linglong 229
(10 June 1936): 762.

25 Yang Xiuqiong in
formal Western gear.
Source: Linglong 243
(1 July 1936): back cover.

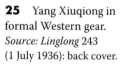

petty urbanites, who could identify with her fashionable appearance and her upward mobility through sports.

Other forms of media attention followed. Yang joined famed sprinter Liu Changchun and tennis player Qiu Feihai as the only athletes featured in biographies. Shanghai journalist Wang Jianming published the highly flattering pop biography titled *Meirenyu Yang Xiuqiong (The Mermaid Yang Xiuqiong)*, in an edition of fifteen hundred copies (see Figure 26). The biography highlighted her popularity among the fans, and her patience, generosity, intelligence, and beautiful eyes. Wang did, however, insert a serious vein by generally following Nationalist policies and applauding Yang's activities on behalf of the New Life Movement in particular.[29]

Yang also received notice in the Western press, though with mixed results. One problem was that a legacy of fake Mermaids had generated much cynicism. When Yang's photograph with her nickname appeared in the *Atlanta Constitution* in 1935, it created a positive change. The American newspaper noticed her two-piece swimsuit. The caption read: "Chinese Mermaid: Conservative authorities in China are trying to prevent women from adopting Western styles, but they cannot keep Miss Yang Hsiu-Chong [a different romanization of Yang's name] out of abbreviated suits when she competes in swimming events and after she won the national swimming title in a meet at Shanghai. If you ask us, she's 'Yang' and pretty."[30] Although Yang did not win anything in Berlin, her beauty attracted the attention of the German audience. The famous filmmaker and photographer Leni Riefenstahl took her picture for a commemorative book on the 1936 Olympics.[31]

Compared with other noted athletic figures, Yang's relationship with the media was dynamic. Her intelligence and education were two reasons for this. Rather than accept media coverage passively, she presented her own voice and story. Her writing ability was cultivated through a solid academic education. Along with her younger brother Changhua, Yang first enrolled at the Xinmin (New Citizenry) Elementary School in Hong Kong when she was nine years old. She transferred to the Zunde (Respecting Virtue) Girls' School two years later, and there she learned Chinese and English. At sixteen, Xiuqiong and her sister Xiuzhen were admitted to St. Paul's French School, where she focused on English for two years. She also studied calligraphy, music, dance, and painting.[32] In a subtle comparison, she likened her rise from local to provincial swimming champion in 1930 to elevation in rank through the civil service examination conducted during China's imperial dynasties.[33]

Her learning and insights gave Yang more media savvy and perhaps a greater democratic sensibility than other athletes. In the aftermath of the Fifth

26 Cover of Yang Xiuqiong's biography by Shanghai journalist Wang Jianming.

National Games, she and her fellow athletes toured Xuanwu Lake in Nanjing. Several men asked for pictures. Her teammate Liu Guizhen said, "We are not doing sports on the athletic field; what are the photographs for?" Yang persuaded Liu, "Why give them a hard time? Once we become athletes, we are just like merchants who have opened a store. Just as we cannot turn away people from buying from the store, it is impossible to avoid photographers. Taking photographs would not cost us much." She smiled and said, "Regardless how they are going to use the photographs, they take pictures of us, which shows they watch us. It is not easy for an athlete to be noticed. If we do not perform well and win championships, even when you invite them to take photographs, they will not. Their negatives cost money as well." Her sister Xiuzhen added, "If they asked with respect, we cannot reject." Thus did the Yang family adjust gracefully to their new fame.[34]

Only success guaranteed favourable coverage. After Yang's defeat in the 1936 Olympics, the media, which had been overly kind to her in the past, turned against her. During the peak of her fame, *Shidai manhua (Modern Sketch/Epoch Cartoons)* carried two cartoons that featured her among national male and female celebrities, including Chiang Kai-shek and the chairman of the Nationalist government Lin Sen. After the Olympics, the special issue of *Modern Sketch* that ridiculed track star Li Sen and her team treated Yang the most harshly. It featured a drawing by the noted cartoonist Lu Shaofei on the back cover, which portrayed her garbed in a red bathing suit while fondling a goose egg with five rings, representing her failure to win any medals, and on a diving board surrounded by Western male photojournalists (see Figure 27). In contrast, the front cover featured the Josephine Baker-inspired drawing of a muscular black woman representing "Victory of Coloured People in the Olympics." Other entertainment magazines launched vulgar attacks on her. One reported Yang's explanation of her defeat to the Chinese community in Singapore as equivalent to "blaming the hard ground for not being able to poop." *Cinematic Tone* noted that the harsh attacks made Yang sob and threaten to quit swimming.[35]

Yang offered her own accounts of her experiences at the Olympics in an article published in the *Tianwentai sanri (Three Days at the Observatory)* journal in Hong Kong. In 1938, she reflected on her achievements and sudden fame in an autobiography (see Figure 28). In both pieces, she wrote positively about her Olympic experience. Noting that the point of participation was not just to win medals but to spread the spirit of the Chinese nation, Yang conveyed the great pride she felt when her country's flag joined those of other nations. She accepted blame for her own defeat but argued that the Olympic debacle stemmed from the nation's poor nutrition and lack of long-term training and experience. In all, she regarded the Olympics as the greatest moment in her life thus far. She explained that the athletes had arrived in Europe out of shape, exhausted, and recovering from seasickness. She had remained cheerful and had striven to enjoy herself. She related a number of personal recollections. During her stay in Venice, for example, she found that

27 A "goose egg" for Yang Xiuqiong after her defeat at the 1936 Olympics.
Source: Shidai manhua 29 (20 August 1936): back cover.

she liked the Italians, whose skin and hair colour were close to hers. They called her *Bella* (beautiful), which quickly became her nickname. She enjoyed German food, especially sausages, and was impressed by the Berlin Zoo and the museums. She traded clothing with athletes from other nations and felt inspired by the German female journalists.[36] She herself worked briefly as a

28   Cover of Yang Xiuqiong's autobiography.

journalist for *Qiaosheng bao* (*Voices of Overseas Chinese*) during the full-scale war with Japan. Because she was a pioneer in that male-dominated profession, the media closely scrutinized her new adventure with cynicism.[37]

Yang's fame drew the attention of the great writer Lu Xun, who sarcastically grouped Yang with other famous Chinese female performers who rose and fell in the court of public opinion:

I feel China is a nation that sometimes loves equality extremely. Whatever stands out a little, there are always people who slice them with big knives to even it out with the rest. As far as human beings are concerned ... Ruan Lingyu was a movie star with relatively good achievements, but "others' words are fearsome," after all she swallowed three bottles of sleeping pills in one gulp ... Naturally, there are exceptions to root for. But this rooting is just before they are smashed into pieces. Probably there are still people remembering the "Mermaid" who was cheered to the point of nausea. Even seeing the name feels funny or absurd. According to Chekov, "praise by wretches is worse than fighting and dying in their hands." These are heart-broken and heart-felt words. But China is a nation that loves the average; therefore there are no extreme wretches. They will not come to fight you, so you cannot die in a courageous and straightforward fight. If one cannot endure, one has to take sleeping pills oneself.[38]

Rather than criticize the female high achievers personally, Lu Xun targeted their compatriots who could not bear their rapid rise across gender and class lines and therefore created treacherous environments that led to the dramatic fall of such young women. Yang was far from committing suicide, but Lu's words reflected the ordeals and complexities she faced once her sexy athletic body was recruited to the nationalist cause.

An Ambivalent Poster Girl for the New Life Movement

The Nationalist government quickly latched onto Yang's fame and guided it into the nationalist discourse, since she personified health, patriotism, education, and beauty. Immediately after the Fifth National Games, on 22 October 1933, Nanjing government official Zeng Zhongming invited Yang to cut the ribbon at the opening of the Yangtze River ferry that was part of the Tianjin-Pudong railroad connection. Recognizing her athletic achievements, the media applauded the use of Yang's athletic skill and beauty for such an event. *Young Companion Pictorial* used this moment, along with the Manchurian Shi sibling's patriotic crossing of the Yangtze River, to refresh the national memory of Japanese military aggression.[39]

Building up a competent air force was a key part of wartime nation building, and Yang lent her fame to this cause. Before she departed for Berling in 1936, Yang and her sister took part in the Shanghai Aviation Association swim meet at the Shanghai Swimming Pool to raise money for warplanes in honour of Chiang Kai-shek's birthday. Despite the high ticket prices, ranging from two yuan to five yuan, amounts ten to twenty times the prices to see the Liangjiang basketball games, the crowd swarmed to her performance.[40] Despite the controversy in Singapore during her trip back from the 1936 Olympics, Yang was recruited to the cause of extending "Greater China" to Southeast Asia as well. In 1938, the Yang sisters travelled to Java and Singapore for swimming exhibitions to raise funds for war refugees.[41]

Most significantly, the New Life Movement adopted Yang as its poster girl to attract greater interest and highlight the New Woman's combination of patriotism and a healthy body. To support the movement, Yang toured Central and South China from 25 July to 8 August 1934, during the scorching summer heat, to demonstrate model womanhood. She was invited to Nanchang, Jiangxi Province, to cut the ribbon at the opening ceremony of a new swimming pool on 25 July. Although she could not accept many of the invitations that poured in after her triumph in the Philippines, she "happily accepted" the invitation to travel to Nanchang, which she described as the "original site of the NLM." In articles that she penned, Yang claimed that she was anxious to "bring swimming to Nanchang, and bring the NLM back to Hong Kong." The NLM's advertisement of her visit coined the phrase "swimming to save the nation." The Nanchang public was enthusiastic. After the opening ceremony, Yang toured Lu Mountain (where Madame Chiang and her husband spent summers). There she met such powerful political figures as Nationalist government chairman Lin Sen, Jiangxi chairman Xiong Shihui, and Wang Jingwei's wife, Chen Bijun, who donated a diving platform in Qingdao the following year to promote swimming. General Zhang Zhizhong, chief of public security at Lu Mountain, treated Yang particularly well. Her presence among the nation's elite was vivid testimony that they regarded her as a major asset to the NLM.[42]

Yang was put to work fundraising for charities nationwide. To spread the spirit of the NLM to the rest of China, Dr. Chu Minyi, general secretary of the Executive Yuan, invited Yang to participate in a Nanjing swim meet to raise funds for refugees. The media noted that Yang attracted more support than the famous film star Hu Die had at a similar fundraising event among cinema professionals.[43] When the Gongyu Lianhua Club invited Dr. Chu to photograph the naval parade and *taiji cao* (a style of collective exercise created by Dr. Chu that combined modern gymnastics with traditional *taiji quan*) performance to celebrate Chiang Kai-shek's return to the capital after worshipping Confucius in Qufu, Shandong Province, he made sure to include Yang's swimming performances. She travelled to Shanghai and Xiamen to perform at a semi-official competition between Shanghai and South China swimmers at public and private swimming sites, before returning to a hero's welcome in Hong Kong. Yang was warmly welcomed everywhere and remained at the centre of attention. She received lavish media attention during her tour of Central and South China. News photographs recorded her every move, including shots of her with the common staff of the NLM. *Linglong, Young Companion Pictorial, Dongfang zazhi (Eastern Miscellany), Shenbao yuekan (Supplementary Monthly Magazine of Shanghai Daily),* and other popular periodicals filled their pages with photographs of Yang, with captions such as "The Active Mermaid." A noted male tiyu scholar and administrator, Jiang Huaiqing, authored an article titled "An Impression of Yang Xiuqiong during Her Tour to the North" for *Lüxing zazhi (Travel Magazine)*. Even the obscure Circle of China Harmonica *(Zhonghua kouqin jie)* placed a photograph of the organization greeting Yang in the Gaoqiao Garden on the cover of its magazine.[44]

At the same time, Yang's personal appearance posed contradictions for government policy. The NLM sought to erase "bizarre" or overly sensual women's dress, yet Yang appeared frequently in swimsuits that revealed her legs, shoulders, and much of her torso. Such athletic dress was scandalous at the time, even in Western nations. When fully clothed, Yang often wore a fashionable *qipao* or donned fashionable Western clothes. Although neither conformed to NLM guidelines, articles complained in detail that she dressed more in the latest Western clothing than in *qipao*. At the very beginning of her fame, the media noted that, although other female athletes used ample Parisian powders and rouge, Yang did not need to do so, and her biographer observed that a woman born jianmei would never need makeup. Yang's choices changed, however, and after becoming the NLM's representative she used facial makeup and permed her hair despite the authorities' disapproval.[45]

Other controversies arose. Most pernicious were the sensual fantasies of powerful, aged male political figures. Yang's physique transfixed top officials of the Nationalist government. They occupied about one-third of the seats during the women's competitions at the Fifth National Games. When Yang and other female swimmers came out of the locker room in their bathing outfits, Chairman Lin Sen blinked and clapped his binoculars to his eyes. When Lin and Minister Wang Zhaoming asked for a photograph with Yang, she declined, a decision that reporters from China's major metropolises such as Beiping, Shanghai, Tianjin, and Wuhan considered a big loss.[46] Lin received the Yang siblings twice during their tour on behalf of the NLM, at Lu Mountain and in the capital, Nanjing. On both occasions, photographs were taken and widely circulated in the media. In one of the press photographs, Lin, holding a fan and sporting a full beard, is seen sitting between the standing Yang sisters (see Figure 29).[47]

While most officials kept their lust in check, one politician behaved scandalously. Amid rumours about numerous powerful and older political figures lusting after the teenage swimmer, Chu Minyi's actions garnered the most attention. The motives behind his enthusiastic promotion of Yang in the NLM were not entirely patriotic. According to a noted Shanghai doctor of traditional Chinese medicine, Chen Cunren, Chu's obsession with sexuality had led him

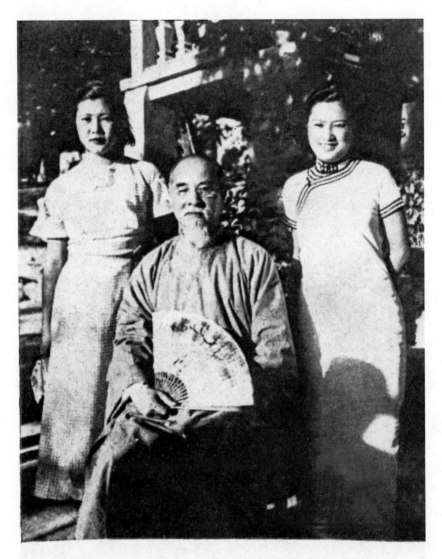

影留時席主林見觀京南在姊珍秀興我

29 The Yang sisters with Lin Sen, chairman of the Nationalist government.
Source: Yang, *Yang Xiuqiong Zizhuan*, 23.

to research the sexual organs of rabbits for his medical degree from the University of Paris School of Medicine. The famous American writer Emily Hahn, who met the "eccentric" Chu in person, confirmed that Chu had first become famous for "his choice of a doctor's thesis" titled "A Study of the Vaginal Vibrations of Female Rabbits." Chu was notorious for his improper involvement with actresses, opera singers, prostitutes, and dancing girls.[48] In the middle of Yang's NLM tour, the print media ran a large photograph of Chu driving a horse cart for the Yangs (see Figure 30), accompanied by sly, suggestive commentary. Along with other photographs of the Yang family, *Linglong, Young Companion Pictorial, Monthly Magazine of Shanghai Daily,* and *Guowen zhoubao (National News [Kuowen] Weekly)* published this notorious photograph, in which Chu, wearing a long Chinese gown and soft cap, is seen sitting high in the driver's seat of a horse cart, holding the reins, while the smiling Yang sisters sit in the front row and their brother on the side. Compared with this image, the Yang sisters' pose with Lin Sen, which appeared next to it in *Young Companion Pictorial,* seems dignified and conventional!

Linglong quipped that "with Chu himself holding the whip to serve as her chauffeur, Miss Yang's honour reached a peak." Newspapers in Shanghai and Beiping wrote:

> The General Secretary of the Executive Yuan, Chu Minyi, who holds a high position as vice president of the Games, ridiculously invited "Mermaid" Yang to tour the banks of Qinghuai River [which was historically associated with courtesans and sing-song girls]. They drove in a wagon, Chu sitting in the driver's seat to control the horse, Yang sitting in the cart.[49]

Chen Bijun, the wife of would-be collaborative government head Wang Jingwei and also Chu's sister-in-law, used the scandalous media coverage to scold Chu. The picture compromised Yang. Famous courtesans attended horse races as a means of boosting their popularity, and in 1923 Lu Xun had published an influential review of Chinese fiction that connected courtesan novels with despicable locales and practices. Despite the Yang family's constant vigilance over their daughter's reputation, riding in the cart with Chu raised cynical eyebrows in the press. At the very least, it created links in the public's mind between the unsuspecting Yang's public sports, her beauty, and traditional courtesan behaviour.[50]

Yang's interactions with Chu Minyi were characteristic of her dealings with the NLM and politicians in general. As noted earlier, she had a personal style of dress and hair at variance with NLM dictates for Chinese women. During the heyday of her success, officials could ignore such contradictions. Morris and Fan have both highlighted the militaristic, semi-fascist character of the NLM.[51] As she recalled in her memoir, during the Berlin Olympics Yang was impressed with the efficiency of the German staff and watched with amazement when a Japanese female athlete asked Adolf Hitler for his autograph

30　Scenes from the Yang family's tour for the New Life Movement: "Nanchang Welcomes Famous Girl Swimmer." The caption to the photograph with Chu Minyi at the centre reads, "Dr. Chu Minyi, Chief Secretary of C.E.C. driving in a carriage with Yang sisters in Nanking," with no mention of their brother.
Source: Liangyou huabao 92 (15 August 1934) A17.

and then kissed him on the cheek. She shared the admiration Zhang Huilan and other members of the delegation felt for German sports and women's participation. Her recollections, published just a year after the Olympics, lack any comments about Nazi behaviour. She certainly did not appear to trumpet German fascist methods,[52] and her public words and appearance on behalf of the NLM offered no evidence of fascism; rather, she appeared eager to display nationalist pride. She may be regarded as naïve in her dealings with Chiang and the NLM, or as a careful guardian of her career and a patriot.

Female leftist critics quickly noted the contradictions between Yang's image and NLM guidelines. Certain officials were criticized for sternly opposing women's "bizarre appearance" and bare legs in public while in private encouraging their concubines, lovers, or prostitutes to dress gaudily. Although they did not explicitly accuse Yang of being an improper sexual partner of these officials, female writers focused on her swimsuits or, equally controversial, her modern Western outfits in challenging both the propriety of her representing the NLM and the legitimacy of the movement itself. One article in *Linglong* argued: "The sumptuary laws are not applied to the Western suits of officials or to the naked legs of celebrities like Yang Xiuqiong"; furthermore, "in terms of morality, the thousands of men and women in short tight swimsuits in one swimming pool do more harm than bare feet and legs."[53]

Conventional motherhood within marriage was an essential part of proper womanhood during the national crisis, and was endorsed by *Young Companion Pictorial* and *Linglong*. The periodicals cited First Lady Madame Chiang as the model of wifely virtue in assisting her husband. With her fame as Miss China, Yang's marriage prospects naturally attracted public attention. Xu Xinqin, a critic at the satirical magazine *Modern Sketch*, expressed outrage at Yang's troubled place in the national media. He noted that as soon as young, unmarried women appeared in the glare of publicity, the first question people asked about their future had to do with the "marriage issue." He linked this question to the harmful rumours circulating about Yang. Xu recommended that Yang and other single women, including actress Li Lili, avoid marriage, which would turn them into "slaves of family" who suffered while their husbands enjoyed other lovers. Rather, he suggested that she choose for herself. Accompanying the article was a cartoon of Yang with a big *ji* (bun) on the side of her head and the body of a fish below her chest.[54] In addition, the media repeatedly circulated rumours about her involvement with foreigners, which was alleged to have occurred on the boat to Berlin despite supervision by female tiyu administrators.[55]

Marriage might be legitimately, or even admirably, forgone by other sportswomen out of devotion to career and nation, but it was essential for Yang, who represented China's model womanhood. Despite Xu's advice, and perhaps to calm rumours, she married Tao Bolin, the top jockey in North China, in 1937. However, widely publicized rumours about her marriage raised questions about Yang's status as poster girl of the NLM and representative of "standard womanhood." While constant rumours of concubinage before her marriage tended to disqualify her as a potential good wife, further rumours of unwanted relationships marred her marriage. These included rumours of her forced concubinage by elderly top officials. For example, days after the Fifth National Games, the Hong Kong press reported that Yang would soon become the eighth concubine of Chen Taiyuan, chief consultant of the Guangxi Bank, and that Yang's mother would receive 30,000 yuan from Chen as dowry. Another rumour linked her with Hu Runjun, a famous Shanghai architect; stories circulated that they were engaged and would be married after the 1936 Olympics. Yang publicly denied these stories but the rumours persisted.[56] In Chongqing, she attracted the attention of Fan Shaozeng, a military official in Sichuan and godson of Madame Chiang. Newspapers reported that, with Chiang Kai-shek's approval, Fan had forced Yang to divorce Tao in order to take her as his eighteenth concubine. The *Chongqing Daily* headlined its story, "Chinese Mermaid Yang Xiuqiong married General of Sichuan Army Fan Shaozeng: Yang Xiuqiong and Tao Bolin divorced." The newspapers printed a divorce decree with the signatures of Tao and Yang, who was just nineteen years old. Domestic and international papers reported the scandal, just as they had covered the activities of courtesans for decades.[57]

The veracity of the concubine story is questionable. Yang had frequently been the target of rumours of concubinage, and it was not unknown for a famous woman to be kidnapped and forced into an unwanted relationship. For example, China's "Movie Queen" Hu Die suffered such a fate from 1944 to 1946 when Dai Li, director of the Chinese Military Council's Investigation and Statistics Bureau (Chiang Kai-shek's secret police), imprisoned her in Sichuan and silenced her husband. Hu regained freedom only after Dai died; understandably, she was later unwilling to discuss her plight. It appears that Yang and Tao did divorce. While modern divorce for ordinary women was rare, her high-profile case caused anxiety in women's periodicals dealing with marriage and family, which had frequently featured Yang as a role model for their readers. They cast a nostalgic look at the perfect moment of her wedding and linked Yang's case with the divorce of noted actress and singer Zhou Xuan in discussing the lessons that women could learn.[58] Following Yang's divorce, there were non-stop rumours over the reasons behind the split and Yang's romantic involvement with figures such as the Shanghai gangster Du Yuesheng and other rich businessmen.[59]

影合生先廷正王隊領及事領林光鄺與宋呂小在表代女四隊泳游國我會運東遠屆十第

31 "The four female swimmers with Consul Kuang Guanglin and Wang Zhengting, the head of China's delegation to the Philippines during the Tenth Far Eastern Games." Yang's mother sits at Wang's right.
Source: Yang, *Yang Xiuqiong Zizhuan*, 29.

Throughout these ordeals, Yang's family was her bedrock. Her mother, who also excelled in swimming, tried to accompany her daughters to all major competitions. She made it to the National Games and to the Far Eastern Games in Manila, and posed for photographs with athletes and officials (see Figure 31).[60] Yang agreed to lend her name to the NLM only after authorities agreed to make it a family project. The entire Yang family braved the summer heat to travel from Hong Kong to Shanghai up the Yangtze River to Nanchang in 1934 (see Figure 32). Except for the mother, the family swam in Nanchang before a huge crowd, and they toured Lu Mountain together.[61] Many photographs that recorded Yang's movements during her NLM tour included her fashionable and apparently affluent family: Yang Xiuqiong, her sister, and their mother in *qipao* or tight Western dress with fancy jewellery, her father in a suit and tie, and her brother, Yang Changhua, in shirt and wide belt. The family atmosphere in those pages helped dilute the sensual flavour of other photographs, such as the one with Chu Minyi.[62]

As Yang prepared to travel to the 1936 Berlin Olympics, she learned that there were no funds for her mother, who had accompanied her on all her

影合時幕開池泳游會運活生新為昌南赴同人家與

32 The Yang family at the opening ceremony of the swimming pool in Nanchang in 1934.
Source: Yang, *Yang Xiuqiong Zizhuan,* 24.

33   Yang Xiuqiong and Lu Lihua at Liangjiang Tiyu School during
Yang's New Life Movement tour in 1934.
Source: Wang Jianming, *Meirenyu Yang Xiuqiong* (Shanghai: Guanghua
shuju, 1935).

previous trips and insisted on continuing to do so. Lu Lihua suggested that
Yang give a swimming exhibition to raise cash for her mother's passage.
Newspapers criticized the event as a publicity stunt for Lu's school, but Yang
defended Lu at the swim meet (see Figure 33). *Linglong* reported that after
the funding request on behalf of Yang's mother was rejected by the CNAAF,
a rich businessman's wife promised to step in.[63] Despite those efforts, it appears unlikely that Yang's mother made the trip. The government ensured that

each female athlete had a mentor who helped provide "accurate direction in terms of Western customs and life." Cabin assignments ensured that mentors had access to the female athletes at all times. Yang's supervised travels both before and during the Olympics raises doubts that these experiences made her wiser in the ways of the world. Unlike Zhang Huilan with her international travels, Lu Lihua with her global ambitions, or even the basketball players and track stars who travelled around China and Asia, Yang was closely supervised when she travelled and was perhaps too young to seek new horizons.

Yang returned to Hong Kong in October 1936. A few months later, her mother was diagnosed with cancer. After futile trips to doctors, Long Lizhen died on 6 September 1937. Without the encouragement of her beloved mother, the grieving Yang initially lost interest in swimming, but despite her sadness, she planned to return to her sport and perhaps open a training club. She also wanted to win glory for her country in a future Olympics, a desire, however, that was thwarted by world war.[64]

Yang and Tao resumed their marriage in 1946 and moved to Hong Kong in 1949 amid rumours alleging domestic violence and speculating that a domineering husband affected her decision to leave Shanghai. Known in Hong Kong as Yvonne Tan Sau King (a Cantonese transliteration of Xiuqiong), Yang organized a philanthropic women's lifeguard society, which led to her being presented to Queen Elizabeth II at Buckingham Palace. The family prospered by operating the well-known Sky Restaurant on Hong Kong's Shouson Hill. When they married in 1937, Yang and Tao decided not to have children for ten years so that Yang could focus on the tiyu cause, but they eventually had four children: Alice, Patrick, Caroline, and Monica. The entire family immigrated to Vancouver, Canada, on 5 March 1977, where Yang became prominent in the local Chinese community. She died as a result of complications from an injury suffered after she fell from a ladder in 1982.[65]

Yang Xiuqiong's Mass Appeal

The media regarded Yang's swimming with a mixture of admiration and conservatism. The noted magazine *Wanxiang (Panorama)* tried to desexualize her image by construing it as healthy and athletic to confirm its nationalist meaning. Its caption to rare photographs documenting Yang's swimming career stated that her triumph in the Far Eastern Games had won "incomparable honour for the nation in the international society," and that "under a clear sky in the south country, diving twenty metres into the transparent sea, one can feel her body and soul flying together. Watching the drops of salty water rolling on her smooth and firm skin, everyone would show healthy and noble [non-sensual] smile. That was how our Mermaid Yang Xiuqiong developed."[66] Just as natural settings purified the bodies of the German nudists, swimming did likewise for Yang.

In contrast to the these romantic and pleasant watery surroundings, just before full-scale war with Japan broke out, the leftist *Modern Sketch* published two photomontage cartoons featuring Yang in a swimsuit above scorched soil. In June 1937, "A life endangered by diving" by noted cartoonists Wang Zimei and Xi Yuqun depicted Yang diving into a region filled with dead trees adorned with corpses on nooses due to famine caused by drought (see Figure 34), while "The sad situation of the Mermaid in Sichuan" showed Yang lying on the cracked, dry bed of a pond (see Figure 35).[67] Reminiscent of Lu Xun's criticism of the nation's treatment of its young female celebrities, the cartoonists' depiction of Yang against the frightening "hell on earth" background of famine and disaster highlighted the decadent, frivolous nature of Yang's celebrity. They suggested that the shallow worship of her sensual *(rougan)* body was irrelevant to the national plight, especially the starvation and privation in the countryside. Consequently, the images challenged the legitimacy of "Miss China" in the nationalist discourse. The cartoons drove home the message by subtly publicizing her marital problems with rumours of forced concubinage and divorce. Other cartoonists, such as the noted Lu Shaofei, shared the cynical attitudes of Wang and Xi toward Yang's fame. The caption to Lu's drawing of Yang for the cover of the first issue of *Shiri zazhi (Ten-Day Magazine)* complained: "Currently, Miss Yang Xiuqiong has been rooted into a supernatural human being."[68]

Fully aware of Yang's vulnerability to such criticism, periodicals with feminist sympathies such as *Linglong* were concerned with exploitation of her sensualized body. *Linglong* was always filled with images of beautiful women who served as lofty, if unmatchable, models for female petty urbanites. It warned that the young, attractive, and promising Yang might be manipulated and used, which would damage her reputation – a reputation representing the power and progress of the New Woman. *Linglong's* major concern was the commercialization of Yang's body and her image as an entertainer. The journal cited successful figures, including movie stars, anti-Japanese generals, and even the once-popular sprinter Sun Guiyun, as examples of those whose reputations plummeted after they allowed their names to be used for profit. Chen Zhenling, the female editor of *Linglong*, worried that curious Shanghai residents were excited about Yang's visit not for her swimming skills but because they viewed her as a popular entertainer. A female author writing in the periodical observed that Yang ran around attending ceremonies fit only

34   "A life endangered by diving."
Source: Shidai manhua 39 (20 June 1937): 1.

for the taste of mediocre male petty urbanites eager to watch "maidens taking bath." She called on Yang to stop serving as a vulgar men's puppet and plaything. Instead, she should contribute to the noble causes of women's liberation, the progress of the nation, and the bright future of mankind.[69]

35 "The sad situation of the mermaid in Sichuan."
Source: Shidai manhua 39 (20 June 1937): 1.

The irony was that Yang's long-term impact lay in her powerful influence on China's popular modernity. In the realm of mass consumerism and the new cinema, with the mass appeal of her reputation as Miss China, Yang's association with the New Life Movement and her scandalous encounter with

Chu Minyi enhanced her fame and marketability. With fame based on her skills, beauty, and alliance with the nationalist cause, she became the focus of the gaze of the male masses.

Even discounting the exaggerated accounts of her biographer, Wang Jianming, one can sense her popularity with the public. Although she attracted the attention of the very few female journalists,[70] male photojournalists were the first group to scrutinize her closely. A foldout photograph, taken from the rear, shows a male media horde ogling her. After Yang won the 50-metre freestyle and 100-metre backstroke at the Fifth National Games, male photographers swarmed toward her before she could wipe her body dry and take a breath. One joked suggestively that it is best to take photographs of a "Mermaid" fresh from the water. Ordinary citizens began imitating these journalists. *Linglong* noted that during the Fifth National Games, an admiring crowd curious about the Yang sisters' unique floating silk pants or bare legs quickly surrounded them whenever they went for food or snacks. One incident at a teahouse at Jiming Temple provides a gauge of the public response to Yang. Wang described how the guests saw the four swimmers (two Yangs, Liang Yongxian, and Liu Guizhen) in modern clothes, with permed hair and high heels and sporting red lipstick and white powder. They wondered about the women's identities: "Who were they, *dajia guixiu* [daughters of big/noble families]? Great scholars, or ... ?" A soldier recognized Yang from the photograph in the newspaper he was holding. He politely approached her and the others to ask for autographs. When other guests asked him who they were, he answered, "Those are the famous swimmers from South China. The one in the silver *qipao* is the Mermaid, Yang Xiuqiong," whereon the room buzzed with excitement.

Yang's performances sparked mass interest in women's competitive swimming, as was evident at the box office. Her future biographer reported:

> There are fathers instructing their sons, "You can miss meals or books, but never miss seeing the 'Mermaid.'" "This is the scene once in a thousand of years," husbands warn their wives. "You can skip combing your hair or applying makeup, but you should never miss the performance of the 'Mermaid.' After you observe that spirit of hers, you will start to understand that not all Chinese women are like the pretentious ones who are meant only for consumption by men."

Generally, the press showed less interest in Wang's comments about consumerism than in those about Yang's bathing suits. His biography also accentuated the uncanny impact of Yang's swim attire and confirmed the erotic nature of the spectatorship. Wang observed that audiences would wait quietly near the pool and stare as Yang slowly removed her bathing gown to reveal her black swimsuit before jumping into the water to practise. Remarkably, despite government disapproval of her attire and makeup, Yang's celebrity and relaxed demeanour inspired awe rather than condemnation in public settings.[71]

Still, sensuality dominated her public events, which began to attract dangerously large crowds. In Shanghai, people in the streets talked of "going to see the Mermaid." The YMCA pool, where she performed, was packed with spectators. When she appeared at Shanghai's Gaoqiao Beach on 6 August 1934, the crowd, consisting mostly of petty urbanites, became so boisterous that Yang became frightened and then felt quite ill. As occurred at the Liangjiang basketball games (see Chapter 3), the crowd was electrified at the sight of the scantily clad young woman. However, despite the risks inherent in such poorly regulated public events, Yang persevered and went on to make appearances and swim at private and school swimming pools, the new symbols of China's modernity.[72]

Yang's enormous appeal became big business. Rumours spread that the Nanjing Central Swimming Pool profited by advertising her appearance to sell tickets for 0.5 yuan each. *Linglong* attributed the rumour to the mentality of mediocre petty urbanites.[73] The reality was that getting Yang into such ventures involved considerable amounts of money. For her trips to Nanchang for the New Life Movement and to Shanghai for the Sixth National Games, authorities paid Yang 1,000 yuan each, a fee other athletes seldom received.[74] Spectators paid to watch such official women's swimming events. Inviting her to opening ceremonies became a smart business move. For example, an overseas Chinese entrepreneur, Huang Da'en, opened a swimming pool at the Xiamen YWCA in 1935; to attract the local youth, he organized a round-trip swimming race between Gulangyu, a small island in Xiamen harbour, and the city from 10 to 12 August, and featured Yang in the opening ceremony.[75] Commercialization could backfire, however, especially after media coverage turned sour following Yang's defeat in Berlin. Also, in contrast to the triumphs of the women's basketball and track teams, the Yang sisters gained a bad reputation in the Southeast Asian tour. They were accused of behaving as uncooperative stars and, worse, demanding large amounts of spending money, and pocketing a portion of the funds raised during their appearances.[76]

Yang's image was featured in an advertisement for *Young Companion Pictorial* in 1935. She was shown reading the magazine while sitting cozily on a sofa with a blanket covering her legs; the ad text read: "The Mermaid is reading the special magazine [for the Sixth National Games]." The domestic scene filled with Western furniture targeted young petty urbanites who found modern consumerism appealing. One of *Linglong*'s advertising ploys was to give magazine subscriptions to female record-breaking athletes at the Fifth National Games. All track and field stars and swimmers were given one-year and half-year subscriptions, respectively, except for Qian Xingsu (two years) and Yang Xiuqiong (one year). Yang's photographs were sold to raise money for flood refugees in 1935 in Shanghai. One print cost 100 yuan, an amount greater than most tiyu teachers' monthly salaries.[77] When the media launched a heated debate over Yang's involvement in advertisements, her father stepped in to defend her. Compared with other female athletes, Yang enjoyed financial success as a smart businesswoman. As early as 1935, she bought a property in Hong Kong, and around 1938 she earned handsome fees as an insurance agent. Unimpressed, the media viewed her involvement with business as degrading and as detrimental to her athletic skill.[78]

In Chapter 2, I discussed the integration between sports and media in popular modernity. I will discuss the fusion of sports and cinema more extensively in the next chapter, but Yang's immediate influence on films merits attention here. Hollywood first made films about swimming. Stars such as swimmer-entertainer Eleanor Holm from Brooklyn, New York, and the world-renowned Olympic champion swimmer and star of six Tarzan films in the 1930s, Johnny Weissmuller, were familiar to Chinese filmgoers and magazine readers.[79] In 1932, *Linglong* reported that the eighteen-year-old Holm raised hopes for the US team's success at the Los Angeles Olympics after she set records in the 200-metre breaststroke and 100-metre backstroke. Her skills translated to the silver screen: "After the Olympics, many studios recruited male and female athletes; however, most lacked sufficient facial expressiveness, despite their jianmei figures. Warner Brothers selected only Holm." The magazine reported that she never used her real name as a film star. In a photograph captioned "Holm's Gentle Gymnastics," she posed near a bush, extending her right leg behind her while holding her right foot near her head, a feat possible only with a jianmei body.[80] The Chinese media held Holm up as the highest standard for Yang. *Linglong* commented that Yang's outstanding swimming skills, well-proportioned body, willowy figure, and beautiful face generally resembled Holm's. It believed that Yang might one day become the Chinese version of Holm.[81]

Swimming made for a natural combination of feminine beauty and Hollywood stardom. One writer aptly synthesized the argument: "Hollywood stars love swimming, and their perfect jianmei bodies make us admire them and feel ashamed to compare ourselves to them."[82] In a move indicating how Yang popularized swimming, *Linglong* published a series of photographs of Hollywood stars in swimsuits and high-heeled sandals on beaches, river banks, and seashore cliffs, sitting, diving, holding balls, playing chess on a drifting raft, or just exhibiting the latest swimsuit styles. One 1931 photograph showed how the Metro Company filmed a swimming movie using special lighting, background, cameras, and sound.[83]

Yang soon entered the world of cinema. As early as 1933, Mingxing Studio filmed her competition in the Fifth National Games. That same year, she played a small role in the feature film *Polang (Breaking the Waves)*. Shot by Lianhua Studio primarily in Hong Kong, it starred Hong Kong actress Guo Wawa and film star Li Zhuozhuo, one of two wives of Lianhua boss Li Minwei. Along with Yang's part, their presence ensured a high profile for the film. It opened at the Grand Beijing Theater in Shanghai on New Year's Day 1934.[84] The New Times Company hired the Mermaid's sister, Yang Xiuzhen, to star in a new comedy called *Wang Xiansheng dao "nongcun qu" (Mr. Wang Goes to the Countryside)*. Guangzhou mayor Liu Jiwen invested 35,000 yuan to transform the Central China Photograph Studio into the Central China Cinematic Company, whose first film was *Shizi jietou (Crossing Road)*. After Liu's wife visited Hong Kong to negotiate with Yang and her parents, the Yang sisters were hired to star in the company's second film, *Shuishang hua (Flowers on the Water)*, which was scheduled for production in 1935, although there is no record that the film was ever made.[85]

Yang's cinema career, limited as it was, stirred controversy. This reflected the traditional prejudice against entertainers and how Yang helped to redefine boundaries. Some journals reported that Yang was happily considering starring in films; others claimed that she "denied that she is entering cinema." "Voice of the Readers" in *Cinematic Tone* asked, "Why cannot Yang Xiuqiong star on silver screen? Is cinema degenerate?"[86] Hearing that the Yilian Studio in Shanghai was interested in Yang, *Linglong* was concerned that Yang would lose her amateur status and miss the more important mission of winning glory for the nation.[87] Around 1940, free of marital restrictions and eager to rise from her failed marriage through a new career, Yang attempted to re-enter cinema in Hong Kong and the "isolated island" of Shanghai through working for the noted Hong Kong filmmaker Zhang Shankun. Later, after she had reconciled with Tao, her family, concerned about complications that might arise from pregnancy and childbirth, and anxious about the complex political environment, convinced her to give up acting. The planned film, *The Mermaid*, starred Hong Kong actress Chen Yunshang (Nancy Chan) instead.[88]

The entertainment periodicals considered Yang's screen image "sensual," and reported her taking up singing and dancing, singing with entertainment stars, learning Beijing opera, and dancing competitively with the noted dancing girls Liang Yuzhu and Liang Saizhu. An article called "The Never-Fading Impression on Shanghainese: Li Huitang Playing Soccer, Yang Xiuqiong Swimming, Mei Lanfang Fundraising for the refugees, and Hu Die's Wedding" appeared in *Zhongguo manhua (China Cartoons).*[89] Yang's portrayal as the equal of the kings of soccer and Beijing opera and the "Movie Queen" confirmed her high status in the intertwined world of sports and entertainment.

Making Swimming Feminine, Glamorous, and Modern

Yang Xiuqiong's career kept pace with rapidly changing social attitudes toward swimming, a sport that had only recently become popular around the world, by redefining it as feminine, fashionable, and modern.[90] Initially, the Nationalist government viewed swimming as a masculine event. Women were excluded from swimming at the Fourth National Games in 1930. Although swimming was not considered as important as track and field or ball games, it was influential in the development of Chinese women's body culture. Despite the dangerously erotic and carnival-like atmosphere associated with women's swimming, the sport was finally included in the Fifth National Games, although there were still fewer women's events offered than men's.[91] Besides receiving government sponsorship, the Fifth National Games were heavily politicized. Exiled swimmers from Manchuria tried to carry an anti-Japanese political message. The Shi siblings from Liaoning performed well, and after the games the family swam across the Yangtze River in an attempt to awaken the nation to the Japanese occupation of Manchuria.[92] Some, who were uncomfortable with swimming as a woman's sport to cultivate feminine beauty while serving the nationalist agenda, defined swimming strictly as a male heroic sport, as demonstrated by the grand adventure of the Shi siblings and later by Mao Zedong's famous crawls across the Yangtze River.

Yang's overwhelming celebrity based on feminine beauty defined the sport as feminine while retaining its heroic dimension. Conquering water in nature appeared essential to defining the gender of swimming. Just as the Shi siblings and Mao used the Yangtze River to convey their masculine and political message, Yang defined her status in swimming through the ocean. For example, just before the Tenth Far Eastern Games, she earned international praise for saving a drowning man by jumping into a harbour in Hong Kong in her school uniform. Yang modestly dismissed the praise: "Learning to swim is basically to guarantee safety in the water. It is a natural obligation for swimmers to rescue those in danger."[93] Yang was presented as a goddess who dominated

36 Yang Xiuqiong's goddess-style dominant image.
Source: Wanxiang 2 (June 1934): 39.

the swimming scene. In one photograph published in *Panorama,* Yang in a swimsuit suit, sitting coolly on a sky-high diving board, dwarfed not only the mountain but also male beachgoers, some of whom were looking up at her (see Figure 36).[94] The theme was echoed in a photograph of Yang taken by the famed Wang Kai Photography Studio, which appeared on the cover of the journal *Nüshen (Goddess).*[95] In part, these ambiguities stemmed from the uncertain status of women's swimming as a legitimate sport. A related anxiety concerned the effect of swimming on women's bodies; like track and field events, competitive swimming relies on strength, speed, and technique.

The American dialogue about gender and swimming affected Chinese attitudes. Yang's impact may be seen in an international debate over the effects of competitive swimming on women's bodies. In 1935, Johnny Weissmuller was quoted as saying that swimming would hurt feminine beauty and that adult women should give up swimming:

> "Swimming is good for women under seventeen for establishing the basis for the future development of jianmei. Women above seventeen should not swim any more because swimming will develop huge shoulder muscles and harm their gentle beauty. Women who are good at swimming are not as attractive as those just walking around the swimming pool in swimsuits. Because their muscles cannot stand being restrained, swimmers wear only comfortable clothes and do not care about their looks. Their bobbed hair, tanned necks, and firm arms have lost their sexiness. Therefore, women who love swimming should absolutely quit. If not immediately, they should reduce their daily swimming time."[96]

What Weissmuller saw as ideal feminine beauty is unclear, but evidently he did not like an athletic figure. Other commentators suggested moderation. According to a famous American bodybuilder, Sylvia Ulbeck, female athletes lost their beauty when they overexercised. She argued: "Although swimming, horseback riding, and tennis are beneficial sports for women, rules need to be followed." A Chinese author who introduced these opinions added that too much swimming caused overly wide shoulders and chests. Vigorous tennis could make the arms too large and thick. He described for readers the "standard Hollywood beauty": "Five feet tall, less than one hundred pounds, with a round figure and smooth skin." "She plays tennis for twenty minutes a day or no more than nine holes of golf, but not both; horseback riding for at most two hours at a time; and mild swimming." Moderation more than athletic training produced this critic's ideal woman.[97]

Chinese women found a role model in Eleanor Holm, who impressed them when she debated Weissmuller in 1933. In a lengthy exchange covered fully by the Shanghai-based *Tiyu zhoubao (Tiyu Weekly)*, Weissmuller and Holm disagreed on the effect of swimming on the female body. Weissmuller repeated his contention that "swimming deprives females of beauty." Asked whether he felt that sports made women more attractive, he responded, "Absolutely not!" He continued stating that while women looked "incredibly beautiful" in swimsuits, they should never let them get wet. Swimming leads to excessive musculature on the neck, shoulders, and thighs, which he deplored. When queried about Holm, the male athlete joked that she was the exception that proved the rule. In words that had to cheer Yang and her supporters, Holm derided Weissmuller as an antique, and advised women: "If you want to be elegant, go swimming." She noted that Olympic glory was far greater than Hollywood fame and that she and other athletes constantly received adoring fan mail.[98] Chinese women made an explicit connection between Holm's advice and local attitudes toward Yang. A female reporter wrote in *Linglong* that women did not lose their feminine and sexy beauty from swimming and that the feminine beauty some Chinese men admired was "out of date." She cited Yang as living proof of her point: "For example, China's Yang Xiuqiong is a very attractive girl." Implicit in such comments about Yang was the view that Weissmuller's and Ulbeck's contentions, though Western, were not progressive, whereas Holm's surely were.[99]

Yang had her own take on the debate over swimming and women's health. In one of several articles that she penned for Hong Kong newspapers, she noted: "Swimming is the most important in tiyu." She argued that all could enjoy it and that it was safe and pleasant and allowed one to purify one's thoughts. It was, she assured readers, "the most beautiful sport in the world."[100] Yang was aware of the potential pitfalls of appearing to be too masculine. In her autobiography, she wrote:

American athlete Helen Stephens attracted attention [at the 1936 Olympics] not only for her championships in the 100-metre dash, but also for the fact that her facial features, stout figure, deep and loud voice, and masculine movements showed no hint of her being a woman. When she came in to ask female athletes to sign her notebook during lunch one day, all other female athletes decided that she was a man. Only I believed that she was a woman, because she wore permed hair and face powder as well. Only when Stephens was assigned to the same group as Li Sen to compete in sprinting did Miss Li realize that Stephens was a woman. We had a good laugh.[101]

Yang's good humour enabled her to defuse public concerns about excessive masculine traits among athletic women, and her response to the Stephens incident also showed affection for a fellow athlete. As the New Life Movement's chief spokesperson, her affable cosmopolitanism also benefited the movement by making it more attractive to the masses.

Ultimately, Yang's influence extended into Chinese society. The sexual appeal of swimmers refuted the allegations of core risks for women – reproductive damage and development of masculine physical characteristics – associated with track and field athletes. Yang's fame began to affect public life in fields beyond cinema, including fashion and such socially sensitive places as swimming pools and beaches. With swimming's rapid rise in popularity and the overwhelming power of cinema, the controversy over pools dissipated. Swimming pools had historically been privately owned and operated by universities and wealthy individuals. Whereas in the United States struggles over swimming pools were about race, in China gender was the contested arena. In 1932, a Beiping businessman named Yang, who was over forty years old and nicknamed "old modern" for his interest in new ideas, opened a commercial swimming pool. Sharp comment over mixed public swimming hurt his business. In 1935, the Beiping government proposed a ban on mixed-gender swimming, and Yang had to divide his pool with rope and a net, with two-thirds of the space for men and one-third for women. Yang's business declined further because after the small pool was split, people could not even turn around. Mixed-gender swimming was also banned in Guangzhou, where three swimming pools (Dongshan, West Suburb, and Shiwei) had opened as early as 1932. The ban applied to children as well. Urban residents petitioned the authorities, saying that it was a pity to separate young lovers who comprised the majority of those using the pools. The Beiping authorities decided not to ban mixed-gender swimming on the grounds that swimming pools were places for tiyu, in which foreign guests sometimes joined, and had nothing to do with morality. The first public swimming pool opened by the YMCA allowed mixed-gender swimming. Soon the Shanghai Transportation University offered separate nude swimming, and Fudan University proposed to follow.[102]

Throughout the decade, scientists strove to reassure the public about the benefits of water sports. *Linglong* reported the activities of a new Chinese Women's Swimming Research Association through a photograph showing two rows of women in swimsuits listening to a male instructor. Using physiological theories, popular magazines advocated swimming as the best tiyu activity and entertainment for women to "develop their minds and bodies" without developing masculine muscles, which they regarded as the disadvantage of tiyu events on land. "In hot summers, swimming is the most suitable, beneficial, cool, and easy exercise."[103]

As swimming became more acceptable, magazines and newspapers provided useful advice about maintaining health while bathing or swimming, publishing frequent articles about hygiene and other scientific information. Swimming began to appear more salubrious. Articles stated that it could help muscles develop evenly and improve one's physique efficiently because the exercise used all the muscles. Swimming was beneficial for the internal organs, especially the lungs, and for nerves, thanks to water pressure. At the same time, the public had to be cautious. Journalists recommended a medical examination to determine whether a person was fit for swimming. To avoid disturbing the digestive and respiratory systems, writers discouraged swimming within two hours after eating, and viewed consumption of alcohol while swimming as absolutely harmful. Swimmers who felt tired and cold were advised to get out of the water immediately. After swimming, one should wipe the skin until it turned red. Beginners were advised to limit their swimming to twenty or thirty minutes. A hot shower was recommended to adjust the body temperature gradually while waiting for the pulse to slow down after fierce exertion and before entering the swimming pool; massage and hot water were prescribed for cramps. Earplugs and Vaseline were recommended to avoid infections. Qualities needed in order to learn how to swim included "confidence, balance, relaxation, skillful breathing, and coordination of arms and legs." Journalists used pictures to illustrate the various stages of diving, and articles noted: "The head, like a boat's rudder, is for direction, knees should always be straight, feet should always be together, hands extended in front of the head, and only the waist can move." One writer described an "American-invented" balloon attached to a swimmer's arms as an "assisting device for swimming," and published a drawing of a Western woman demonstrating its use.[104]

After swimming was deemed appropriate and beneficial for women by "science," abetted by Yang's fame and cinematic interest in the sport, swimming became a fashionable and romantic tiyu activity for average "modern" youth, especially women, in big cities. Its popularity in China exploded in the early 1930s. Chinese women took to swimming pools and ocean beaches to show off modern swimsuits and to display newly acquired aquatic skills. According to a 1935 editorial in *Linglong:* "Summer is swimming time, and we advocate swimming for women as both *yundong* [exercise] and entertainment to improve women's health. Swimming is also significant in showing the differences between modern and old-fashioned women. We hope sisters swim more and read more to pass the long summer."[105]

The swimming pool also became associated with literary and cinematic romance. In a photograph in *Linglong,* Shi Manyong, a female member of the famous left-wing Roaring Waves Drama Club *(Nuchao jushe),* posed in a bathing suit while holding a dragon statue.[106] In a letter to the editor of *Linglong,* a female student asked for help with an adolescent love problem at a swimming pool: Two girls went to learn how to swim and a male stranger volunteered to teach them. Mixed signals, misunderstanding, and confusion ensued – which of them did he like? The letter noted:

> Although he said "[see you] tomorrow" to the second girl when he left, he did not come on the following day, which seems to show that he was not really interested in her, and yesterday perhaps he was only seeking revenge against

the first girl. Do you think he loves the first girl? If so, why did he seek revenge, since a courting man should try to please?

The editor commented: "When two girls are taught by one young man, how could you know that man is not to be suspected of taking advantage of them?"[107]

A Shanghai woman linked swimming with tourism: "[After you travel to Shanghai] I can only recommend swimming, which will strengthen your body and combat the hot weather, as summer entertainment here, since fans blow only hot air in dance halls, theatres, and other places." Women in Hong Kong and Guangdong, especially schoolgirls, began to swim in early spring.[108]

The Yang effect on cinema and swimming pools soon showed up in fashion. Swimming became a common part of modern young women's fashion culture. Numerous swimming-related photographs submitted to *Linglong* by ordinary readers appeared on front pages or were distributed across various issues. At times, swimming, along with dancing, was called simply the virtue of a "popular lady." Jin Shaozhen, with heavy makeup and permed hair and wearing a fancy *qipao*, was described as a "model woman, with jianmei physique, good at socializing, dancing, and swimming. It is a pity that she, well known in Hong Kong, did not demonstrate swimming in Shanghai." In a "go swimming" photograph, two sisters were dressed in *qipao*, Western shirts, vests, and long pants, and one of them carried a small suitcase. Stairs and fences near swimming pools or lawns were frequently used as backgrounds for women posing in swimsuits and caps under the heading of "modern ladies." Women were shown diving from cliffs and showering in waterfalls. Some images featured Hollywood stars wearing high-heeled leather sandals with their swimsuits, a soft towel draped across their body, and, under a big summer hat, a long ponytail fluttering in the wind.[109]

During her life as a sports figure, celebrity, and model for Chinese womanhood, Yang Xiuqiong powerfully advanced women's roles. She accepted her role as a symbol of the New Life Movement and thus as a representative of the Chinese state. She met the criteria of patriotism, obedience to the law, and high moral character. She was industrious and innovative, qualities that Chinese society of her time required of illustrious women. Later, with the arrival of children, she realized the sole attribute of female virtue that had been missing during her career years. She was not a clay model moulded by politics. Her personal life, public persona, and intelligence matched her accomplishments as a champion swimmer. Even as political figures, aggressive males, and an adoring public strove to channel her public identity, Yang demonstrated that poise, a strong family, and integrity made possible a solid career and personality. As a charming modern female athlete, she was portrayed as an attractive and erotic woman. She was a pioneer in athletics and in fashion, where she exemplified the physicality and implicit sexuality of modern femininity. Young female athletes like Yang helped to shape new beauty standards based on a more sexual female body. As a popular sports figure, she exuded a concentrated and influential appeal for the thousands of Modern Girls walking the streets of Shanghai.[110] Of all the athletes discussed in this book, Yang was best able to establish her own identity and that of her sport. Her impact is demonstrated in films, one of the most powerful and influential social forces.

Not surprisingly, her reputation in China suffered after the Communist takeover in 1949. In the 1950s, writers in the *People's Daily*, the official state newspaper, used her accomplishments to illustrate the superiority of sports in the New China. Articles compared her triumphs under the Nationalist government with those of later athletes in order to show the positive effect of socialism. Such criticism notwithstanding, Yang may be seen as a precursor of China's Olympic champion swimmers from the 1980s to the present.[111]

6 Sportswomen on Screen: The "Athletic Movie Star," Li Lili (1915-2005)

In Stanley Kwan's 1992 film *Ruan Lingyu (Center Stage),* a homage to the legendary actress Ruan Lingyu (Lily Yuen, 1910-35), actress Li Lili (played by Carolina Lau) is portrayed as a close friend and patriot. Li teaches Ruan how to speak Mandarin, is a close confidant, and leads fellow actors in singing anti-Japanese songs. The real Li Lili, then in her late seventies, appears in the film reminiscing about the sad and famous funeral after Ruan's suicide in 1935. Although Li's character in the film was a strong supporting role, in Chinese film and sports history her contribution was much greater and more significant. This chapter shows how Li, in concert with filmmakers, created a cinematic version of the athletic woman. Her performances were timely because of the Japanese invasion and the concomitant national crisis in China. Li's athletic female persona supported Chinese nationalist visions of a fit female citizenry. Her film appearances added the power of this influential medium to the government's edicts.[1]

The Japanese invasion of Manchuria in 1931 and attack on Shanghai in late January 1932 exacerbated a sense of national crisis already pervasive in China. In response to the invasion, Communists, Nationalists, and leftist intellectuals made building a strong military a joint priority. In the cultural realm, overcoming their earlier suspicions of cinema, they viewed films as a promising vehicle with which to convey political ideology and construct a modern discourse of the body and physical fitness. In this chapter, I will show how filmmakers and actors connected *tiyu* (physical education, sports, and physical culture) with cinematic representations of female bodies.

As shown in Chapter 2, concepts of "robust/healthy beauty" (*jianmei*) penetrated various fields of popular culture in the 1930s, including cinematic stardom. Fan magazines began calling for actresses of a new athletic type, and dissatisfaction with the older female film personae was evident in their appeals. In 1933, a *Linglong* magazine article ridiculed domestic actresses for "their gentle and foxy charms," with their "Lin Daiyu-style beautiful faces, sick and fragile bodies, and depressed personalities; their ability to ride the heart of the director rather than a horse; and their wearing sexy swimsuits ...

to show off their beautiful curves rather than for swimming." The article called for a modern "masculine gallant" *(xiong jiujiu)* style of actress comparable to the athletic and jianmei actresses of dynamic and active Western nations.[2]

To pursue the goal of a national cinema, Chinese nationalists of every political stripe promoted the movie actress Li Lili (Qian Zhenzhen) as an "athletic movie star" *(tiyu mingxing)*.[3] She became the model of the physically fit woman, a model that suited the discursive needs of China's wartime nationalism. All sides in the political struggles of the time found ways to appropriate her screen image of athletic robustness for their own agendas. Communists sought to construct strong female working-class citizens through Li's screen image, while the Nationalist government used her performances to project an international image of strong, healthy middle-class Chinese female citizens to represent the new modern nation. Communists, Nationalists, and Li herself found ways to deal with both the sexuality exuding from depictions of her athletic body and the persistent cultural biases against and suspicions of actresses. Nationalists and Communists competed to legitimize the body codes that emerged from their differing versions of female citizenry.[4]

While the Nationalist government controlled Shanghai and its cinema during the 1930s, leftist filmmakers, actors, and critics were able to maintain a public presence, provided they espoused educational values, social responsibility, and the patriotic struggle against Japanese imperialism. The Nationalist Party's law and regulations regarding cinema gave its officials direct influence and control. As Zhang Zhen has argued, leftist film creators, including writers, directors, critics, and actors, commingled with Nationalists in a "broad, democratic forum."[5]

In this chapter, I explore the career of Li Lili to demonstrate how Nationalist and Communist filmmakers collaborated in the construction of her cinematic persona as an athletic film star. I use the term "athletic" very broadly to include organized competitive sports, physical exercise, and such social graces as dancing. I also demonstrate how her performances enabled Lianhua Studio's leading director, Sun Yu (1900-90), to move beyond the martial arts and female-centred melodrama that dominated the films of the late 1920s, into making politically important cinema. Far from seeing her as a pawn of these various forces, however, my approach emphasizes Li Lili's sense of political agency in her films. I show how she structured her public and private life to respond to the competing demands of powerful ideological forces and to create her own model of female citizenship. Li's background, as well as both her public and private life, coalesced around athleticism, political rights, and patriotism. Despite the cinematic exposure of her body, Li presented herself as sexually innocent and fervently anti-Japanese. She furthered her nationalist credentials and fostered national unity by using *guoyu* (the official language of the nation)[6] in her films, plays, and other public presentations. Zhiwei Xiao suggests that "on the whole, few actors and actresses were as politically committed as their screen-writing and film critic counterparts," but this was not the case with Li. Along with male directors and screen-writers, she actively participated in negotiating the meaning of her strong and heroic onscreen image and facilitated the nationalist agendas.[7]

Until recently, Li has escaped the notice of most scholars of Chinese film. Zhang Zhen has highlighted Li's role in *Tiyu huanghou (Queen of Sports)* as the embodiment of the moral lesson of the importance of collective efforts over individual glamour. Zhang argues that the "didactic message about the need to harness the individual body – in particular the female body – for nation building, is not to be missed." Such is also the argument of Sean MacDonald, who notes that Li's naturalistic acting style enabled her to create her own persona, one tied with national aspirations.[8] I view Li's career as crucial in the making of the cinematic trope of the athletic movie star. By merging athletics and beauty, Li and her favourite director, Sun Yu, created the athletic movie star as an important archetype for Chinese film, at a time when competitive sports had become central to Chinese culture. In Chapter 2, I demonstrated how concepts of female physical fitness were frequently reflected in 1930s Chinese magazines. This fascination with sports is characteristic of modern Chinese national identity to the present. Li's performances fused sensuality and melodrama with sports to produce a modern, nationalistic female persona that appealed to the masses while serving the nation-building goals of China's major political parties.[9]

Li's career presents contradictory meanings. This is hardly surprising given the multiple meanings invested in actresses from the very beginning of Chinese cinema. Michael Chang interprets the contradictions and anxiety over the social mobility of movie actresses as an issue of both class and gender in the broad context of "a shifting social structure – the slow decline of former gentry elites and the rise of a professionalized urban middle class."[10] In other words, as social transformations created a rising urban, professional middle class, which included actresses, the declining gentry tried to defend the patriarchal order that underlay their social power. I argue that institutional political powers contributed to the contradictions and anxieties over the rise of film actresses. The sexuality of movie actresses had always been suspect and placed under scrutiny. To counter these suspicions, the first and second generations of movie stars worked hard to appear as chaste and moral women. Since the sexy body of the athletic movie star was not automatically assumed to be clean, Nationalists, Communists, and Li herself had to maintain a public aura of chastity. While patriarchal control made her physically less dangerous and less threatening and her innocent girlish image masked a sexual appeal, the patriotic spirit of a sacrificing woman justified the display of her body.

Promoting Li Lili as the Athletic Movie Star

Li Lili was born in Beijing on 2 June 1915 to Qian Zhuangfei (1896-1935), a doctor who would become an important underground Communist activist, and Zhang Zhenhua, who was also a physician and Communist.[11] She made her film debut at the age of eleven, starring in *Yanshan xiaying (Invisible Swordsman)*, directed and written by her father and featuring her whole family. Since both her parents devoted themselves to clandestine Communist activities, Li grew up adrift, like many actresses from lower-class backgrounds. When the Nationalist Party purged the Communists in 1927, her parents fled Shanghai. She studied Beijing opera for a short time, then left, partly in response to an instructor's harassment. Li joined the singing and dancing troupes of Li Jinhui's (1891-1967) Bright Moon Association (Mingyue she), where she trained and worked for about four years.[12] During that time, the troupe travelled to Singapore. To comply with immigration and residency requirements, the young Qian Zhenzhen took Li's surname and became "Li Lili," but maintained contact with her birth parents. Leo Ou-Fan Lee suggests that dance schools such as Li Jinhui's were viewed as "little more than glorified brothels." Andrew F. Jones, in contrast, describes the Bright Moon Song and Dance Troupe as "imbued with the May Fourth spirit of humanist enlightenment, antifeudalism, and nationalism." As Jones and Zhang Zhen have noted, the Bright Moon Association became one of the most important suppliers of musical materials and talent to the emerging sound film industry.[13] All of the troupe members learned *guoyu* for use in singing parts. Since Li spoke the Beijing dialect, she began to teach *guoyu* soon after she joined the association.[14]

After the Mingxing Studio released China's first full-length sound movie, *Genü Hong Mudan (Sing-song Girl Red Peony)*, starring Hu Die in early 1931, Lianhua's founder and manager, Luo Mingyou (1900-67) proposed a merger between the Bright Moon Song and Dance Troupe and Lianhua Studio. In May of that year, the troupe changed its name to Lianhua Song and Dance Group (Lianhua gewu ban) and became part of the studio. In 1932, the group left the studio, but Wang Renmei (1914-87) and Li Lili remained with Lianhua. Lianhua needed an actress with Li's fluency in *guoyu* to make profitable sound movies that could compete with the likes of *Sing-song Girl Red Peony*. Li's professional training in dance and strong athletic skills were ideal for the construction of an athletic body image connected with tiyu, a modern alternative to the traditional martial arts-type costume represented by *Red Peony.* During the golden years of her career, from 1932 to 1937, Li made thirteen films for Lianhua and established her on- and off-screen image as the athletic movie star.

Lianhua Studio pioneered the athletic type, marking an important shift in the way women were represented in film. Athletic women were radically different from the female characters who typically appeared in films adapted from the "Mandarin Ducks and Butterflies" school *(yuanyang hudie pai),* "scholar and beauty romances" *(caizi jiaren),* or "knight-errant, spirit, and ghost films" *(wuxia shenguai pian),* all of which were popular among petty urbanites *(xiaoshimin)* during the 1920s. The ideal gendered images of the "scholar and beauty romances" were "pale-faced scholarly youth" *(bailian xiaosheng)* and sickly and fragile beauties such as Xishi or Lin Daiyu.[15] In typical fan magazine photographs of the 1920s, a movie actress "struck fragile poses of femininity – eyes turned demurely away and hands delicately drawn inwards."[16] Since male bodies were less morally sensitive than female bodies, Lianhua began promoting athletic screen images with male roles. By the 1930s, more masculine actors, such as the "King of Cinema" Jin Yan (of Korean ethnicity), Gao Zhanfei, and Zheng Junli, had replaced the effeminate-looking pale-faced, scholarly youth actors of the 1920s.[17]

The feminine beauty of 1920s movie stars – elegant, slender, weak, even sickly – continued to enjoy popularity in roles of young, oppressed urban women. For example, Ruan Lingyu in the films *Yecao xianhua (Wild Grass and Idle Flowers), Gudu chunmeng (Glorious Days), Rendao (Humanity), Xin nüxing (New Woman), Shennü (Goddess), Xiao tianshi (Little Angel),* and *San ge modeng nüxing (Three Modern Women)* was "forever holding a wounded smile."[18] With her slim body and elegant facial features, Ruan epitomized this type. The onscreen image also spilled over into reality. Fan magazines stressed the weakness of the real Ruan. In 1933, for example, *Linglong* reported that, while shooting *Muxing zhi guang (Glory of Motherhood),* Ruan fainted one evening due to overwork and a cold.[19]

Although the frail feminine type remained popular, Lianhua's radical May Fourth intellectuals began to endow these weak-bodied, oppressed, tragic female characters with strong wills and a spirit of national consciousness. In so doing, they explored the possibilities of a new female image (the "New Woman") to meet the political needs of the nation. Following a speech by the character Zhou Shuzhen (the embodiment of a real modern woman) on the plight of those in Manchuria under Japanese occupation, the male protagonist (an actor) in *Three Modern Women* defines the "real modern woman" as "independent, rational, and courageous, with the welfare of the masses and national affairs in mind," rather than the type presented in women's fashion magazines. The female protagonist in *New Woman* echoes this sentiment by highlighting the value of work and economic independence for women: "New women ... don't waste away their time dreaming about love and they have self-respect; they are not parasites – instead, they work; new women rise in suffering and awakening." Yet, Ruan's 1935 suicide, an act that appeared to resemble the fate of her cinematic roles, confirmed the fragility of the onscreen images of New Women with sickly bodies.

To represent strong and healthy female citizens, Lianhua Studio and Li Lili created and propagated the athletic movie star. From 1928 to 1936, Sun Yu directed and edited approximately twenty films and built up a new group of physically fit actors and actresses. Films such as *Yu guang qu (Song of Fishermen)* and *Dalu (Big Road),* which were popular in cities and helped legitimize strong, athletic actors, began to dominate the screen.[20] The female protagonists in these two movies, played by Wang Renmei and Li, respectively, represented a "new style" that displayed bare feet, young and healthy bodies, casual dress, and lively personalities. Fan magazines frequently paired the two and described their off-screen images as consistent with their onscreen personae. As Sean MacDonald has pointed out, Li's past experience with the Bright Moon Song and Dance Troupe instilled in her a stage-performance style with direct contact with the audience. Paul Pickowicz has shown how Sun Yu infused his political themes with audience-gratifying melodrama.[21] Thanks to her natural style and fluency in *guoyu*, dancing, and sports, Li was chosen from among the new generation of strong, lively young actresses to serve as a model for the athletic movie star.

This construction of the athletic movie star also enabled Lianhua to circumvent the Nationalist government's desire to reduce film into "ice cream for the eyes," or a cinema with no social commentary. Li's films and other Lianhua productions promoted anti-imperialism and class antagonisms while not urging radical social change. Rather, Li's athletic persona supported the government's hopes for a sturdy female citizenry, and the studio could identify the Nationalists as the primary force against Japanese imperialism. Jubin Hu has pointed out how Lianhua distanced itself from other left-wing studios, which advocated sharp class struggle.[22] I argue that Lianhua and Li created a radical new type of female film character: the sportswoman. The film persona of the sportswoman further popularized athletic competitions and the jianmei body type.

Li's own film persona contrasted with the older style epitomized by Ruan Lingyu, with whom she co-starred in *Xiao wanyi (Little Toys)* in 1933 and *Guo feng (The Nation)* in 1935, two patriotic films. Unlike Ruan, Li had a large round face and a strong athletic body, with arms twice as thick as Ruan's. Whereas Ruan typically played characters with sad, oppressed, and tragic personalities, Li performed roles that were open, lively, a little rough, and mentally healthy. Li's "modern beauty" reinforced her athletic appeal both on- and off-screen. Accordingly, jianmei of the whole body beyond facial features further reinforced athleticism as an essential feature of female beauty. As a result, the 1920s image of vulnerable female beauty became dated. *Jianmei* became a popular term to describe movie stars, and physically strong and athletic looks became expected of actresses.[23]

Although Li had little formal training in cinematic performance beyond her experience with the Bright Moon Song and Dance Troupe, her natural talents facilitated her transition into an athletic movie star. Lianhua designed roles based on her personality and physical appearance. Li's "natural performance" *(bense biaoyan)* was critical to the establishment of her image. After she joined the studio, Sun Yu made six consecutive films with her from 1932 to 1937, three of which were directly related to tiyu and were designed to promote her athletic image. Critics argued that Sun's work with Li created a perfect blend of jianmei and "sweetness and fragrance."[24] Among these films, *Huoshan qingxie (Revenge in the Volcano's Shadow)* took advantage of her dancing skills, *Tiyu huanghou Queen of Sports* demonstrated her ability in modern sports, and *Dao ziran qu (Back to Nature)* incorporated reformed martial arts into her athletic image.[25]

As Li's first movie at Lianhua, *Revenge in the Volcano's Shadow* spoke to contemporary social attitudes. As observed earlier, Zhang Huilan was part of the movement to introduce Western-style dancing into the physical education curriculum of modern Chinese schools. When tiyu was introduced in the early twentieth century, non-competitive and "feminine" dancing served as the first step in liberating and freeing women's bodies from these traditional restrictions.[26] Li received professional dance training while she was with the Bright Moon Association. The formal training in the association was gendered: boys were trained mainly as musicians, girls as dancers and singers. Li was listed in newspapers as one of the "Four Holy Queens" *(Sida Tianwang)* of the association for her dancing skills.[27]

In *Revenge in the Volcano's Shadow*, Li plays a dancing girl in a tropical overseas club, which appears to be in Southeast Asia – an essential site for constructing the "Greater China." The indigenous tropical women are portrayed in the popular imagination of Republican China to be fit and strong.

Her powerful dancing is the female counterpart to a masculine boxing match between two bare-chested men that is offered as entertainment for sailors as they ate and drank. When Li appears on the stairs next to the stage on which the boxers are fighting, everyone, including the two boxers, stops and stares at her, stunned. She removes her shoes and dances, moving her hips quickly with arms held high above her head, jumping back and forth, kicking her legs high. She is wearing a pair of high-cut shorts and her strong, bare legs are the focus of the camera. This is true when she is dancing as well as when she pulls aside her striped skirt to salute the audience, wipes her legs in her upstairs bedroom, or pulls back her fur coat to walk. In 1932, *Linglong* reviewed the three major domestic film studios, criticizing Mingxing's "old medieval atmosphere" and Tianyi's "wandering and hesitating." But because of *Revenge in the Volcano's Shadow, Humanity,* and *Xu Gudu chunmeng (Continuing for the Glorious Days),* Lianhua was praised for "following the steps of the time from both artistic and ideological perspectives."[28]

Li, aware of the studio's expectations, worked to improve her modern athletic skills. In her memoir, she recalled that "besides dancing and singing, we had to learn other skills such as swimming, horseback riding, and running so that we could play more roles." While Li worked at the Lianhua Studio, she was a full-time student in the English Department at Southern Ocean Business School (Nanyang gaodeng shangye zhuanke xuexiao, or "Nangao" for short), where she honed her athletic skills and developed into a real athlete. Every morning, carrying her school bag and tennis racket, Li rode her bicycle from Xu jiahui (Zikawei) down Shanzhong Road to the school. Bicycling was a mode of transportation and enhanced her image as the athletic movie star. She participated in the school's athletic competitions and took first place in the 50-metre dash at a track meet. While few other actresses could swim, Li swam regularly at a pool in the Hongkou District and displayed her diving skills at the opening ceremony of the Shanghai Swimming Pool. Li was also a member of Nangao's women's basketball team, which was famous in Shanghai. In a publication dedicated to the Fifth National Games in 1933, a photograph shows Li being coached in running by male track athlete Wang Jingxi.[29]

Images in fan magazines confirmed Li's status as a genuine athlete with professional skills. Photographs from *Linglong* show her posing, in appropriate sports attire, with her school basketball team or alone on a running track.[30] It was fashionable for movie stars to be associated with sports in order to promote their jianmei images. While fan magazines reported other "actresses visiting sports games," only Li was respected and admired as an athlete. In a *Linglong* movie column, among the movie stars who visited the Second Shanghai Middle School Games in 1933, Li Jinhui's daughter, Li Minghui, who had had similar singing and dancing experience before entering the cinema, was shown in a fancy Western-style long coat as a male fan gawked at her. On the same page, Li Lili was shown crouching along with female athletes from Guanghua Middle School, wearing similar athletic garb.[31]

The 1934 film *Queen of Sports* showcased Li's athletic skills and firmly established her onscreen image as an athletic movie star. Sun Yu highlighted her sprinting, a track event that required speed and power. Track and field, a masculine domain in the West,[32] had become, as demonstrated in Chapter 4, a legitimate exercise for women in the context of the national crisis. As war loomed, China's urgent need for physically strong citizens justified the cinematic representation of a competitive and powerful female body. Sun Yu began shooting this film on 26 November 1933, right after Qian Xingsu replaced Sun Guiyun as the track queen in the Fifth National Games. In a contemporary interview, Sun articulated a vision for the film that stressed its realistic portrayal of tiyu, something that was important to counter the image of China as a "sick man," and to encourage exercise that would contribute to national development. Sun added that "strengthening the body will not necessarily save the nation, but the citizens who are to save the nation must have strong bodies."[33] At the same time, Li's dancing in *Revenge in the Volcano's Shadow*, her sex appeal, and other consciously constructed off-screen images assured the audience of her femininity. In addition to sports, Li played the piano, a skill that was a modern version of one of the four essential traditional skills for Chinese ladies – playing a musical instrument (the other three were chess, calligraphy, and painting). After Nangao was disbanded by the authorities in 1935, Li transferred to the National Music School (Guoli yinzhuan) to study piano. In a photograph captioned (piano rhythm and sadness) "*Qinyun xinyuan*" published by *Linglong*,[34] Li is seen resting her left arm on the piano frame, her head on that arm, with her face toward the piano keys. Rather than the usual innocent, happy, and lively girl, Li poses here as a quiet lady in a reflective mood. A gossip column reported that "since Li loved to play piano, especially late at night, she was always scolded by neighbours." As such, ignoring accusations that she was too masculine, Sun Yu chose to depict her in the sprint rather than more feminine sports such as tennis and swimming, despite the unprecedented popularity gained by Yang Xiuqiong at the Fifth National Games.[35]

In *Queen of Sports*, images of Li crouching at the starting line and running among a group of strong and tough girls, played by students from Lu Lihua's Private Liangjiang Women's Tiyu Normal School in Shanghai, are repeated numerous times.[36] The image of her powerful athletic body, accentuated by tight shorts and a short-sleeved shirt, fuelled the popularity and influence of the movie. Similar types of images of women athletes were popular among college and middle-school students and can be found in a variety of publications, such as leftist cartoon magazines, including *Shidai manhua (Modern Sketch/Epoch Cartoons).*[37] The popular *Liangyou huabao (Young Companion Pictorial)* featured such an image of Li taken by the noted photographer Lang Jingshan and proclaimed that "the ultimate goal of tiyu" is to cultivate healthy citizens who could "contribute to the greatest work for the happiness of mankind" (see Figure 37).[38]

Since women represented the immutable "national essence" amid the wartime disorder, women's track and field became defined as local and indigenous at the same time. Highlighting the contrast between the country roots of Li Lili's lively character, Lin Ying, and the stiff foreign manners of her Western-educated suitor, Mr. Gao, in *Queen of Sports*, American-trained director Sun Yu took pains to project the origin of the track queen as running and jumping in the open country field. The Westernized modern treaty port of Shanghai, portrayed as exotic and alienating, only reshaped and disciplined her natural and indigenous physical capacity. Consistent with the spirit of the film, nationalists and media strove to portray track and field as indigenous sport by highlighting the humble roots of the real-life track queens, as discussed in Chapter 4.

The Chinese media had already done some early work to create a celebrity network among the track and field athletes. For example, the American Fox Company made film news at the Second Shanghai Middle School Games when its Western and Chinese journalists recorded Chen Baixue, the Liangjiang basketball player, in shot put gestures.[39] *Queen of Sports* crystallized the stardom of the track queen. By interweaving images of track stars with fashion, the film further popularized the sport among the public. There were moments of unreality, however. Lang Jingshan filmed actresses Wu Guiying and Hu Ping wearing high-heeled sandals and formal *qipao* dresses, crouching on the lawn imitating the start of a dash. There was no sense of irony in these mass-appeal photographs carried in *Young Companion Pictorial.*[40]

Other crossovers between athletic competitions and Li's film persona appeared. *Linglong* published a special issue on swimming that included an article called "The Sweet Sister and the Mermaid," making a direct correlation between Li Lili and Yang Xiuqiong. Li's pose of swimming in water occupies the front page of the issue. A popular musical booklet with music and lyrics of the most popular songs of the day was named after Sun Yu's film: *Tiyu huanghou: Modeng mingge xuan (Queen of Sports: Selections of Modern Popular Songs)*. On its cover was a drawing of a crowned, fit woman with muscular legs in tight gym shorts and T-shirt. A recently composed song

運動的目標 標的動運

。成是的經爲全的運都每的競民—我應我康義他飛演地悲，膝技
是一工賞全的：動應——奪，選們體們健是們面在是，失利的
一把作眾人身是的謀個個場耶健憲育不。在體前廣演他妝者廣在標決終是體用滋
而金，最瓶體在最平運。中怕全必是需　身育，大員們者不妝運。不的體育是標
穗戈而帶的，有轉配動　最他的的后悲　體的告的，同不必上動　是目育，很的
旗，不大幸來健日：員　末是國是，什　的意訴民粉樣必喜，競　鎬的最但恁年

37   "Li Lili appearing in *Queen of Sports.*" The caption reads: "The Goal of Tiyu: competition supports tiyu, but the ultimate goal of tiyu is definitely not competition. In athletic competition, the winners do not have to be overjoyous, and the losers do not have to cry, because they are both actors who perform in front of the masses to show that physical health is the true meaning of tiyu. We do not need a so-called 'queen of sports.' What we need are healthy citizens, even though they may finish last in athletic competitions. Every athlete should firmly remember: the ultimate goal of tiyu is to cultivate healthy bodies, in order to contribute to the greatest work for the happiness of mankind, not a gold spear or a silk banner."
Source: Liangyou huabao 82 (November 1933): 11.

called "Queen of Sports" (not from the movie), which called on women to pursue tiyu, including practising martial arts for their military significance, occupied the first page of the booklet. Similarly, Pathé Records *(Baidai changpian)* used the title "Queen of Sports" and an image of muscle-legged Li holding a 78-rpm record in a shot put pose to promote her songs. By making "Queen of Sports" a coveted title and making women's sports central to its narrative, the film sent the message that competitive sports were a legitimate part of womanhood.[41]

The box office success of Li's films is difficult to determine. Laikwan Pang's valuable compilation of newspaper advertisements mentions *Back to Nature* but not the others. *Back to Nature* was a decent hit, playing for twenty-eight days, a figure above average on Pang's list but far below the eighty-four-day run of *The Song of Fishermen*, which played in an air-conditioned theatre in the torrid Shanghai summer of 1934. Pang argues that the petty urbanite audience for Chinese films ranged from bored businessmen, couples on dates, and idle women tired of stage performances to the lower classes, who could not afford any other kind of entertainment. The breadth in social class of such cinema-goers suggests that Li's personification of the Chinese jianmei beauty and the athletic film star had a wide reception. Combined with the print media, her persona influenced many Chinese female urbanites and their male companions. Moreover, as Zhang Yingjin points out, Chinese films did far better than Hollywood products in the interior of China, where Li's message complemented the tiyu message of the educational system.[42]

As an athletic movie star, Li also transformed traditional cinematic physicality. Her image incorporated traditional martial arts, which were an essential part of tiyu, although from the perspective of a nation obsessed with promoting a modern, scientific, and healthy spirit, martial arts were tainted by their connections with folk beliefs and local religions. The May Fourth Movement's enthusiasm for modern scientism continued to shape nationalist ideological control during the 1930s, and the Nationalist Party launched an anti-superstition movement, whose targets included folk beliefs and religions. At the end of the 1920s, the National Film Censorship Committee ordered the country's studios and movie theatres to popularize films pertaining to "science, patriotism, and adventure"; at the same time, the government gradually banned "knight-errant, spirit, and ghost films."[43] The plots in the latter category were traditional stories associated with folklore and popular beliefs, and martial arts masters with magical *gongfu* (power) served as their heroes. Besides the fact that the close connection between the display of martial arts skills and superstitions made the Nationalist government leery of martial arts, the traditional dress and body codes in those movies also widened the gap between martial arts and modernity. Although Mingxing's *Huo shao Honglian si (Burning the Red Lily Temple)* achieved unprecedented popularity for its display of masterful martial arts skills, it fell into the "knight-errant, spirit, and ghost films" classification and was criticized by Nationalist officials for its folk tale plot and traditional clothing. Luo Mingyou was determined to "revive Chinese film by getting rid of superstitious ghost movies as well as violent knight-errant ones."[44]

Following *Queen of Sports, Back to Nature* continued the construction of Li as an athletic movie star. Her image in this film was that of an athlete scantily clad in animal skins and carrying a quiver of arrows, set against a background of beautiful mountains and rivers. By replacing traditional clothing with a barely covered athletic body, and featuring a modern class-struggle plot tied to nature, *Back to Nature* made martial arts modern and integrated their power and strength with modern dancing and sports to forge the image of the athletic movie star.

Serving Contending Versions of the Nation

Li's performances merged conventional film genre with ideology, although the politics were not always clear. In reality, relationships among the various forces were characterized by conflict intertwined with cooperation; struggles in the field of cinema among the various political and intellectual forces and Li herself were not clear-cut. Her movies did not support one party over another, but each party manoeuvred for as much space as possible in the shared project. Luo Mingyou was a cagy, politically adept yet committed filmmaker with great ambitions to promote Chinese filmmaking and distribution. He stated that the studio's mission was "to promote education and bring Lianhua's films to the interior of China ... make more newsreels, and resist the cultural and economic invasion of foreign countries; champion the virtues embedded in our national culture and show the right way to our people." Luo's good intentions were insufficient for some intellectuals, who called for artistic films dealing with the life of the poor, especially peasants and workers.[45] The growing patriotic feelings among the Chinese public as a result of Japanese aggression in Manchuria opened the film world to leftist intellectuals. During the 1930s, the three major studios in Shanghai – Lianhua, Mingxing, and Yihua – were all under the influence of the Communist Party.[46] In their screenplays, the Communist/leftist screenwriters subtly navigated between their political ideology and the demands of the commercial cinema, avoiding forceful and explicitly radical messages.

Communist notions such as "urban proletariat, worker strikes, theories of socialism and revolutionary literature, above all, the peasantry and its revolutionary potential" were generally absent from mainstream print media.[47] While government censors knew that the small numbers of studios made surveillance easier, they also considered the cinema to be a more powerful and influential medium than print. By working around these limitations, cinema offered a window into the metropolitan world that the Communists could use to construct and disseminate their visions. In *Revenge in the Volcano's Shadow, Queen of Sports,* and *Back to Nature,* class consciousness and class struggle are important aspects of the image of the athletic movie star. As will be shown below, the power dynamics centred on class backgrounds in *Back to Nature,* the egalitarian "true tiyu spirit" in *Queen of Sports,* and the volcanic revolution of the oppressed class in *Revenge in the Volcano's Shadow.* These factors support the argument that the image of the athletic movie star was based on class egalitarianism and heroic class struggle. In *Queen of Sports,* the male coach and the director of the school persuade Li's character to replace one of her teammates, who had died of a heart attack due to ignorance of "the true tiyu spirit" and excessive obsession about the tournament, rather than concentrating on the common, public good. Eventually she agrees, but because she has the true tiyu spirit, she yields first place to her rival and gives up the title: "Queen? All those who want to be queen, and everyone who roots for the queen, we will burn them some day. All their unreasonable, elitist, individualist competitiveness will be abandoned in the future. For the 'true tiyu spirit,' we can only struggle and go forward." These typical Communist slogans struck the same chords as the words of a well-known Communist song ("Unity Is Power") *("Tuanjie jiushi liliang")* about the end of unjust systems and the struggle toward a new egalitarian Chinese nation. While all of these arguments were political, they also retained the heightened moral claims, extravagant representation, and rhetorical excess of melodrama. Paul Pickowicz contends that such a mixture allowed the audience of petty urbanites to make sense of the changing political settings within messages about good and evil that played out just below the surface of their daily lives.[48]

"Anti-feudal" class struggle is explicit in *Revenge in the Volcano's Shadow,* the story of a young farmer named Song Ke (played by Zheng Junli), who, after years of drifting and suffering, seeks revenge against a local rich and powerful man who killed his family and drove him from his idyllic and peaceful village. In Southeast Asia, Song Ke meets a dancing girl, played by Li, who falls in love with him and stands by him when he eventually kills his foe after a struggle at the foot of a volcano. The film ends with the young man shouting, "Explode! Volcano, burn! Get rid of another devil amidst humans." In Communist vocabulary, "devil" stands for the oppressing class and "volcano" for the strength of the oppressed masses. Li was proud of these roles in her late years.

Treating cinema exclusively as a cultural form to represent cosmopolitanism, Zhang Zhen interprets films with countryside themes as being about "how country girls and boys transform into sophisticated urban subjects." Leo Ou-Fan Lee points out that the country/city narrative structure created by the leftist screenwriters was to construct contrasting worlds of good and evil.[49] I argue that the idealized rural figures subtly conveyed this binary in other contexts as well as in Communist ideology. The clothing, face, and body in the roles played by Li – Zhu'er in *Small Toys*, Moli in *Big Road*, Yu'er in *Langshan diexue ji (Bloodshed on Wolf Mountain)*, and Lingling in *Tianming (Daybreak)*[50] – defined the standard of the natural physical beauty of working-class women based on their youth and physical fitness. Such characters have healthy and bright faces and thick, dark hair, and display bare and strong athletic limbs accentuated by simple, unstylish, and worn clothes. They appear in various styles of shorts and short-sleeved shirts, shirts with the sleeves carelessly rolled all the way up to expose their arms, or homemade but well-fitting pants and shirts.[51] The beauty of these working-class female characters lies in their hardworking, rough, aggressive, brave, and resourceful qualities. For example, in the film *Big Road*, Moli's courage, wit, and calmness serve her well as she rescues the imprisoned road construction worker Jinge (played by Jin Yan) from a landlord. A strong body and determined mind defined the ideal female citizenry for the coming Communist nation.

The Communist ideology of class struggle was in direct conflict with the Nationalist nation-building agenda. At the Fourth Plenum of the Second Central Executive Committee, Chiang Kai-shek proposed replacing class struggle ideology with the spirit of mutual help and cooperation.[52] The National Film Censorship Committee moved to ban class struggle movies and to control cinematic vocabulary and expression. For example, censors asked filmmakers to change typical Communist terms such as "continuously struggle" *(jixu fendou)* to the more neutral "continuously strive" *(jixu nuli)*, and "with the support of the masses" to "protect the public interest."[53] In February 1934, the "League for Removing Communism from Chinese Youth" sent a second lengthy letter to newspapers. The following quotation gives us a sense of the league's intentions:

> Studios must not make films that advocate class struggle and communism, harm harmony, and damage the nation. Especially, do not confuse class-theme films with nationalist films. For the purpose of social education, try to avoid

showing the sick and dark side of the society ... Scenes that portray bonfires [symbolizing class struggle], physical fighting, national survival, or the roaring waves of the China Sea must be cut ... Cinemas showing Communist films and newspapers carrying Communist film reviews will be banned.[54]

The Nationalists expected films to contribute to the improvement of China's international image and to the promotion of patriotism among the citizenry.

Such attitudes affected the Nationalist response to contemporary Hollywood films. During the 1920s and 1930s, foreign films, especially Hollywood movies, dominated China's film market. Over 90 percent of the films shown were of foreign origin, and Chinese films never reached more than 15 percent of market share in any one year.[55] Chinese characters in many foreign films appeared physically weak and morally corrupt. Chinese men were usually depicted as ugly opium smokers, gamblers, servants, and thieves, with tiny physiques and queues hanging down their backs. Women were exotically dressed servants or prostitutes. Fighting such negative images in "films insulting to Chinese/China" *(ru Hua pian)* became the central task in the Nationalist agenda and the public responded excitedly. Students from Nanjing created the Organization to Forever Resist Films Insulting to China, in order to discourage theatres from showing them and to do academic research on their social background.[56] Fan magazines became actively involved in the campaign. *Linglong* argued that Hollywood "made up absurd and distorted stories to insult the Chinese" because "Westerners forever view the Orient as mysterious and inferior." Evoking an imagined racial hierarchy, the author was anxious that the "treacherous propaganda" in *Roar of the Dragon* made by RKO would hurt the international status of the Chinese nation, because "it almost treats Chinese like the barbarian African natives." The magazine was outraged with the misrepresentation of Chinese womanhood by a Japanese actress in the American film *The Bitter Tea of General Yen.*[57]

The Nationalist government banned the 1925 film *Thief of Bagdad* because it was a "ghost story."[58] Even more upsetting to the Nationalists was the 1932 motion picture *Shanghai Express,* which included the remark that "time and life have no value in China." Both films emphasized the Chinese American actress Anna May Wong's exotic, sensual body, a factor the Nationalists viewed as a sign of weakness. Wong's Oriental, weak, and sexually available image, so popular internationally, represented China poorly in the Nationalist and Communist views, a perception that became especially troubling after the Japanese invasion. During the war, Japanese studios promoted Li Xianglan

(Yamaguchi Yoshiko, Ri Koran), a Japanese actress who had been born and brought up in Manchuria, as Chinese. Her roles depicted similarly weak and sexually available Chinese women controlled by powerful Japanese men.[59]

Most offensive of all foreign films, however, was MGM's *The Good Earth*, based on Pearl Buck's award-winning novel. *Linglong* charged that the film "distorted the rural economic situation of our nation ... by hiring hooligans to wear strange clothing, speak weird English, and perform all kinds of unbearable scenes." While most "films insulting to China" were shot abroad, "now the treacherous foreigners came to our land to shoot them."[60] After Paramount was kicked out of China due to controversies over the film *Shanghai Express* and regained access to the market only through diplomatic negotiation, a concerned MGM consulted the Nationalist government and gained official permission to shoot *The Good Earth* in China.[61] The government ultimately approved the film, but condemned it for its depictions of Chinese weakness. "Weak nations have no diplomacy, and Chinese foreign affairs authorities can do nothing. Can we just sit by and watch this dangerous behaviour [by MGM]?" Mingxing Studio decided to shoot the same movie with a different name, *Dadi (The Grand Earth)*, to counter the damage caused by MGM's film, which was translated into Chinese as *Fudi (The Lucky Earth)*.[62] Doubtless, the performances of male lead Paul Muni and female start Luise Rainer, who appeared in "yellow face" (Western actors imitating Asians), bothered the Nationalists.

Much as the film irritated Chinese nationalists, the roles played by Anna May Wong caused the most resentment. As her biographer tells it: "Her popularity was so widespread that she frequently graced the pages of movie magazines in America, Europe, Australia, South America, and the Far East, especially China and Japan." Her international reputation and popularity raised the perception globally that Wong was the image of Chinese women, whereas both Nationalists and Communists viewed her as the product of American Orientalism (as we would now put it) and as the pawn of powerful men representing Western nations. They were ashamed and angry that her exotic and sexually promiscuous body appeared to represent the Orient, especially Chinese women. Her roles as servants or prostitutes and her exotic and sexy outfits (sometimes based on traditional Chinese costumes) established her image of an untrustworthy, dangerous Oriental sexual object. At the same time, Wong's international fame and extraordinary fashion sensibility made her alluring to Chinese female petty urbanites. Judging by the large crowds who thronged to see her and the open arms of the Chinese diplomatic elite who hosted her at numerous dinner parties when she visited China in 1936, Wong overcame political criticism of her roles.[63]

To counter Hollywood's stereotypical and offensive casting, the Nationalists used the athletic movie star Li's patriotic, clean, and athletic body and mind to represent the female citizens of the Chinese nation. Through some powerful figures on the board of trustees of Lianhua Studio, the Nationalist government maintained an effective influence on her image. Lianhua cooperated with the Nationalists in their nation-building agenda, which contrasted with Mingxing Studio's refusal, on more than one occasion, to serve the Nanjing government.[64] More importantly, Lianhua filmmakers and Li herself shared the Nationalists' dissatisfaction with the image of China in foreign films, as well as a patriotic response to the Japanese invasion.[65]

Playing roles depicting middle-class women in the context of the rise of Japanese imperialism in China and heroines who oppose superstition in the films *Gui (Ghost)* and *Bloodshed on Wolf Mountain,* the athletic movie star contributed to the promotion of a physically fit female citizenry armed with modern national culture and patriotic ideas for nation building. The context of *Queen of Sports* is China's resistance against the Japanese invasion. In the scene depicting a preparatory meet for the Far Eastern Games, the teams from each province march before the audience. When the banners of the three provinces of Manchuria, under Japanese occupation since 1931, appear, the audience in the film rises in anger and sadness. The impetus for the coach, Mr. Yun, to devote himself to training female athletes in a women's tiyu school is "to save the nation through tiyu." When the director of the school tries to persuade Li's character, Lin Ying, to participate in a track race, he says, "You need to think about the glory of the whole school, the whole city, and the whole nation, which all rest on your participation." The message is that the glory of the nation depends on a woman's strong athletic body and her willingness to struggle for that glory. Lin Ying sports permed, bobbed hair and wears a long scarf and tightly fitting *qipao,* indicating a woman who conforms to patriotic ideas while sporting modern hair styles. The narrative allows her to combine patriotism and personal style.

Li Lili showed her patriotism during the grave national crisis. After Japanese forces attacked Shanghai in August 1937, she resigned from the Lianhua Studio to help injured soldiers in the hospitals of Shanghai's Zhabei District. Soon she joined the newly established China Studio, run by Zhang Zhizhong, the Nationalist general who supervised the Cultural Department of the Nationalist Military Committee. The Communist cinema bureau, under the leadership of Guo Moruo, was incorporated into the China Studio. Luo Jingyu (1911-70), whom Li would marry in late 1937, was appointed as vice president in charge of cinema. In 1938, the studio relocated to Chongqing. Poshek Fu sees the choices made by film personnel during the war mainly in terms of economic survival; however, Li endured financial and material difficulties while with the China Studio and was motivated by deep political commitment. As early as 1936, during Lianhua's dispute about whether, in the face of financial woes, to turn "left" or "right," Li accepted a lower salary to support the studio's production of leftist films. *China at War*, a magazine designed for American supporters of China during the Second World War, pointed out that since the top salary for actors at China Studio was about 300 yuan a month, "it requires fortitude and courage to do art work at such low pay and under most trying conditions." The journal praised Li as "the number one actress" of the studio and "a versatile, vivacious daughter of modern China who gave up a comfortable home in Shanghai and considerably higher pay to work in the capital city."[66]

The wartime Anti-Japanese United Front of Communists and Nationalists made sure that the athletic movie star would play patriotic and strong-minded heroines in "national defence films" *(guofang dianying)* made by China Studio. In 1936, she starred in *Bloodshed on Wolf Mountain*, often seen as the first national defence film. After her performance in *Rexue zhonghun (The Patriotic Family)*, made in Wuhan in 1938, the newly formed Dadi Studio called her to Hong Kong to appear in *Gudao tiantang (Paradise on the Isolated Island)*.[67] She later went to Inner Mongolia to star in *Saishang fengyun (Storm on the Border)*. In 1944 and 1945, Li starred in two other films with resistance themes: *Qi zhuang shanhe (To Die a Heroic Death)* and *Xue jian yinghua (Blood on the Cherry Blossoms)*.

The wolves in *Bloodshed on Wolf Mountain* evidently refer to the Japanese. Although the character Yu'er is a country girl, her class background is not emphasized. Echoing the Nationalist anti-superstition movement and anti-Japanese propaganda, the disagreement among the villagers over whether or not to fight the wolf (the Japanese enemy) centres on religious belief intertwined with gender dynamics rather than any class struggle between the rich landlord and poor farmers. The character Mr. Zhao Er urges the villagers to put Daoist divine paper on their doors and draw white circles to repel the wolves, who are protected by the mountain spirit, without offending them. As the wolves become more and more aggressive, however, the villagers unite to fight them under the leadership of Yu'er, a tough, determined, and courageous girl whom the fan magazines viewed as representing the nation's millions of compatriots.[68] Side by side with the advertisement in a fan magazine that promoted Li's new patriotic film, an article denounced Anna May Wong's half-brother for defending her in appearance in "films insulting to China." He had argued that if Wong had not taken the parts, Hollywood would have hired a Japanese or Korean. The article extended its harsh criticism to the brother and went so far as to portray his statement as that of a traitor *(hanjian)* who claimed, "If I did not sell out the country, others would." Wong herself was warned to stop selling out the country or her soul for dollars.[69]

As the territories controlled by the Nationalists and Communists shrank during the war, the heroic female warriors played by the athletic movie star were deployed to solidify the political and cultural boundaries of the threatened Chinese nation. Japanese scholars had argued that close racial ties between Japanese and Mongolians justified Japan's territorial expansion into Inner Asia and North China. In *Storm on the Border,* the Mongolian girl Jinhua, played by Li with Mongolian braids and tiara, singing Mongolian songs and dancing Mongolian dances, showed the nationalist efforts to incorporate minorities in the construction of the national body politic. The roughness of the strong nomadic girl with a rosy face, galloping on a big white horse, added dramatically to the image of patriotic strong women representing Nationalist China. This heroic gesture and style served as the genealogical root of the "iron girl" image of the Maoist era.

Li's career coincided with a revolution in film technology that had major implications for national language. Her promotion as an athletic movie star occurred during the transition from silent to sound movies, when modern cinema became an essential tool in popularizing *guoyu* and building a new national culture. Li's fluency in guoyu and her experience in the movement to promote it as the national language legitimized her role as an athletic movie star representing a united, strong nation. Whereas guoyu was identified with the Chinese nation-state, dialects represented not only regional autonomy, especially in Guangdong and Guangxi, but also a competing transnational Chinese identity in Southeast Asia and Chinatowns in North America.[70]

In 1931, the National Film Censorship Center ruled that guoyu be the only spoken language in films, and banned dialects. It ordered that the newly developed phonetic symbol chart should be displayed at the beginning of each film, with the characters in subtitles marked with standard pronunciation. From 1936 to 1937, the National Central Film Review Commission denounced Cantonese films as "superstitious," "frivolous," and "feudal," and banned them repeatedly. As the Nationalist government needed to shift its energy and attention to the more urgent task of resisting Japanese aggression and came under pressure to compromise with the Pan-Cantonese community in order to recruit support for the resistance, it granted a three-year transition period for the shift from Cantonese to guoyu films, on the condition that the studios affected would pay for a Film Review Bureau in Guangzhou to review dialect films.[71]

From late 1937 to 1940, Cantonese films were made in Hong Kong and their market in Chinese communities in Southeast Asia and Chinatowns in North America grew. Poshek Fu argues these films "became a site in which a Hong Kong identity was projected and contested."[72] In *Paradise on the Isolated Island,* the athletic movie star image was invoked to insert an anti-colonial state-building discourse and ensure the Chineseness of Hong Kong. Li had established her stardom among the Chinese diaspora in Southeast Asia in the earlier guoyu movements. This film was intended to spread the centralizing nationalism among the pan-Chinese population and counter the obstacles caused by the "vulgar," "frivolous," and "treasonable" Cantonese films.

In occupied Shanghai, Cantonese film actress Chen Yunshang and later Li Lihua, with robust physiques and athletic charms, rose to stardom. After Xinhua Studio's costume drama *Mulan congjun (Mulan Joins the Army)* became a hit in 1939, Chen's athletic body competed against Li Lili's as a patriotic icon. Leftist intellectuals in Chongqing highlighted Xinhua's association with the collaborationist Wang Jingwei regime and *Mulan Joins the Army* of being "treasonous." The movie was burned by a mob in Chongqing in early 1940 and Chen's jianmei body was stigmatized. Consequently, Li's warrior images in the national defence films stood unambiguously for the centralizing nationalism of the legitimate Nationalist state.[73]

Making the Sexy Athletic Body Chaste and Moral

How could Li Lili's sexy and bare athletic body be made chaste, moral, and controlled in order to serve lofty nationalist goals? Even more than for their male counterparts, actresses' bodies defined their role. Their physicality and visibility made them morally dangerous, and were often associated with prostitution. Movie actresses in the 1920s were viewed as little more than prostitutes and dancing girls in disguise. Until then, only the bodies of such women had been shown in public. Electing a cinematic queen was likened to the pleasure quarter's election of the "queen of the flowers" *(huakui).* According to Michael Chang, this association of actresses with prostitution in the 1920s served to maintain boundaries of gender and class. Actresses' photographs never appeared alongside those of "genteel ladies of high society, writers, painters, socialites [*dajia guixiu* or *minggui*], the educated, and the wealthy."[74]

Leo Ou-Fan Lee observes that the "fashionable femininity" exhibited by Chinese movie stars in long Chinese gowns with bare arms does not convey the same strident sexuality and body fetishism of the Hollywood stars with "the face glamorously made up, a half-revealed torso, and most frequently a

38 A sexy scene performed by "athletic movie star" Li Lili and "King of Cinema" Jin Yan in *Back to Nature.*
Source: Shidai manhua 33 (20 January 1937).

pair of exposed legs." Lee interprets the difference in terms of cultural distinction in "aesthetics of the feminine" and degrees of "high capitalism" represented by commercialized female bodies;[75] however, the new generation of jianmei Chinese film stars represented by Li exhibited a similar skin-revealing sensuality. Li's typical costume as an athletic movie star – short-sleeved shirt and high-cut shorts showing most of her thighs – was still controversial and sometimes considered scandalous. For example, in *Back to Nature*, she wears a bikini-style costume made of sexy leopard skin. The image of Li sitting near the roaring ocean leaning back on her hands, with the male character (played by Jin Yan) in a swimsuit standing in front of her, the two staring into each other's eyes, was particularly suggestive. *Modern Sketch* features a photograph showing the bare-skinned Jin tickling the toe of Li in her typical athletic movie star outfit in the wild nature. Its caption ridicules the film for simply imitating the popular Hollywood film *King Kong* to make easy money by selling sex in the name of "going back to nature" (see Figure 38).[76]

When performed in urban settings such as ballrooms or nightclubs, the innocent athletic activity of dancing is transformed into sexually charged pleasure. *Gewu ban (Song and Dance Troupe)* shows the filmmaker's awareness of the sexual exposure of athletic dress in a dance club setting, although the ostensible theme of the film is to criticize such exposure and defend the dignity of art. In the film, Li leads a group of girl dancers in high-cut shorts and sleeveless shirts, kicking their legs high, as male onlookers use magnifying glasses to gaze at them. Next to them are advertisements on which appear words such as "delicious," "mysterious," and "sensual." In *Revenge in the Volcano's Shadow,* Li plays a barefoot cabaret performer adorned with heavy makeup and wearing an exotic hula skirt and fur coat. She shows off her strong legs by performing an erotic dance and flirts with the male patrons.[77]

Some critics have claimed that, as one of the first popular film stars to expose most of her body, Li Lili's appeal was sensual. She has been dubbed the Chinese Mae West. Zhang Zhen and Paul Pickowicz note the powerful sexuality displayed by the onscreen image of the athletic movie star, but offer more culturally inflected interpretations. Zhang observes that Li's performance in a grass (hula) skirt and bare feet in *Revenge in the Volcano's Shadow* echoes similar performances by Marlene Dietrich in *The Blue Angel* (1930) and *Dishonored* (1931), and marks Li as the femme fatale type of Modern Girl. Pickowicz refers to scenes from *Queen of Sports,* including Li climbing a "phallus-like smokestack as the breeze whips her skirt to and fro" and female student-athletes in tight shorts and revealing T-shirts gazing reverently at their handsome male teacher, to suggest that the wholesome, frisky, and spontaneously sexual athletic movie star image developed not from dance hall heroines but from the chaste athletes promoted by the YWCA. I argue that the athletic movie star image was multifaceted and complex, at once sexual, cultural, and political.[78]

As Michael Chang suggests, public discourse on movie actresses was a function of power and discipline through moral scrutiny. Prominent and independent women such as Hu Die and Ruan Lingyu could be especially threatening during uncertain times. Li's physically strong and fit image made her scarcely clad body even more threatening. Sun Yu's new style of film is a tribute to chaste yet lively womanhood. On one level, the film evokes a powerful sexuality, and cultural officials associated with both the Communists and Nationalists took steps to control the threatening and sexual aspect of the athletic movie star by making her body appear clean and chaste. On another level, her sexual appeal was maintained and exploited to expand its influence among the masses.

Nationalist roles in early-twentieth-century China allowed women to establish a more egalitarian relationship to the state than in many other countries. Still, the contradictions between feminism and nationalism were shown by the patriarchal power relations within the Communist Party and by the

Nationalist Party's retreat to traditional patriarchal gender values and its prosecution of female Communists after 1927. The Nationalist government perpetuated suspicious attitudes toward the power of film to morally and sexually corrupt its female citizens. The display of women's bodies and sexual intimacy were attacked as "obscene," "unchaste," and "harmful to public morality" *(you shang fenghua)*. As early as 1929, the Shanghai municipal government decreed that kissing scenes be kept to less than twenty frames, or just over a second, of film in length, and prohibited showing of the unclothed human body from the breasts to above the thighs. The Communists shared the Nationalists' paternalistic attitude and looked to film to maintain traditional values of chastity and gender norms. The patriarchal forces sought to desexualize the athletic movie star image, thus allowing it to serve lofty nationalist rhetoric.[79]

In the United States, male coaches were viewed as morally dangerous for sexually exploiting female athletes and prescribing programs that were too masculine.[80] In contrast, during China's national crisis, male figures were employed to tame and desexualize the competitive bodies of female athletes, to make them respectable and channel them to the nationalist discourse, despite Zhang Huilan's insistence that male teachers should be excluded from women's tiyu. Consistent with the use of male coaches for noted female athletes in real life, in Li's films an authoritative and "correct" male mentor often serves to keep the sensuality of her body under patriarchal constraint. In *Queen of Sports,* the coach, Mr. Yun, with his square and handsome face, tall and strong body, and silent but authoritative personality, is the "sports expert" *(tiyu jia)* who guides the "queen." After Mr. Yun criticizes Li for not being serious and solemnly instructs her to "work harder and talk less," she repeats his exact words twice sheepishly and with assurance: "Mr. Yun, as long as you teach me and instruct me, I will listen to everything you say and will be obedient." The serious, authoritative, and "correct" male role in these films is sometimes transformed from a director to a protector of the lively and naughty young girl. When Mr. Yun fights the fake and corrupt sports expert; when Song, representing the oppressed masses, fights the bullying rich and powerful man in *Revenge in the Volcano's Shadow;* and when an intellectual with May Fourth ideals fights with the troupe manager who "destroyed art without consciousness" in *Song and Dance Troupe* – in all three instances, Li's characters stand aside, scared, running back and forth to watch, before being embraced protectively.

According to Leo Ou-Fan Lee, Neo-Sensationalist writers of the 1930s constructed an image of the Modern Girl as a foreign and exotic femme fatale to represent the modern city itself. She constantly outwitted and overpowered the thin, slender, and much weaker male narrator-protagonist with his "eager behavior like a boy." Lee discusses how "SPORTIVE" (original in English) modern women with short hair, protruding breasts, and tanned "light dark" skin began to emerge as one prototype of the femme fatale. Zhang Zhen argues that "while the left-wing screen writers embraced a form of revolutionary masculinity hardened by nationalism, the modernists (led by the 'neo-sensationalist' writers) were preoccupied with apotheosizing the Modern Girl as the hybrid emblem of the machine age and cosmopolitan consumption." When the mature male mentor in the previously discussed films, strengthened by nationalist masculinity, replaced the boyish narrator-protagonist in the Neo-Sensationalist literature, the "athletic movie star" was "rescued" from becoming a free, daring, and promiscuous urban femme fatale and transformed into a patriotic, chaste, and sweet girl. At the same time, cinematic presentations of the Modern Girl's pleasurable indulgences objectified her into what Xiaobing Tang refers to as a consumer and material commodity. The mentor figure tamed the femme fatale and transformed her into a national subject with spiritual goals.[81]

Leo Ou-Fan Lee also theorizes that the ballroom patronized by the femme fatale stood for material glamour and the pleasures of the urban landscape. Automobiles, representing time and speed, key values of Western modernity, were equated or associated with the femme fatale to show the seduction and commodification of urban "mechanical civilisation." Smoking, an erotic symbol, "is combined with eating and drinking to provide a perfect 'tease' for sex." When a modern femme fatale smoked a cigarette, it signalled irresistible sexual invitation.[82] In contrast to these trappings of Western modernity, a plain appearance marked by simple clothing and no makeup, an integral part of jianmei, was associated with frugality and signalled not only the authenticity of an innocent girl but also good morals and patriotism. The authoritative male mentors in Li's films instructed the athletic movie star to remain pure and simple. In *Queen of Sports,* Yun symbolically saves Li's character from the danger of corruption by dragging her away from a sports car and from a ballroom. In *Revenge in the Volcano's Shadow,* echoing Yun's instruction that makeup is not proper for athletes, Song grabs a cigarette from the lips of Li's dancing girl character, who is associated with the smoking and drinking of the dance club culture, and scolds her: "Smoking, painted eyebrows, face powder – people nowadays are all fashionable!" Then he lifts her chin and asks, "Why must you paint your lips blood-red? How are they beautiful?" In fan magazines, Li was never shown in a fancy *qipao* and high heels. Next to a photograph of Li in a plain, slightly wrinkled cotton *qipao*, one *Linglong* author commented: "I have never seen such plain clothes, even for the 'frugal star' *[jianyue mingxing]*." In neglecting the correcting and reforming power of the male mentor, Zhang Zhen interprets the dancing girl played by Li in *Revenge in the Volcano's Shadow* as the femme fatale type. Vivien Shen has ably discussed the importance of fancy clothing among Shanghai starlets, but Li's use of athletic clothing has gone unnoticed.[83]

Michael Chang suggests that the second and third generations of Chinese actresses were depicted as "good girls" and expected to show "true character" *(bense)*, or "authenticity," in their acting. This "true character" standard functioned as a gendered constraint, because it was based on the socially constructed ideal of "good girls" who were "natural" *(ziran)*, "innocent" *(tianzhen)*, and "pure" *(chunjie)*. Therefore, the "true character" standard of acting dominated screenwriting and casting practices. The onscreen and off-screen discourses of "true character" and the "good girl" virtually guaranteed that the sexual display of Li as an athletic movie star would not be judged in terms of her moral character as a woman. All of Li's athletic movie star roles are innocent girls rather than threatening, mature, and sophisticated women. The pure body of an innocent girl could be legitimately displayed in public, whereas a married woman's body was supposed to be concealed inside the family's private domestic space. Li played a married woman or a mother only once, in *Qiu shan mingdeng (Autumn Fan and Bright Lights)*; such roles were rare for Anna May Wong as well. For Wong, this meant she could be more easily manipulated as an Oriental and exotic sexual object deprived of motherhood or wifehood; for Li, it was a way to maintain girlish purity and innocence so as to justify the public display of her body.

Li's performances emphasized the innocence of her characters. In a scene from *Ghost*, for instance, she stands next to a tree, listening to a group of men talking about ghosts; her hands are resting against the tree, her head tilted to one side, an innocent smile on her face. When she is asked whether or not she believes in ghosts, she jerks her head and thrusts her chin forward with the air of a confident little girl: "Yes, I do; my mother always said yes." When she is invited, in the same scene, to drink alcohol and eat peanuts, she responds that she does not know how to drink, picks up a peanut, and looks down at it while working off the shell with both hands. In *Queen of Sports*, on two occasions when her family and one of her admirers talk about her winning the title of "queen of sports," she runs around the room, a white dog following her or riding on her shoulder, scampering over tables and a bed like a spoiled girl who does not care about how people view her. If these manifestations of innocence in the performance are not enough, the authoritative mentors are there to guarantee the pure and girlish image. When Lin Ying follows the serious and silent Yun after he drives off the fake sports expert, she peeks at him to gauge his mood with a childish, wily, and naughty smile, looking like a guilty girl scanning her parents' faces for their reactions.

The films' sensuality overrode Li's half-child/half-woman image. In *Queen of Sports*, Lin Ying naughtily lifts her bare legs above and beyond her head while lying in bed. In *Big Road*, when Moli flirts with the landlord, her smiling baby face and hands clasped behind the chair make her appear like a little girl. Her noble friendship with the road workers, portrayed as comradely love, helps to maintain this image of purity. In *Daybreak*, dressed in worn-out shorts and a shirt full of holes, Lingling sprawls in a canoe, one bare foot reflected in the water and the other idly dangling in the air. Her downcast eyes are fixed on a crab, with which she is playing in a childlike manner. Playing with the crab softens the sensuality of her sprawling body. In *Revenge in the Volcano's Shadow*, the dancer's girlish innocence emerges when she gets angry and runs to bed, kicking her legs in the air, talking baby talk, and making faces at her pet parrot. The construction of such innocent and girlish characters reflected a need to mitigate the potential threat posed by strong, independent, and sexually suggestive images of Li's body. One might argue that girlish leg kicking was a sexualization of youth. At the very least, the overt sensuality of her characters made stronger connections between sports and sex than any of the athletes discussed in this book.

Off-screen, Li was projected as a "sweet girl" *(tian jie'er)*, which served as the title of a cartoon portrait of her by leading cartoonist Ye Qianyu. Her girlish sweetness was first acknowledged by her colleagues at the Lianhua Studio and then by the press and the public. In a photograph accompanying a 1934 *Linglong* article titled "Eating Expressions," Li, along with two other girlish movie stars with naughty expressions, pose eating noodles. Another fan magazine, *Diansheng (Cinematic Tone)*, described Hu Die's singing pose as "standing quietly, no special gesture after singing, with 'the style of a lady from an upper-class family' *[guige zhi feng]*." In contrast, Li was described as "singing and playing naturally; if she is satisfied with herself, she will jump up with both feet; otherwise she will burst out 'doesn't count, doesn't count, this time it doesn't count!'"[84] In the photographs circulated among fans, innocent, girlish, naughty, and lively features are constantly presented to diminish the sexy appeal of a young woman. In a photograph in *Linglong*'s 1933 movie column, Li is shown bending forward in a swimsuit, her cleavage revealed. The caption reads: "Offering her virgin chastity to him; overcoming male seduction; who should be responsible for divorce?" At the same time, her sweet smile, straight hair, dainty slippers, and especially the frog-imitating gestures she makes with her open hands serve to depict her as an innocent, sweet girl, despite the sensual and alluring pose and the language of the caption. The combination of sexuality and innocence is present in various ways in other photographs of Li published in *Linglong*. In "Near Bright Star River," Li stands in water up to her knees, holding her cotton *qipao* high up with both hands to reveal her muscular legs. The sensual image of her bare skin is overshadowed, however, by her childishly naughty smile and a piece of clothing carelessly flung over her head like a hood.[85]

While the fan magazines stressed Li's youth and physical power to represent a new and strong nation, they emphasized Anna May Wong's age and wrinkles, calling her "a woman without the colour of youth, with a mother's figure, fatigued face, wrinkles at the corners of her eyes." Wong's status as a single woman was a sensitive topic for the public. She could not find a spouse because anti-miscegenation laws in California prohibited her from marrying a Caucasian, and Chinese prejudices against actresses reduced her chances of securing a proper Chinese husband. Nationalist and leftist critics ridiculed her for confessing to be a bachelorette and dreaming about a honeymoon. In contrast, Li's romantic life remained low-key. Whereas other actresses were romantically involved with powerful businessmen or other actors, Li's husband, Luo Jingyu, was a behind-the-scenes cinematic technician without any celebrity to generate gossip.[86]

George Mosse suggests that "nationalism helped control sexuality, yet also provided the means through which changing sexual attitudes could be absorbed and tamed into respectability, and that nationalism produced a stereotype of supposedly 'passionless' beauty for both men and women." In their early days, Chinese films, as Zhiwei Xiao argues, were not characterized by the kind of nationalism discussed by Mosse. During the national crisis, however, the sensuality of women's bodies was appropriated for the cause of national strengthening and resistance. Just as female warriors had used patriotism to justify taking male roles, the athletic movie star employed wartime nationalism to make her body clean and legitimate. In fact, patriotism served as a standard by which to judge the sexuality of an actress's body. Chinese nationalists regarded the sensual body of Anna May Wong as dangerous because the roles she played were harmful to Chinese "national dignity" *(guoti)*. Nationalists regarded her as a traitor. Alongside a still photograph from *Shanghai Express,* in which Wong plays a prostitute with tough street hairdo, heavy makeup, and sharply drawn eyebrows, ran the caption "the Chinese in America all call her 'traitor'" *(maiguozei)*. When she refused roles insulting to China after her visit there, the mass media in China offered a gesture of forgiveness. In 1938, she was called a good patriotic daughter of the Chinese nation after she sold her clothing and jewellery and donated sizable amounts of money to the anti-Japanese cause.[87]

Li was very aware of the need for patriotic gestures. When performing in the street play *Wei ziyou heping er zhan (Fighting for Freedom and Peace)* in Tongliang, Sichuan, she reached an agreement with fellow actress Shu Xiuwen to maintain the patriotic spirit of the performance by refusing to sing irrelevant songs and by objecting to a sensual advertisement put up by the director, which proclaimed, "Look at the stars: they are delicious." In a scene from *The Patriotic Family*, two women, one of them played by Li, are tied up by Japanese soldiers; the *qipao* worn by Li's character is torn, revealing her leg and part of her undershirt and neck. The eroticism of this image is mitigated by the political commitment of the character.[88]

Li's films frequently referred to the need of a woman's sacrifice for the nation to legitimize yet control her physically strong and sensual image. Just as Anna May Wong's film characters usually die or commit suicide, so do most of Li's; however, while Wong's deaths show the effects of racial oppression, Li's deaths symbolize Chinese women's self-sacrifice for the nation. Although Lin Ying does not die in *Queen of Sports*, her teammate's death in a competition inspires in the "queen of sports" the true tiyu spirit. All the other characters played by Li die an optimistic and brave death for the sake of the nation and the public. Before the dancing girl in *Revenge in the Volcano's Shadow* dies, she tells Song, "I will not die. I am going to see you get rid of the devils among humans." Similarly, when Zhu'er in *Little Toys*, Moli in *Big Road*, and Jinhua in *Storm on the Border* die in Japanese attacks in the arms of a mother, in the arms of a female comrade, and in front of rival Chinese ethnic groups, respectively, they are happy to see that their deaths inspire their survivors to fight the Japanese and save the nation.

These systematic control measures to make the sensual body of the athletic movie star acceptable were powerful and effective. Despite her onscreen Mae West-style sexuality, the off-screen Li was rarely the subject of romantic gossip of the sort that overwhelmed other actresses, such as Ruan Lingyu.[89] Among the new generation of jianmei stars, those who failed to desexualize their athletic bodies suffered the fate of the actresses who had played the physically fragile New Women. Ying Yin, known as a "robustly beautiful female star" *(jianmei de nüxing)*, was constantly rumoured to be "enjoying her fit young college student boyfriends." Ying joined the left-wing theatre group Roaring Waves Drama Club (Nuchao jushe) and wrote plays that helped give her a serious intellectual reputation. Portrayed in *Linglong* in a plain *qipao* as a member of the association, Ying appears with a restrained nervous gesture, her hands held palms down in front of her abdomen. Ultimately, however, she committed suicide because of the ceaseless rumours about boyfriends.[90]

Seeking New Opportunities in Hollywood without Success

Competing images of modern Chinese women in popular culture crossed national boundaries. During its wartime occupation, Japan tried to mobilize the Shanghai cinema world to support its "Greater East Asia" discourse against Western imperialism, represented by Hollywood. This was not always successful. For example, the athletic movie star image was used to counter the "films insulting to Chinese/China." The athletic "movie queen" Chen Yunshang in occupied Shanghai was inspired partly by the cult of "health" and "beauty" in Hollywood stars.[91] After the United States became an ally of China in 1941, the Nationalists and Communists saw a good opportunity to expand the market for China's resistance films and export a positive and heroic image. Luo Jingyu gave a speech titled "Motion Picture Industry in China" at the fifty-second semi-annual meeting of the Society of Motion Picture Engineers in the United States in 1941-42 as the vice president of China Studio and the deputy chief of the Film Section of the Political Department of the Chinese Military Affairs Commission.[92] He brought with him national defence films, including two films starring Li Lili: *The Patriotic Family* and *Paradise on the Isolated Island*. Guo Moruo arranged for Luo to connect with James Wong Howe (Huang Zongzhan, 1899-1976), one of the top cinematographers in Hollywood, and confirmed the relationship within a nationalist paradigm by writing Howe a banner reading "Win glory for the nation."[93]

In 1944, an American performance company headed by a friend of Luo Jingyu's invited Li to the United States to perform in a Chinese historical play. During her stay in that country from early 1945 to 1947, Li attempted to develop new professional skills and transform her athletic movie star image from innocent girl to sexy, mature, and liberal middle-class woman in her thirties.[94] She took every chance to watch plays and even observed the Miss America pageant. She was impressed with the American view of beauty, fitness, and sexual attractiveness, and the tendency to regularize and standardize fitness and beauty by carefully measuring the whole body. Howe tried to steer Li away from simply playing herself toward acting in roles that required real performance skills. He also tried to change Li's image by taking various types of photographs from different perspectives. Using special lighting and shooting in black and white, he made Li's round athletic movie star face look thinner, and therefore more serious and classic. Li's opportunities in Hollywood were limited because "yellow face" practices were the norm in an America that had prohibited Chinese immigration and stereotyped all non-white races. Li also learned a lesson from Anna May Wong, whose exotic sexual image was notorious among the Chinese due to the "bad" roles she played. Li was aware that despite her sexy display as an athletic movie star, the patriotic and nationalistic roles she played were key to purifying her athletic body and giving her a good reputation. Besides maintaining a patriotic and nationalistic image, Li was careful to avoid being associated with Wong. Since Howe and Wong were both celebrated Hollywood figures with roots in Taishan, Guangdong, they were close friends. Li became friends with Howe during her visit to Hollywood, so it is likely that the two women met, but in her memoirs she avoided any mention of Wong even while detailing her interaction with Howe. Asked in a telephone interview in 2002 whether Li knew Wong, Ai Zhongxin, Li's second husband (her first, Luo Jingyu, had committed suicide during the Cultural Revolution) became very alert and responded that they were different and had nothing to do with each other. He stated that Wong's "fame was not the equivalent of true status or achievement."[95]

Li did not get the chance to act in any play or film in the United States. Howe's plan to make a film based on *Rickshaw Boy* by Lao She and starring Li collapsed because of the civil war in China. In the spring of 1946, he recommended her for a role in a Warner Brothers film about the air war between the United States and Japan, but Li worried that playing a Japanese woman in an American film might raise questions about her Chinese patriotism.[96] Her chances faded even further when her Hollywood connections came under attack for their association with the Popular Front as the debate over "who lost China" developed.

After returning to China in 1947, Li and Luo stayed in Nanjing and waited out the civil war. They went to Beijing to attend the First Conference in Culture and Art in 1949. Li was assigned to the Beijing Film Studio but there was no filmmaking as the new Communist government needed to sort out the cinematic circle first. Instead, Li and her colleagues took part in political campaigns and thought reforms, including meetings to read and discuss newspapers and put on live performances for workers and farmers. In 1953, she starred in her only postwar film, *Zhi qu Huashan (Capturing Mount Hua by Stratagem)*, playing a Nationalist officer's wife. In her three brief scenes, her athletic body was well covered by fancy clothes, and her acting career ended with this role. In 1955, she began studying performance at the Central Academy of Cinema in Beijing, where she became a professor after graduating. During the Cultural Revolution (1966-76), Li, her family, and many of her close friends and colleagues were suppressed or tortured to death because of the rivalry between Li and Mao Zedong's wife, Jiang Qing (who as Lan Ping had been an actress in Shanghai in the 1930s), which had developed while shooting *Bloodshed on Wolf Mountain*. Jiang has a minor role in this film, in which Li was the lead actor. Li's last appearance was in *Center Stage* in 1992, as described at the beginning of this chapter.[97]

After the Communist takeover in 1949, the ideology of rural populism replaced the older paradigm that contrasted images and values of the city and countryside. The urban Communist culture of the war period was overcome by the Yan'an rural style in post-revolutionary socialist construction, and Li's exposed athletic body was no longer appreciated. The few films made in the early People's Republic focused on Communist military and collective masculine power. For example, *Zhonghua nü'en* (*Daughters of China*), released in January 1949 from Manchuria after the Communists took over the region, marked a transition from the exposed athletic body to images of self-sacrificing, heroic anti-Japanese female farmers, whose strong bodies were fully covered by drab, masculine clothing. These films were about the collective achievements of serious and brave military men with strong wills, wise hearts, handsome faces, and bright, determined eyes. They depicted suffering and shabbily dressed working-class women who needed protection or liberation. Nevertheless, although the sexual dimension of Li's athletic body was suppressed, its legacy would be found in the working-class and masculine physical codes of the female ideals during the Maoist era. Poshek Fu argues that "women's service is needed only when the nation is in crisis, and once the emergency is over, they should go back home, where they belong."[98] I argue that gender and nation were radically reshaped during the war, and that the legacy of the athletic movie star could not be completely suppressed as the meaning of modern womanhood continued to be negotiated.

Li Lili's athletic movie star image was a site where ideological values and political systems constructed and contested notions of nation and state. While playing a central role in reconciling the contradictions in nation building, Li broke through the hierarchical divisions of gender norms – in which the male body is the focal point of public, political, and collective causes and the female body the focal point of individual, private, and sexual concerns – by projecting an athletically trained female body into public and national view. Her portrayal of the athletic female body reflected complex interactions between the nationalist agenda and feminism in the modernizing discourse of Chinese nationhood – that is, the strong female bodies featured in wartime cinema both symbolized nationalist mobilization and celebrated womanhood with a new public persona that projected confidence and strength.

Conclusion

On 1 October 1949, the Chinese Communist Party (CCP) gained full power and created the People's Republic of China (PRC), a socialist, independent state that continues to the present day. The CCP emphasized sports as part of its drive to construct a centralized ideological, political, and economic system, and to develop its economy and national defence. Sports became a mass phenomenon and the CCP encouraged women, who, as we have seen, had been enthusiastic participants and followers of sports, to become mass participants. Over the next few years, the CCP took firm control over all aspects of sports, as in other areas of social production, and in 1952 created a National Sports Commission that worked closely with other ministries, such as Education and National Defense. The CCP developed in sport, as generally in other areas, a vast, top-down hierarchy of power that remains in place today. For Chinese women, mass participation in education and sports was truly emancipating, as the vast majority had little previous experience in either. CCP sports organization was the successful culmination of efforts begun under the Nationalists. The political instability of the national crisis, world war and civil war, shortage of funds, and an immature sports industry doomed the Nationalist efforts. The CCP, having expelled the imperialist powers, consolidated control over the Chinese nation and people, unified the sports movement, and succeeded where the Nationalists had only dreamt.[1]

In concert with the People's Liberation Army, the CCP developed specialized, elite sports teams in the early 1950s. With this platform, the CCP soon opened elite sports schools and hired professional coaches with the goal of developing athletes who could perform successfully in national and international competitions. China sent a delegation that included twenty-four male basketball and football players and two female swimmers to the 1952 Helsinki Summer Olympic Games. Because the International Olympic Commission (IOC) issued invitations to the PRC late, only one male swimmer, Wu Chuanyu, actually took part. The IOC, initially confused by the prospect of two Chinas, acceded to American pressure after the Olympics, recognized the Republic of China in Taiwan as the proper representative of the Chinese, and barred the PRC from future Olympics, a ban not lifted until 1979. Observing the boycott of the Moscow Olympics in 1980, China did not participate in an Olympics until the Los Angeles Games in 1984. It did, however, compete in numerous other international sports competitions, most notably in the Games of the Newly Emerging Forces (GANEFO) in 1963 and 1966, which enabled it to champion developing nations, revolution, and sports without the presence of the Taiwan Chinese.[2]

Except during the Cultural Revolution (1966-76), China sustained its vast internal efforts at sports education and involvement in international competitions outside of the Olympics. Dong Jinxia has ably chronicled those complex years. Matters changed drastically in 1979 with the advent of market reforms in China, full ties with the United States, and the Chinese government's initiatives to ramp up its international athletic competition and win gold medals at the Olympics, a process that Dong, Xu Guoqi, and Susan Brownell have discussed fully. As indicated earlier, in the Introduction, China finally achieved Olympic glory in Beijing in 2008.[3]

The CCP still rigorously controls China's athletes, limits their profits from their work, and seldom allows them independent action. If that were the entire story, the histories of the individual athletes and administrators recounted in this book would be antiques, of interest to the historian but with little relevance to contemporary life. To be sure, their fame generally did not last once their glory days faded; however, in a nation where women have generally faced obstacles to social mobility, the life experiences of most of the sportswomen still appear to have been positive. If sports elevated their individual lives, what was the significance of these female athletes for Chinese history? As I have argued in this book, sportswomen contributed heavily to the emerging Chinese nation-state during the national crisis from 1931 to 1945. Zhang Huilan established the intellectual basis for women's competitive sports. As a private entrepreneur, Lu Lihua created a sports network. The basketball players of the Private Liangjiang Women's Tiyu Normal School brought fame to their school and made their sport into a national and regional spectacle. The track queens directly supported government initiatives during their brief moments of fame; one of them, Li Sen, and swimmer Yang Xiuqiong became the first two female Chinese Olympians. In the final chapter, I showed how Li Lili became the "athletic movie star" and thereby further enhanced the importance of *tiyu* and sportswomen.

By using these biographical sketches and linking the lives of athletes with their competitive achievements, I have shown that female athletes strove for more individual independence than previous scholars have acknowledged. Although the print media could be fickle and the government was often arbitrary, the sportswomen created places for themselves in the collective consciousness of the public. I have also argued that sportswomen must be considered as part of the Modern Girl movement. Yang Xiuqiong is the best example of this, but other female athletes also showed modernity through their public presence in competitions, their body types, and their occasional larks, even as they guarded their innocence. Whether they won gloriously or lost ignobly, and as they began, ended, or fended off romances, the sportswomen were part of the public space in ways that few ordinary Chinese women had ever been, sustaining a female agency even as they competed and worked within a harsh patriarchal society and dealt with slippery, even predatory men.[4]

Their collective efforts established the platform from which future female Chinese athletes would launch their careers. Such an achievement occurred despite the revolutionary turmoil in Chinese society. As Susan Brownell has observed, the Communist takeover brought new meaning to the training of the body to benefit the nation. Rather than striving for a moment of competitive victory, the active body was in continuous revolution, forever in motion and in service to the Communist state.[5] The changes that the Communist Party wrought might appear to be so far-reaching as to have eliminated any traces of the nation-building efforts of the 1930s, but some things endured. The sense of crisis continued during the Cold War, and increased after China's alienation from the Soviet Union since the late 1950s. The CCP used sports as a vehicle for instilling national pride and celebrating national achievement, and except during the Cultural Revolution, it developed elite teams for competitive sports. Shut out of the Olympics by international politics, China and its allies organized their own games.

The 2008 Beijing Olympics symbolized China's ascent to power, the future extent of which no one can predict. Since the initiation of market reforms in 1979, the Chinese nation and its Communist government have embarked on creating sports organizations and goals that are direct descendants of the Nationalist efforts of the 1930s. Tiyu schools and their advanced, specialized academies prepared the athletes, who then rise through a series of national and regional games with aspirations for Olympic glory. If anything, elite athletes in China today are descendants of the basketball players, track stars, and swimmers encountered in this book.

Today's female Chinese athletes embrace life's meaning through the nation-state, much as their counterparts did in the 1930s. Well cared for during their competitive years, as state employees they are paid very little and are expected to earn glory for China, not themselves. Often, they are discarded after defeats or injuries. Western-style superstardom and lucrative contracts are absent.

Tellingly, the female Chinese athlete with the most medals at the 2008 Olympics was swimmer Pang Jiaying, who won a bronze medal in the 200-metre freestyle, another bronze medal in the 4 × 100-metre medley, and a silver in the 4 × 200-metre freestyle. No male or female Chinese athlete won anything close to the array of medals awarded to the American swimmer Michael Phelps. Female Chinese athletes enjoy the trappings of female modernity, dressing well but not luxuriously. In this they remain closer in style to the Modern Girl as petty urbanites, or ordinary people, rather than living the extravagant lifestyles that Western female celebrity athletes enjoy. Any one of them would admire Yang Xiuqiong for her athletic achievements, fame, independence and agility in negotiating with government and officials, and Modern Girl persona. The recent case of Li Na, the tennis star who captured the title in the women's singles tournament at the French Open in 2011 is illustrative. She broke away from the state-owned system and represented China as a private citizen. Advertisements featuring Li's taut, *jianmei* figure cocking a backhand return adorn the main streets of Beijing, Shanghai, and other major Chinese cities. The official media show tolerance of the newly gained freedom of athletes like her, as long as they win glory for the nation.[6]

This saga of female athletes in the 1930s and their descendants in the present demonstrates the complexity of women's roles in Chinese society over the past century. Female athletes combined devotion to the nation during times of great crisis with personal ambition and fascination with the allurement of modern style and dress. Scholars must consider the role of sports and sportswomen in discussions of the roles played by the Modern Girl or the New Woman in the creation of contemporary Chinese womanhood. The female athletes and administrators discussed in this book demonstrated drive and agency despite obstacles placed in their way by government, media, and predatory personalities, and earned their freedoms both on the playing fields and in public culture.

Notes

Introduction

1 Xu Guoqi, *Olympic Dreams: China and Sports, 1895-2008* (Cambridge, MA: Harvard University Press, 2008). See also Gao Yunxiang, "China and the Olympics," and "2008 Olympics," in *Encyclopedia of Modern China*, 4 vols., edited by David Pong (Detroit: Gale/ Scribners, 2009).

2 For a good overview of the crisis, see Rana Mitter, *A Bitter Revolution: China's Struggle with the Modern World* (New York: Oxford University Press, 2004), 157-63.

3 Ono Kazuko, *Chinese Women in a Century of Revolution, 1850-1950* (Stanford, CA: Stanford University Press, 1982), 102; Louise Edwards, "Chinese Women's Campaigns for Suffrage: Nationalism, Confucianism and Political Agency," in *Women's Suffrage in Asia: Gender, Nationalism, and Democracy*, edited by Louise Edwards and Mina Roces (London: Rout- ledge, 2004), 59-79; Lin Yutang, *My Country and My People* (New York: Reynal and Hitchcock, 1935), 172.

4 Zhonghua tiyu xiejin hui, ed., *Chuxi di shiyi jie shijie yundong hui Zhonghua daibiao tuan baogao* (abbreviated as *Baogao*) (Shanghai: n.p., 1937), [section 1] 11-66, 24-32, 53-58, [section 3] 94-96; Chen Yongsheng, *Ouzhou tiyu kaocha riji* (Shanghai: Nansheng chuban- she, 1938), 36-37, 106-94. On *qipao*, see Antonia Finnane, *Changing Clothes in China: Fashion, History, and Nation* (New York: Columbia University Press, 2008), 149-52. On the national goods campaign, see Karl Gerth, *China Made: Consumer Culture and the Creation of the Nation* (Cambridge, MA: Harvard University Press, 2003). On the colour white, see Tina Mai Chen, "Proletarian White and Working Bodies in Mao's China," *Positions: East Asia Cultures Critique* 11, 2 (Fall 2003): 361-93. White, as Chen notes, "signified discontinuity with the past through themes of professionalism, modernization, and technical experience." On the exhausting sea voyage, see "Ge xuanshou chijin fenglang kui: Chuguo shi yinggai zou lulu," *Diansheng* 5, 31 (7 August 1936): 796. On Chinese rela- tions with Germany and dislike of racist propaganda, see William C. Kirby, *Germany and Republican China* (Stanford, CA: Stanford University Press, 1984), 167-69; Zhang Huilan, "Pianren de jiaxiang: di shiyi jie Aoyunhui xiaoyi," *Tiyu shiliao* 4 (June 1981): 38-39. *Cinematic Tone* praised the Chinese delegation's intelligience in salutation – facing right, hats off, and right hands resting on the heart to avoid the Nazi salute. "Zhongguo dui zhi xingli," *Diansheng* 5, 31 (7 August 1936): 797. On the documentary, see "Di qi ci changwu dongshi huiyi jilu," *Tiyu jikan* 3, 2 (June 1937): 232; "Yingyan di shiyi jie shiyun yingpian jilue," *Tiyu jikan* 3, 2 (June 1937): 254.

5 After full-scale war broke out, Zhai from Taixing, Jiangsu Province, moved to Sichuan and taught at the National Second Middle School. In 1938, she wrote to Madame Chiang Kai- shek, expressing her wish to compete in swimming in the 1940 Olympics to wash away the shame the nation suffered in 1936. Zhai claimed that senior Nationalist leader Dai Jitao was her godfather. Second National Archives of China in Nanjing, vol. 5, file 15164. Liu remained active in the field of martial arts. In 1957, she published an ideologically charged

article that initiated the politicization of martial arts and *tiyu*. In 1980, she published a short memoir on her experience in Berlin. Liu Yuhua, "Duiyu Wang Xinwu 'Kaizhan wushu yundong de yixie yijian' de yijian," *Tiyu wencong* 7 (1957): 10; "Yi di shiyi jie Aoyunhui Zhongguo wushu dui fu Ou biaoyan," *Tiyu shiliao* 2 (August 1980): 29-30.

6 Despite the Nationalist government's commitment to a sizable delegation, the budget was tight. For example, for almost half a year after Chiang Kai-shek received the delegation, the Shanghai municipal government and the Ministry of Education each insisted that the other was obligated to pay the delegation's 661.2 yuan fare for the round trip from Shanghai to Nanjing. In January 1937, the Nationalist government intervened and ordered the Ministry of Education to make the payment to the Department of Transportation. The Henan provincial government contributed 1,500 yuan to help cover the trip to Berlin of three Henan marital arts performers (including Liu Yuhua). Second National Archives of China in Nanjing, vol. 2, file 2707. Enthusiasm was so high, however, that two female *tiyu* teachers paid their own way, and Chen Yongsheng, in order to accompany the observers, contributed 2,000 yuan that she won in a lottery. See Wang Zheng, *Women in the Chinese Enlightenment: Oral and Textual Histories* (Berkeley: University of California Press, 1999), 271. *Baogao*, [section 1] 21-22, [section 3] 96. Toward the delegation's total budget of 220,000 yuan, the Nationalist government contributed 170,000 yuan and the CNAAF raised 30,560.88 yuan from various ministries of the central government and local politicians. The soccer team raised the rest through their tour in Southeast Asia and India. The CNAAF ended up with a 17,000 yuan surplus. "Di qi ci changwu dongshi huiyi jilu," *Tiyu jikan* 3, 2 (June 1937): 232.

7 An all-male delegation composed of a soccer team, a basketball team, three track and field athletes (one from Taiwan and one from Singapore), and swimmer Wu Chuanyu from Indonesia competed in the Fourteenth Olympics in London in 1948 on a razor-thin budget. Zhang Banglun, "Canjia di shisi jie Aoyunhui zhuiyi," *Tiyu shiliao* 2 (August 1980): 32-43. Li Zhenzhong, "Zhongguo lanqiu daibiao dui canjia di shisi jie Aoyunhui jingguo," *Tiyu shiliao* 2 (August 1980): 44-47.

8 "Yang Xiuqiong, Li Sen heyan shiyun lunzhong yimu yaju," *Yule* 2, 28 (1936): 547.

9 Jizhe, "Wo guo canjia Shiyunhui xiangmu ji renxuan jiantao," *Qinfen tiyu yuebao* 3, 6 (March 1936): 517-18.

10 Linling, "Canjia shijie yundong hui tandao woguo nüzi tiyu shifou jinbu," *Linglong* 262 (18 November 1936): 3488-89.

11 Andrew D. Morris, *Marrow of the Nation: A History of Sports and Physical Culture in Republican China* (Berkeley: University of California Press, 2004), 5, 141; Fan Hong, *Footbinding, Feminism and Freedom: The Liberation of Women's Bodies in Modern China* (London: Frank Cass, 1997); Yu Chien-ming, *Yundong chang nei wai: Jindai Huadong diqu de nüzi tiyu, 1895-1937* (Taipei: Institute of Modern History, Academia Sinica, 2009).

12 Prasenjit Duara, "The Regime of Authenticity: Timelessness, Gender, and National History in Modern China," *History and Theory* 37, 3 (October 1998): 297-99. See also Edmund S.K. Fung, *Intellectual Foundations of Chinese Modernity: Cultural and Political Thought in the Republican Era* (New York: Cambridge University Press, 2010), 6-8, 12; and Mitter, *A Bitter Revolution*, 146-48.

13 Xu, *Olympic Dreams*; Morris, *Marrow of the Nation*, 2-3; Fan, *Footbinding*; Susan Brownell, *Training the Body for China: Sports in the Moral Order of the People's Republic* (Chicago: University of Chicago Press, 1995), 34-36; Prasenjit Duara, *The Global and Regional in China's Nation-Formation* (New York: Routledge, 2009), 121-22.

14 "The Feminist Movement in China," *People's Tribune* (edited by Tang Liangli) 25, 5 (1 June 1935): 301-14; Lin, *My Country and My People*, 269-71.

15 Morris, *Marrow of the Nation,* 3-4.
16 Susan Mann, "Scene-Setting: Writing Biography in Chinese History," *American Historical Review* 114, 3 (June 2009): 631-39; Wang, *Women in the Chinese Enlightenment;* Danke Li, *Echoes of Chongqing: Women in Wartime China* (Urbana: University of Illinois Press, 2010); Joan Judge, *The Precious Raft of History: The Past, the West, and the Woman Question in China* (Stanford, CA: Stanford University Press, 2008), 94-95.
17 Joan Judge, *Print and Politics: "Shibao" and the Culture of Reform in Late Qing China* (Stanford, CA: Stanford University Press, 1996), 22; Catherine Vance Yeh, *Shanghai Love: Courtesans, Intellectuals and Entertainment Culture, 1850-1910* (Seattle: University of Washington Press, 2006), ch. 4. On the emergence of print capitalism in China, see Christopher A. Reed, *Gutenberg in Shanghai: Chinese Print Capitalism, 1876-1937* (Vancouver: UBC Press, 2004).
18 "Jiaoyu bu tiyu weiyuanhui baogao," in *Kangzhang shiqi peidu tiyu shiliao,* edited by Chongqing shi tiyu yundong weiyuanhui and Chongqing shizhi zongbian shi (Chongqing: Chongqing chubanshe, 1987), 11.
19 Ibid., 11; *Yule* 2, 31 (1936): 613; *Diansheng* 5, 31 (7 August 1936): 788.
20 Leo Ou-Fan Lee, *Shanghai Modern: The Flowering of a New Urban Culture in China, 1930-1945* (Cambridge, MA: Harvard University Press, 1999), 46, 63; Morris, *Marrow of the Nation,* 70, 157.
21 According to "The Survey of Women's Magazines and Journals across the Nation," printed in *Linglong* in June 1933, there were twenty-three women's periodicals of various kinds in China. The thirteen in Shanghai included *Women's Daily,* the weekly *Linglong,* the biweekly *Women's Voice* and *Women's Pictorial,* the monthly *Women (Nüzi), Modern Women (Xiandai funü), Women Youth (Nü qingnian), Women's Bugle/Bell (Nüduo), New Family,* and *Modern Parents; Woman and Family,* a periodic supplement to the daily *Morning News (Chenbao),* the weekly *Modern Domestic Affairs* supplement to *Xinbao,* and the "Woman and Family" column in *Eastern Miscellany (Dongfang zazhi).* The four in Beiping included *New Women (Xin funü),* a periodic supplement to the *North China Daily;* the weekly *Women and Youth (Funü qingnian)* in the daily *Morning News (Chenbao); Women Weekly (Funü zhoukan),* a supplement to *World Daily (Shijie ribao);* and the weekly *Family Paradise,* a supplement to the *Morning News.* The two in Hong Kong included the monthly *Modern Women (Dangdai funü)* and *Women's Weekly,* a supplement to *Oriental Daily.* Nanjing had the monthly *Women's Shared Voice (Funü gongming);* Hangzhou had the thrice-monthly *Funü xunkan;* Zhengzhou had *Women's Weekly,* a supplement to *Zhengzhou Daily;* and Tianjin had the weekly *Family. Linglong* 100 (21 June 1933): 964. On development of a similar women's magazine genre in Japan, see Sarah Frederick, *Turning Pages: Reading and Writing Women's Magazines in Interwar Japan* (Honolulu: University of Hawai'i Press, 2006).
22 On the *xiaoshimin* generally, see Lu Hanchao, *Beyond the Neon Lights: Everyday Shanghai in the Early Twentieth Century* (Berkeley: University of California Press, 1999); and Wen-Hsin Yeh, *Shanghai Splendor: Economic Sentiments and the Making of Modern China, 1843-1949* (Berkeley: University of California Press, 2007). Neither Lu nor Yeh mentions sports in discussions of the *xiaoshimin.*
23 Fan, *Footbinding.* See Fung, *The Intellectual Foundations of Chinese Modernity,* 7, for an admonition to combine social and political histories of modern China.
24 See in particular the essays in Madeleine Yue Dong and Joshua Goldstein, eds., *Everyday Modernity in China* (Seattle: University of Washington Press, 2006); Frank Dikötter, *Things Modern: Material Culture and Everyday Life in China* (London: Hurst, 2007), and *Exotic Commodities: Modern Objects and Everyday Life in China* (New York: Columbia University Press, 2006); Ruth Rogaski, *Hygienic Modernity: Meaning of Health and Disease in Treaty-Port China* (Berkeley: University of California Press, 2004).

25 On the uncanny in Chinese life, see Lee, *Shanghai Modern*, 181-82.

26 The Modern Girl around the World Research Group, eds., *The Modern Girl around the World: Consumption, Modernity and Globalization* (Durham, NC: Duke University Press, 2008), 1-25. The New Life Movement was "a set of beliefs, that were part fascist, part Confucian, and were formulated by Chiang Kai-shek's government during the 1930s to change the moral character of the Chinese and create an alert, 'militarized' society." Jonathan Spence, *The Search for Modern China*, 2nd ed. (New York: W.W. Norton, 1990), A59.

27 On images of women as weak, see E. Perry Link Jr., *Mandarin Ducks and Butterflies: Popular Fiction in Early Twentieth-Century Chinese Cities* (Berkeley: University of California Press, 1981). On physical education, see Joan Judge, "Citizens or Mothers of Citizens: Gender and the Meaning of Modern Chinese Citizenship," in *Changing Meanings of Citizenship in Modern China*, edited by Merle Goldman and Elizabeth J. Perry (Cambridge, MA: Harvard University Press, 2002), 32.

28 On the Modern Girl, see the essays by Madeleine Dong and Tania Barlow in particular, in The Modern Girl around the World Research Group, *The Modern Girl around the World*, and Hsiao-pei Yen, "Body Politics, Modernity and National Salvation: The Modern Girl and the New Life Movement," *Asian Studies Review* 29, 2 (June 2005), 165-86. On maternal celebrity characteristics, see Yingjie Guo, "China's Celebrity Mothers: Female Virtues, Patriotism, and Social Harmony," in *Celebrity in China*, edited by Louise Edwards and Elaine Jeffreys (Hong Kong: Hong Kong University Press, 2010), 45-66.

29 On fame in China, see Edwards and Jeffreys, *Celebrity in China;* and Mary Farquhar and Yingjin Zhang, eds., *Chinese Film Stars* (New York: Routledge, 2010). In general, see Leo Braudy, *The Frenzy of Renown: Fame and Its History* (New York: Oxford University Press, 1986). On print media, see Reed, *Gutenberg in Shanghai*. On sports celebrity in Japan, see Dennis J. Frost, *Seeing Stars: Sports Celebrity, Identity and Body Culture in Modern Japan* (Cambridge, MA: Harvard University Press, 2011).

30 Elisabeth Croll, *Feminism and Socialism in China* (London: Routledge, Keegan and Paul, 1978), 155-58.

31 Sarah E. Stevens, "The New Woman and the Modern Girl in Republican China," *NWSA Journal* 15 (Autumn 2003): 82-103. See also Yen, "Body Politics." I agree with Yen that the New Life Movement did not border on the fascist, as suggested in Fan Hong, "Blue Shirts, Nationalists and Nationalism: Fascism in 1930s China," in *Superman Supreme: Fascist Body as Political Icon-Global Fascism*, edited by J.A. Mangan (London: Frank Cass, 2000), 205-26. Morris also emphasizes the militaristic qualities of the New Life Movement. See *Marrow of the Nation*, 133-34.

32 Wang, *Women in the Chinese Enlightenment;* and Li, *Echoes of Chongqing;* Mann, "Scene-Setting"; Judge, *The Precious Raft of History*, 94-95.

33 Paola Zamperini, *Lost Bodies: Prostitution and Masculinity in Chinese Fiction* (Leiden: Brill, 2010); Yeh, *Shanghai Love*, esp. 220-48.

34 Fan, *Footbinding*, 9-10, 262, 270-72, 296.

35 Morris, *Marrow of the Nation*, 16; Brownell, *Training the Body for China*, 16-17.

36 Brownell, ibid., 17.

37 Prasenjit Duara, *Sovereignty and Authenticity: Manchukuo and the East Asian Modern* (Lanham, MD: Rowman and Littlefield, 2003), 26.

38 Morris, *Marrow of the Nation*, 17.

39 Zhang Huilan, interviewed by Qiu Weichang and Zheng Yuangao, "Shanghai Nüqingnian-hui tiyu shifan xuexiao," in *Titan xianfeng* (Shanghai: Shanghai renmin chubanshe, 1990), 190, 195, and in *Tiyu shiliao* 9 (January 1983): 8-9; Zhang Huilan, "Zaoqi peiyang nüzi tiyu shizi de xuexiao," in *Titan xianfeng* (Shanghai: Shanghai renmin chubanshe, 1990), 192-96. Lu Lihua, Duan Gangcheng, and Zhou De, interviewed by Chu Jianhong, "Shanghai Zhongguo nüzi ticao xuexiao jieshi," in *Tiyu shiliao* 6 (April 1982): 4-5. On introduction

of YMCA, see Gunsun Hoh, *Physical Education in China* (Shanghai: Commercial Press, 1926), 208-20; and Shirley S. Garrett, *Social Reformers in Urban China: The Chinese YMCA, 1895-1926* (Cambridge, MA: Harvard University Press, 1970), ch. 5.

40 Hung Chang-tai, *War and Popular Culture: Resistance in Modern China, 1937-1945* (Berkeley: University of California Press, 1994), 271.

41 Zhang Jiwu, *Feichang shiqi zhi guomin tiyu* (Shanghai: Zhonghua shuju, 1937); Zhongguo Guomindang zhongyang zhixing weiyuanhui xuanchuan weiyuanhui, ed., *Tiyu yu jiuguo*; Xiao Zhongguo, "Tichang nüzi tiyu yu Zhonghua minzu zhi fuxing," *Tiyu jikan* 3, 2 (June 1937): 145-47.

42 Wang Zhenya, *Jiu Zhongguo tiyu jianwen* (Beijing: Renmin tiyu chubanshe, 1984), 3-4, 13, 112.

43 On sport in areas under Communist control, see Fan, *Footbinding*, 149-225; Su Xiaoqing, *Xin minzhu zhuyi tiyu shi* (Fuzhou: Fujian jiaoyu chubanshe, 1999); Zeng Biao, *Zhongyang suqu tiyu shi* (Nanchang: Jiangxi ga oxiao chubanshe, 1999). For discussion of the problem of the term "China" in modern women's history, see Gail Hershatter, "State of the Field: Women in China's Long Twentieth Century," *Journal of Asian Studies* 63, 4 (November 2004): 991-1065.

Chapter 1: Zhang Huilan (1898-1996): The "Mother of Women's Modern Physical Education"

1 Liu Jun, "Zhang Huilan yisheng zhili fazhan tiyu, jiushi gaoling huo Lianheguo Rongyu Jiang," *Renmin ribao*, 3 January 1987; Mao Ruiqing. "Zhang Huilan huo Lianheguo Jiaokewen Zhuzhi Tiyu Jiang," *Renmin ribao*, 6 June 1987.

2 Although Zhang suffered during the Cultural Revolution, she was eventually rehabilitated. In 1984, before the UNESCO award, the National Tiyu Commission of China awarded her an honorary medal for her contributions to national tiyu. *Renmin ribao*, 23 September 1984.

3 See, for example, the comments in the oral history of Chen Yongsheng in Wang Zheng, *Women in the Chinese Enlightenment: Oral and Textual Histories* (Berkeley: University of California Press, 1999), 262, 279-80. See also Joan Judge, "Talent, Virtue, and the Nation: Chinese Nationalisms and Female Subjectivities in the Early Twentieth Century," *American Historical Review* 106, 3 (June 2001): 765-803, esp. 766, 788. On the importance of American degrees, see Leo Ou-Fan Lee, *Shanghai Modern: The Flowering of a New Urban Culture in China, 1930-1945* (Cambridge, MA: Harvard University Press, 1999), 51.

4 Only after the Qing government published *Charters on Girls Elementary Education* and *Charters on Women's Normal School* in 1907 was women's education integrated into the official educational system for the first time in Chinese history. Zhang attended missionary schools a couple of years before the laws were published. E-mail from Lu Aiyun (Zhang's former student, chief librarian and professor at Shanghai Athletic University), 13 October 2012, based on information from the archives of the Shanghai Athletic University.

5 Second National Archives of China in Nanjing, vol. 668, file 34; interview with Lu Aiyun, December 2006 and April 2008, Shanghai. On YMCA, see Shirley S. Garrett, *Social Reformers in Urban China: The Chinese YMCA, 1895-1926* (Cambridge, MA: Harvard University Press, 1970).

6 Zhang Huilan, interviewed by Qiu Weichang, and Zheng Yuangao, "Shanghai Nüqing-nianhui tiyu shifan xuexiao," in *Titan xianfeng* (Shanghai: Shanghai renmin chubanshe, 1990), 188-91; Xu Songtao, "Woguo di yi wei nü tiyu jiaoshi," *Tiyu shiliao* 3 (February 1981): 30-31. Fan Hong, *Footbinding, Feminism and Freedom: The Liberation of Women's Bodies in Modern China* (London: Frank Cass, 1997), 88, 232-34; and Andrew D. Morris, *Marrow of the Nation: A History of Sport and Physical Culture in Republican China* (Berkeley: University of California Press, 2004), 32-34, argue that women's physical exercise was

largely limited to calisthenics during this period.

7   Second National Archives of China in Nanjing, vol. 668, file 34.

8   Weili Ye, *Seeking Modernity in China's Name: Chinese Students in the United States, 1900-1927* (Stanford, CA: Stanford University Press, 2001), 115-16, 146-52. See also Wang, *Women in the Chinese Enlightenment,* 44-50, 80-83; "Liu Mei Zhongguo xueshenghui xiaoshi," *Dongfang zazhi* 14, 12 (December 1917); "Zenyang chazhao Minguo chuqi liu xuesheng mingdan," *Minguo chunqiu* 4 (25 July 1988): 62.

9   On Japan, see Judge, "Talent, Virtue, and the Nation," 783, and "Between *Nei* and *Wai:* Chinese Women Students in Japan in the Early Twentieth Century," in *Gender in Motion: Divisions of Labor and Cultural Change in Late Imperial and Modern China,* edited by Bryna Goodman and Wendy Larson (Lanham, MD: Rowman and Littlefield, 2005), 121-44; Cheng Jun, "Zhongguo nüzi guanfei liuxue zhi shi," *Minguo chunqiu* 6 (25 November 1990): 38.

10 Zhang, "Shanghai Nüqingnianhui tiyu shifan," 190.

11 Jin Feng, *The Making of a Family Saga: Ginling College* (Albany, NY: SUNY Press, 2010), 4. On missionary schools and elite status, see Xiaoping Cong, *Teachers' Schools and the Making of the Modern Chinese Nation-State* (Vancouver: UBC Press, 2007), 35-37. On makeup of faculty, see Second National Archives of China in Nanjing, vol. 668, file 34. The forty-three-member faculty and administrative staff consisted of eleven men and thirty-two women, with thirteen foreign teachers of unspecified gender. On her hiring, see Mrs. Lawrence Thurston and Ruth M. Chester, *Ginling College* (New York: United Board for Christian Colleges in China, 1955), 48. On male theorists, see Andrew D. Morris, *Marrow of the Nation: A History of Sports and Physical Culture in Republican China* (Berkeley: University of California Press, 2004), 86-87. On influence of the churches, see Ryan Dunch, "'Mothers to Our Country': Conversion, Education, and Ideology among Chinese Protestant Women, 1870-1930," in *Pioneer Christian Women: Gender, Christianity, and Social Mobility,* edited by Jessie G. Lutz (Bethlehem, PA: Lehigh University Press, 2010), 342-44.

12 Feng, *Family Saga,* 81-86.

13 On Thurston, see folder on her career in Second National Archives of China in Nanjing, vol. 668, file 34. On turmoil and decision to change leadership, see Feng, *Family Saga,* 120-27. On Ginling's early years and faculty, see Thurston and Chester, *Ginling College,* 5-37, 44-46; Gale Graham, "Exercising Control: Sports and Physical Education in American Protestant Mission Schools in China, 1880-1930," *Signs* 20 (Autumn 1994): 23-48.

14 *Ginling College Magazine* 5, 1 (March 1929), found in Second National Archives of China in Nanjing, vol. 668, file 26. On bitterness, see Feng, *Family Saga,* 124-28.

15 "Jiaoyu bu tiyu weiyuanhui baogao," in *Kangzhan shiqi peidu tiyu shiliao,* edited by Chongqing shi tiyu yundong weiyuanhui and Chongqing shizhi zongbian shi (Chongqing: Chongqing chubanshe, 1987), 73-76.

16 Fan, *Footbinding,* 230-33, 321-22; Cong, *Teachers' Schools,* 135-38.

17 Two other female faculty members, Sun Zhenghe and Lin Yunsheng, held lesser positions on a part-time basis. Sun was hired as assistant professor in 1932 for 130 yuan. All three were graduates of the Shanghai YWCA Tiyu Normal School. The university supplemented salaries with subsidies for rice and housing, again based on rank and with an upward adjustment for those with families. Second National Archives of China in Nanjing, vol. 648, files 1574 and 1478; on supplements, see vol. 668, file 39.

18 Charles H. McCloy taught Du Longyuan for one year at the Shanghai YWCA Tiyu Normal School before he returned to the United States and she transferred to Ginling. Du Longyuan, recorded by Meng Pu, "Tiyu jiaoyuan duiyu xiao xuesheng de zhuyi," *Tiyu zhoubao* 28 (13 August 1932): 5; 34 (24 September 1932): 30. Du served as the vice president of the Amateur Athletic Federation in Tianjin in 1932.

19 Interview with Lu Aiyun, December 2006 and April 2008, Shanghai; interview with Zhang Hongguang (Du Longyuan's great-nephew and a retired math professor from Nankai University in Tianjin), December 2004 and January 2005, Tianjin; interview with Zheng Yuangao (Zhang Huilan's interviewer, a journalist for the "tiyu column" of *Jiefang ribao* [Liberation Daily]*, July 2001, Shanghai; *Hebei shifan daxue tiyu xueyue yueshi*, 1931-2002 (draft, 2002), 3-4; Wang Jinsheng, *Bainian dongren* (Shijiazhuang: Hebei jiaoyu chubanshe, 2002), 229; An Shuqing, "Tianjin nüzi shifan xueyuan tiyu xi jieshi," *Tiyu shiliao* 8 (September 1982): 47. Charles H. McCloy attributed the poor performance of Chinese swimmers at the Sixth Far Eastern Games in 1923 to the lack of swimming pools in China. He advised that the athletes should not take "having lost face" personally. Mai Kele, "Di liu jie Yuandong yundong hui de jiaoxun," *Tiyu jikan* 2, 2 (July 1923): 1-6.
20 *Qinfen tiyu yuebao* 1, 3 (10 December 1933): 63, 67; 2, 4 (10 January 1935): 281. *Tiyu zhoubao* 36 (8 October 1932): 28.
21 *Tiyu zhoubao* 31 (3 September 1932): 6-23; 39 (29 October 1932): 7-8.
22 *Qinfen tiyu yuebao* 1, 3 (10 December 1933): 63, 67; 1, 7 (10 April 1934): 5-6, 29; 2, 4 (10 January 1935): 281.
23 Ibid., 2, 2 (10 November 1934): 154.
24 Zhonghua tiyu xiejin hui, ed., *Chuxi di shiyi jie shijie yundong hui Zhonghua daibiao tuan baogao* (abbreviated as *Baogao*) (Shanghai: n.p., 1937), [section 3] 3, 22, 60-62, 87, 89, 90, 92, 94; Chen Yongsheng, *Ouzhou tiyu kaocha riji* (Shanghai: Nansheng chubanshe, 1938), 8-9.
25 Zhang Huilan, "Pianren de jiaxiang: di shiyi jie Aoyunhui xiaoyi," *Tiyu shiliao* 4 (June 1981): 38-39; Zhang, Faculty Information Sheet, 1948, in Second National Archives of China in Nanjing, vol. 668, files 34; *Baogao*, [section 1] 21-24, [section 3] 3, 22, 47-50, 60-62, 87-94.
26 Chen, *Kaocha riji*, 8-9, 51-52.
27 Zhang, Faculty Information Sheet, 1948.
28 Hongshan Li, *US-China Educational Exchange: State, Society, and Intercultural Relations, 1905-1950* (New Brunswick, NJ: Rutgers University Press, 2008), 116-20.
29 Fan, *Footbinding*, 232-33; Morris, *Marrow of the Nation*, 95.
30 On early games and attitudes, see Morris, *Marrow of the Nation*, 86-90. See also Fan, *Footbinding*, 171-75; Susan Brownell, *Training the Body for China: Sports in the Moral Order of the People's Republic* (Chicago: University of Chicago Press, 1995), 42-43.
31 Zhang Huilan, "A Colligation of Facts and Principles Basic to Sound Curriculum Construction for Physical Education in China" (PhD diss., University of Iowa, 1944), 35.
32 William C. Kirby, *Germany and Republican China* (Stanford, CA: Stanford University Press, 1984), 102-45.
33 *Baogao*, [section 3] 3, 22, 60-62, 87, 89, 90, 92, 94; Wu Wenzhong, *Tiyu shi* (Taipei: Guoli bianyiguan, 1962), 20, 77, 321-25.
34 *Linglong* 58 (13 July 1932): 375; 104 (26 July 1933): 1240; 107 (23 August 1933): 1416; 222 (24 June 1936): 243-46; 283 (28 April 1937): 1205-6.
35 Zhang, "A Colligation of Facts and Principles," 35.
36 Zhang, "Pianren de jiaxiang."
37 Charles H. McCloy, "New Wine in New Bottles," *Journal of Physical Education* 25 (October 1927): 43-52; Charles H. McCloy, "Some Fundamental Considerations in Physical Education," *Physical Training* 17 (November 1919): 4-11; Charles H. McCloy, "What Is Modern Physical Education," *University of Iowa Extension Bulletin* 505 (1 April 1941): 2-16; James R. Little, "Charles Harold McCloy: His Contributions to Physical Education" (PhD diss., University of Iowa, 1968), 1, 62, 190-210.
38 Little, "McCloy," 123, 126, 150. Susan K. Cahn, *Coming on Strong: Gender and Sexuality in Twentieth-Century Women's Sports* (Cambridge, MA: Harvard University Press, 1994), 62-65.

39 Morris, *Marrow of the Nation*, 55-62; Fan, *Footbinding*, 257-58.

40 Feng, *Family Saga*, 81-86.

41 Ibid., 93-94; Brownell, *Training the Body for China*, 225-26. On views in America, see Cahn, *Coming on Strong*, 58-65.

42 Hwai Lan Chang (Zhang Huilan), "Chinese Women Leaders in Physical Education," *The Chinese Student's Monthly* 18, 8 (June 1923): 36-40.

43 Zhang, "A Colligation of Facts and Principles," 30-31; Mai Kele, "Nüzi jingzheng yundong," *Tiyu jikan* 2, 2 (July 1923): 1-8.

44 Zhang Huilan, "Tige jianyan ji tiyu fenzu wenti," *Qinfen tiyu yuebao* 2, 12 (September 1935): 801.

45 Zhang, "A Colligation of Facts and Principles," 30-31.

46 Charles H. McCloy, "A Study of Landing Shock in Jumping for Women," *Bulletin of the State University of Iowa*, 15 August 1931, 101-11; Found in Box 2, Charles H. McCloy Papers, Special Collections Department, University of Iowa Libraries; Ibid; *Philosophical Bases for Physical Education* (New York: F.S. Crofts, 1940), 287-88; Little, "McCloy," 128-29, 150.

47 On beliefs about menstruation in general, see Frank Dikötter, *Sex, Culture and Modernity in China: Medical Science and the Construction of Sexual Identities in the Early Republican Period* (Honolulu: University of Hawai'i Press, 1995), 41-44.

48 Zhang Huilan and Sun Zhenghe, *Hehuan yundong* (Shanghai: Qinfen shuju, 1935), 3-15, 23-31, 35-37.

49 Zhang, "A Colligation of Facts and Principles," 31-37.

50 Cahn, *Coming on Strong*, 8, 32, 44-48, 57.

51 Zhang and Sun, *Hehuan yundong*, 1. On textbooks, see Lee, *Shanghai Modern*, 52-55.

52 On Zhang's years of teaching at National Central University, see Second National Archives of China in Nanjing, vol. 668, files 34 and 338. Zhang Huilan, interviewed by Qiu Weichang, "Wo zai Zhongda tiyu xi shenghuo pianduan," *Tiyu shiliao* 10 (October 1984): 85-87.

53 Cahn, *Coming on Strong*, 26.

54 Zhang and Sun, *Hehuan yundong*, 1, 3-15, 23-31, 35-37.

55 Feng, *Family Saga*, 81-86; for Wuchang dancing, see Gunsun Hoh, *Physical Education in China* (Shanghai: Commercial Press, 1926), 155.

56 Chen, *Kaocha riji*, 8-9.

57 Zhang, "Shanghai Nüqingnianhui tiyu shifan."

58 Zhang, "Zhongda tiyu xi," 85-87.

59 Zhang, "Chinese Women Leaders in Physical Education," 36-40; Shishi, "Nü zhuanjia Zhang Huilan tan nüzi tiyu," *Nüduo* 21, 5 (February 1932): 66.

60 *Tiyu zhoubao* 31 (3 September 1932): 10; 39 (29 October 1932): 7.

61 Shishi, "Nü zhuanjia Zhang Huilan tan nüzi tiyu," *Nüduo* 21, 5 (February 1932): 66.

62 Feng, *Family Saga*, 10-14.

63 Suping Lu, ed., *Terror in Minnie Vautrin's Nanjing: Diaries and Correspondence 1937-38* (Urbana: University of Illinois Press, 2008).

64 Zhang Huilan to C.K. Chu, 14 October 1944, box 69, stack 14, James Yen Papers, Butler Library, Columbia University, New York (all the subsequent letters cited come from the same source).

65 Zhang to James Yen, 18 January 1945. On Lu and Needham, see Simon Winchester, *The Man Who Loved China: The Fantastic Story of the Eccentric Scientist Who Unlocked the Mysteries of the Middle Kingdom* (New York: HarperCollins, 2008).

66 On Zhang's resume, see Second National Archives of China in Nanjing, vol. 668, file 34. Interview with Lu Aiyun, December 2006 and April 2008, Shanghai; Zhang to Tang Chiyi (James Yen's secretary), 31 November 1947; Tang to Zhang, 11 October 1947.

67   Zhang Huilan, "The Development of a Program of Hygiene for the National Teachers College for Women" (thesis for a Certificate in Public Health, Massachusetts Institute of Technology, 1941), 14-16, 31, 59, 173, 192.

68   Kirby, *Germany and Republican China*, 181-83; Laura Tyson Li, *Madame Chiang Kai-shek: China's Eternal First Lady* (New York: Atlantic Monthly Press, 2006), 106-10.

69   On Du's stationery and letter to Wu, see Second National Archives of China in Nanjing, vol. 668, file 87.

70   Zhang, "A Colligation of Facts and Principles," 2-3.

71   Zhang, "The Development of a Program of Hygiene," 23-26, 44, 69-70, 77, 83-85, 95-97, 106, 156-67; "A Colligation of Facts and Principles," 81-87.

72   Du was one year older than Zhang, and the older student and younger teacher became very close friends. Zhang Hongguang described Du Lunyuan as "the guide of education" among his family. His father and uncle, who were studying in Tianjin, lived together with Du, Zhang, and Zhang's mother. Interview with Zhang Hongguang, December 2004 to January 2005, Tianjin.

73   Wang, who later became a professor of anatomy at Shanghai Athletic University, died on 14 April 2008. Lu Aiyun wrote her obituary. She was born to Wang Jianru and Liu Yunzhen and had two brothers. Both her father and older brother, Wang Rujun, worked in the textile sector, and her younger brother was a surgeon in Chicago. E-mails from Lu Aiyun, 15 April 2008 and 23 October 2012. Zhang had extended her unconditional love to close family members. Far away across the Pacific Ocean, she was worried about whether her nephew received sufficient nutrition and sent him vitamin pills. After her brother died of tuberculosis, the obligation to her brother's widow and three children was part of the reason Zhang had to leave the MEM, when "things were getting much higher every day." Zhang to Tang, 31 November 1947.

74   Wang, *Women in the Chinese Enlightenment*, 162-65, 262, 279-80.

75   Dikötter, *Sex, Culture and Modernity*, 137-45; Tsz-lan D. Sang, *The Emerging Lesbian: Female Same-Sex Desire in Modern China* (Chicago: University of Chicago Press, 2003), 99-163, esp. 100-3; Gail Hershatter, *Dangerous Pleasures: Prostitution and Modernity in Twentieth-Century Shanghai* (Berkeley: University of California Press, 1997), 118; Ono Kazuko, *Chinese Women in a Century of Revolution* (Stanford, CA: Stanford University Press, 1989), 122-23.

76   Estelle B. Freedman, *Maternal Justice: Miriam Van Waters and the Female Reform Tradition* (Chicago: University of Chicago Press, 1996), 180, 273, 283, 331-32; Lillian Faderman, *Odd Girls and Twilight Lovers: A History of Lesbian Life in Twentieth-Century America* (New York: Columbia University Press, 1991), 150-57.

77   Zhang to Chu, 14 October 1944.

78   James Yen to Zhang, 15 August 1947.

79   Typical female endearment letters are found in *Nüshu*, the local writing used exclusively by women in Hunan province. Cathy Silber, "From Daughter to Daughter-in-Law in the Women's Script of Southern Hunan," in *Engendering China: Women, Culture, and the State*, edited by Christina K. Gilmartin et al. (Cambridge, MA: Harvard University Press, 1994), 47-69.

80   In her autobiography, *A Woman Soldier's Own Story*, female soldier Xie Bingying (1906-2000) wrote: "At the time we did not really know the meaning of the term 'homosexual love.' Yet it was very strange how all our friends paired up in couples, inseparable whether in action or at rest. When two people met they fell in love. From love they moved to 'marriage' (When they slept together they were married)." Evidently, Xie and her classmates did not then categorize the "pairing up" as homosexual. Only under the influence of her daughter and (American) son-in-law, who translated her book, does Xie now apply the current

category of "homosexual love" to the female friendship then, and label "sleeping together" in the dorm as "marriage." Xie Bingying, *A Woman Soldier's Own Story,* translated by Lily Chia Brissman and Barry Brissman (New York: Columbia University Press, 2001), 40.

81 On *qipao*s, see Antonia Finnane, *Changing Clothes in China: Fashion, History, Nation* (New York: Columbia University Press, 2008), 115-16, 119, esp. 141-56. On high-heeled bound shoes, see Dorothy Ko, *Cinderella's Sisters: A Revisionist History of Footbinding* (Berkeley: University of California Press, 2005), 130, 191, 193, 206, 207. On sexiness, see Valerie Steele, *Shoes: A Lexicon of Style* (London: Scriptum Editions, 1998), 25-28.

82 Zhang, "Zhongda tiyu xi."

83 Zhang, "The Development of a Program of Hygiene," 22, 47, 142.

84 Ibid., 36, 59, 143-47; Zhang, "Health Education in the Public Health Program," 1945, James Yen Papers, 8-10, 19.

85 Zhang and Sun, *Hehuan yundong,* 1, 3-15, 23-31, 35-37.

86 Zhang, "The Development of a Program of Hygiene," 36, 78, 139-42.

87 Zhang, "A Colligation of Facts and Principles," 36, 45-56, 78, 92, 139-42.

88 Zhang, "The Development of a Program of Hygiene," 36, 73-77, 139-42.

89 Among the three "intellectual demons," were Li Jinghui for his song and dance troupes, and Liu Haisu, for introducing nude models in the Shanghai Artistic Vocational School. Zhang Yongjiu, *Minguo sanda wenyao jizhuan: shangxin de jitan* (Beijing: Dongfang chubanshe, 2010), 8; Charles Leary, "Sexual Modernism in China: Zhang Jingsheng and 1920s Urban Culture" (PhD diss., Cornell University, 1994).

90 Yang Buwei, *Yi ge nüren de zizhuan* (Taipei: Zhuanji wenxue chubanshe, 1967), 201-11, and *Zaji Zhao jia* (Taipei: Zhuanji wenxue chubanshe, 1972), 65, 204.

91 Interview with Lu Aiyun, December 2006 and April 2008, Shanghai. Due to her close attachment to the Nationalist government, Gao left for Taiwan with Hao Gengsheng in 1949.

92 See in particular Susan Glosser, "'Women's Culture of Resistance': An Ordinary Response to Extraordinary Circumstances," in *In the Shadow of the Rising Sun: Shanghai after Japanese Occupation,* edited by Christian Henriot and Wen-Hsin Yeh (New York: Cambridge University Press, 2004), 302-25; Danke Li, *Echoes of Chongqing: Women in Wartime China* (Urbana: University of Illinois Press, 2010).

93 Little, "McCloy"; Paul August Knipping, "Clair E. Turner and the Growth of Health Education" (PhD diss., University of Wisconsin, 1970); Charles Hayford, *To the People: James Yen and Village China* (New York: Columbia University Press, 1990).

94 McCloy served as the honorary secretary of CNAAF from 1923 to 1924, chairman of its Rules Committee from 1921 to 1925, chairman of the Rules Committee of the Far Eastern Athletic Association from 1921 to 1925, and the basketball official at the Fifth Far Eastern Championship Games in Shanghai in 1921. Little, "McCloy," 89-90, 99, 161, 163, 166-68, 181, 184.

95 Ibid., 146, 156-59, 162, 179.

96 Knipping, "Turner," 36-38; Zhang to Chu, 14 October 1944; Zhang, "The Development of a Program of Hygiene."

97 Zhang learned this later "from an unofficial but reliable source," although the scholarship committee officially recommended that she find a remunerative position near Iowa City to save on travel expenses and avoid the high cost of living in Boston. Zhang to Chu, 14 October 1944.

98 Yen to Zhang, 30 August 1944; Zhang to Clair E. Turner, 25 August 1944; Zhang to Chu, 14 October 1944; note by Hong (Yen's secretary), 19 August 1944; Agreement between Zhang Huilan and James Yen, 19 August 1944, James Yen Papers.

99 Ibid.

100 Hayford, *To the People,* x, 65, 83, 88, 111, 132-33; James Yen Papers, Box 69, stack 14.

101 Zhang, "Health Education in the Public Health Program."
102 Zhang to Turner, 25 August 1944; note by Hong, 19 August 1944; Yen to Zhang, 30 August 1944. Yen's wife, Alice, was a daughter of Huie Chin (Xu Qin), who was born in Guangdong province and worked as the minister at the First Chinese Presbyterian Church in New York's Chinatown, and an Irish woman from Brooklyn. Mrs. Yen had studied PE at Columbia Teachers College and won the 1917 Women's Swimming Championship of the Eastern Chinese Students Association at a meet organized by T.V. Soong (Song Ziwen, Madam Chiang's older brother) of Harvard. Hayford, *To the People*, 21.
103 Hong to Zhang, 24 October 1944 and 1 November 1944.
104 Zhang to Hong, 29 October 1944; Hong to Zhang, 1 November 1944; Zhang to Tang, 23 September 1945; Tang to Zhang, 29 September 1945; Zhang to Tang, 11 March 1946 and 26 April 1946; Tang to Zhang, 6 June 1946.
105 Zhang to Tang, 31 November 1947.
106 Yen to Zhang, 30 August 1944; Zhang to Turner, 25 August 1944; note by Hong, 19 August 1944.
107 Turner to Zhang, 1 September 1944; Turner to Yen, 1 September 1944; Yen to Zhang, 23 September 1944.
108 Zhang to Yen, 19 September 1944; Yen to Zhang, 23 September 1944.
109 Yen to Turner, 4 November 1944.
110 Hayford, *To the People*, 115.
111 Zhang to Tang, 30 June 1947.
112 The honorary chairmen of the committee included H.H. Kung (Kong Xiangxi, Madame Chiang's brother-in-law), T.V. Soong, Chen Li-fu, Wei Daoming (Chinese ambassador to the United States), and Hu Shi. Tang to Zhang, 10 May 1945.
113 Zhang to Yen, 2 June 1945; Yen to Zhang, 13 June 1945; Yen to US Department of State, 12 June 1945; Tang to Zhang, 10 May 1945.
114 Tang to Wei Daoming, 20 May 1946; Zhang to Yen, 2 June 1945; Yen to Zhang, 13 June 1945; Yen to US Department of State, 12 June 1945; Zhang to Tang, 11 March 1946.
115 Zhang to Tang, 1 April 1946 and 13 May 1946.
116 Ibid., 1 April 1946 and 3 May 1946.
117 Bryna Goodman, "The Vocational Woman and the Elusiveness of 'Personhood' in Early Republican China," in *Gender in Motion: Divisions of Labor and Cultural Change in Late Imperial and Modern China*, edited by Bryna Goodman and Wendy Larson (Lanham, MD: Rowman and Littlefield, 2005), 265-87.
118 Christina K. Gilmartin, *Engendering the Chinese Revolution: Radical Women, Communist Politics and Mass Movements in the 1920s* (Berkeley: University of California Press, 1995), 204.
119 *Renmin ribao*, 26 October 1956; Zhonghua quanguo tiyu zonghui choubei weiyuanhui, ed., *Xin minzhu zhuyi de guomin tiyu* (Beijing: 1949), 1-12. On the People's Republic of China government's willingness to continue with Nationalist educational officials into the new era, see Douglas A. Stiffler, "Creating 'New China's First New-Style Regular University,' 1949-50," in *Dilemmas of Victory: The Early Years of the People's Republic of China*, edited by Jeremy Brown and Paul G. Pickowicz (Cambridge, MA: Harvard University Press, 2007), 288-308.
120 *Xin minzhu zhuyi de guomin tiyu*, 24.
121 *Renmin ribao*, 15 September 1956, 21 October 1958, 12 March 1959, 13 June 1960, 14 February 1964, 27 September 1964, 13 December 1964, 26 February 1978, 17 July 1979, 12 March 1979, 1 and 19 September 1983, 6 November 1987.

Chapter 2: Nationalist and Feminist Discourses on *Jianmei*

 1 Leo Braudy, *The Frenzy of Renown: Fame and Its History* (New York: Oxford University Press, 1986); Charles L. Ponce de Leon, *Self-Exposure: Human-Interest Journalism and the*

Emergence of Celebrity in America, 1890-1940 (Chapel Hill: University of North Carolina Press, 2004), 15-18, 28.

2 Leo Ou-Fan Lee, *Shanghai Modern: The Flowering of a New Urban Culture in China, 1930-1945* (Cambridge, MA: Harvard University Press, 1999), 86-88.

3 Sarah Frederick, *Reading and Writing Women's Magazines in Interwar Japan* (Honolulu: University of Hawai'i Press, 2006), 4-6.

4 Prasenjit Duara, *Sovereignty and Authenticity: Manchukuo and the East Asian Modern* (Lanham, MD: Rowman and Littlefield, 2003), 133, 141.

5 Michael Hau, *The Cult of Health and Beauty in Germany: A Social History, 1890-1930* (Chicago: University of Chicago Press, 2003), 2, 178; George Mosse, *Nationalism and Sexuality: Respectability and Abnormal Sexuality in Modern Europe* (New York: Howard Fertig, 1997), 10.

6 Lee, *Shanghai Modern*, 64, 67.

7 On list, see "Introduction," n19.

8 *Linglong* 58 (13 July 1932): 375.

9 Ibid., 94 (10 May 1933): 574, 602-3.

10 Ibid., 128 (17 January 1934): 157-64.

11 Ibid., 186 (5 June 1935): 1295, 1274. The company headquarters enjoyed a prestigious address at 56 Nanjing Road, Shanghai.

12 The estimated monthly social expenses, including movies, for an average dance hostess in Shanghai came to twenty Chinese yuan. One yuan equalled one hundred copper coins. This confirms Lee's assertion that books in the 1920s and 1930s were relatively cheap, in order to promote new culture and education for those who could not afford to go to school. *Shanghai Modern*, 27, 47.

13 *Linglong* 234 (29 April 1936): 1224-25; 232 (24 June 1936): 1056-57.

14 Madeleine Yue Dong, "Who's Afraid of the Chinese Modern Girl," in *The Modern Girl around the World: Consumption, Modernity, and Globalization,* edited by The Modern Girl around the World Research Group (Durham, NC: Duke University Press, 2008), 199.

15 "Bianji zhe yan," *Linglong* 196 (7 October 1935): 1985. The famous writer Zhang Ailing (Eileen Chang) stated that every female student in the 1930s read *Linglong*. Zhang Ailing, "Tan nüren," in *Zhang Ailing dianchang wenji,* by Zhang Ailing (Harbin: Harbin Publishing House, 2005), 4: 64.

16 "Yi jiu san qi nian dui funüjie de xiwang," *Linglong* 268 (6 January 1937): 5-8.

17 The term *nüquan* (women's rights/power) first entered public discourse when reformers began to address the "women problem" for national strengthening after China's defeat in the Sino-Japanese war in 1895. See Mizuyo Sudo, "Concepts of Women's Rights in Modern China," in *Translating Feminisms in China,* edited by Dorothy Ko and Wang Zheng (New York: Blackwell, 2008), 13-34. In the May Fourth period (1915-25), Chinese terms, including *nüzi zhuyi* (female-ism), *nüxing zhuyi* (feminine-ism), *funü zhuyi* (womanism), *nüquan zhuyi* (the ism of women's rights) and *fumineishimu* (feminism) appeared to "grasp the complexity of Western feminism." Wang Zheng, "Feminism: China," in *Routledge International Encyclopedia of Women: Global Women's Issues and Knowledge,* edited by Cheris Kramarae and Dale Spender (New York: Routledge, 2000), 2: 736-37.

18 *Linglong* 81 (11 January 1933): 22.

19 Nora became a familiar symbolic figure after Henrik Ibsen's *A Doll's House* was translated into Chinese in the May Fourth Movement as part of the discussion of the "women problem."

20 *Linglong* 133 (21 March 1934): 455-56; 159 (31 October 1934): 2163-66; 182 (8 May 1935): 905-6; 283 (28 April 1937): 1270-72; Shi Minyu, "Xitele dui Deguo funü de qiwang," *Linglong* 128 (17 January 1934): 131-34; "Ducai xia de funü," *Linglong* 148 (25 July 1934): 1451-52.

21 *Linglong* 104 (26 July 1933): 1216.

22 Moli, "Yundong yu Zhongguo," *Linglong* 1 (18 March 1931): 24-25; 41 (22 December 1931): 1631; 58 (13 July 1932): 360-61; 61 (3 August 1932): 527; 78 (14 December 1932): 1326; 88 (22 March 1933): 362-63; 89 (29 March 1933): 308-9.

23 Maureen Turim, "High Angles on Shoes: Cinema, Gender, and Footwear," in *Footnotes on Shoes*, edited by Shari Benstock and Suzanne Ferriss (New Brunswick, NJ: Rutgers University Press, 2001), 58-93.

24 See Mosse, *Nationalism and Sexuality,* 48, 50-53, 139, illustration 16 between 96 and 97.

25 *Linglong* 29 (30 September 1931): 1076-77; 35 (11 November 1931): 1368; 183 (15 May 1935): 997-99; 191 (3 July 1935): 1527.

26 "Mosuolini chang jianmei," *Linglong* 91 (12 April 1933): 405. See also George Mosse, *The Image of Man: The Creation of Modern Masculinity* (New York: Oxford University Press, 1996), 95; Mosse, *Nationalism and Sexuality,* 48-65, on the integration of the cult of the physique into Nazi and Fascist ideology.

27 Whether Mussolini and Garbo actually made these remarks is beside the point. What is significant here is the way the *Linglong* writers used the influential Western figures in their efforts to popularize the translated concept of jianmei.

28 *Linglong* 10 (20 May 1931): 352, 359; 27 (15 September 1931): 1011; 52 (2 June 1932): 77; 62 (10 August 1932): 552-53; 67 (14 September 1932): 797; "Nü yundong jia de mingxing," *Linglong* 102 (12 July 1933): 1134; 148 (25 July 1934): 1484, 1494; 162 (28 November 1934): 2398; 172 (20 February 1935): 352-53; 183 (15 May 1935): 997-98; "Shijie biaozhun meiren zhaoxing," *Linglong* 168 (16 January 1935): 98-99; "Gelantai Jiabao de huazhuang tan," *Linglong* 264 (2 December 1936): 3683-84; "Jianshen yundong," *Linglong* 283 (28 April 1937): 1205-6.

29 Hau, *Cult of Health and Beauty in Germany,* 6-7, 32-44, 183.

30 "Jianmei de biaozhun," *Linglong* 74 (16 November 1932): 1112.

31 "Weilai zhi guoji biaozhun meiren," *Linglong* 150 (15 August 1934): 1589.

32 "Yi jiu san liu nian mei de tiaojian," *Linglong* 196 (7 October 1935): 1941-42.

33 *Linglong* 181 (1 May 1935): 846.

34 Ibid., 39 (9 December 1931): 1534; 136 (11 April 1934): 645-47; 229 (10 June 1936): 805-6.

35 None of the five female athletes who participated in the Berlin Olympics in 1936 was taller than 1.60 m or weighed more than 55 kg. It was argued that the "disadvantage in natural physique," in addition to "inactive advocacy, incomplete measures and poor organisation" were attributed to "the limitation that only two women participated [in competition], and they did not win anything." The athletes were Li Sen (1.58 m, 55 kg), Yang Xiuqiong (1.57 m, 52 kg), Zhai Lianyuan (1.56 m, 53 kg), Fu Shuyun (1.60 m, 54 kg), and Liu Yuhua (1.55 m, 54 kg). Zhonghua tiyu xiejing hui, ed., *Chuxi di shiyi jie shijie yundong hui Zhonghua daibiao tuan baogao* (Shanghai: n.p., 1937), [section 1] 56-58. Linling, "Canjia Shijie Yundong Hui tandao woguo nüzi tiyu shifou jinbu," *Linglong* 262 (18 November 1936): 3488-89.

36 In photographs of short-haired women leaping over hurdles, the camera focused on their well-muscled legs. At the finish line, one sees the winner's outstretched arms and twisted, gasping facial expression. In the javelin and shot put competition, images depicted the power of muscles with the body leaning far backward. Photographs singled out individual ball players for their aggressive gestures under the label *jianjiang* (robust athletes). High-jumpers going over the pole were shot from above with the audience, dwarfed, on the other side, looking up into the sky at the athletes. *Linglong* 28 (23 September 1931): 1028; 52 (1 June 1932): 76; 85 (15 February 1933): 216-17; 94 (10 May 1933): 601; 168 (16 January 1935): 96-97; 189 (26 June 1935): 1399; 217 (1935): 4223.

37 Ibid., 51 (25 June 1932): 24-25; 56 (29 June 1932): 265; 61 (3 August 1932): 508; 95 (17 May 1933): 662-63; 159 (31 October 1934): 2192-93.

38 Ibid., 28 (23 September 1931): 1018, 1024, 1026, 1047; 72 (26 October 1932): 1032-33; 94 (10 May 1933): 604; 127 (10 January 1934): 84; 135 (4 April 1934): 578; 145 (25 April 1934): 1252; 161 (21 November 1934): 2318-19; 168 (16 January 1935): 96-97; 186 (5 June 1935): 1238-39; 189 (26 June 1935): 1398-99; 242 (24 June 1936): 1839.

39 Ibid., 63 (17 August 1932): 599; 97 (31 May 1933): 780; 89 (29 March 1933): 307; 101 (5 July 1933): 1041; 134 (18 March 1934): 543; 161 (21 November 1934): 2318-19; 169 (23 January 1935): 158; 171 (6 February 1935): 276; 172 (20 February 1935): 322; 173 (27 February 1935): 415; 174 (6 March 1935): 450; 177 (27 March 1935): 662; 182 (8 May 1935): 912; 194 (24 July 1935): 1767; 284 (5 May 1937): 1302. On *qipao,* see Antonia Finnane, "What Should Chinese Women Wear? A National Problem," in *Dress, Sex and Text in Chinese Culture,* edited by Antonia Finnane and Anne McLaren, (Clayton, Australia: Monash Asia Institute, 1999), 3-36.

40 *Linglong* 71 (19 October 1932): 1006.

41 Cao Xueqin (1717-63), *Honglou meng.*

42 Chen Zhenling, "Xiandai nanzi dui nüxing mei muguang zhi zhuanyi," *Linglong* 95 (17 May 1933): 635-37.

43 *Quanyun hui teji* (Shanghai: Tiyu shenghuo chubanshe, 1948), 56; Miss Peifang, "Xin nüxing de liangda xunlian," *Linglong* 76 (30 November 1932): 1203-4; Feisi, "Zhe shidao xuyao na yi zhong nüxing?" *Linglong* 259 (28 October 1936): 3256-58.

44 Zhu Yaoxian, "Cong nüzi tiyu kandao nüzi jianglai de mingyun," *Linglong* 94 (10 May 1933): 575-76; Shen Yixiang, "Xiandai funü heyi bi congqian funü haokan," *Linglong* 25 (2 September 1931): 901-2.

45 "Mianbu taishou bujiu fa," *Linglong* 104 (26 July 1933): 1216; "Shaonü men de qieshen wenti, zenyang shi shenti jianmei," *Linglong* 136 (11 April 1934): 645-47.

46 Chen Zhenling, "Xiandai nanzi dui nüxing mei muguang zhi zhuanyi"; "Haolaiwu nüxing de jianshen meirong shu," *Linglong* 148 (25 July 1934): 1489.

47 See Gao Yunxiang, "Sports, Gender, and Nation-State during China's 'National Crisis' from 1931 to 1945" (PhD diss., University of Iowa, 2005), 307-10, for the rich literature discussing jianmei of specific parts of the female body by *Linglong's* male and female readers and editors.

48 Zhang Guiqin, "Wo de jianshen shu," *Linglong* 7 (29 April 1931): 221-22; Ping'er, "Jiaozheng zitai," *Linglong* 30 (10 October 1931), 1152; 25 (2 September 1931): 927-29; Miss Liu Meiying, "Jianbian de jianshen shu," *Linglong* 29 (30 September 1931): 1073; "Weisheng guicheng," *Linglong* 59 (20 July 1932): 399; Aimei, "Huanfei yanshou ruhe shizhong," *Linglong* 232 (24 June 1936): 1051-53; Miss Shi Yunfang, "Tan jianmei de tujing," *Linglong* 241 (17 June 1936): 1734-37; "Jianbian er youxiao de jianmei fa," *Linglong* 258 (21 October 1936) 3203-4; Miss Liuying, "Shouren zeng fei fa," *Linglong* 261 (11 November 1936): 3443-47.

49 *Linglong* 42 (1 January 1932): 1652; 43 (13 January 1932): 1719; 50 (18 May 1932): 2054; 73 (9 November 1932): 1058.

50 Ibid., 40 (16 December 1931): 1580; 68 (21 September 1932): 841; 137 (18 April 1934): 733; 145 (25 April 1934): 1250; 179 (10 April 1935): 728.

51 Ibid., 39 (9 December 1931): 1530; 151 (29 August 1934): 1684; 182 (8 May 1935): 921; 184 (22 May 1935): cover.

52 He Jing'an, "Funü caiyi shi ying zhuyi zhi yaodian," *Linglong* 192 (3 July 1935): 1619.

53 *Linglong* 43 (21 November 1932): 1724; 51 (25 May 1932): 23; 61 (3 August 1932): 507; 66 (7 September 1932): 767; 68 (21 September 1932): 845; 69 (5 October 1932): 894; 78 (14 December 1932): 1323; 100 (21 June 1933): 974; 107 (23 August 1933): 1442; 155 (3 October 1934): 1967; 174 (6 March 1935): 480-81.

54 In 1935, the Film Star Photograph Company (Yingxing zhaopian she), based in central Shanghai, released a special jianmei issue for its mass circulation series *Album of Stars,* with each volume selling for 0.2 yuan. The issue included not only well-known younger

jianmei stars who were once trained in song and dance troupes but also older stars who had never revealed their skin. This showed how much jianmei had become a generally appealing quality for Chinese cinema stars to possess. *Linglong* 189 (26 June 1935): 1444.

55 *Hu Die nüshi xiezhen ji*, vol. 12 (Shanghai: Liangyou tushu yinshua gongsi, 1933), 8; Li Lili, *Xingyun liushui pian: huiyi, zhunian, yingcun* (Beijing: Zhongguo dianying chubanshe [private imprint], 2001), 168.

56 *Linglong* 127 (10 January 1934): 123.

57 Lee, *Shanghai Modern*, 46, 63.

58 Ibid., 65, 74.

59 Here I am influenced by the ideas on female writers and readers contained in Janice Radway, *Reading the Romance: Women, Patriarchy, and Popular Literature* (Chapel Hill: University of North Carolina Press, 1984).

60 "Guangzhou xuanju datui meiren," *Linglong* 198 (21 October 1935): 2042.

61 "Xuanju Shanghai xiaojie," *Linglong* 198 (21 August 1935): 2074.

62 See Fan Hong, *Footbinding, Feminism, and Freedom: The Liberation of Women's Bodies in Modern China* (London: Frank Cass, 1997), 235-37, for a succinct discussion of the NLM.

63 For example, the Nationalists considered Communism, the original target of the NLM, illegitimate on the grounds that the physical appearances of Communist women did not fit into state codes. After the split between the Nationalist Party and the Communist Party in 1927, Nationalist Party forces killed thousands of "modern" women because they were accused of "free love" or sometimes simply because they had bobbed hair, unbound feet, or a local reputation for opposing familial authority. Duara, *Sovereignty and Authenticity*, 137. When the actress Li Lili travelled across Shaanxi to Inner Mongolia to make a movie in 1940, she was told that some foot-bound women wearing heavy makeup dancing on the streets in Xi'an were Communists. Li, *Xingyun liushui pian*, 114, 119.

64 Zhongguo di'er lishi dang'an guan, ed., *Zhonghua Minguo shi dang'an ziliao huibian*, vol. 5, no. 1: Wen Huan [Culture] 2. (Nanjing: Jiangsu guji chubanshe, 1991), 930.

65 "Nüzi shouruo de yuanyin," *Linglong* 137 (18 April 1934): 727-28; Zhao Liang, "Cong chanzu shuodao luozu," *Linglong* 151 (29 August 1934): 1654-56; "Shanghai nüzhong qudi nüsheng shuru," *Linglong* 206 (9 October 1935): 3393-94; "Gaogen xie de haichu," *Linglong* 234 (1936): 1215.

66 The tabloids rumoured that Huang had dressed inappropriately to attract newspaper attention and promote her film, which was to be shown in Chongqing. See "Huang Jing yixiang tiankai de xuanchuan fangfa," *Diansheng* 5, 26 (19 June 1936): 590.

67 "Funü yu xufa yundong," *Linglong* 171 (6 February 1935): 259-60; "Xin shenghuo yundong zhi funü xufa yundong," *Linglong* 171 (6 February 1935): 306-7; "Qudi funü shimao fuzhuang," *Linglong* 221 (22 January 1936): 157-58.

68 "Xu Lai wei modeng pohuai," *Linglong* 136 (11 April 1934): 700. William C. Kirby, "The Internationalization of China: Foreign Relations at Home and Abroad in the Republican Era," in *Reappraising Republican China*, edited by Frederic Wakeman Jr. and Richard L. Edmonds (Oxford: Oxford University Press, 2000), 179-204, here 190, 195, suggests that Chinese young men's militaristic organizations, such as the Blue Shirt Society (resembling the Italian Blackshirts), played an important role in the NLM, which combined Confucianism with fascism. It seems that the "modern fashion destruction troupes" were inspired by the Blue Shirt Society.

69 Similarly, popular hygiene literature of the European life reform movement doubted the legitimacy of cosmetics and cosmetic surgery as contradictory to a person's real character. Hau, *Cult of Health and Beauty in Germany*, 180.

70 Cao Xiulin, "Xin nüzi ying you zhi zhunbei," *Linglong* 3 (1 April 1931): 79; 4 (8 April 1931): 124; Zhiying, "Yao xian mei de liliang," *Linglong* 3 (1 April 1931): 89-91; Miss Xiuling, "Nü

yundong jia zhuji," *Linglong* 50 (18 May 1932): 2074-75; Li Mingxia, "Zuo yi wei xiandai nüzi," *Linglong* 196 (7 August 1935): 1911-12.

71 As a common style of dress, *qipao* can be categorized as either "fancy" and "bizarre dress" incompatible with jianmei or plain clothing consistent with jianmei based on fabric, cut, and decorations. Karl Gerth, *China Made: Consumer Culture and the Creation of the Nation* (Cambridge, MA: Harvard University Press, 2003), 22, suggests that "the conditions of production rather than the national origins of the style or type of good defined product-nationality." For comments on German opposition to women's fashion associated with corrupt, artificial, urban life, see Mosse, *Nationalism and Sexuality*, 55.

72 Qiong, "Tan Deguo jin nüzi tu zhifen," *Linglong* 107 (23 August 1933): 1399-1401; Jiang Xinlang, "Fufen ye shi yishu," *Linglong* 3 (1 April 1931): 91; Miss Yunfang, "Fufen fengchao: wo guo jiaoyu jie youwu ganxiang," *Linglong* 13 (10 June 1931): 443; "Xuefu bianwei zhifen chang," *Linglong* 130 (31 January 1934): 263; Huasheng, "Cong Deguo de weisheng fuzhuang yundong tandao Zhongguo shimao funü de yanghua," *Linglong* 221 (22 January 1936): 167-69.

73 Chen Mulan, "Tan funü yu shechi ping," *Linglong* 240 (10 June 1936): 1669-71.

74 Lian, "Zai guoshi weidai zhong, xin nüxing yinggai zenyang," *Linglong* 260 (4 November 1936): 3328-30.

75 Gail Hershatter, *Dangerous Pleasures: Prostitution and Modernity in Twentieth-Century Shanghai* (Berkeley: University of California Press, 1997), 246-70, suggests that, since late Qing, nationalist and feminist writers linked prostitution with national weakness and the quest for modernity. This connection was more explicit during the national crisis.

76 "Changsha jinü pei taozhang," *Linglong* 173 (27 February 1935): 445; "Taiyuan fandui jinü tangfa gelü," *Linglong* 184 (22 May 1935): 1131-32; "Taiyuan jinü shixing tangfa he chuan gaogen xie," *Linglong* 185 (29 May 1935): 1210; "Hankou jiang huading changji qu," *Linglong* 191 (3 July 1935): 1574; "Qudi funü shimao fuzhuang," *Linglong* 221 (22 January 1936): 157-58; "Guangdong funü buyong toujin," *Linglong* 221 (22 January 1936): 186-87.

77 "Nanbei ji," *Linglong* 153 (19 September 1934): 1805.

78 "Riben yiji he nü zhaodai yiqi jiaru guofang yundong," *Linglong* 283 (28 April 1937): 1225-26.

79 As part of the efforts to embrace a new modest image, they tried to learn modern, socially relevant plays *(huaju)* in addition to the traditional *pingju* romances. "Guanyu shoudu genü de xunlian," *Linglong* 240 (10 June 1936): 1645-46; "Shoudu jinü zhi jinbu," *Linglong* 137 (18 April 1934): 726.

80 'Zhenjiang zuzhi jiaofang nüzi minzhong xueshe miaowen," *Linglong* 190 (26 June 1935): 1525-26.

81 "Taiyuan fandui jinü tangfa gelü," *Linglong* 184 (22 May 1935): 1131-32.

82 "Qudi funü shimao fuzhuang," *Linglong* 221 (22 January 1936): 157-58; "Zhenjiang zuzhi jiaofang nüzi minzhong xueshe miaowen," *Linglong* 189 (26 June 1935): 1526.

83 "Funü yu xufa yundong," *Linglong* 171 (6 February 1935): 259-60; Pengzi, "Zhengqi tangfa zai Hangzhou," *Linglong* 221 (22 January 1936): 184. During the radical Maoist years in the People's Republic of China, *ji*-chignons were attacked as feudal and backward. Only the evenly cropped "liberation hair style" was considered modern and revolutionary.

84 Pingzi, "Qudi nanzi qizhuang yifu," *Linglong* 158 (24 October 1934): 2101-3; "Nannü luti fa zuo kugong," *Linglong* 197 (14 August 1935): 2061-62. On bare feet and pornography, see Dorothy Ko, *Cinderella's Sisters: A Revisionist History of Footbinding* (Berkeley: University of California, 2005), 41-42.

85 Several telegrams from Beiping appealed to the minister of education to stop Mayor Yuan Liang's ban on coeducation, in order to protect equality in education. At the same time, the head of the Henan Bureau of Education announced that the bureau would combine

girls' and boys' middle schools in 1935 in order to save money and develop general education. Ni, "Biekai shengmian de jinling," *Linglong* 151 (29 August 1934): 1651-53, 1709; "Pingshi choushe nüzi gongyu," *Linglong* 191 (3 July 1935): 1572; "Nannü luoti youyong," *Linglong* 191 (3 July 1935): 1573; "Yu shixing nannü tongxue," *Linglong* 198 (21 October 1935): 2143.

86 Jingzi, "Waiguo zuojia de Zhongguo nüxing guan," *Linglong* 194 (24 July 1935): 1760-62.

87 "Jinzhi luozu sheng zhong yi fansheng," *Linglong* 151 (29 August 1934): 1664-65, 1709; Linjun, "Qudi funü luotui," *Linglong* 152 (20 September 1934): 1715-16; Miss Liu Mei, "Shehui fugu qingxiang zhong funü ying you de zijue," *Linglong* 157 (17 October 1934): 2035-38.

88 "'Sancun jinlian' yu Xin Shenghuo," *Linglong* 158 (24 October 1934): 2114.

89 Shanxi yi cungu, "Qing jiuji chizu luotui," *Linglong* 154 (26 September 1934): 1856; "Jinzhi luozu sheng zhong yi fansheng," *Linglong* 151 (29 August 1934), 1664-65; Miss Liu Mei, "Shehui fugu qingxiang zhong funü ying you de zijue," *Linglong* 157 (17 October 1934): 2035-38. On bare feet, see Janet Lyon, "The Modern Foot," in *Footnotes on Shoes*, edited by Shari Benstock and Suzanne Ferris (New Brunswick, NJ: Rutgers University Press, 2001), 272-75.

90 "Jinzhi luozu sheng zhong yi fansheng," *Linglong* 151 (29 August 1934): 1664-65, 1709.

91 Xiujuan, "Luti fasheng wenti," *Linglong* 4 (8 April 1931): 112.

92 Miss Qixiu, "Luoti wenxian," *Linglong* 191 (3 July 1935): 1519-22; Yingwu, "Luoti mei suyuan," *Linglong* 186 (5 June 1935): 1034.

93 *Linglong* 29 (30 September 1931): 1076-77; 39 (9 December 1931): 1532-33; 50 (18 May 1932): 2069; 53 (8 June 1932): 120-21; 60 (27 July 1932): 460; Lisha, "Ziran shenghuo yu Deguo funü," *Linglong* 88 (22 March, 1933): 344-45.

94 Zeng Na, "Luoti da jihui zhi canju," *Linglong* 56 (29 June 1932): 281; "Daojie luoti zhuyi zhe," *Linglong* 197 (14 August 1935): 2060; Fenzhen, "Fenlan zhi luoti zhuzhi," *Linglong* 221 (22 January 1936): 178-79; "Xiangfen liao de dongji yundong chang," *Linglong* 271 (27 January 1937): 311-14.

95 Ma Xiaojin, "Tan Luoti," *Linglong* 189 (26 June 1935): 1441-42; 191 (3 July 1935): 1528; Xiangcun, "Luoti jiating," *Linglong* 241 (17 June 1936): 1794-98; "Meiguo de luoti xueyuan," *Linglong* 271 (27 January 1937): 312-13.

96 *Linglong* 2 (25 March 1931): 46-47; Lisha, "Ziran shenghuo yu deguo funü," *Linglong* 88 (22 March 1933): 344-45; "Huabu zhi Yadang Xiawa," *Linglong* 97 (31 May 1933): 763; "Dongjing wu chunü," *Linglong* 169 (23 January 1935): 143-44.

97 *Linglong* 43 (13 January 1932 [wrongly dated 1931]): 1723; 102 (12 July 1933): 1103; 206 (9 October 1935): 3344; Zhaoliang, "Luoti yu fushi," *Linglong* 225 (26 February 1936): 463-66.

98 Tan Xishan, "Luoti, bansu, shi hewu: yiguo qingdiao," *Linglong* 232 (24 June 1936): 1025-27; "Qingshi zhi liubing yundong," *Linglong* 225 (26 February 1936): 526-27; 228 (18 March 1936): 724-25; Yaofang, "Guangxi Yaoren funü de shenghuo," 97 (31 May 1933): 760.

Chapter 3: The Basketball Team of the Private Liangjiang Women's Tiyu Normal School

1 Arthur J. Daley, "On Basketball Courts: Chinese Play Basketball," *New York Times*, 21 January 1939, 10.

2 On the introduction of basketball into China, see Jonathan Kotlach, *Sports, Politics and Ideology in China* (New York: Jonathan David, 1972), 29. See also Yao Ming, *Yao: A Life in Two Worlds* (New York: Miramax, 2004).

3 See Wang Zheng, *Women in the Chinese Enlightenment: Oral and Textual Histories* (Berkeley: University of California Press, 1999), 145-87. Lu mentions the basketball team on 156-58. Wang's commentary does not mention the sport at all.

4 Lu established the school with her personal savings. In her interview with Wang Zheng, she repeatedly referred to Liangjiang as "my school." On women and travel, see Susan Mann, "The Virtue of Travel for Women in the Late Empire," in *Gender in Motion: Divisions of Labor and Cultural Change in Late Imperial and Modern China,* edited by Bryna Goodman and Wendy Larson, (Lanham, MD: Rowman and Littlefield, 2005), 55-74.

5 Yu Chien-ming, *Yundong chang nei wai: jindai Huadong diqu de nüzi tiyu, 1895-1937* (Taipei: Institute of Modern History, Academia Sinica, 2009); Yu Chien-ming, "Jindai huadong diqu de nü qiuyuan: yi baokan zazhi weizhu de taolun," *Zhongyang yanjiu yuan jindai shi yanjiu suo jikan* 32 (1999): 57-125.

6 Wang, *Women in the Chinese Enlightenment,* 146-53; Zhang Zhiliu, "Fang Liangjiang Nütizhuan yuan xiaozhang Lu Lihua," *Shanghai tiyu shihua* 11, 28 (1985); *Shanghai tebie shi jiaoyu ju jiaoyu zhoubao* 30 (1929): 3; *Nüduo* 18, 6 (1929): 85.

7 The *People's Tribune* used Liangjiang as the exemplar institution for physical education in China, having "in its fourteen years of existence turned out over 300 trained women physical instructors, and today, has 100 students in residence taking a three-year course." "The Feminist Movement in China," *People's Tribune* 25, 5 (1 June 1935): 301-14. Twenty-two classes of more than a thousand students graduated from Liangjiang from 1922 to 1950. Liangjiang remained active and influential until just before the outbreak of full-scale war. On 1 February 1936, the Social Bureau of Beiping sent an official letter to Liangjiang requesting the acceptance of two students from Duzhi Girls' Secondary School, with a tuition waiver. Beijing Municipal Archives, vol. J2, no. 3, file 557. In June 1936, Lu Lihua sailed through Hong Kong to Guangzhou to establish a branch of the alumni association there: *Qinfen tiyu yuebao* 3, 9 (June 1936): 871; *Tiyu zhoubao* 2, 20 (24 June 1933): 1; *Yule* 2, 23 (1936): 448; *Pingmin yuekan* 12, 10 (1936): 19; *Shishi yuebao* 22, 3 (1940): 136; *Xuesheng shenghuo* 1, 3 (1940): 10; *Haiguang* 15 (1946): 12; *Xinbao zhoukan* 12 (1946): 4.

8 *Shenbao,* 18 September 1929, 18 January 1931, and 8 February 1931; *Nü pengyou* 1, 6 (1932): 24-25.

9 "Zhonghua nü'er guo wei xumei tuqi," *Shibao,* 23 March 1934; *Nü pengyou* 1, 5 (1932): 26-27; *Qinfen tiyu yuebao* 1, 7 (10 April 1934): 60-61. Huang Shufang, Long Jingxiong, Yang Ren, Xiang Dawei, Cheng Baixue, Chang Mingzhen, et al., interviewed by Wu Zhiming, "Liangjiang nüzi tiyu zhuanke xuexiao xiaoshi," *Tiyu shiliao* 6 (April 1982): 7-8.

10 Lu Lihua, "Zhongguo nü lanqiu zai quanyunhui geiyu women de yinxiang" (abbreviated as "Yinxiang"), *Qinfen tiyu yuebao* 1, 2 (10 November 1933): 7-8.

11 *Qinfen tiyu yuebao* 3, 5 (February 1936): 447; Zhao Yukun, "Jijian xiaoshi," *Tiyu shiliao* 6 (April 1982): 36.

12 For the national games' regulations on the amateur status of participating athletes, see *Zhonghua minguo ershi'er nian quanguo yundong dahui jinian ce* (Shanghai: Zhonghua shuju, 1933), 9, 17-20; "Zhonghua quanguo tiyu xiejin hui shending xiuzheng yeyu yundong guize (ershiliu nian wuyue xiuzheng)," *Tiyu jikan* 3, 2 (June 1937): 240-41.

13 *Shenbao,* 23 November 1929.

14 Ibid., 15 March 1930.

15 Lu, "Yinxiang."

16 *Tiyu zhoubao* 2, 22 (8 July 1933): 27; 2, 26 (5 August 1933): 2-5; 2, 28 (19 August 1933): 2-5; *Qinfen tiyu yuebao* 3 (5 February 1936): 447; *Shenbao,* 18 January 1931.

17 Susan K. Cahn, *Coming on Strong: Gender and Sexuality in Twentieth-Century American Women's Sports* (Cambridge, MA: Harvard University Press, 1994), 87.

18 *Shenbao,* 19 March 1929 and 28 November 1933.

19 *Linglong* 104 (26 July 1933): 1233.

20 *Young Companion Pictorial* featured the dancing scenes of the Liangjiang games in 1929, which Minxin (民新) Studio shot among its very first films featuring natural scenes, politics, and the birth of the studio itself. *Beiyang huabao,* 11 June 1927 and June 1928; *Liangyou*

huabao 37 (July 1929): 20-21; *Hong Meigui* 4, 36 (1928): A4, A6; *Funü zazhi* 14, 2 (1928): 1; *Xiandai xuesheng* 1 (1930): 1; *Zi luolan* 1, 15 (1926): 1; 1, 16 (1926): 1; 2, 21 (1927): 3; *Qinfen tiyu yuebao* 3, 10 (July 1936): 929.

21 *Dushu qingnian* 2, 8 (1937): 3; 2, 12 (1937): 40-42; *Funü shenghuo* 4, 5 (1937): 1; *Funü Xinshenghuo yuekan* 4 (1937); *Kangjian shijie* 2 (1935): 1; *Libai liu* 691 (1937): 23; *Nü xuesheng* 2 (1931): 29-30; *Qinfen tiyu yuebao* 2, 4 (10 January 1935): 300; 12 (September 1935): 31-32; *Shidai zimei* 1 (1934): A6; 1 (1934): B47; *Shishi yuebao* 2, 5 (1930): 5; *Jiaoyu zazhi* 27, 5 (1937): 1; *Xuexiao shenghuo* 7 (1930): 27; *Xiandai funü* 1, 1 (1933): 1; *Xiandai jiating* 7 (1937): 1; *Zhonghua huabao* 1, 59 (18 September 1931); *Zhufu zhiyou* 1, 2 (1937): 1; *Zhongguo xuesheng* 3, 6 (1936): 15; 3, 7 (1936): front and back covers; 3, 19-22 (1937): 1; 4, 5 (1937): 14-15.

22 Lu Lihua, "Jie wo huazhou," *Guoshu zhoukan* 158-60 (1936): 5; Lu Lihua, "Sichuan kaocha hou zhi yinxiang," *Zhonghua guohuo chanxiao xiehui meizhou huibao* 3, 37 (1937): 3; *Diansheng* 7, 42 (21 October 1938): 837.

23 *Linglong* 40 (16 December 1931): 1578-79; 68 (21 September 1932): 862.

24 *Shenbao*, 29 October, 30 October, and 1 November 1930; *Liangyou huabao* 53 (30 January 1931): 32; *Nankai daxue zhoukan* 92 (1930): 37; 94 (1930): 36-37; *Nankai shuangzhou* 6, 3 (1930): 48-49, 54.

25 *Beiyang huabao*, 18 November 1930.

26 *Dagong bao* (Tianjin), 31 October 1930.

27 Lu, "Yinxiang," 7-8.

28 Bryna Goodman and Wendy Larson, "Introduction," in *Gender in Motion: Divisions of Labor and Cultural Change in Late Imperial and Modern China*, edited by Bryna Goodman and Wendy Larson (Lanham, MD: Rowman and Littlefield, 2005), 6-7.

29 *Tiyu zhoubao* 2, 22 (8 July 1933): 27; *Nüduo* 22, 3-4 (1933): 99.

30 In Fujian, the team was received by representatives from *Jiangsheng* newspaper, the Provincial Tiyu Association, Jimei School, and Xiamen University, and by alumni teaching at Yude Girls' School. In Guangdong, the head of Experimental District of Mass Tiyu received the team. *Tiyu zhoubao* 2, 22 (8 July 1933): 27.

31 *Tiyu zhoubao* 2, 24 (22 July 1933): 27; 2, 26 (5 August 1933): 2-5; 2, 28 (19 August 1933): 2-5; *Shenbao*, 22 June and 11 August 1933.

32 *Tiyu zhoubao* 2, 26 (5 August 1933): 25.

33 *Qinfen tiyu yuebao* 2, 4 (10 January 1935): frontispieces, 299-300; *Shenbao*, 10, 14, 18, and 21 December 1934, and 26 December 1936; *Funü yuebao* 3, 1 (1937): 19-20.

34 Due to a lack of equipment, the Fourth National Games still employed the English system rather than the metric system. Women were allowed to compete in volleyball, tennis, and track and field for the first time as well. *Quanguo yundong dahui zong baogao: shijiu nian siyue Hangzhou juxing* (1930) 2, 9-10; *Quanyun hui teji* (Shanghai: Tiyu shenghuo chubanshe, 1948), 17, 19-21, 29-30; *Linglong* 6 (22 April 1931): 188.

35 *Qinfen tiyu yuebao* 1, 2 (10 November 1933): 72-73; *Linglong* 133 (21 March 1934): 481; *Quanyun hui teji*, 37-41, frontispieces; *Di wu jie quanyun zhuanji* (Shanghai: Wenhua meishu tushu gongsi, 1933), 3. *Minguo ershi'er nian quanguo yundong dahui zong baogao shu* (Shanghai: Zhonghua shuju, 1934), [section 2] 22.

36 *Qinfen tiyu yuebao* 3, 2 (November 1935): 175.

37 *Linglong* 117 (25 October 1933): cover, 2010.

38 *Quanyun hui teji*, 37-41, frontispieces; *Diliu jie quanyun shimo ji* (Beiping: Pingbao tiyu bu, 1935), 47-53, 141, 152.

39 Wang Jianming, a Shanghai journalist and the author of a biography of Yang Xiuqiong, noted that "in the heavy traffic to the site of the Fifth National Games, women from Liangjiang walked among rickshaws and cars and arrived first." *Meirenyu Yang Xiuqiong*

(Shanghai: Guanghua shuju, 1935), 5; *Di wu jie quanyun zhuanji* 33; Lu, "Yinxiang," frontispiece, 7-8, 74-76.

40 Lu Lihua, "Liangjiang Nüxiao canjia wanguo lanqiu sai de jingguo" (abbreviated as "Jingguo"), *Shanghai tiyu shihua* 2 (1984): 15; Lu Lihua, "Woguo zuizao chuguo bisai de nüzi lanqiu dui" (abbreviated as "Lanqiu dui"), *Tiyu shiliao* 3 (February 1981): 40; Cai Yangwu and Liu Yali, eds., *Shanghai tiyu zhi* (Shanghai: Shanghai shehui kexue yuan chubanshe, 1996), 184; Li Jingchang and Li Fan, eds., *Shanghai tiyu jingcui* (Beijing: Dadi chubanshe, 1989): 162; Wu Chih-kang, "The Influence of YMCA on the Development of Physical Education in China" (PhD diss., University of Michigan, 1956), 34; Wu Zhiming and Wu Jian, "Nülan wuhao – ji Chen Baixue," *Tiyu shiliao* 6 (April 1982): 7-8, and 8 (1982): 41; *Linglong* 58 (13 July 1932): 358; 67 (14 September 1932): 795; *Shenbao*, 12 March 1930; 18 January and 8, 15, and 22 February 1931; 22 January 1935; *Zhonghua zhoubao* 10 (1932): 198.

41 *Shenbao*, 15 and 20 February 1930.

42 Ibid., 25 and 27 February 1933.

43 *Qinfen tiyu yuebao* 3, 2 (November 1935): 207.

44 Andrew D. Morris, "Native Songs and Dances: Southeast Asia in a Greater Chinese Sporting Community, 1920-1948," *Journal of Southeast Asian Studies* 31, 1 (March 2000): 48-69.

45 *Qinfen tiyu yuebao* 2, 3 (10 December 1934): 251; Lu, "Lanqiu dui," 40; Wang, *Women in the Chinese Enlightenment*, 157-58.

46 See the essays generally in Bryna Goodman and Wendy Larson, eds., *Gender in Motion: Divisions of Labor and Cultural Change in Late Imperial and Modern China* (Lanham, MD: Rowman and Littlefield, 2005).

47 "The Feminist Movement in China," *People's Tribune* 25, 5 (1 June 1935): 301-14.

48 *Linglong* 117 (25 October 1933): 2010.

49 *Tiyu zhoubao* 2, 22 (July 8, 1933): 27; 2, 24 (22 July 1933): 27; 2, 26 (5 August 1933): 2-5; *Shenbao*, 22 June and 11 August 1933. On Shandong women, see Ellen R. Judd, "Women on the Move: Women's Kinship, Residence, and Networks in Rural Shandong," in *Gender in Motion*, edited by Goodman and Larson, 91-120.

50 In July 1932, the Guangzhou Athletic Association organized the South China men's and women's basketball and volleyball teams, consisting of thirteen male and seventeen female players, for a tour of Southeast Asia, including the Philippines and Singapore. Both women's teams won their games against local teams and generated excitement in the local athletic circle in both countries. *Tiyu zhoubao* 32 (10 September 1932): 25. *Linglong* 67 (14 September 1932): 795, carried a photograph of the South China women's basketball team beating the American public school girls' basketball team in the Philippines, 38 to 8, in 1932. The basketball team of Dongya Tiyu Vocational School in Shanghai gained fame after it performed and encouraged women's tiyu in the hinterlands of Jiangxi at the invitation of the Jiangxi Bureau of Education in October 1934. The Malayan basketball and volleyball association and the Chinese communities in Singapore telegraphed to invite the team to tour Southeast Asia from January to February 1935. *Qinfen tiyu yuebao* 2, 5 (10 February 1935): 377; 3, 5 (February 1936): 447; *Shenbao*, 21 and 29 March, 4 May, and 24 December 1937.

51 Lu Lihua, "Lu Lihua nanyou guangan lu," *Shibao*, 6 June 1935.

52 *Shenbao*, 27 May 1935; *Shishi xunbao* 25 (1935): 27; *Funü gongming* 4, 3 (1935): 73; 6 (1935): 29; *Libai liu* 592 (1935): 22.

53 Lu Lihua, "Liangjiang nütishi lanqiu dui yuanzheng nanyang ji" (abbreviated as "Nanyang ji"), *Qinfen tiyu yuebao* 2, 10 (10 July 1935): 677-78, frontispiece photograph; 3, 5 (February 1936): 447.

54 *Tiyu zhoubao* 2, 24 (22 July 1933): 27; 2, 28 (19 August 1933): 2-5; *Shenbao*, 22 June 1933.

55 Lu, "Lanqiu dui," 40.
56 Ibid.; Lu, "Yinxiang," 7-8.
57 Gu Zhenglai was a lifelong coach for the Boy Scouts, a head teacher of Jimei School, and later the principal of the Chinese Tiyu School in Shanghai. The two met during the annual conference of the nationwide Education Improvement Society created by noted educators Cai Yuanpei and Tao Xingzhi. Wang, *Women in the Chinese Enlightenment,* 163-64.
58 *Tiyu zhoubao* 2, 3 (25 February 1933): 4. On Mei Lanfang's visit, see Joshua Goldstein, *Drama Kings: Players and Publics in the Re-creation of Peking Opera, 1870-1937* (Berkeley: University of California Press, 2007), 272-82.
59 *Tiyu zhoubao* 2, 2 (18 February 1933): 1-2; 2, 3 (25 February 1933): 6; 2, 5 (25 February 1933): 26.
60 Ibid., 2, 2 (18 February 1933): 1-2; 3 (25 February 1933): 4-7; Lu Lihua, "Fuxing hou de Liangjiang nüzi tiyu shifan xuexiao shinian qian de huisu" (abbreviated as "Huisu"), *Qinfen tiyu yuebao* 1, 10 (10 July 1934): 31-32.
61 Pan Gongzhan, "Wei ju chengbao sili Liangjiang nüzi shifan xuexiao mujuan fuxing xuexiao jianshe yi an zhunyu bei'an you," *Shanghai shi zhengfu gongbao* 155 (1935): 83-84.
62 *Tiyu zhoubao* 2, 3 (25 February 1933): 6; 2, 5 (25 February 1933): 26.
63 *Tiyu zhoubao* 2, 2 (18 February 1933): 1-2.
64 Ibid., 2, 3 (25 February 1933): 4; 2-5 (25 February 1933): 26; *Zhongguo kangjian yuebao* (March 1933): 38-40.
65 *Shenbao,* 8, 9, 10, 12, and 13 February 1933; *Tiyu zhoubao* 2, 2 (18 February 1933): 1-2; 2-3 (25 February 1933): 4.
66 When Lu first established the Liangjiang Tiyu School, she was encouraged by Ma Xiangbo and Zhang Boling, both significant educators, and Yu Youren, a dominant leader of the Nationalist government. Dong Shoujing, Wang Rutang, and Zhang Boling served as Liangjiang's trustees over different periods. Lu, "Huisu," 31-32; Wang, *Women in the Chinese Enlightenment,* 146-53.
67 *Tiyu zhoubao* 2, 2 (18 February 1933): 1-2; 2, 3 (25 February 1933): 4-6.
68 Ibid., 2, 2 (18 February 1933): 1-2; 2-3 (25 February 1933): 4-7.
69 *Tiyu zhoubao* 2, 3 (25 February 1933): 7; 2, 4 (4 March 1933): 2; 2, 7 (25 March 1933): 21; *Shenbao,* 21, 24, and 27 February 1933.
70 *Tiyu zhoubao* 2, 7 (25 March 1933): 24.
71 Ibid., 2, 4 (4 March 1933): 2; 9 (8 April 1933): 4.
72 *Da gongbao* (Tianjin), 26 February 1933.
73 *Tiyu zhoubao* 2, 26 (5 August 1933): 2-5; 2, 28 (19 August 1933): 2-5.
74 Lu, "Yinxiang," 7-8; Wang, *Women in the Chinese Enlightenment,* 145-86.
75 *Qinfen tiyu yuebao* 3, 5 (February 1936): 447.
76 Lu, "Nanyang ji."
77 Wang Jianwu, "Lanqiu de zhexue," *Tiyu zhoubao* 35 (1 October 1932): 20.
78 Lu, "Huisu" 31-32.
79 *Shenbao,* 12 January 1931.
80 Popular magazines indicated that opening the somewhat mysterious female students' dormitories to the curious public on certain days was a fashionable form of public relations for schools. Jiangsu shengli zhenjiang gonggong tiyu chang, ed., *Tiyu yanjiu yu tongxun* 1, 3 (June 1933); Lu, "Huisu," 31-32; *Qinfen tiyu yuebao* 1, 5 (10 February 1934): 7; 9 (10 June 1934): 34.
81 *Dashanghia jiaoyu* 2, 1 (1934): 1; *Libai liu* 573 (1934): 1; *Zhongguo xuesheng* 2, 19 (1936): back cover.
82 "The Feminist Movement in China," *People's Tribune* 25, 5 (1 June 1935): 301-14.
83 *Shenbao,* 3 February 1931.

84 A noted doctor of Chinese medicine, Chen Cunren, recalled that when an orphanage that he took over after Japan bombed Shanghai in August 1937 was overwhelmed, he asked Lu for help. Believing that Chen's "gentle demeanor could not sustain the situation," Lu saved the day with a thousand scouts from Liangjiang. An official from the orphanage later told Chen: "Fortunately, we have the 'dragon lady' *(e niangzi)* Lu Lihua in command to survive the most difficult three days." Chen, who described Lu as a straightforward woman "with stout physique and manly temperament," was amused by the phrase "*e niangzi*." Chen Cunren, *Kangzhang shidai shenghuo shi* (Guilin: Guangxi shifan daxue chubanshe, 2007), 16-17.

85 Frederic Wakeman Jr., *Policing Shanghai, 1927-1937* (Berkeley: University of California Press, 1995), 268.

86 *Tiyu zhoubao* 41 (21 November 1932): 2-3.

87 In the games of the Construction Division of Zhejiang Province, the three joined Liangjiang's Cheng Rongming, Yang Sen, and Huang Shuhua to form the Shanghai squad, which played impressively against the Hangzhou team. *Tiyu zhoubao* 2, 2 (18 February 1933): 1-2; 2, 5 (25 February 1933): 26; 2, 3 (25 February 1933): 5. Female leaders of those women's tiyu schools worked together. For example, in 1935, Lu, Du Yufei, and Yu Ziyu participated in organizing the Shanghai Municipal Amateur Athletic Association *(tixiehui)*. *Qinfen tiyu yuebao* 2, 5 (10 February 1935): 371.

88 *Tiyu zhoubao* 2, 5 (25 February 1933): 26.

89 "Pan Yueying shang Liangjiang xiaozhang Lu Lihua shu," *Shenbao*, 16 February 1933.

90 *Tiyu zhoubao* 2, 3 (25 February 1933): 2.

91 *Shanghai zhoubao* 1, 16 (1933): 307-9.

92 *Shenbao*, 19 January and 21 February 1931; Wang, *Women in the Chinese Enlightenment,* 155-56.

93 Fundraising was one purpose of the ill-fated competitions between Liangjiang and the Western team in Shanghai that directly led to the failure of the world tour, but *Tiyu Weekly* noted that the trip budget benefited little from the meagre ticket sales. *Tiyu zhoubao* 2, 2 (18 February 1933): 1-2.

94 *Beiyang huabao,* 18 and 19 November 1930.

95 Ibid.

96 *Shenbao*, 29 and 30 October, 1 November, and 5 December 1930.

97 *Shenbao*, 19 January 1935; *Qinfen tiyu yuebao* 2, 5 (10 February 1935): 377.

98 *Tiyu zhoubao* 2, 24 (22 July 1933): 27; 2, 26 (5 August 1933): 2-5; 2, 28 (19 August 1933): 2-5.

99 Cahn, *Coming on Strong,* 87.

100 Lu, "Yinxiang," 7-8.

101 *Tiyu zhoubao* 2, 24 (22 July 1933): 27; 2, 26 (5 August 1933): 2-5; 2, 28 (19 August 1933): 2-5.

102 On crowds, see Haun Saussy, "Crowds, Number, and Mass in China," in *Crowds,* edited by Jeffrey T. Schnapp and Matthew Tiews (Stanford, CA: Stanford University Press, 2006), 262-65. On the Harbin riot, see James H. Carter, *Creating a Chinese Harbin: Nationalism in an International City, 1916-1932* (Ithaca, NY: Cornell University Press, 2002), 120-25.

103 *Shenbao*, 25 November 1934.

104 *Tiyu zhoubao* 2, 2 (18 February 1933): 1-2; 2, 3 (25 February 1933): 5. For more on Lin Kanghou, see Chen, *Kangzhan shidai shenghuo shi,* 247-48.

105 *Tongji xunkan* 134 (1937): 5-6.

106 *Shenbao*, 18 October and 5 December 1930.

107 *Beiyang huabao,* 28 October, 6 and 20 November 1930; *Hong meigui* 7, 30 (1932): A2.

108 *Shenbao*, 29 and 30 October, and 1 November 1930; *Liangyou huabao* 53 (30 January 1931): 32.

109 *Beiyang huabao,* 9 December 1930.

110   Huang Jiping, "Liangjiang nüxiao lanqiu dui dongzheng ji," *Shenbao*, 22 May 1931; *Liangyou huabao* 60 (August 1931): 33; 61 (September 1931); Lu, "Nanyang ji," 677-78; *Qinfen tiyu yuebao* 3, 5 (February 1936): 447; *Zhongguo xuesheng* 3, 4 (1931): 8.

111   *Qinfen tiyu yuebao* 3, 2 (November 1935): 207; *Yule* 1, 24 (1935): 581.

112   *Minzhong shenghuo* 1, 32 (1931): cover, 3; *Shenghuo* 6, 29 (1931): 626; *Shenghuo huabao* 13 (1932): 1; *Dongfang zazhi* 32, 12 (1935): 1; *Tianxin* 26 (1931): 10; *Linglong* 15 (24 June 1931): 512; *Yule* 1, 23 (1935): 554; *Libai liu* 485 (1933): 22; 490 (1933): 12; 506 (1933): 10; 532 (1933): 12; *Xuexiao shenghuo* 1 (1929): 13; 29 (1933): 7; 55 (1933): 7; *Tiyu xinsheng* 2 (1931): 18.

113   On Berenson and her influence, see Pamela Grundy and Susan Shackelford, *Shattering the Glass: The Remarkable History of Women's Basketball* (New York: New Press, 2005), 8-21. On Chinese American teams, see Kathleen S. Yep, "Playing Rough and Tough: Chinese American Basketball Players in the 1930s and 1940s," *Frontiers: A Journal of Women's Studies* 31, 1 (2010): 123-41.

114   Cahn, *Coming on Strong*, 87.

115   This game used the basic basketball skills of passing the ball. Teams did not gain points by shooting but by successfully passing the ball to their own commander. There were usually seven players on each side, with three players, including the commander, in the circle. Zhang Huilan, interviewed by Qiu Weichang, and Zheng Yuangao, "Shanghai Nüqingnian-hui tiyu shifan xuexiao," *Tiyu shiliao* 9 (January 1983): 8-9; *Zhejiang zhongdeng xuexiao di er ci lianhe yundong hui baogao* (n.p.: n.p., 1919).

116   In February 1916, the Shanghai YMCA translated the American version of basketball rules into Chinese, but teams still needed to negotiate and agree on details before each competition. In 1936, the International Basketball Federation set up universal rules, but some courts still followed American rules. Women officially began using the same rules as men in the Shanghai Basketball Games in 1948, with five players on each side. The only difference was that the women's game was divided into four eight-minute sessions and the men's game into ten-minute sessions. The fan-shaped basketball board was changed into a rectangle in 1950. Cai and Liu, *Shanghai tiyu zhi*, 185; Chengdu tiyu xueyuan tiyu shi yanjiu shi, ed., *Zhongguo jindai tiyu shi jianbian* (Beijing: Renmin tiyu chubanshe, 1981), 56. On American rules, see Grundy and Shackelford, *Shattering the Glass*, 26-28.

117   *Tiyu zhoubao* 42 (19 November 1932): 9; *Qinfen tiyu yuebao* 2, 1 (10 October 1934): 73; *Shibao*, 10, 13, 17, 18, 20, 21, 22, 25, and 28 October, and 1 November 1938; "Gongbu yi jiu san liu-yi jiu san qi nian nanzi lanqiu guize genggai," *Tiyu jikan* 3, 2 (June 1937): 246-53; "Gongbu yi jiu san liu-yi jiu san qi nian nüzi lanqiu guize genggai," *Tiyu jikan* 3, 2 (June 1937): 253.

118   *Tiyu zhoubao* 42 (19 November 1932): 9, 43 (26 November 1932): 1-2.

119   For discussions of the new rules in all their complexity, see *Tiyu zhoubao* 42 (19 November 1932): 9; *Qinfen tiyu yuebao* 1, 7 (10 April 1934): 59; 2, 3 (10 December 1934): 251. In her study of Chinese American women's teams, Yep suggests that a larger court space facilitated rapid ball movement and passing. See Yep, "Playing Rough and Tough," 125-26.

120   *Tiyu zhoubao* 42 (19 November 1932): 9.

121   *Qinfen tiyu yuebao* 1, 7 (10 April 1934): 59.

122   Ibid., 2, 3 (10 December 1934): 251.

123   *Tiyu zhoubao* 43 (26 November 1932): 1-2; 2, 8 (6 Feburary 1933): 1-2; 2, 10 (15 April 1933): 2.

124   Wu Bangwei, "Zuijin gexiang yundong guize zhi zhaiyao," *Tiyu yanjiu yu tongxun* 1, 2 (March 1933): 191-200.

125   *Tiyu zhoubao* 2, 8 (1 April 1933): 1; 2, 9 (8 April 1933): 2-3.

126   Ibid., 2, 10 (15 April 1933): 4.

127   For many advertisements of basketball regulation books, see *Qinfen tiyu yuebao* 1, 5 (10 February 1934): 48; 1, 3 (10 December 1933): 34; 2, 1 (10 October 1934): 73.
128   *Shenbao*, 3 May 1930.
129   *Quanyun hui teji*, 37-41, frontispieces; *Di liu jie quanyun shimo ji* (Beiping: Pingbao tiyu bu, 1935), 47-53; *Quanguo yundong dahui zong baogao*, 9-10.
130   Cahn, *Coming on Strong*, 88-89.
131   Nüxia, "Yuxuan," *Shenbao*, 18 September 1929.
132   *Shenbao*, 18 January, 22 February, and 6 March 1931.
133   Lu, "Huisu" 31-32; "Liu Mei yundong jia Hu Zhengqu fanguo," *Qinfen tiyu yuebao* 1, 5 (10 February 1934): 65; "Hu Zhengqu renjiao Liangjiang nü tishi," *Qinfen tiyu yuebao* 1, 6 (10 March 1934): 65.
134   *Qinfen tiyu yuebao* 2, 5 (10 February 1935): 380.
135   *Quanyun hui teji*, 37-41, frontispieces; *Liangyou huabao* 110 (October 1935): 6.
136   *Qinfen tiyu yuebao* 3, 2 (November 1935): 207.
137   *Shenbao*, 22 and 31 January 1935, and 26 February 1936.
138   *Tiyu zhoubao* 2, 2 (18 February 1933): 1-2; 2, 3 (25 February 1933): 4; 2, 24 (22 July 1933): 27.
139   *Shenbao*, 19 May 1931, 27 May 1935.
140   In 1932, for example, Wu Meixian and Wang Yuan, great track stars from Harbin who gained national fame in the Fourth National Games of 1930, organized the Nanqiang basketball team of Nankai Girls' Secondary School. In October 1932, the team easily won its first game by beating the staff team of its own school. It then encountered confusion and delay over rules. The scheduled first game against the Black and White women's team team was cancelled because the latter insisted on using the men's regulations. The second scheduled game, against the Jin team, was cancelled due to lack of referees who could interpret the rules. *Tiyu zhoubao* 40 (5 November 1932): 4.
141   *Tiyu zhoubao* 43 (26 November 1932): 1-2.
142   Ibid., 2, 9 (8 April 1933): 1.
143   *Liangyou huabao* 36 (March 1929): 22-23.
144   Zhou Wenjuan, "Nüzi lanqiu ying yong nanzi guize yi," *Shibao*, 30 November 1934.
145   *Shenbao*, 14 February 1931.
146   "Xiao xuexiao gezhong tiyu huodong de xiangdui jiazhi," translated by Zhang Jinjian, *Tiyu zhoubao* 2, 13 (6 May 1933): 12.
147   "Lanqiu shi jilie yundong ma?" *Tiyu zhoubao* 41 (12 November 1932): 13.
148   Jianmei, "Lanqiu shi julie yundong ma?" *Tiyu zhoubao* 2, 4 (4 March 1933): 7.
149   Wen Huaiyu, "Guanyu nüzi lanqiu: yinyong nanzi guize zhi chuyi," *Shibao*, 13 November 1934.
150   Liu Shao Jinying, "Tichang nüzi tiyu zhi wujian," *Qinfen tiyu yuebao* 2, 3 (10 December 1934): 212-13.
151   Wang Jianwu, "Lanqiu de zhexue," *Tiyu zhoubao* 35 (1 October 1932): 20.
152   *Qinfen tiyu yuebao* 2, 3 (10 December 1934): 251.
153   *Dagong bao* (Tianjin), 24 October 1930.
154   *Shenbao*, 5 December 1930.
155   Zeng Naidun, *Nü xuesheng shenghuo sumiao* (Shanghai: Nüzi shudian, 1936), 45; *Dagong bao* (Tianjin), 17 April 1934; *Shenbao*, 14 May 1934.
156   Wen, "Guanyu nüzi lanqiu."
157   *Daxia* 9, 24 (1 May 1933): 495-96.
158   Zhou, "Nüzi lanqiu ying yong nanzi guize yi."
159   *Tiyu zhoubao* 43 (26 November 1932): 1-2.
160   Ibid., 2, 3 (25 February 1933): 2.

161 *Shenbao*, 17, 18 June and 14 August 1930, and 17 May 1933; *Yougong yuekan* 2, 4 (1929): 3. Yep reports that Chinese American women also played against men. See Yep, "Playing Rough and Tough," 126.

162 "Hangzhou Zhejiang Jianshe yundong hui kaimu," *Shenbao*, 7 January 1933; Cheng Dingyuan, "Xin Zhejiang jianshe yundong hui zhuanzai," *Zhejiang tiyu banyue kan* 24 (1933): 41-45.

163 *Shenbao*, 19 January 1935; *Qinfen tiyu yuebao* 2, 5 (10 February 1935): 377.

164 Lu, "Nanyang ji," 677-78, frontispiece; *Qinfen tiyu yuebao* 3, 5 (February 1936): 447; *Shenbao*, 27 May 1935.

165 *Shenbao*, 26 August 1930.

166 *Dagong bao* (Tianjin), 16 and 17 August 1930.

167 Ibid., 11 May 1928.

168 *Chenbao* (Beiping), 22 and 24 January 1932.

169 Lu Lihua, "Duiyu muqian chubanjie de yijian: xiezuo, chuban, dushu – sanwei yiti," *Dushu* 1, 1 (1937): 16-18.

170 Lu Lihua: "Jiqie xuyao zhi Zhongguo nüzi tiyu," *Tiyu zhoubao* 2, 20 (24 June 1933): 1; "Shanghai nüzi tiyu yingyou de gaijin," *Shanghai jiaoyu jie* 4 (1933): 26-27; "Weixie de quxian," *Shaonü* 2, 1 (1949): 21-24; "Shanghai jidai juban de shiye," *Zhongguo Hongshizihui yuekan* 37 (1938): 4-9.

171 Liu Shao Jinying, "Tichang nüzi tiyu zhi wujian," *Qinfen tiyu yuebao* 2, 3 (10 December 1934): 212-13.

172 *Tiyu zhoubao* 2, 3 (25 February 1933): 4.

173 Lengxue (Chen Baixue's pen name), "Liangjiang lanqiu dui nanzheng riji," *Shibao*, 18 February 1935.

174 *Tiyu zhoubao* 2, 2 (18 February 1933): 2.

175 Ibid., 1-2; 3 (25 February 1933): 4-6.

176 Ibid.; 5 (25 February 1933): 26.

177 Chen Zhenling, "Liangjiang lanqiu zheng Ou Mei," *Linglong* 87 (11 March 1933): 295.

178 *Tiyu zhoubao* 2, 22 (8 July 1933): 27; 26 (5 August 1933): 2-5; 28 (19 August 1933): 2-5.

179 Ibid.

180 *Di liu jie quanyun shimo ji* (Beiping: Pingbao tiyu bu, 1935), 140-41, 152, 173.

181 Lu, "Yinxiang," 7-8.

182 *Tiyu zhoubao* 2, 24 (22 July 1933): 27; 2, 26 (5 August 1933): 2-5; 2, 28 (19 August 1933): 2-5.

183 *Shenbao*, 8 February 1931.

184 *Nankai shuangzhou* 7, 2 (1931): 50.

185 Huang Jiping, "Liangjiang nüxiao lanqiu dui dongzheng ji," *Shenbao*, 22 May 1931, 10, 14, 18, and 21 December 1934, and 26 December 1936; *Liangyou huabao* 60 (August 1931): 33; 61 (September 1931); *Zhongyang ribao*, 22 April 1931; Lu "Nanyang ji"; *Qinfen tiyu yuebao* 2, 4 (10 January 1935): frontispiece, 299-300; 3, 5 (February 1936): 447.

186 *Tiyu zhoubao* 2, 2 (18 February 1933): 1-2; 2, 3 (25 February 1933): 4-5. On the campaign to use national goods, see Frank Dikötter, *Exotic Commodities: Modern Objects and Everyday Life in China* (New York: Columbia University Press, 2006), 39-42, 63, 67, 71.

187 *Shenbao*, 18 December 1929.

188 Pei Shunyuan and Shen Zhenchao, eds., *Nü yundong yuan* (Shanghai: Shanghai tiyu shubao she, 1935).

189 "Dongya jinguo liezhuan," *Shibao*, 14 March 1936.

190 *Shibao*, 24 February 1935.

191 *Shenbao*, 8, 9, 10, 12, and 13 February 1933; *Tiyu zhoubao* 2, 2 (18 February 1933): 1-2; 2, 3 (25 February 1933): 4.

192 *Qinfen tiyu yuebao* 1, 7 (10 April 1934): 60; 1, 6 (10 March 1934): 54; 2, 4 (10 January 1935): 285; "Zhonghua nu'er guo wei xumei tuqi," *Shibao,* 23 March 1934.

193 Hangong, "Tiyu waishi (xu)," *Tiyu zhoukan* 2 (30 October 1931): 11.

194 *Tiyu zhoubao* 2, 4 (4 March 1933): 2; 2, 9 (8 April 1933): 4.

195 See *Liangyou huabao* 36 (March 1929): 22-23 for an image of a men's team that toured overseas, sponsored by a wealthy businessman. For another, later plan, see "Hu Guigeng deng faqi Hubao Tiyuhui," *Shibao,* 12 October 1938.

196 The Liangjiang basketball team's involvement in the "greater China sports community" turned out to be the only moment of extravagance. Player Chen Baixue wrote in *Shibao* that the tour to Southeast Asia used a luxury vessel with modern facilities. Lengxue, "Liangjiang lanqiu dui nanzheng riji," *Shibao,* 18 February 1935; *Yule* 1, 15 (1935): 1; 18 (1935): 435; *Shehui xinwen* 13, 2 (1935): 1.

197 *Tiyu zhoubao* 2, 3 (25 February 1933): 4.

198 Qiuying, "Yougan yu mouxiao nüsheng saiqiu," *Shijie ribao,* 22 April 1935.

199 *Beiyang huabao,* 12 May 1931.

200 *Liangyou huabao* 106 (June 1935): cover.

201 *Shenbao,* 13 January 1934.

202 On crowd control problems at men's games, see *Shenbao,* 22 February 1931.

203 *Beiyang huabao,* 18 November 1930.

204 Ibid., February 1931 and 4 April 1931.

205 *Tiyu zhoubao* 2, 20 (24 June 1933): 3; 2, 22 (8 July 1933): 1-2.

206 Ibid., 2, 2 (18 February 1933): 1-2.

207 Ibid., 2, 28 (19 August 1933): 2-5.

208 *Beiyang huabao,* 18 November 1930.

209 *Honglü* 1, 6 (1936): 144; *Zhongguo xuesheng* 3, 1 (1931): 10.

210 *Qinfen tiyu yuebao* 1, 2 (10 November 1933): 72-73; *Quanyun hui teji,* 37-41, frontispieces.

211 *Tiyu zhoubao* 43 (26 November 1932): 2.

212 Zeng Naidun, *Nü xuesheng shenghuo sumiao.*

213 *Nü qingnian yuekan* 13, 6 (June 1934): 33; Shiyi, "Jinri nü yundong yuan de bingtai," *Guomin tiyu huikan* 1 (January 1936): 32.

214 Cahn, *Coming on Strong,* 170-94.

215 For Lu's discussions of her marriages, see Wang, *Women in the Chinese Enlightenment,* 162-64.

216 "Lu Lihua xiaojie shengde feichang di piaoliang," *Xuexiao shenghuo* 10 (1930): 23; *Hong Meigui* 5, 14 (1929): A2; *Xiandai jiating* 2 (1937): 1; *Xianxiang* 13 (1936): 2; *Shehui xinwen* 1, 1 (1932): 17; Lu Lihua, "Nannü jihui zhi jundeng," *Xing zazhi* 1 (1927): 1-2; Lu Lihua, "Shejiao gongkai zhi zheng yiyi," *Xing zazhi* 2 (1927): 1-3; Lu Lihua, "Jiankang de zhufu yu jiating," *Zhufu zhiyou* 1, 3 (1937): 5-8; Lu Lihua, "Tiyu yu jiating, renlei jiankang de xin faxian," *Kuaile jiating* 1, 6 (1937): 90-92; Lu Lihua, "Nüzi tiyu yu jiating xingfu," *Funü yuebao* 3, 3 (1937): 8.

217 The other rare case of combining a career as a tiyu teacher and administrator with a happy marriage to a male tiyu professor and administrator was Gao Zi, a classmate of Zhang Huilan, who married Hao Gengsheng (see Chapter 1). When the China Athletic Referee Association in Shanghai recruited basketball referees, Shao and Bao Xiuzhen were hired to maintain women's rules, while six men did the same for men's rules. *Tiyu zhoubao* 2, 5 (25 February 1933): 26.

218 *Linglong* 58 (13 July 1932): 358; *Furen huabao* 46 (February 1937).

219 *Tiyu zhoubao* 2, 22 (8 July 1933): 27; 2, 26 (5 August 1933): 2-5; 2, 28 (19 August 1933): 2-5; "Nüzi lanqiu jianjiang Shao Jinying hunbian ji," *Qinfen tiyu yuebao* 1, 8 (10 May 1934): 64. Copied from *Tiyu pinglun* 81 (21 April 1934): 217.

220   *Qinfen tiyu yuebao* 2, 11 (10 August 1935): 764.

221   Yu, *Yundong chang nei wai,* 87-88.

222   See Francesco Alberoni, "The Powerless 'Elite': Theory and Sociological Research on the Phenomenon of the Stars," in *The Celebrity Culture Reader,* edited by P. David Marshall (New York: Routledge, 2006), 108-23.

223   Wang, *Women in the Chinese Enlightenment,* 159, 165-67.

Chapter 4: The Evanescent Glory of the Track Queens

1   Jizhe, "Wo guo canjia shiyunhui xiangmu ji renxuan jiantao," *Qinfen tiyu yuebao* 3, 6 (March 1936): 515-17.

2   The noted female writer Xiao Hong (1911-42) attended the same school around the same time. Xiao Hong, *Xiaohong jingxuan ji* (Beijing: Beijing Yanshan chubanshe, 2006), 1; *Qinfen tiyu yuebao* 2, 5 (10 February 1935): 379; "Ha'erbin shi zhi: tiyu zhi" (1997), http://218.10.232.41:8080/was40/search?channelid=4279.

3   *Quanyun hui teji* (Shanghai: Tiyu shenghuo chubanshe, 1948), 17, 29-30; *Quanguo yundong dahui zong baogao: shijiu nian siyue Hangzhou juxing* (1930) 36, 38, 39-40, 59, 85, 87-89; Shi Xia, "Hafu si jiemei," *Tiyu shiliao* 4 (June 1981): 38; Dong Shouyi, "Aolinpike jiushi," *Tiyu shiliao* 2 (August 1980): 10.

4   *Beiyang huabao,* 15 April 1930, 27 June 1930; *Liangyou huabao* 46 (April 1930): Cover, 1; 50 (October 1930): 34-35.

5   Huang Jingwan, "Nü yundong jia Sun Guiyun," *Wenhua* 9 (1930): 22-23; *Funü zazhi* 16, 4 (1930): 1.

6   Javelin was also added to track and field, and softball throwing became a real softball tournament, involving nine teams. *Quanyun hui teji,* frontispieces, 37-41, 59, 63, inserts between 21 and 22; Shi Xia, "Qian Xingsu," *Tiyu shiliao* 5 (December 1981): 44.

7   Ge Min, "Yidai tianjing nüjie Qian Xingsu" (abbreviated as "Qian Xingsu"), in *Titan xianfeng* (Shanghai: Shanghai renmin chubanshe, 1990), 35-38.

8   Yue, "Yundong nüjie Qian Xingsu" (abbreviated as "Qian Xingsu"), *Qinfen tiyu yuebao* 1, 1, (10 October 1933): 59; *Quanyun hui teji,* frontispiece, 37-41, 59, 63, inserts between 21 and 22; *Linglong* 28 (23 September 1931): 1019-22; *Liangyou huabao* 63 (November 1931): 24-25; *Tiyu zhoubao* 2, 26 (5 August 1933): 2-5; *Nü pengyou* 1, 10 (1932): 24-25; *Tiyu xinsheng* 2 (1931): 20.

9   Ge, "Qian Xingsu," 35-38; Ye Qianyu, ed., *Mingguo ershi'er nian quanguo yundong hui zhuankan* (abbreviated as *Zhuankan*) (Shanghai: Shidai tushu gongsi, 1933); "Tianjing nüjiang Qian Xingsu," *Linglong* 117 (25 October 1933): 2037; 1190 Zhenyan, "Quanyun nü tianjing lun yingxiong," *Linglong* 117 (25 October 1933): 2002-5.

10   Ge, "Qian Xingsu," 35-38; *Libai liu* 503 (1933): 6.

11   Shi, "Qian Xingsu," 44; Yue, "Qian Xingsu," 59; Ge, "Qian Xingsu," 35-38; *Tiyu zhoubao* 2, 26 (5 August 1933): 2-5.

12   *Di liu jie quanyun shimo ji* (Beiping: Pingbao tiyu bu, 1935), 47-53, 89; *Quanyun hui teji,* frontispieces, 37-41, 59, 63, inserts between 21 and 22; *Linglong* 208 (23 October 1935): cover, 3607, 3610, 3647; *Shenbao yuekan* 4, 11 (1935): 1; *Xianxiang* 11 (1935): 1.

13   Ye, *Zhuankan.*

14   *Qingqing* 1, 5 (1933): 1.

15   Yue, "Qian Xingsu," 59.

16   *Rensheng xunkan* 1, 9-10 (1935): cover; *Qinfen tiyu yuebao* 1, 1 (10 October 1933): cover; 2, 3 (10 December 1934): 260.

17   *Qianqiu* 13 (1933): inside front cover.

18   Jin Chuan, "Nü pao wang Li Sen" (abbreviated as "Li Sen"), in *Titan xianfeng* 33-34, says that Li was born in 1914, but Li's autobiographical piece in October 1935 says that she

was then eighteen, which indicates that she was born in 1917. Li Sen, "Wo de tiyu shen-ghuo," *Liangyou huabao* 110 (October 1935): 17.

19 *Di liu jie quanguo yundong hui shimo ji*, 47-53, 89; *Quanyun hui teji*, frontispieces, 37-41, 59, 63, inserts between 21 and 22; Wan Tianshi, "Yi ge nüzi duanpao mingjiang de zhaoyu – ji Li Sen" (abbreviated as "Ji Li Sen") *Tiyu shiliao* 6 (April 1982): 33-34.

20 Feng Yuxiang, "Wo de ruwu qianhou," *Liangyou huabao* 101 (January 1935): 12-13; Gan Naiguang, "Wo de xingzheng yanjiu de kaishi," *Liangyou huabao* 102 (February 1935): 12-13; Chen Gongbo, "Shaonian shidai de huiyi," *Liangyou huabao* 106 (June 1935): 14-16; "Ming jizhe Ge Gongzhen zhi zhuiyi," *Liangyou huabao* 110 (October 1935): 7; Anna May Wong, "Wo de zishu," *Liangyou huabao* 114 (February 1936): 24.

21 Li Sen, "Wo de tiyu shenghuo."

22 Dazheng, "Li Sen fangwen ji," in *Di liu jie quanguo yundong dahui huabao*, edited by Ma Chongjin and Hu Bozhou (Shanghai: Qinfen shuju, 1935), 1.

23 *Liangyou huabao* 106 (June 1935): 8.

24 Shen Kunnan, "Zhongguo tianjing daibiao dui canjia di shiyi jie Aoyunhui bisai qingkuang," *Tiyu shiliao* 2 (August 1980): 19; Zhonghua tiyu xiejing hui, ed., *Chuxi di shiyi jie shijie yundong hui Zhonghua daibiao tuan baogao* (abbreviated as *Baogao*) (Shanghai: n.p., 1937), [section 1] 14-16, 56-58; Jin, "Li Sen," 33-34.

25 Jizhe, "Wo guo canjia shiyunhui xiangmu ji renxuan jiantao," *Qinfen tiyu yuebao* 3, 6 (March 1936): 517-18.

26 Shen, "Zhongguo tianjing daibiao dui canjia di shiyi jie Aoyunhui bisai qingkuang," 20; *Baogao*, [section 1] 36-37.

27 *Shidai manhua* 29 (20 August 1936); *Zhongguo xuesheng* 3, 7 (1936): 17-18; *Yule* 2, 35 (1936).

28 Lu Lihua, Duan Gangcheng, and Zhou De, interviewed by Chu Jianhong, "Shanghai Zhongguo nüzi ticao xuexiao jieshi," *Tiyu shiliao* 6 (April 1982): 4-5; Zhang Huilan, interviewed by Qiu Weichang and Zheng Yuangao, "Shanghai Nüqingnianhui tiyu shifan xuexiao," *Tiyu shiliao* 9 (January 1983): 8-9; Zhang Huilan, "Zaoqi peiyang nüzi tiyu shizi de xuexiao," in *Titan xianfeng* 195.

29 *Liangyou huabao* 15 (30 May 1927): 28.

30 *Beiyang huabao*, August 1931.

31 "Nandao yongyuan zuo bingfu?" *Linglong* 59 (20 July 1932): 430; "Riben: tamen qiangguo de yuanyin," 96 (24 May 1933): 722-23.

32 *Qingfen tiyu yuebao* 1, 5 (10 February 1934): 44; 2, 1 (10 October 1934): 18; *Tiyu zhaobao* 30 (27 August 1932): 19. For more on Hitomi, see Dennis J. Frost, *Seeing Stars: Sports Celebrity, Identity, and Body Culture in Modern Japan* (Cambridge, MA: Harvard University Press, 2011).

33 *Jindai funü* 22 (October 1930): 9.

34 Xing, "Renjian yaowang yi zhounian jinian," *Tiyu zhoubao* 30 (27 August 1932): 19; *Nü xuesheng* 1 (1931): 8; *Tiyu xinsheng* 1 (1931): 20-21; Kinue Hitomi, *Nü yundong yuan lingzhen zhiqian*, translated by Liu Jiaxiong (Shanghai: Qinfen shuju, 1931); *Qinfen tiyu yuebao* 1, 5 (10 February 1934): 44; 2, 1 (10 October 1934): 18; Kinue Hitomi, "Nüzi yundong ying zhuyi zhi shixiang," *Qinfen tiyu yuebao* 3, 7 (10 April 1936): 674-76.

35 *Qinfen tiyu yuebao* 1, 5 (10 February 1934): 44.

36 Prasenjit Duara, *Sovereignty and Authenticity: Manchukuo and the East Asian Modern* (Lanham, MD: Rowman and Littlefield, 2003), 180.

37 "Successful Field Day by Local Chinese: Happy Social Function," *Manchuria Daily News*, 15 May 1923.

38 *Beiyang huabao*, 15 April 1930 and 27 June 1930; *Liangyou huabao* 46 (April 1930): 1; 50 (October 1930): 34-35. Shi Xia. "Fu Baolu," *Tiyu shiliao* 4 (December 1981): 38.

39 For Liu's records, see *Quanguo yundong dahui zong baogao*, 36, 38, 39-40, 59, 85, 87-89.

40   "Liu Changchun de riji," *Tiyu zhoubao* 32 (10 September 1932): 21-24; 33 (17 September 1932): 17-18; 34 (24 September 1932): 27-28; Liu Changchun, "Canjia shijie yundong hui ganyan," *Tiyu zhoubao* 40 (5 November 1932): 18-19.

41   *Qinfen tiyu yuebao* 2, 6 (10 March 1935): 458; 3, 1 (October 1935): 111; 5 (February 1936): 447.

42   *Beiyang huabao*, 15 April 1930, 27 June 1930; *Xuexiao shenghuo* 7 (1930): 15.

43   *Quanyun hui teji*, 17, 29-30; *Quanguo yundong dahui zong baogao*, 36, 38, 39-40, 59, 85, 87-89.

44   *Zhonghua minguo nian nian di shiwu jie Huabei yundong hui* (1933), 21; *Guowen zhoubao* 8, 22 (1931): 1.

45   *Quanyun hui teji*, 17, 29-30; *Quanguo yundong dahui zong baogao* (1930), 36, 38, 39-40, 59, 85, 87-89; Shi, "Hafu si jiemei," 38; Dong, "Aolinpike jiushi," 10.

46   On Zhang Xueliang and education, see Rana Mitter, *The Manchurian Myth: Nationalism, Resistance and Collaboration in Modern China* (Berkeley: University of California Press, 2000), 68-70; *Tiyu zhoubao* 2, 23 (15 July 1933): 5-6.

47   *Quanyun hui teji*, 17, 29-30; Shi, "Hafu si jiemei," 38; *Beiyang huabao*, 5 November 1929.

48   *Tiyu zhoubao* 2, 23 (15 July 1933): 5-6.

49   *Beiyang huabao*, 3 June 1930.

50   Ibid., 17 June 1930; *Minzhong shenghuo* 1, 3 (1930): 3-4.

51   Lu Xun, "Xu Maoyong zuo 'Daza Ji' xu," in *Lu Xun wencui* (Beijing: Wenhua yishu chubanshe, 2003), 350.

52   *Beiyang huabao*, 17 June 1930.

53   *Quanyun hui teji*, frontispieces, 37-41, 59, 63, inserts between 21 and 22.

54   Yao, "Di shijie Yuandong woguo youyong tianjing nüzi lixiang dui," *Linglong* 117 (1933): 2030; 133 (21 March 1934): 480-1.

55   Liu Changchun, "Yundong chang shang shi'er nian," *Liangyou huabao* 110 (October 1935): 16.

56   Andrew Morris, *Marrow of the Nation: A History of Sports and Physical Culture in Republican China* (Berkeley: University of California Press, 2004), 154.

57   Some noted female basketball players excelled in track and field events. In the Sixth National Games, Chen Baixue placed sixth in the 80-metre hurdles, while Chen Rongtang placed first in the discus throw and set a national record in the shot put. *Quanyun hui teji*, 37-41, frontispieces; *Di liu jie quanguo yundong hui shimo ji*, 47-53, 110; *Qinfen tiyu yuebao* 3, 2 (November 1935): 150-53. Sun Guiyun and her fellow runners from Harbin took up basketball. In the Fifth National Games, Sun captained the Beiping basketball team and led it to easy victories over Anhui in the second round of the games. *Diligent Tiyu Monthly* attributed the team's victory to Sun's skills. Later, Sun took up skating briefly as well. Wu Meixian and Wang Yuan organized the Nanqiang basketball team in late 1932, when they attended Nankai Girls' Secondary School. *Tiyu Weekly* proclaimed the team "very competitive" under the leadership of two "great athletes." "Nüzi lanqiu," *Qinfen tiyu yuebao* 1, 2 (10 November 1933): 72; *Shishi xunbao* 19 (1935): 20; *Tiyu zhoubao* 40 (5 November 1932): 4. Li Sen was praised for "being good at all kinds of ball games, in addition to track and field events. Dazheng, "Li Sen fangwen ji."

58   *Tiyu zhoubao* 2, 7 (25 March 1933): 2-3.

59   *Qinfen tiyu yuebao* 2, 6 (10 March 1935): 458; 3, 1 (October 1935): 111; 5 (February 1936): 447.

60   Li Sen, "Wo de tiyu shenghuo."

61   *Qinfen tiyu yuebao* 3, 6 (March 1936): 533.

62   "Quanguo nannü tianjing zuigao jilu," *Tiyu jikan* 3, 2 (June 1937): 234-35; *Diansheng* 6, 13 (2 April 1937): 628; Wan, "Ji Li Sen," 33-34; Jin, "Li Sen," 33-34; Wang Zhenya, *Jiu Zhongguo tiyu jianwen* (Beijing: Renmin tiyu chubanshe, 1984), 159-60.

63 *Tianxin* 11 (1931): 3; *Tiyu zhoubao* 2, 25 (29 July 1933): 26.
64 *Qinfen tiyu yuebao* 2, 2 (10 November 1934): 186; 3, 5 (February 1936): 454.
65 *Beiyang huabao*, 13 August 1931.
66 *Tiyu zhoubao* 2, 26 (5 August 1933): 2-5.
67 *Shenbao*, 24 April 1936; *Qinfen tiyu yuebao* 3, 8 (May 1936): pictorials, 792; *Yule* 2, 17 (1936): 327. *Liang you huabao* 119 (August 1936): cover.
68 *Qinfen tiyu yuebao* 2, 10 (10 July 1935): 686; 3, 5 (February 1936): 454; *Yule* 1 (1935): 9; *Nüduo* 24, 11 (1936): 45; *Guomin tiyu huikan* 1 (1936): 24.
69 Jin, "Li Sen," 34.
70 *Liangyou huabao* 53 (30 January 1931): 32.
71 "Sun Guiyun dilan shiyi, Zhang Suhui yiming jingren," *Zhonghua minguo nian nian di shiwu jie Huabei yundong hui*, 21.
72 *Qinfen tiyu yuebao* 2, 9 (10 June 1935): 629, 642; *Shishi yuebao* 9, 4 (1933): 16-17; *Xuexiao shenghuo* 7 (1930): 7.
73 *Libai liu* 526 (1933): 4.
74 *Tiyu zhoubao* 2, 23 (15 July 1933): 5-6.
75 Susan K. Cahn, *Coming on Strong: Gender and Sexuality in Twentieth-Century American Women's Sports* (Cambridge, MA: Harvard University Press, 1994), 110-12, 117-39.
76 *Linglong* 63 (17 August 1932): 622.
77 *Shidai manhua* 29 (August 1936): cover.
78 Cahn, *Coming on Strong*, 173, 179.
79 *Keda zazhi* 2, 8 (1931): 8; *Guowen zhoubao* 7, 15 (1930): 1; 8, 22 (1931): 1; *Shishi yuebao* 2, 5 (1930): 2; *Xuexiao shenghuo* 7 (1930): 23, 26.
80 *Linglong* 114 (10 October 1933): cover.
81 *Liangyou huabao* 106 (June 1935): 8; 110 (October 1935): 4-5; Ye *Zhuankan*; *Linglong* 208 (23 October 1935): 3631.
82 *Liangyou huabao* 60 (August 1931): 8-9; *Beiyang huabao*, 18 June 1931; *Qinfen tiyu yuebao* 3, 2 (November 1935): 144; *Di wu jie quanyun zhuanji* (Shanghai: Wenhua meishu tushu gongsi, 1933): 1; *Shishi yuebao* 9, 5 (1933): 23; *Weisheng yuekan* 5, 12 (1935): 12.
83 *Qinfen tiyu yuebao* 3, 2 (November 1935): 144.
84 *Xuexiao shenghuo* 7 (1930): 7; *Liangyou huabao* 62 (October 1931): 49.
85 *Qinfen tiyu yuebao* 2, 5 (10 February 1935): 379; *Beiyang huabao*, 28 June 1930; "Ha'erbin shi zhi: tiyu zhi" (1997), http://218.10.232.41:8080/was40/search?channelid=4279.
86 The arrangement continues in the People's Republic China and is widely present in tiyu theme cinema in the twentieth-century China.
87 Yue, "Qian Xingsu," 59; Ge, "Qian Xingsu," 35-38; Li, "Wo de tiyu shenghuo," 642; Dazheng, "Li Sen fangwen ji."
88 *Xuexiao shenghuo* 7 (1930): 7; *Beiyang huabao*, 6 June 1931.
89 *Zhonghua huabao* 1, 59 (18 September 1931).
90 *Henan jiaoyu* 2, 23 (1930): 60-61.
91 Yue, "Qian Xingsu," 59; *Qinfen tiyu yuebao* 3, 6 (March 1936): 533; Ge, "Qian Xingsu," 35-38.
92 Sun Hebin, "Ping di wu jie quanguo yundong hui nüzi tianjing sai," *Qinfen tiyu yuebao* 1, 2 (10 November 1933): 6; Yue, "Qian Xingsu," 59.
93 "Nüzi tianjing," *Qinfen tiyu yuebao* 3, 2 (November 1935): 150-53; "Nüzi erbai gongci juesai," in *Di liu jie quanguo yundong hui shimo ji*, 110; Dazheng, "Li Sen fangwen ji."
94 Once she arrived in Shanghai in 1931, Chen emerged as a basketball star with the Liangjiang team. She continued to excel in track and field, placing second in javelin and fourth in the broad jump at the Second Multi-national Games in Shanghai in 1932, and setting a national record in javelin and taking second place in softball throwing at the Fifth National Games.

Di liu jie quanguo yundong dahui huabao, 1, 34; *Qinfen tiyu yuebao* 2, 2 (10 November 1934): 175-76; *Tiyu zhoubao* 2, 22 (8 July 1933): 27.

95 Li Sen, "Wo de tiyu shenghuo," 629, 642; Jin, "Li Sen," 33-34.

96 Dazheng, "Li Sen fangwen ji."

97 *Qinfen tiyu yuebao* 2, 2 (10 November 1934): 175-76.

98 Event officials viewed female competitiveness in this event respectfully. During the Fourth National Games, a dispute between the Harbin team and the Guangdong team over the 200-metre relay halted the games for half a day. While national leaders Zhang Jingjiang, Zhu Jiahua, Chu Minyi, and Dai Jitao watched from the judges' platform, the authorities deliberated carefully, granted championships to both teams, and awarded them silver cups. Qian Xingsu was hailed when her performance saved the gold medal for the Shanghai team in the 400-metre relay in the Fifth National Games, against the Guangdong team that possessed equal capacities. The media dramatized how she bested her opponent step by step. The two teams met again at the Sixth National Games, in which the Shanghai team, led by Li Sen, won first place; refusing to accept defeat, however, the Guangdong team accused Li Sen of veering out of her lane. After reviewing photographs taken by Wang Kai Photography Studio, chief referee Zhang Boling decided to annul Shanghai's championship and grant it to the Guangdong team. *Xuexiao shenghuo* 7 (1930): 7, 20, 26; *Quanyun hui teji*, 17, 29-30; Shi, "Hafu si jiemei," 38; Dong, "Aolinpike jiushi," 10; Ge, "Qian Xingsu," 35-38; *Qinfen tiyu yuebao* 3, 2 (November 1935): 150-53; "Nüzi erbai gongci juesai," 110; Dazheng, "Li Sen fangwen ji"; Jin, "Nü pao wang Li Sen," 33-34.

99 Sun Yu, "Daoyanzhe yan," *Lianhua huabao* 3, 15 (15 April 1934).

100 Zhu Shifang, "Zhongdeng xuexiao nüzi tianjing wenti," *Qinfen tiyu yuebao* 1, 5 (10 February 1934): 37-38.

101 *Quanyun hui teji*, 17, 29-30; *Quanguo yundong dahui zong baogao*, 36, 38, 39-40, 59, 85, 87-89; Shi, "Hafu si jiemei," 38; Dong, "Aolinpike jiushi," 10; *Yiyuan* 1, 19 (1931): 189.

102 *Linglong* 28 (23 September 1931): 1019-22; *Liangyou huabao* 63 (November 1931): 24-25; *Tiyu zhoubao* 2, 26 (5 August 1933): 2-5; Yue, "Qian Xingsu," 59; Ge, "Qian Xingsu," 35-38; Shi, "Qian Xingsu," 44.

103 Li, "Wo de tiyu shenghuo," 642; Dazheng, "Li Sen fangwen ji."

104 Fei'e, "Lu Lihua kouliu Li Sen," *Yule* 1, 16 (1935): 390.

105 Li Sen, "Wo de tiyu shenghuo"; Xing, "Renjian yaowang yi zhounian jinian," *Tiyu zhaobao* 30 (27 August 1932): 19.

106 Zhang Huilan, "A Colligation of Facts and Principles Basic to Sound Curriculum Construction for Physical Education in China" (PhD diss., University of Iowa, 1944), 35.

107 Zhu, "Zhongdeng xuexiao nüzi tianjing wenti," 37-38.

108 *Beiyang huabao*, September 1931.

109 *Qinfen tiyu yuebao* 2, 5 (10 February 1935): 377; 7 (10 April 1935): 495; Ge, "Qian Xingsu," 35-38.

110 Ge, "Qian Xingsu," 35-38.

111 Li, "Wo de tiyu shenghuo."

112 While fans mistook her for the sister of another basketball player, Chen Rongtang from Dongya, because of their similarly robust physiques and top basketball skills, the media tried to distinguish them by highlighting the latter's transnational background. *Di liu jie quanguo yundong dahui huabao*, 6; *Qinfen tiyu yuebao* 2, 2 (10 November 1934): 175-76; *Tiyu zhoubao* 2, 22 (8 July 1933): 27.

113 Sun, "Ping di wu jie quanguo yundong hui nüzi tianjing sai."

114 *Qinfen tiyu yuebao* 2, 2 (10 November 1934): 175-76; *Tiyu zhoubao* 2, 22 (8 July 1933): 27.

115 *Qinfen tiyu yuebao*, ibid.

116 *Tiyu zhoubao* 2, 2 (18 February 1933): 3; 2, 8 (1 April 1933): 2.

117 Li Sen, "Wo de tiyu shenghuo," 642.

118 Fan Hong, *Footbinding, Feminism and Freedom: The Liberation of Women's Bodies in Modern China* (London: Frank Cass, 1997), 246.

119 *Qinfen tiyu yuebao* 2, 3 (10 December 1934): 262; 4 (10 January 1935): 288; Ge, "Qian Xingsu," 35-38; *Zhonghua yuebao* 2, 11 (1934): 1; *Libai liu* 582 (1934): 1. On arguments about militarization and fascism of the NLM, see Morris, *Marrow of the Nation*, 134, 140.

120 *Liangyou huabao* 117 (June 1936): 16-17, 118 (July 1936): 16; "Wuguo chuxi shijie tianjing xuanshou mingdan," *Qinfen tiyu yuebao* 3, 9 (June 1936): 862; 3, 10 (July 1936): cover; *Libai liu* 647 (1936): 1.

121 *Guanghua yiyao zazhi* 1, 6 (1934): 57-58.

122 *Libai liu* 596 (1935): 1; *Weisheng yuekan* 5, 6 (1935): 17.

123 Li Sen, "Gao xi yapian de tongbao," *Xiandai nongmin* 3, 1 (1940): 6.

124 Cahn, *Coming on Strong*, 173, 179, 194, 215.

125 *Diansheng* 5, 35 (11 September 1936): 916.

126 *Beiyang huabao*, 18 June 1931 and 6 August 1931; *Zhongguo xuesheng* 3, 5 (1931): 11.

127 Ye, *Zhuankan*.

128 Li Sen, "Wo de tiyu shenghuo"; *Liang you huabao* 119 (August 1936): cover; *Yule* 1, 19 (1935): 460.

129 *Quanyun hui teji*, 17, 29-30; Shi, "Hafu si jiemei," 38. *Tiyu jikan* 3, 1 (March 1937): frontispieces.

130 Dazheng, "Li Sen fangwen ji," *Tiyu jikan* 3, 1 (March 1937): 128.

131 *Qinfen tiyu yuebao* 1, 1 (10 October 1933): 4.

132 *Liangyou huabao* 104 (April 1935): 43-44.

133 *Tiyu zhoubao* 38 (22 October 1932): 3, 26.

134 Ye, *Zhuankan*.

135 *Beiyang huabao*, 18 June and 6 August 1931.

136 Ibid., 6 June 1931.

137 *Diansheng* 4, 13 (29 March 1935): 269.

138 *Yule* 1, 1 (1935): 4; 1, 16 (1935): 399; 1, 18 (1935): 442; 1, 22 (1935): 530; 1, 23 (1935): 553; "Liu jie quanyun bisai huaxu: Qian Xingsu pole," *Linglong* 208 (23 October 1935): 3634-35.

139 Dazheng, "Li Sen fangwen ji."

140 *Qinfen tiyu yuebao* 3, 10 (July 1936): cover, pictorial, 952.

141 *Diansheng* 5, 33 (21 August 1936): 851; 6, 9 (5 March 1937): 468; 6, 21 (28 May 1937): 949.

142 Fan, *Footbinding*, 276.

143 *Tiyu zhoubao* 2, 1 (11 February 1933): 2-3; 2, 2 (18 February 1933): 5; 2, 3 (25 February 1933): 2-3; *Liangyou huabao* 76 (May 1933): 22; *Qinfen tiyu yuebao* 1, 6 (10 March 1934): 65. As late as 1936, *Cinematic Tone* covered Wang Yuan's rumoured romance and her activities in public swimming pools with a sensual atmosphere. *Diansheng* 5, 31 (7 August 1936): 795.

144 Wan, "Ji Li Sen," 33-34.

145 Zhong Qi, "Wang Yuan nüshi de zuo yitaitai wenti," *Tiyu zhoubao* 2, 1 (11 February 1933): 2.

146 Sun, "Ping di wu jie quanguo yundong hui nüzi tianjing sai," 6.

147 *Tiyu zhoubao* 2, 2 (18 February 1933): 5.

148 Ibid., 2, 3 (25 February 1933): 2-3.

149 Cahn, *Coming on Strong*, 114-16, 136, 139.

150 Zhu, "Zhongdeng xuexiao nüzi tianjing wenti."

151 Zhu Minzhi, "Nü yundong jia bu jiehun," *Linglong* 70 (12 October 1932): 921.

152 According to Susan Cahn, some American media tried to soften Didrikson's image by reporting her domestic skills. Didrikson tried to escape the masculine and homosexual stigma and transform herself into a "real woman" by marrying the professional wrestler George Zaharias in 1938, taking up the more socially respectable game of golf in 1947 after quitting track and field and basketball, and carefully cultivating a more feminine image through longer hair, makeup, and dresses. Cahn, *Coming on Strong*, 4, 115, 173, 179, 194, 214-15.

153   Zhu Minzhi, "Nü yundong jia bu jiehun."

154   Liao Jiemin, "Guonan qijian qingnian bu dang tan lian'ai," *Linglong* 231 (24 June 1936): 955-57.

155   "Mingyan huibian – Niu Yongjian," *Zhongyang Guoshu Guan liu zhounian jinian tekan* (Nanjing: Zhongyan guoshugan, 1934), 22.

156   Sun Guiyun, "Wo de jinzhuang," *Linglong* 2 (25 March 1931): 49.

157   *Linglong* 204 (2 October 1935): 327-38.

158   *Qinfen tiyu yuebao* 2, 2 (10 November 1934): 175-76; *Tiyu zhoubao* 2, 22 (8 July 1933): 27.

159   "Qian Xingsu ai kan xiaoshuo," in *Di liu jie quanguo yundong dahui huabao*, edited by Ma Chongjin and Hu Bozhou (Shanghai: Qinfen shuju, 1935), 1; Ge, "Qian Xingsu."

160   Li Sen, "Wo de tiyu shenghuo."

161   Throughout Sun's brief celebrity, her elder brother, Sun Guiji, was omnipresent. In the same month that Sun gained national fame, the photograph of the little-known actor in a play appeared in *Young Companion Pictorial*, in which he was introduced as "the brother of Sun Guiyun." She went to Shanghai for university in order to be near her brother, who worked in the Central Studio in Nanjing. When she married, Guiji, then the head of the department of acting at Central Studio, attended her wedding. *Liangyou huabao* 46 (April 1930): 1; 50 (October 1930): 34-35; 62 (October 1931): 49; *Shenbao*, 24 April 1936; *Qinfen tiyu yuebao* 2, 2 (10 November 1934): 186; 3, 5 (February 1936): 454; 3, 8 (May 1936): 792.

162   Li, "Wo de tiyu shenghuo."

163   *Tiyu zhoubao* 2, 2 (18 February 1933): 5.

164   *Beiyang huabao*, 17 June 1930.

165   Li, "Wo de tiyu shenghuo."

166   *Liangyou huabao* 62 (October 1931): 49.

167   "Qian Xingsu ai kan xiaoshuo," 1.

168   *Yule* 1, 16 (1935): 390; 1, 17 (1935): 418.

169   *Linglong* 59 (20 July 1932): 430; 96 (24 May 1933): 722-23.

170   *Liangyou huabao* 117 (June 1936): 16-17; *Qinfen tiyu yuebao* 3, 9 (June 1936): 862; 3, 10 (July 1936): 95.

171   *Qinfen tiyu yuebao* 3, 2 (November 1935): 144.

172   *Liangyou huabao* 46 (April 1930): cover.

173   *Jindai funü* 28 (May 1931): 1.

174   *Qinfen tiyu yuebao* 2, 2 (November 1934): 175-76; *Liangyou huabao* 110 (October 1935): 4-5.

175   *Quanyun hui teji*, advertisements between 21-22.

176   Zhong, "Wang Yuan."

Chapter 5: "Miss China," Yang Xiuqiong (1918-82): A Female Olympic Swimmer

1   *Liangyou huabao* 92 (15 August 1934); 99 (1 December 1934): 22.

2   Although there were other notable contemporary female swimmers, including Shi Ruisheng, the youngest of the Shi siblings from Manchuria; Lui Guizhen, Liang Yongxian, and Chen Huanqiong from Hong Kong; and the four He sisters (Yulan, Wenjing, Wenya, and Wenjin) from Shandong, Yang Xiuqiong received by far the most attention. For previous coverage of her, see Andrew Morris, *Marrow of the Nation: A History of Sports and Physical Culture in Republican China* (Berkeley: University of California Press, 2004), 156-57, 194; and Hsiao-pei Yen, "Body Politics, Modernity and National Salvation: The Modern Girl and the New Life Movement," *Asian Studies Review* 29, 2 (June 2005): 165-86.

3   For the ordinariness of American stars in this period, see Joshua Gamson, *Claims to Fame: Celebrity in Contemporary America* (Berkeley: University of California Press, 1994), 35.

4   Fan Hong, *Footbinding, Feminism and Freedom: The Liberation of Women's Bodies in Modern China* (London: Frank Cass, 1997), 275, 277.

5 Yang Xiuqiong, *Yang Xiuqiong zizhuan* (abbreviated as *Zizhuan*) (Hong Kong: Xinhua chubanshe, 1938), 3-4.

6 Following her father's example, Yang set up a school to teach swimming in 1935. While training for the Olympics, she also coached swimming at the Nanhua Swimming Association. Zhen, "Yang Xiuqiong he tade youyong jiating," *Linglong* 117 (25 October 1933): 2031; 118 (1 November 1933): 1; 146 (16 October 1935): cover, 1372-73; *Qinfen tiyu yuebao* 2, 1 (10 October 1934): 10; *Yule* 1 (1935): 18; *Libai liu* 562 (1934): 23; 611 (1935): 21.

7 *Liangyou huabao* 67 (March 1932): 24-25; *Jindai funü* 22 (October 1930): 9; Yang, *Zizhuan*, 5-9. For a later review of her early career, see *Qinfen tiyu yuebao* 3, 1 (10 October 1935): 763.

8 *Di wu jie quanyun hui teji* (1933), 37-41; *Di wu jie quanyun zhuanji* (Shanghai: Wenhua meishu tushu gongsi, 1933), cover; Yang, *Zizhuan*, 13-14; *Xuexiao shenghuo* 56 (1933): cover.

9 *Qinfen tiyu yuebao* 1 (10 June 1934): 17; Yang, *Zizhuan*, 18-19; *Minjian zhoubao* 62 (1934): 1; *Guowen zhoubao* 11, 21 (1934): 1, 15; 11, 22 (1934): 1; *Kangjian zazhi* 2, 5 (1934): 1; *Shishi yuebao* 10, 6 (1934): 3; 11, 1 (1934): 2; Wang Jianming, *Meirenyu Yang Xiuqiong* (Shanghai: Guanghua shuju, 1935), 8-10, 12-13. On men's teams, see Fan Hong, ed., *Sport, Nationalism and Orientalism: The Asian Games* (New York: Routledge, 2007), xxii.

10 *Shishi xunbao* 5 (1934): 10; *Libai liu* 557 (1933): 13; *Tiyu jikan* 1, 1 (1935): 8.

11 Yang, *Zizhuan*, 23-24; *Linglong* 209 (30 October 1935): 3714; *Shenbao yuekan* 4, 11 (1935): 1; *Chunse* 21 (1935): inside back cover; *Shiri zazhi* 3 (1935): 1; *Guoheng* 1, 13 (1935): 84; *Guowen zhoubao* 12, 43 (1935): 1; *Jiankang shenghuo* 5, 2 (1935): 1; *Kangjian shijie* 2 (1935): 1; *Kangjian zazhi* 3, 11 (1935): 1; *Shidai dianying* 1 (1935): 10; *Shidai shenghuo* 3, 1 (1935): 23; *Shishi yuebao* 13, 5 (1935): 4; *Xiandai qingnian* 1, 2 (1935): 5, 13; *Wanxiang* 11 (1935): 1; *Yule* 1, 16 (1935): 387; 17 (1935): inside front cover, 414-15; 18 (1935): 1, 434-36; *Libai liu* 611 (1935): 21; *Diansheng* 6, 30 (30 July 1937): 1309.

12 *Diansheng* 4, 30 (26 July 1935): 629; *Tiyu jikan* 1, 2 (1935): 7.

13 *Jincheng* 1, 1 (1934): 49.

14 Zhonghua tiyu xiejing hui, ed., *Chuxi di shiyi jie shijie yundong hui Zhonghua daibiao tuan baogao* (Shanghai: n.p., 1937), [section 1] 56-58; "Quanguo youyong zuigao jilu," *Tiyu jikan* 3, 2 (June 1937), 236-37; *Yule* 2, 31 (1936): 607, inside back cover; *Libai liu* 646 (1936): 23; *Diansheng* 6, 27 (9 July 1937): 1189.

15 Jizhe, "Wo guo canjia shiyunhui xiangmu ji renxuan jiantao," *Qinfen tiyu yuebao* 3 (March 1936): 517-18. *Yule* notes, however, that Yang's speed of backstroke could surpass that of Japanese female swimmers. *Yule* 1, 18 (1935): 438.

16 Xu Guoqi, *Olympic Dreams: China and Sports, 1985-2008* (Cambridge, MA: Harvard University Press, 2008), 44-48; and Morris, *Marrow of the Nation*, 171-81; Yang, *Zizhuan*, 29-30.

17 *Wenshi jinghua* 10 (2006); *Diansheng* 6, 32 (13 August 1937): 1381.

18 "Sports in China: Enthusiasts Face Lack of Equipment," *China at War* 7, 4 (April 1944): 62; *Xiangxue hai* 1 (1946): 6; *Jian li mei* 2 (1941): 22; *Zazhi* 13, 3 (1944): 199-200; *Tushu zhanwang* 2, 7 (1937): 9; *Huguang* (1946): 8; *Dongnan feng* 15 (1946): 9; *Xiaojie* 10 (1937): 24; *Jinghua* 2, 10 (revised version, 1946): 6; *Zhongmei zhoubao* 227 (1947): 43-44; 245 (1947): cover; 295 (1948): cover; *Kuaihuo lin* 24 (1946): 5.

19 *Guomin tiyu huikan* 1 (1936): 33; Susan K. Cahn, *Coming on Strong: Gender and Sexuality in Twentieth-Century Sport* (Cambridge, MA: Harvard University Press, 1994), 129-30.

20 *Minjian zhoubao* 63, 80, and 81 (1934): 1; *Wanxiang* 2 (June 1934): 38; *Linglong* 117 (25 October 1933): 2051; *Weisheng yuekan* 5, 12 (1935): 13.

21 Wang, *Meirenyu*, 11, 14-15.

22 *Linglong* 117 (25 October 1933): 1998, 2011, 2015; *Diansheng* 5, 26 (19 June 1936): 625.

23 *Liangyou huabao* 67 (March 1932): 24-25; 77 (June 1933): cover; 110 (October 1935): 8; *Linglong* 117 (25 October 1933): 2051-52; 150 (15 August 1934): 1585; *Dongfang zazhi* 32,

20 (1935): cover; *Hanxue zhoukan* 5, 15 (1935): cover; *Renyan zhoukan* 2, 31 (1935): cover, 609; *Yule* 2, 25 (1936): 487; 1, 19 (1935): 1; Lin Yutang, *My Country and My People* (New York: Reynal and Hitchcock, 1935), 170. On changes in swimsuits in this period, see Patricia Campbell Warner, *When Girls Came Out to Play: The Birth of American Sportswear* (Amherst: University of Massachusetts Press, 2006), 79-81.

24 *Jindai funü* 22 (October 1930): 9; Yang, *Zizhuan*, 5-9.

25 *Liangyou huabao* 110 (October 1935): 8; *Linglong* 155 (4 April 1934): cover; *Guoshu tongyi yuekan* 1, 3-4, (1934): 65-67; *Choumou yuekan* 1, 2 (1934); *Libai liu* 577 (1934): 1. On the Chinese Modern Girl's use of makeup and social condemnation, see Madeleine Yue Dong, "Who Is Afraid of the Modern Chinese Girl," in *The Modern Girl around the World*, edited by The Modern Girl around the World Research Group (Durham, NC: Duke University Press, 2008), 194-219.

26 Yang, between 26 and 27; *Rensheng xunkan* 1, 6 (1935): 26; *Shenbao yuekan* 4, 10 (1935): 1; *Chunse* 21 (1935): inside back cover; *Diansheng* 4, 41 (11 October 1935): 890; 4, 43 (25 October 1935): 930; *Funü yuebao* 1, 8 (1935): 25; 1, 9 (1935): 16, 30-31; *Yule* 1, 19 (1935): cover.

27 *Di liu jie quanyun shimo ji* (Beiping: Pingbao tiyu bu, 1935), 47-53; *Linglong* 155 (3 October 1934): 1923-24; 202 (18 September 1935): 2307; 229 (10 June 1936): 762.

28 *Linglong* 243 (1 July 1936), front and back covers.

29 Wang, *Meirenyu.*

30 "Chinese Mermaid," *Atlanta Constitution,* 12 November 1935. On cynical attitudes about Chinese Mermaids, see, for example, "Recalls Old Humbugs," *Washington Post,* 7 June 1903.

31 *Diansheng* 5, 33 (21 August 1936): 858. For the photography, see Leni Riefenstahl, *Schönheit im Olympischen Kampf. Mit zahlreichen Aufnahmen von den Olympischen Spielen 1936* (Berlin: Deutscher Verlag, 1937).

32 Yang, *Zizhuan,* 3-4; *Jinghua* 2, 7 (1946): 2.

33 *Liangyou huabao* 67 (March 1932): 24-25; *Jindai funü* 22 (October 1930): 9; Yang, *Zizhuan,* 5-9.

34 Wang, *Meirenyu,* 28-30.

35 *Shidai manhua* 1 (15 April 1934); 29 (20 August 1936): front and back covers; *Yule* 2, 35 (1936): 688; *Xianshi bao* 17 (1938): 11; *Haichao zhoubao* 15 (1946): 10; 19 (1946): cover; *Haiguang* 20 (1946): 6; *Diansheng* 5, 43 (30 October 1936): 1157-58; 5, 47 (27 November 1936): 1275; 6, 16 (23 April 1937): 749.

36 Yang, *Zizhuan,* 33-36.

37 "Sports in China," 62; *Diansheng* 6, 2 (15 January 1937): 189; *Haiyan* 12 (1946): 6; *Haiguang* 23 (1946): 9; *Piao* 4 (1946): 9-10; *Daguanyuan zhoubao* 26 (1946): 3; *Yizhou jie* 7 (1946): 2; *Kuaihuo lin* 12 (1946): 1; *Chunhai* 2 (1946): 3, 6.

38 Lu Xun, "Xu Maoyong zuo 'Daza Ji' xu," in *Lu Xun wencui* (Beijing: Wenhua yishu chuban-she, 2003), 350.

39 *Liangyou huabao* 82 (November 1933): 4-5, 13; *Dongfang zazhi* 30, 22 (1933): cover; *Linglong* 117 (25 October 1933): 2015; *Libai liu* 527 (1933): 13; *Shishi daguan* 1 (1934): 1. Yang's autobiography and Wang Jianming's biography of her suggest that she cut the ribbon in 1934, in the middle of her NLM tour. Yang, *Zizhuan,* 16; Wang, *Meirenyu.*

40 *Libai liu* 646 (1936): 23; *Diansheng* 4, 36 (6 September 1935): 766; *Linglong* 243 (1 July 1936): 1941-42; "Yang Xiuqiong de tuoche wenti," *Linglong* 243 (1 July 1936): 1891; Wang, *Meirenyu,* 59, 62-63, 67-72.

41 *Diansheng* 7, 25 (24 June 1938): 494-95; 7, 31 (5 August 1938): 618.

42 Yang, *Zizhuan,* 21-22; *Liangyou huabao* 92 (15 August 1934): 17; Wang, *Meirenyu,* 59, 62-63, 67-72; *Funü yuebao* 1, 8 (1935): 24-25; *Shishi xunbao* 1 (1934): 10; 3 (1934): 10; 4 (1934): cover; 5 (1934): 1; *Libai liu* 568 (1934): 1; *Lunyu* 49 (1934): 68.

43 *Yule* 1, 15 (1935): 370, 383.

44 *Liangyou huabao* 92 (15 August 1934); 99 (1 December 1934): 22; *Dongfang zazhi* 31, 17 (1934): 193; *Shenbao yuekan* 3, 8 (1934): 1; *Qiantu* 2, 9 (1934): cover; Jiang Huiqing, "Yang Xiuqiong beiyou yinxiang ji," *Lüxing zazhi* 8, 9 (1934): 57-60; *Zhonghua yuebao* 2, 9 (1934): 1; *Zhonghua kouqin jie* 4-5 (1934): cover; *Linglong* 150 (15 August 1934): cover; *Guoshu tongyi yuekan* 1, 2 (1934): 43-59; *Guoxun* 75 (1934): 264; *Jiankang shenghuo* 1, 1 (1934): 1, 6-8, 15; *Dushu guwen* 2 (1934): 9; Yang, *Zizhuan*, 21-22.

45 On clothing restriction, see Antonia Finnane, *Changing Clothes in China: Fashion, History, Nation* (New York: Columbia University Press, 2008), 171-75. On government policy, see Yen, "Body Politics," 178. On controversies over swimsuits and women's participation in events, see Warner, *When Girls Came Out to Play*, 91-96; Wang, *Meirenyu*, 82-87; *Taishan* 24 (new version) (1947): cover.

46 Wang, *Meirenyu*, 8-13, 16-17, 56-57.

47 *Liangyou huabao* 92 (15 August 1934): 17; *Qiantu* 2, 9 (1934): 1; *Jiankang shenghuo* 1, 1 (1934): 1. Yang, *Zizhuan*, 23.

48 Chen Cunren, *Kangzhang shidai shenghuo shi* (abbreviated as *Shenghuo shi*) (Guilin: Guangxi shifan daxue chubanshe, 2007), 65-86; Emily Hahn, *China to Me: A Partial Autobiography* (Philadelphia: Blakiston, 1944), 21-22.

49 *Linglong* 150 (15 August 1934): 1587-89, 1614-15; *Liangyou huabao* 92 (15 August 1934): 17; *Shenbao yuekan* 3, 8 (1934): 1; *Guowen zhoubao* 11, 32 (1934): 1; Wang, *Meirenyu*, 16-17; Wang Zhenya, *Jiu Zhongguo tiyu jianwen* (Beijing: Renmin tiyu chubanshe, 1984), 159.

50 Chen, *Shenghuo shi*, 65-86; Hahn, *China to Me*, 21-22. Chu's muddle-headed involvement with Wang's puppet government as its ambassador to Japan led to his execution by the Nationalist government in 1946. On Lu Xun, courtesan behaviour, and public understanding, see Paola Zamperini, *Lost Bodies: Prostitution and Masculinity in Chinese Fiction* (Leiden: Brill, 2010), 11.

51 Morris, *Marrow of the Nation*, 246; Fan, *Footbinding*, 235-42.

52 Yang, *Zizhuan*, 33-36.

53 *Linglong* 153 (19 September 1934): 1779-81; 151 (29 August 1934): 1664-65.

54 Xu Xinqin, " Shidai xiaojie de jianglai," *Shidai manhua* 1 (15 April 1934): 2.

55 *Lingxiao* 1 (1946): 6; *Yule* 1, 15 (1935): 366; 18 (1935): 436; 19 (1935): 459; 2, 28 (1936): 547; *Yingju* 6 (1943): 7; *Diansheng* 4, 29 (19 July 1935): 608; 4, 45 (8 November 1935): 985; 5, 43 (30 October 1936): 1156; 5, 45 (13 November 1936): 1215; 6, 14 (9 April 1937): 669.

56 On Chen, see Wang, *Jiu Zhongguo tiyu jianwen*, 159-60, and *Qinfen tiyu yuebao* 1 (10 December 1933): 75. On Hu, see *Qinfen tiyu yuebao* 2 (10 August 1935): 763; *Linglong* 121 (1933): 2295; *Shanghai shenghuo* 1, 4 (1937): 53; 5, 10 (1941): 1; *Diansheng* (anniversary version) (1939): 1; *Xuanmiao guan* 5 (1939): 93; *Qingqing dianying* 4, 40 (1940): 20. Yang Xiuzhen married around 1938. *Wufeng* 10 (new version) (1938): 19-20; 2, 5 (1938): 14; *Diansheng* 9, 5 (3 February 1940): 1.

57 After the Communist takeover in 1949, Fan converted to the Communist side and served as consultant to the Military and Political Committee of South and Central China, senior consultant within the People's Liberation Army system, vice chairman of the Tiyu Commission of Henan, committee member of the provincial government, and Representative of the Provincial People's Congress and Political Consultative Conference. He died at Zhengzhou in 1977 at the age of 83. On scandal, see *Wenshi jinghua*, no. 10 (2006). On courtesan coverage, see Catherine Vance Yeh, *Shanghai Love: Courtesans, Intellectuals and Entertainment Culture, 1850-1910* (Seattle: University of Washington Press, 2006,) 246-47.

58 *Jiating yu funü* 5, 1 (1941): 6; *Jiating zhoukan* 115 (1936): cover; *Lixiang jiating* 2 (1941): 14; *Kuaile jiating* 1 (1936): cover. On kidnapping and forced concubinage, see Gail Hershatter, *Dangerous Pleasures: Prostitution and Modernity in Twentieth-Century Shanghai* (Berkeley: University of California Press, 1997), 181-91; Hu Die and Liu Huiqin, *Hu Die huiyi lu* (Beijing: Wenhua yishu chubanshe, 1988).

59 *Yizhou jian* 11 (1946): 9; *Shanghai tan* 11 (1946): 6; "Yang Xiuqiong yu Du Yuesheng," *Dadi* 17 (1946): 10; *Dongnan feng* 4 (1946): 1; 22 (1946): 8; *Jinghua* 1, 20 (1946): cover.

60 *Qinfen tiyu yuebao* 1 (10 June 1934): 17; Yang, *Zizhuan,* 18-19.

61 Yang, *Zizhuan,* 21-22; *Liangyou huabao* 92 (15 August 1934): 17.

62 *Linglong* 150 (15 August 1934): 1585, 1614-15; 155 (3 October 1934): 1923-24; 202 (18 September 1935): 2307; 229 (10 June 1936): 762.

63 *Yule* 2, 25 (1936): 487; Wang, *Women in the Chinese Enlightenment,* 170; "Yang Xiuqiong de tuoche wenti," *Linglong* 243 (1 July 1936): 1891.

64 Yang, *Zizhuan,* 42-43.

65 *Shanghai tan* 2 (1946): 6; *Piao* 8 (1946): 10; 11 (1946): 8; *Haifeng* 29 (1946): 7; 30 (1946): 12; 34 (1946): 2; *Haixing* 13 (1946): 11; 14 (1946): cover; *Haichao zhoubao* 32 (1946): 10; 65 (1947): 7; *Fengguang* 26 (1946): 2-3; *Shanghai tan* 12 (1946): 10; *Qingqing dianying* 5, 5 (1940): 4; "Sports in China," 62. For obituary and family details, see "'China's Mermaid' Dies," *Vancouver Sun,* 13 October 1982, and "Yvonne Tan Sau King," *Globe and Mail,* 14 October 1982. On the restaurant, see *Far Eastern Economic Review* 18 (1955): 381.

66 "Nanguo tiankong xia de Meirenyu," *Wanxiang* 2 (June 1934): 38.

67 *Shidai manhua* 39 (20 June 1937): 1.

68 *Shiri zazhi* 1 (1935): cover.

69 *Linglong* 153 (19 September 1934): 1779-81; 151 (29 August 1934): 1664-65; 196 (7 October 1935): 1985; 207 (1935): 3413-15; 3477-78; Jingzi, "Guan Yang Xiuqiong biaoyan hou," *Linglong* 243 (1 July 1936): 1888-91; *Yongjin* 3, 4 (1934): 598; *Huanghou* 9 (1934): 4-5; *Funü gongming* 2, 11 (1933): 35-36; *Jiankang shenghuo* 1, 1 (1934): 9; *Yule* 1, 15 (1935): 369; 16 (1935): 399; *Yishi gonglun* 22 (1934): 12-13; *Daxia hun* 7, 7-8 (1938): 1275.

70 *Wenhua yuekan* 8 (1934): 121-24.

71 Wang, *Meirenyu.* For photographs, see Ye Qianyu, ed., *Minguo ershi'er nian quanguo yundong hui zhuangkan* (Shanghai: Shidai tushu gongsi, 1933), 8-13, 16-17, 50-51, 56-57; *Linglong* 117 (25 October 1933): 1998, 2015-16.

72 Wang, *Meirenyu,* 59, 62-63, 67-72; Yang, *Zizhuan.* On crowd, see the comments in Allen Gutman, "Sports Crowds," in *Crowds,* edited by Jeffrey T. Schnapp and Matthew Tiews (Stanford, CA: Stanford University Press, 2006), 111-33.

73 *Linglong* 153 (19 September 1934): 1779-81; 151 (29 August 1934): 1664-65.

74 Yang, *Zizhuan,* 21-22; *Liangyou huabao* 92 (15 August 15 1934): 17; Wang, *Meirenyu,* 59, 62-63, 67-72; *Diansheng* 4, 40 (4 October 1935): 870.

75 *Linglong* 58 (13 July 1932): 363; 197 (14 August 1935): 2059-60; 117 (1933): 2040.

76 *Diansheng* 7, 27 (8 July 1938): 536; 29 (1938): 578; *Mingxing* 2 (1938): 16.

77 *Liangyou huabao* 111 (November 1935): 56; *Diansheng* 4, 36 (6 September 1935): 767; *Haixing* 19 (1946): 9.

78 *Yule* 1, 16 (1935): 399; 19 (1935): 459; *Nandao fengguang* 1, 1 (1936): 39; *Diansheng* (1938): 76; 8, 30 (28 July 1939): 1; *Fengguang* 27 (1946): 7; *Kuaihuo lin* 33 (1946): 12.

79 Later known as Eleanor Holm Jarrett (1914-2004), the Olympic champion went to Hollywood under a movie contract with Warner Brothers that paid her $500 a week. She often posed at swimming pool edges in publicity stills. Worried about losing her amateur status, Jarrett refused an offer to swim for the silver screen despite a raise to $750 a week. Richard D. Mandell, *The Nazi Olympics* (New York: Macmillan, 1971), 243-48; "Eleanor Holm Whalen, 30's Swimming Champion, Dies," *New York Times,* 2 February 2004.

80 *Linglong* 57 (6 July 1932): 330; 58 (13 July 1932): 374; 75 (23 November 1932): 1195; 90 (5 April 1933): 366; 117 (25 October 1933): 2048.

81 Ibid., 117 (25 October 1933): 2011, 2031.

82 Ibid., 98 (7 June 1933): 841.

83 Ibid., 11 (27 May 1931): 39; 19 (22 July 1931): 695; 20 (29 July 1931): 732; 25 (2 September 1931): 914; 59 (20 July 1932) 412-13; 68 (21 September 1932): 846; 89 (29 March 1933):

314; 90 (5 April 1933): 366; 101 (5 July 1933): 1057; 148 (25 July 1934): 1494; 197 (14 August 1935): 2049-50.

84 Ibid., 117 (1933): 2006; *Lianhua huabao* 2 (17 December 1933): 24.

85 Yang, *Zizhuan*, 20-22; "Chu Minyi she dianying," *Linglong* 154 (26 September 1934): 1900; 192 (3 July 1935): 1632-33; 150 (15 August 1934): 1587-89. *Shalemei* 2 (1935): 1. On announcement of the film *Flowers on the Water*, see *Diansheng* 4, 27 (5 July 1935); *Dianying xinwen* 1, 2 (1935): 9; *Yule* 1, 1 (1935): 29; 1, 19 (1935): 479.

86 *Dianying xinwen* 1, 2 (1935): 9; 1, 4 (1935): 3; *Diansheng* 3, 30 (27 July 1934): 589; 4, 33 (16 August 1935): 681; *Shalemei* 2 (1935): 1.

87 *Linglong* 117 (25 October 1933): 1998.

88 *Dianying xinwen* 4 (1941): 15; "Yang Xiuqiong mingxing meng cheng paying," *Dianying ribao* 38 (14 September 1940): 1.

89 *Diansheng* 4, 44 (1 November 1935): 948; 10, 1 (5 January 1940): 8; *Dianying* 101 (1940): 3-4; 102 (1940): 6; *Dianying shenghuo* 17 (1940): 2; *Dianying xinwen* 124 (1941): 493; *Haixing* 2 (1946): 2; *Haichao zhoubao* 8 (1946): 3; *Mingxing* 3, 1 (1935): 1-2; *Piao* 7 (1946): 10; *Yingju* 6 (1943): 7; *Yingwu xinwen* 3, 1 (1936): 8; 4, 4 (1937): 6; *Yule* 1, 11 (1935): 266; 18 (1935): 448; 25 (1935): 602; *Zhongguo manhua* 4 (1935): 25; *Zhongguo yingxun* 1, 27 (1940): 209; *Zhongwai yingxun* 2, 4 (1941): 8.

90 On world popularity of swimming, see Jean-Didier Urbain, *At the Beach* (Minneapolis: University of Minnesota Press, 2003), 67-95.

91 *Quanguo yundong dahui zong baogao: Shijiu nian siyue Hangzhou juxing* (n.p., 1930); *Di wu jie quanyun zhuanji*, 29, 43.

92 One of the brothers, Shi Xinglu, taught at Dalian Ocean Transportation College in the 1980s. Shi Xia, "Shijia xiongmei," *Tiyu shiliao* 6 (April 1982): 37; *Linglong* 104 (26 July 1933): 1235.

93 *Qinfen tiyu yuebao* 1 (10 June 1934): 17; Wang, *Meirenyu*, 8-10, 12-13; Yang, *Zizhuan*, 18-19.

94 *Wanxiang* 2 (June 1934): 39.

95 *Nüshen* 6 (1935): 1-2.

96 "Youyong neng fang'ai nüxing ma?" *Linglong* 198 (21 October 1935): 2103-4; Heng, "Taishan youyong tan," *Tiyu zhoubao* 2, 19 (17 June 1933): 10-11.

97 *Linglong* 24 (26 August 1931): 894; 25 (2 September 1931): 931.

98 Lin, trans. "Yongyong duiyu nüxing mei de bianlun," *Tiyu zhoubao* 2, 26 (5 August 1933): 17-18. For other articles on the benefits of swimming for women, including a few authored by one of the Shi siblings, Shi Xinglong, see *Tiyu zhoubao* (24 September 1932); 2, 11 (22 April 1933): 8-10; 2, 15 (20 May 1933): 9-13; 2, 22 (8 July 1933): 17, 21-23.

99 "Youyong neng fang'ai nüxing ma?" *Linglong* 198 (21 October 1935): 2103-4.

100 Wang, *Meirenyu*, 163-64.

101 Yang, *Zizhuan*, 32-33.

102 *Linglong* 60 (27 July 1932): 440; 190 (26 June 1935): 1529; 191 (3 July 1935): 1573, 1575-76; *Diansheng* 4, 25 (21 June 1935): 509; *Renyan zhoukan* 1, 26 (1934): 1; *Shishi xunbao* 6, 1 (1934): 1. On swimming pool controversies in the United States, see Jeff Wiltse, *Contested Waters: A Social History of Swimming Pools in America* (Chapel Hill: University of North Carolina Press, 2007).

103 *Linglong* 19 (22 July 1931): 688; 60 (27 July 1932): 478; 61 (3 August 1932): 495; 21 (2 June 1937): 1627.

104 Ibid., 17 (8 July 1931): 594-95; 75 (23 November 1932): 1194; 103 (19 July 1933): 1162-64; 104 (26 July 1933): 1227-29; 243 (1 July 1936): 1899, 1920; Di liu jie quanguo yundong dahui wesheng zhu, ed., *Weisheng tekan* (Shanghai: n.p., 1935), 14-17, 48-53.

105 *Linglong* 196 (7 October 1935): 1985.

106 Ibid., 135 (4 April 1934): 622.

107 Ibid., 260 (4 November 1936): 3349-52.
108 Ibid., 20 (29 July 1931): 734; 103 (19 July 1933): 1169; 136 (11 April 1934): 660; 148 (25 July 1934): 1482; 37 (2 October 1935): 3208.
109 Ibid., 19 (22 July 1931): 660; 42 (1 January 1931): 1651; 57 (6 July 1932): 290; 59 (20 July 1932): 409; 61 (3 August 1932): cover; 62 (10 August 1932): 529; 66 (7 September 1932): 745-46; 68 (21 September 1932): 841; 99 (14 June 1933): 874; 151 (29 August 1934): 1711; 192 (3 July 1935): 1608; 197 (14 August 1935): 2010, 2027; 198 (21 October 1935): 2088.
110 *Liangyou huabao* 111 (November 1935): 56.
111 For articles making unfavourable comparisons, see *Renmin ribao*, 14 September 1957 and 26 November 1959. On Chinese swimmers, see Susan Brownell, *Training the Body for China: Sports in the Moral Order of the People's Republic* (Chicago: University of Chicago Press, 1995).

Chapter 6: Sportswomen on Screen: The "Athletic Movie Star," Li Lili (1915-2005)

1 For film details, go to http://www.imdb.com/title/tt0102816/. For a discussion of the film emphasizing Ruan Lingyu but with a sole mention of Li Lili, see Shuqin Cui, *Women through the Lens: Gender and Nation in a Century of Chinese Cinema* (Honolulu: University of Hawai'i Press, 2003), 30-50.
2 "Guochan nüxing he waiguo nüxing," *Linglong* 91 (21 April 1933): 450.
3 In Republican China, the term *mingxing* referred to cinematic actors exclusively, rather than outstanding figures in various fields as we understand it today. Since *mingxing* was the literal translation of "star" in the Hollywood context, I suspect that in English, "star" also referred exclusively to cinematic actors at the very beginning. Only with the development of other popular media did individuals in fields beyond cinema begin to gain celebrity like actors; consequently, the term "star" began to be applied more generally. *Tiyu mingxing* was the nickname for actress Li Lili. For outstanding figures and celebrities in athletic fields, the terms were *yundong jia* (top athletes) or *tiyu jia* (top administrators, educators, or scholars who specialized in tiyu). For more discussion of the development of Chinese film stars, see Mary Farquhar and Yingjin Zhang, *Chinese Film Stars* (New York: Routledge, 2010).
4 Prasenjit Duara, *Sovereignty and Authenticity: Manchukuo and the East Asian Modern* (Lanham, MD: Rowman and Littlefield, 2003), 137.
5 Zhang Zhen, *An Amorous History of the Silver Screen: Shanghai Cinema, 1896-1937* (Chicago: University of Chicago Press, 2005), 246-50.
6 After the establishment of the Republic in 1911, conscious nation building proclaimed that what had been the spoken language of officials (*guanhua*, thus "Mandarin"), based on the Beijing dialect, would now be the official language of the nation – *guoyu*. Y.R. Chao [Zhao Yuanren], "Some Contractive Aspects of the Chinese National Language Movement," in *Aspects of Chinese Sociolinguistics: Essays by Yuen Ren Chao*, edited by Anwar S. Dil (Stanford, CA: Stanford University Press, 1976), 97.
7 Zhiwei Xiao, "Film Censorship in China, 1927-1937" (PhD diss., University of California at San Diego, 1994), 40. For a recent work also indicating Li's independence, see Sean MacDonald, "Li Lili: Acting a Lively *Jianmei* Type," in *Chinese Film Stars*, edited by Mary Farquhar and Yingjin Zhang (New York: Routledge, 2010), 52-53.
8 Zhang, *An Amorous History,* 78; MacDonald, "Li Lili," 50-67.
9 Andrew D. Morris, *Marrow of the Nation: A History of Sports and Physical Culture in Republican China* (Berkeley: University of California Press, 2004), 75, 80, 104, 110, 157; Xu Guoqi, *Olympic Dreams: China and Sports, 1895-2008* (Cambridge, MA: Harvard University Press, 2008). On melodrama, see Paul G. Pickowicz, "Melodramatic Representation and the 'May Fourth' Tradition of Chinese Cinema," in *From May Fourth to June*

Fourth: Fiction and Film in Twentieth-Century China, edited by Ellen Widmer and David Der-wei Wang (Cambridge, MA: Harvard University Press, 1993), 295-326.

10   Michael G. Chang, "The Good, the Bad, and the Beautiful: Movie Actresses and Public Discourse in Shanghai, 1920-1930s," in *Cinema and Urban Culture in Shanghai, 1922-1943*, edited by Yingjin Zhang (Stanford, CA: Stanford University Press, 1999), 128-59, quote at 131.

11   Qian Zhuangfei was named one of "three heroes in white areas" by the prominent Communist leader Zhou Enlai. Qian had informed Zhou of the betrayal of Gu Shunzhang, the Comintern-appointed Communist general secretary, which saved the whole underground Communist organization from Chiang Kai-shek's purges. Li's family maintained personal/political associations with Zhou throughout the war. For these and other details of her life, see Li Lili, *Xingyun liushui pian: huiyi, zhuinian, yingcun* (Beijing: Zhangguo dianying chubanshe [private imprint], 2001), 10, 13-14.

12   Li Jinhui was a young brother of Li Jinxi, a famous linguist who advocated a national language with phonetic symbols *(guoyu zhuyin yundong)*. In order to cooperate with Li Jinxi's linguistic movement and educate Chinese citizens and overseas Chinese in *guoyu*, Li Jinhui organized the Bright Moon Association, in which Wang Renmei and Li Lili were leading figures. The younger brother of Li Jinhui and Li Jinxi, Li Jinyang (C.Y. Lee) was the author of the famous Broadway play and later Hollywood film *Flower Drum Song*. Li, *Xingyun liushui pian*, 46-47; Andrew F. Jones, *Yellow Music: Media Culture and Colonial Modernity in the Chinese Jazz Age* (Durham, NC: Duke University Press, 2001), 73-104.

13   Leo Ou-Fan Lee, *Shanghai Modern: The Flowering of a New Urban Culture in China, 1930-1945* (Cambridge, MA: Harvard University Press, 1999), 24, 26; Jones, *Yellow Music*, 83, 90; Zhang, *An Amorous History*, 408-42; MacDonald, "Li Lili," 53.

14   Li, *Xingyun liushui pian*, 46-47.

15   Xishi is a legendary beauty of the Warring States period who was known for having heart disease; Lin Daiyu is the consumptive beauty from *Hong lou meng (Story of Stone)* by Cao Xueqin. Their frailty and sickness constituted important parts of their feminine beauty.

16   Chang, "The Good, the Bad," 141.

17   A survey suggested that a common trait among popular male stars was their athletic looks. Some even suggested that what women enjoyed most in going to the movies was "seeing their male stars weight lifting." Xiao, "Film Censorship in China," 250. In 1933, *Linglong* carried a full-page portrait of Jin Yan titled "The Timely Male Star Jin Yan in Chinese Cinematic Circles." He was praised for his "perfectly fit *[jianquan]* body, strong will, and developed mind." *Linglong* 95 (17 May 1933): 674; 101 (5 July 1933): 1071-72.

18   *Qingqing dianying*, September 1934.

19   *Linglong* 96 (24 May 1933): 749.

20   In February 1935, the Nationalist government sent these two movies to Moscow for an international cinema festival. Due to its anti-Japanese scenes, *Big Road* was sent by sea, rather than by train through Manchuria with *Song of Fishermen*, and did not arrive at the festival in time. *Song of Fishermen* won the first international honour for a Chinese film, however. See Li, *Xingyun liushui pian*, 88.

21   MacDonald, "Li Lili," 55; Pickowicz, "Melodramatic Representation."

22   Jubin Hu, *Projecting a Nation: Chinese National Cinema before 1949* (Hong Kong: Hong Kong University Press, 2003), 98-100; Laikwan Pang, *Building a New China in Cinema: The Chinese Left-Wing Cinema Movement, 1932-1937* (Lanham, MD: Rowman and Littlefield Publishers, 2002); Vivien Shen, *The Origins of Left-Wing Cinema in China, 1932-1937* (New York: Routledge, 2005), 17.

23   For a fuller discussion, see Chapter 2. My emphasis on Li's use of jianmei is more pronounced than in MacDonald, "Li Lili," 50-66.

24 *Lianhua huabao* 17 (22 October 1933): 2, 3.

25 Morris has explained that the Jingwu Tiyu Association strove in the 1930s to reform and modernize martial arts by combining it with Western sports and body building, and adopted relevant clothing. Morris, *Marrow of the Nation*, 189-97.

26 According to Zhang Huilan, female students in the 1920s, including some with bound feet, had little background in tiyu. Dancing constituted the majority of instruction. For more information on Zhang Huilan and dancing in Western physical education, see Chapter 1.

27 Li, *Xingyun liushui pian*, 16, 45.

28 "Guopian sanda gongsi de xianzhuang," *Linglong* 74 (16 November 1932): 1149.

29 Li, *Xingyun liushui pian*, 167; *Zhonghua minguo ershi'er nian quanguo yundong hui tekan* (n.p.: n.p., 1934). *Linglong* 117 (25 October 1933): 1999, 2049.

30 *Linglong* 158 (24 October 1934): 2156.

31 Ibid., 94 (10 May 1933): 608.

32 Susan K. Cahn, *Coming on Strong: Gender and Sexuality in Twentieth-Century Women's Sports* (Cambridge, MA: Harvard University Press, 1994), 164-84.

33 *Lianhua huabao* 2, 22 (25 November 1933): 4; 2, 23 (3 December 1933): 3-4; 3, 15 (15 April 1934): 2-4.

34 *Linglong* 227 (11 March 1936): 687.

35 Ibid., 35 (1934): 2283.

36 *Lianhua huabao* 24 (1933): 3.

37 Li drew cartoon pictorials herself and befriended well-known cartoonists such as Shao Xunmei, Ye Lingfeng, and Ye Qianyu, who were major contributors to *Modern Sketch*, as well as Ding Song and his son Ding Cong. See Li, *Xingyun liushui pian*, 20.

38 *Liangyou huabao* 82 (November 1933): 11.

39 *Linglong* 94 (10 May 1933): 607; 104 (26 July 1933): 1224.

40 *Liangyou huabao* 82 (November 1933): 26.

41 *Linglong* 243 (1 July 1936): front and back covers, 1882. *Di liu jie quanguo yundong dahui zhixu ce* (Shanghai: n.p., 1935), 1. In the film, the title of "queen of sports" is something admirable that female athletes compete for. When other female athletes read about how Lin Ying (Li's character) could potentially be the "queen of sports," they comment that "this is the *Great China Daily* rooting for *[peng]* Lin Ying." The term *peng* was used historically for rich or powerful people promoting actors and actresses. Here, fame as a female athlete thus resembles fame as an actress. Lin's teammate said before her abrupt death that her poor mother and little brother in the countryside counted on her to gain fame through sports to better their lives, which suggests that sports careers and activities such as cinema were seen as a legitimate means for women's social advancement.

42 Pang, *Building a New China in Cinema*, 153-57; Zhang Yingjin, *Chinese National Cinema* (New York: Routledge, 2004), 72-73.

43 Daniel W.Y. Kwok, *Scientism in Chinese Thought, 1900-1950* (New Haven, CT: Yale University Press, 1965); Xiao, "Film Censorship in China," 65, 233.

44 Zhongguo dianying jia xiehui, ed. *Zhongguo dianying jia liezhuan* (Beijing: Zhongguo dianying chubanshe, 1982), 1: 183-90.

45 Zhang, *Chinese National Cinema*, 60-62, 66; *Zhongguo dianying jia liezhuan*, 1: 82, 183-90.

46 In 1932, Communists Xia Yan (1900-99), Zheng Boqi (1895-1979), and Qian Xingcun (1900-77) were hired by Mingxing Studio to guide its script department. In 1933, the Chinese Communist Party's Cultural Committee appointed Xia as head of "the Communist Cinema Group." In 1936, the Communist Tian Han (1898-1968) began working as a screenwriter for the Lianhua Studio and a script consultant for the Yihua Studio. See Lee, *Shanghai Modern*, 101, and Chen Bo, "Zhongguo zouyi dianying yundong de dansheng chengzhang yu fazhan," *Dangdai dianying* 4 (1991): 4-13.

47 Lee, *Shanghai Modern,* 62.

48 Pickowicz, "Melodramatic Representation," 301.

49 Zhang, *An Amorous History,* 290; Lee, *Shanghai Modern,* 102; Pickowicz, "Melodramatic Representation," 307.

50 According to the review in *Linglong,* Sun Yu made impressive progress in his directing skills. Ideologically, daybreak means the arrival of revolutionary daylight. *Linglong* 86 (1 March 1933): 284.

51 In *Daybreak,* the short-sleeved shirt with a big hole in the shoulder focuses the viewer's gaze on Lingling's young and healthy body. For further discussion of the contrast between the country girl and urban corruption in these films, see Shen, *Orgins of Left-Wing Cinema in China,* 38-41, 56-57.

52 C. Martin Wilbur, "The Nationalist Revolution: From Canton to Nanjing, 1923-1928," in *The Cambridge History of China,* vol. 12, pt. 1 (Cambridge: Cambridge University Press, 1983), 527-721.

53 *Zhongyang dianying jiancha weiyuanhui gongbao* 1, 11 (1934): 89.

54 *Diansheng* 3, 5 (2 February 1934): 66.

55 Xiao, "Film Censorship in China," 189.

56 *Diansheng* 5, 23 (29 May 1936): 505.

57 *Linglong* 11 (1933): 446; 76 (1932): 1004; "Gedi dangju dui wairen shepian ying yanjia zhuyi," *Diansheng* 5, 30 (31 July 1936): 713; "Xiren zai Beiping paishe ru Hua yingpian cailiao," *Diansheng* 5, 30 (31 July 1936): 749; Huang Qingshu (report from Hollywood), "Haolaiwu ge dianying gongsi shezhi zhong de Zhongguo Beijing yingpian neirong," *Diansheng* 5, 30 (31 July 1936): 755-57.

58 Xiao, "Film Censorship in China," 186.

59 The racial and ethnic twists of Li Xianglan in the Japanese wartime cinema and Anna May Wong in Hollywood in promoting a stereotypical Chinese womanhood are worth noting. Although Wong was born and brought up in the United States, Hollywood singled out her racial background to identify her, referring to her as "Chinese." Li was ethnically Japanese, but her Chinese birthplace and upbringing were highlighted in her onscreen and off-screen identities.

60 *Linglong* 76 (30 November 1932): 1004; 86 (1 March 1933): 286; 91 (12 April 1933): 446.

61 Graham Russell Gao Hodges, *Anna May Wong: From Laundryman's Daughter to Hollywood Legend* (New York: Palgrave Macmillan, 2004), 124, 151.

62 *Linglong,* 86 (1 March 1933): 286; 91 (12 April 1933): 446.

63 Hodges, *Anna May Wong,* xv, 164-66.

64 Xiao, "Film Censorship in China," 51, 53, 186. For instance, in 1933, the Propaganda Committee of the Central Committee of the Nationalist Party signed a contract with Lianhua Studio to shoot several newsreels every month and send them to Lianhua for distribution. "Zhongxuan yu Lianhua hezuo," *Linglong* 96 (24 May 1933): 749. In 1935, Lianhua released *Little Angel* and *The Nation* to advance the New Life Movement's goal of turning the masses into modern citizens. In 1937, the Ministry of Education asked Mingxing Studio to produce a film called *Dadi huichun (The Return of Spring).* Mingxing rejected the request and returned the film script. During the full-scale war against Japan, Luo Mingyou, the secretary-general of the Hong Kong Chapter of the Wartime Chinese Movie Workers' League, negotiated on behalf of the Nationalist government to purchase advanced cinematic equipment from the United States. See *China at War* 4 (1940): 96.

65 Lianhua's screenwriter, Hong Shen, initiated a movement against "films insulting to Chinese/China" by staging a protest in Da Guangming Theatre against the screening of *Welcome Danger* on 23 February 1930, and he continued to be active thereafter. In 1932, his denunciation of *Shanghai Express* in front of a theatre audience led to the banning of the film

in China. To settle the dispute, the theatre contributed 5,000 yuan to local schools, as demanded by Hong Shen. See *Shenbao,* 10 and 11 February 1931; Hodges, *Anna May Wong,* 124.

66 Li, *Xingyun liushui pian,* 25-27; Poshek Fu, *Between Shanghai and Hong Kong: The Politics of Chinese Cinema* (Stanford, CA: Stanford University Press, 2003), 1, 30; "Progress despite Difficulties: China's Young Movie Industry," *China at War* 7, 4 (October 1941): 68.

67 Tang Nan, "Fakan ci," *Kangzhan dianying* 1 (March 1938): 1; Yang Hansheg, Shi Dongshan et al., "Guanyu guofang dianying zhi jianli," *Kangzhan dianying* 1 (March 1938): 2-5; Zheng Yongzhi, "Quanguo de yinse zhanshi qilai," *Kangzhan dianying* 1 (March 1938): 6-7. On how Li Lili contributed to the genre of "national defence films," see Yuan Congmei, "'Rexue zhonghun' zhi hua," *Kangzhan dianying* 1 (March 1938): 15.

68 *Da wanbao,* 19 November 1936, 1252.

69 *Diansheng* 5, 47 (27 November 1936): 47.

70 Sheldon H. Lu and Emilie Yueh-yu, eds., *Chinese Language Film: Historiography* (Honolulu: University of Hawai'i Press, 2005), 144-145; Fu, *Between Shanghai and Hong Kong,* 56-58.

71 For information about the battle against Cantonese films, see Xiao "Film Censorship in China," 212-58, and Fu, *Between Shanghai and Hong Kong,* 51-92.

72 Fu, *Between Shanghai and Hong Kong,* 90.

73 Ibid., 12-14, 44, 46, 127; *Dianying ribao* 19 (26 August 1940): 4; 30 (6 September 1940): 4; 38 (14 September 1940):2; 59 (5 October 1940): 3.

74 Chang, "The Good, the Bad," 41, 133, 141.

75 Lee, *Shanghai Modern,* 93-94.

76 For a more extended discussion, see Gao Yunxiang, "Sports, Gender, and Nation-State during China's 'National Crisis' from 1931 to 1945" (PhD diss., University of Iowa, 2005), 323-40. The enormous popularity of *King Kong* in China and the connection between the two films will be discussed in a separate article. *Shidai manhua* 33 (20 January 1937).

77 Anna May Wong wore the exact same dancing dress in *Across to Singapore,* and, topless, wore the hula skirt on a fifteen-foot-high Austrian poster for *Piccadilly* to show her exotic sexiness. This image was particularly scandalous in the United States and Asia. See Hodges, *Anna May Wong,* 204.

78 Zhang Yingjin and Xiao Zhiwei, *Encyclopedia of Chinese Film* (New York: Routledge, 1998), 3; Zhang, *An Amorous History,* 293-94; Paul Pickowicz, "The Theme of Spiritual Pollution in Chinese Films of the 1930s," *Modern China* 17, 1 (January 1991): 38-75, quote at 51-52.

79 Christina K. Gilmartin, *Engendering the Chinese Revolution: Radical Women, Communist Politics and Mass Movements in the 1920s* (Berkeley: University of California Press, 1995); *Shenbao,* 18 January 1929.

80 Susan K. Cahn, *Coming on Strong,* 4, 25.

81 Lee, *Shanghai Modern,* 26, 28, 172, 194-96, 209; Zhang, *An Amorous History,* 284; Xiaobing Tang, *Chinese Modern: The Heroic and the Quotidian* (Durham, NC: Duke University Press, 2000), 109.

82 Lee, *Shanghai Modern,* 28, 92, 205-7, 212, 264; Shu-mei Shih, "Gender, Race, and Semicolonialism: Liu Na'ou's Urban Shanghai Landscape," *Journal of Asian Studies* 55, 4 (1996): 934-56, quote at 947-48.

83 Zhang, *An Amorous History,* 285; Shen, *Orgins of Left-Wing Cinema in China,* 80-83.

84 *Linglong* 152 (12 September 1934): 1743; *Diansheng* 5, 24 (5 June 1936): 544.

85 *Linglong* 85 (15 February 1933): 288; 100 (21 June 1933): 987; 221 (22 January 1936): 212; 127 (10 January 1934): 128; 81 (11 January 1933): 27.

86 *Diansheng* 4, 2 (15 January 1935): 41; 5, 9 (21 February 1936): 166-67; *Xin yinxing,* September 1928, 14; Hodges, *Anna May Wong,* 36-38.

87 George Mosse, *Nationalism and Sexuality: Respectability and Abnormal Sexuality in Modern Europe* (New York: Howard Fertig, 1997), 10; Xiao, "Film Censorship in China," 191; "Bu wang qi ben de aiguo nü'er," *Mingxing,* 13 November 1938, 12.
88 Li, *Xingyun liushui pian,* 29.
89 "Li Lili xianyu sanjiao lian'ai," *Linglong* 206 (9 October 1935): 3369-70.
90 *Diansheng* 5, 40 (9 October 1936): 1025; *Linglong* 101 (5 July 1933): 1048.
91 Fu, *Between Shanghai and Hong Kong,* 106-17.
92 *China at War* frequently advertised Chinese resistance films available to American audiences. After the meeting and following the outbreak of the Pacific War, Zhang Zhizhong appointed Luo to work with the China National Defense Materials Committee (Zhongguo guofang wuzi gongying weiyuanhui) in Washington, DC, as the representative of the Military Industry Bureau (Binggong shu) of the Nationalist government until October 1945. *China at War* 10, 1 (January 1943): 30-36; Li, *Xingyun liushui pian,* 77.
93 Howe was a member of the authoritative professional group American Society of Cinematographers. He shot 125 films in his lifetime, received ten Oscar nominations for best cinematographer, and won the Oscar twice, for *Rose Tattoo* in 1953 and for *Hud* in 1963. In 1942, he helped the Chinese Board of Information, the Chinese News Service, and the China Institute in America, Inc., to form an Advisory Council on China Motion Pictures (these institutes were all based in New York City). Its aim was to "encourage American producers to make motion pictures about China having cultural value at the same time correctly presenting China, the people and the background." "Advisory Council on China Films," *China at War* 8, 1 (January 1942): 50. The contrasting attitudes of Chinese nationalists toward Anna May Wong (a woman who was defined by her onscreen image) and Howe (a man who was defined by his off-screen skills) are worth studying from a gender perspective.
94 Li, *Xingyun liushui pian,* 32, 67, 76-77.
95 Ibid., 35, 69, 71-72; Ai Zhongxin, telephone interview by the author, September 2002; Hodges, *Anna May Wong,* 155, 213.
96 *Zhongwai chunqiu* 48 (1947): 8; Li, *Xingyun liushui pian,* 68. It seems that Li's concern was real. Sixty years later, the Hollywood film *Memoirs of a Geisha,* starring China's best-known actresses, Gong Li and Zhang Ziyi, was banned in China in late January 2006. Chinese actresses playing Japanese entertainers, particularly along with Japanese actors, evoked the memory of Japanese violation of China during the War of Resistance.
97 Li, *Xingyun linshui pian,* 37, 99-108, 165, 170.
98 Fu, *Between Shanghai and Hong Kong,* 73.

Conclusion
1 Dong Jinxia, *Women, Sport and Society in Modern China: Holding Up More than Half the Sky* (London: Frank Cass, 2003), 22-23.
2 Xu Guoqi, *Olympic Dreams: China and Sports, 1895-2008* (Cambridge, MA: Harvard University Press, 2008), 51-53.
3 Xu, *Olympic Dreams;* Dong, *Women, Sport and Society;* Susan Brownell, *Training the Body for China: Sports in the Moral Order of the People's Republic* (Chicago: University of Chicago Press, 1995).
4 Here I am influenced by the arguments in Walter Johnson, "On Agency," *Journal of Social History* 37, 2 (Autumn 2003): 113-24.
5 Dong, *Women, Sport and Society;* Brownell, *Training the Body for China,* 57.
6 Christopher Clarey, "Li Na Dethrones Schiavone at French Open," *New York Times,* 4 June 2011.

Glossary of Chinese Terms, Titles, and Names

Newspaper, Magazine, Journal, and Book Titles

Beiyang huabao 北洋画报 *(Peiyang [North Ocean] Pictorial News)*

Chenbao 晨报 *(Morning News)*

Choumou yuekan 绸缪月刊 *(Proactive Monthly)*

Chunhai 春海 *(Spring)*

Chunse 春色 *(Spring)*

Da Shanghai jiaoyu 大上海教育 *(Education in Grand Shanghai)*

Dadi 大地 *(Grand Earth)*

Dagong bao 大公报 *(Impartial [Takung] Daily)*

Daguanyuan zhoubao 大观园周报 *(Panorama Garden Weekly)*

Dangdai dianying 当代电影 *(Contemporary Cinema)*

Daxia 大夏 *(Daxia University)*

Daxia hun 大侠魂 *(The Soul of Grand Chivalry)*

Diansheng 电声 *(Cinematic Tone)*

Dianying ribao 电影日报 *(Movie Daily News)*

Dianying shenghuo 电影生活 *(Cinematic Life)*

Dianying xinwen 电影新闻 *(Cinematic News)*

Dongfang zazhi 东方杂志 *(Eastern Miscellany)*

Dongnan feng 东南风 *(Southeast Wind)*

Dushu 读书 *(Reading)*

Dushu guwen 读书顾问 *(Reading Consultant)*

Dushu qingnian 读书青年 *(Reading Youth)*

Fengguang 风光 *(Views)*

Funü gongming 妇女共鸣 *(Women's Communal Voices)*

Funü qingnian 妇女青年 *(Female Youth)*

Funü shenghuo 妇女生活 *(Women's Lives)*

Funü xinshenghuo yuekan 妇女新生活月刊 *(Women's New Life Movement Monthly)*

Funü yuebao 妇女月报 *(Women's Monthly)*

Funü zazhi 妇女杂志 *(Women's Magazine)*

Furen huabao 妇人画报 *(Women's Pictorial)*

Guanghua yiyao zazhi 光华医药杂志 *(Grand China Pharmaceutical Journal)*

Guomin tiyu huikan 国民体育汇刊 *(Comprehensive Journal of Citizens' Tiyu)*

Guoshu tongyi yuekan 国术统一月刊 *(Universal Monthly of National Skills)*

Guoshu zhoukan 国术周刊 *(National Skills Weekly)*

Guowen zhoubao 国闻周报 *(National News [Kuowen] Weekly)*

Guoxun 国讯 *(National News)*

Haichao zhoubao 海潮周刊 *(Ocean Tide Weekly)*

Haifeng 海风 *(Ocean Wind)*

Haiguang 海光 *(Ocean View)*

Haixing 海星 *(Ocean Stars)*

Haiyan 海燕 *(Seagualls)*

Hanxue zhoukan 汗血周刊 *(Sweat and Blood Weekly)*

Hehuan yundong 和缓运动 *(Gentle Exercise)*

Henan jiaoyu 河南教育 *(Education in Henan)*

Hong meigui 红玫瑰 *(Red Roses)*

Honglü 红绿 *(Red and Green)*

Huanghou 皇后 *(Queen)*

Jian li mei 健力美 *(Health, Power, and Beauty)*

Jiankang shenghuo 健康生活 *(Healthy Life)*

Jiao yu xue 教与学 *(Teaching and Learning)*

Jiaoyu zazhi 教育杂志 *(Education Magazine)*

Jiating yu funü 家庭与妇女 *(Family and Women)*

Jiating zhoukan 家庭周刊 *(Family Weekly)*

Jincheng 金城 *(Golden Metropolis)*

Jindai funü 今代妇女 *(Contemporary Women)*

Jinghua 精华 *(Essences)*

Kangjian shijie 康健世界 *(Health World)*

Kangjian zazhi 康健杂志 *(Health Magazine)*

Kangzhan dianying 抗战电影 *(National Defence Films)*

Kuaihuo lin 快活林 *(Tavern)*

Kuaile jiating 快乐家庭 *(Happy Family)*

Liangyou huabao 良友画报 *(Young Companion Pictorial)*

Lianhua huabao 联华画报 *(Lianhua Pictorial)*

Libai liu 礼拜六 *(Saturday)*

Linglong 玲珑 *(Linglong Women's Magazine)*

Lingxiao 凌霄 *(Heavenly Sky)*

Lixiang jiating 理想家庭 *(Ideal Family)*

Lunyu 论语 *(Analects)*

Lüxing zazhi 旅行杂志 *(Travel)*

Mingxing 明星 *(Bright Stars)*

Minjian zhoubao 民建周刊 *(Citizenship Weekly)*

Minzhong shenghuo 民众生活 *(Masses' Lives)*

Nandao fengguang 南岛风光 *(Scenes of Southern Islands)*

Nankai daxue zhoukan 南开大学周刊 *(Nankai University Weekly)*

Nankai shuangzhou 南开双周 *(Nankai Biweekly)*

Nü pengyou 女朋友 *(Girlfriend)*

Nü qingnian yuekan 女青年月刊 *(Female Youth Monthly)*

Nü xuesheng 女学生 *(Female Students)*

Nü yundong yuan linzhen zhiqian 女运动员临阵之前
   (Female Athletes before Competition)

Nüshen 女神 *(Goddess)*

Nüzi 女子 *(Ladies)*

Piao 漂 *(Drifting)*

Pingmin yuekan 平民月刊 *(Commoners' Monthly)*

Qianqiu 千秋 *(Varieties)*

Qiantu 前途 *(Future)*

Qiaosheng bao 侨声报 *(Voices of Overseas Chinese)*

Qinfen tiyu yuebao 勤奋体育月报 *(Diligent Tiyu Monthly)*

Qingqing dianying 青青电影 *(Evergreen Cinema)*

Qingqing 青青 *(Evergreen)*

Renmin ribao 人民日报 *(People's Daily)*

Rensheng xunkan 人生旬刊 *(Life Ten-Daily)*

Renyan zhoukan 人言周刊 *(People's Voice Weekly)*

Shalemei 莎乐美 *(Salome)*

Shanghai jiaoyu jie 上海教育界 *(Circle of Shanghai Education)*

Shanghai shenghuo 上海生活 *(Shanghai Life)*

Shanghai shi zhengfu gongbao 上海市政府公报 *(Shanghai Municipal
   Government Bulletin)*

Shanghai tan 上海滩 *(Shanghai Bund/Metropolis)*

Shanghai tebie shi jiaoyu ju jiaoyu zhoubao 上海特别市教育局教育周报
   (Education Weekly of Shanghai Bureau of Education)

Shanghai tiyu shihua 上海体育史话 *(History of Tiyu in Shanghai)*

Shaonü 少女 *(Young Girls)*

Shehui xinwen 社会新闻 *(Social News)*

Shenbao 申报 *(Shanghai Daily)*

Shenbao yuekan 申报月刊 *(Supplementary Monthly Magazine of Shanghai Daily)*

Shenghuo 生活 *(Life)*

Shenghuo huabao 生活画报 *(Life Pictorial)*

Shibao 时报 *(Eastern Times)*

Shidai dianying 时代电影 *(Modern Cinema)*

Shidai manhua 时代漫画 *(Modern Sketch/Epoch Cartoons)*

Shidai shenghuo 时代生活 *(Modern Life)*

Shidai zimei 时代姊妹 *(Modern Sisters)*

Shijie ribao 世界日报 *(World Daily)*

Shiri zazhi 十日杂志 *(Ten-Day Magazine)*

Shishi daguan 时事大观 *(Overview of Current Affairs)*

Shishi xinbao 时事新报 *(New Newspaper of Current Affairs)*

Shishi xunbao 时事旬报 *(Current Affairs Ten-Daily)*

Shishi yuebao 时事月报 *(Current Affairs Monthly)*

Taishan 泰山 *(Tai Mountain)*

Tianwentai sanri 天文台三日 *(Three Days at the Observatory)*

Tianxin 甜心 *(Sweetheart)*

Tiyu jikan 体育季刊 *(Physical Education Quarterly)*

Tiyu Jikan 体育季刊 *(The Chinese Journal of Physical Education)*

Tiyu pinglun 体育评论 *(Tiyu Review)*

Tiyu shiliao 体育史料 *(Historical Materials of Tiyu)*

Tiyu wencong 体育文丛 *(Tiyu Literature)*

Tiyu xinsheng 体育新声 *(New Voice in Tiyu)*

Tiyu yanjiu yu tongxun 体育研究与通讯 *(Research and Communication on Tiyu)*

Tiyu zhoubao 体育周报 *(Tiyu Weekly)*

Tongji xunkan 同济旬刊 *(Tongji Ten-Daily)*

Tushu zhanwang 图书展望 *(Book Prospect)*

Wanxiang 万象 *(Panorama)*

Weisheng yuekan 卫生月刊 *(Hygiene Monthly)*

Wenhua 文华 *(Essences of Literature)*

Wenhua yuekan 文化月刊 *(Culture Monthly)*

Wenshi jinghua 文史精华 *(Essences of Culture and History)*

Wufeng 舞风 *(Dance)*

Xiandai funü 现代妇女 *(Modern Women)*

Xiandai jiating 现代家庭 *(Modern Family)*

Xiandai nongmin 现代农民 *(Modern Farmers)*

Xiandai qingnian 现代青年 *(Modern Youth)*

Xiandai xuesheng 现代学生 *(Modern Students)*

Xiangxue hai 香雪海 *(Sea of Fragrant Flowers)*

Xianshi bao 现世报 *(Contemporary Affairs Newspaper)*

Xianxiang 现象 *(Phenomenon)*

Xiaojie 小姐 *(Miss)*

Xin funü 新妇女 *(New Women)*

Xin yinxing 新银星 *(New Silver Screen Stars)*

Xinbao 新报 *(New Newspaper)*

Xinbao zhoukan 新报周刊 *(Supplementary Weekly Magazine of the New Newspaper)*

Xing zazhi 性杂志 *(Magazine of Sexuality)*

Xuanmiao guan 玄妙观 *(Xuanmiao Daoist Temple)*

Xuesheng shenghuo 学生生活 *(Students' Lives)*

Xuexiao shenghuo 学校生活 *(Campus Life)*

Yingju 影剧 *(Movie and Play)*

Yingwu xinwen 影舞新闻 *(Cinema and Dance News)*

Yishi bao 益世报 *(Social Welfare)*

Yishi gonglun 医事公论 *(Public Forum for Medical Issues)*

Yizhou jian 一周间 *(Week)*

Yongjin 勇进 *(Forward)*

Yougong yuekan 邮工月刊 *(Postal Staff Monthly)*

Yule 娱乐 *(Entertainment)*

Zazhi 杂志 *(Magazine)*

Zhejiang tiyu banyue kan 浙江体育半月刊 *(Zhejiang Tiyu Biweekly)*

Zhongguo Hongshizihui yuekan 中国红十字会月刊 *(China Red Cross Monthly)*

Zhongguo kangjian yuebao 中国抗建月刊 *(China's Resistance and Reconstruction Monthly)*

Zhongguo manhua 中国漫画 *(China Cartoons)*

Zhongguo xuesheng 中国学生 *(Students of China)*

Zhongguo yingxun 中国影讯 *(Chinese Cinematic News)*

Zhonghua huabao 中华画报 *(China Pictorial)*

Zhonghua kouqin jie 中华口琴界 *(Circle of China Harmonica)*

Zhonghua yuebao 中华月报 *(China Monthly)*

Zhonghua zhoubao 中华周报 *(China Weekly)*

Zhongmei zhoubao 中美周报 *(Chinese-American Weekly)*

Zhongwai chunqiu 中外春秋 *(Chinese and Foreign Annals)*

Zhongwai yingxun 中外影讯 *(Chinese and Foreign Cinematic News)*

Zhongyang dianying jiancha weiyuanhui gongbao 中央电影检查委员会公报 *(Bulletin of the Central Censorship Committee)*

Zhufu zhiyou 主妇之友 *(Friend of Housewives)*

Zi luolan 紫罗兰 *(Violet)*

Film Names

Dadi huichun 大地回春

Dalu 大路

Dao ziran qu 到自然去

Genü Hong Mudan 歌女红牡丹

Gewu ban 歌舞班 (in *Yi hai fenghuang* 艺海风光)

Gudao tiantang 孤岛天堂

Gudu chunmeng 故都春梦

Gui 鬼 (in *Lianhua jiaoxiang qu* 联华交响曲)

Guo feng 国风

Huo shao Honglian si 火烧红莲寺

Huoshan qingxie 火山情血

Jianmei yundong 健美运动

Langshan diexue ji 狼山喋血记

Mulan congjun 木兰从军

Muxing zhi guang 母性之光

Polang 破浪

Qi zhuang shanhe 气壮山河

Qiu shan mingdeng 秋扇明灯

Rendao 人道

Rexue zhonghun 热血忠魂

Ruan Lingyu 阮玲玉

Saishang fengyun 塞上风云

San ge modeng nüxing 三个摩登女性

Shennü 神女

Shizi jietou 十字街头

Shuishang hua 水上花

Tianming 天明

Tiyu huanghou 体育皇后

Wang Xiansheng dao "nongcun qu"
王先生到"农村去"

Xiao tianshi 小天使

Xiao wanyi 小玩意

Xin nüxing 新女性

Xu gudu chunmeng 续故都春梦

Xue jian yinghua 血溅樱花

Yecao xianhua 野草闲花

Yu guang qu 渔光曲

Zhi qu Huashan 智取华山

Zhonghua nü'er 中华女儿

Personal Names

Ai Zhongxin 艾中信

Bao Guancheng 鲍观澄

Cao Xiulin 曹秀琳

Chen Baixue 陈白雪

Chen Bijun 陈璧君

Chen Cunren 陈存仁

Chen Gongbo 陈公博

Chen Jiageng 陈嘉庚

Chen Jucai 陈聚才

Chen Rongming 陈荣明

Chen Rongtang 陈荣棠

Chen Yingmei 陈英梅

Chen Yongsheng 陈咏声

Chen Yunshang 陈云裳

Chen Zhenling 陈珍玲

Cheng Tianfang 程天放

Chu Minyi 储民谊

Ding Ling 丁玲

Dong Chengkang 董承康

Dong Shouyi 董守义

Du Longyuan 杜隆元

Du Yuesheng 杜月笙

Fan Shaozeng 范绍曾

Feng Yuxiang 冯玉祥

Fu Baolu 符保卢

Fu Shuyun 付淑云

Gan Naiguang 甘乃光

Gao Zhaolie 高兆烈

Gao Zi 高梓

Ge Gongzhen 戈公振

Guan Liuzhu 关柳珠

Guo Moruo 郭沫若

Guo Wawa 郭娃娃

Guo Xiaofen 郭效纷

Hao Chunde 郝春德

Hao Gengsheng 郝更生

He Buyun 何步云

He Jian 何健

He Xiangning 何香凝

He Yingqin 何应钦

Hou Tianqi 候天淇

Hu Die 胡蝶

Hu Mulan 胡木兰

Hu Wenhu 胡文虎

Hu Zhengqu 胡正渠

Hu Zhenxia 胡震夏

Huang Jingwan 黄警顽

Huang Liushuang 黄柳霜

Huang Shufang 黄淑芳

Huang Zongzhan 黄宗霑

Jiang Gaodi 姜高弟

Jiang Huaiqing 蒋槐青

Jiao Yulian 焦玉莲

Jin Yan 金焰

Lang Jingshan 郎静山

Li Huitang 李惠堂

Li Jinhui 黎锦晖

Li Jiwen 刘纪文

Li Lihua 李丽华

Li Lili 黎莉莉

Li Minwei 黎民伟

Li Na 李娜

Li Sen 李森

Li Xianglan 李香兰

Li Zhuozhuo 黎灼灼

Liang Desuo 梁得所

Liang Yongxian 梁詠娴

Lin Kanghou 林康候

Lin Pengxia 林鹏侠

Lin Sen 林森

Lin Ying 林樱

Lin Yutang 林语堂

Lin Zecang 林泽苍

Lin Zemin 林泽民

Liu Changchun 刘长春

Liu Guizhen 刘桂珍

Liu Jingzhen 刘静贞

Liu Xiang 刘翔

Liu Xuesong 刘雪松

Liu Yuhua 刘玉华

Long Jingxiong 龙竞雄

Long Lizhen 龙丽真

Lu Guizhen 鲁桂珍

Lu Lihua 陆礼华

Lu Shaofei 鲁少飞

Lu Xueqin 陆雪琴

Lu Xun 鲁迅

Luo Jingyu 罗静予

Luo Mingyou 罗明佑

Ma Sicong 马思聪

Ma Xiangbo 马相伯

Mai Kele 麦克乐

Mei Lanfang 梅兰芳

Pan Gongzhan 潘公展

Pan Meng 潘梦

Pan Yueying 潘月英

Pan Yuliang 潘玉良

Pang Jiaying 庞佳颖

Peng Aipu 彭爱浦

Qian Xingsu 钱行素

Qian Yiqin 钱一勤

Qian Zhenzhen 钱蓁蓁

Qian Zhuangfei 钱壮飞

Qin Xingshi 秦醒世

Qiu Feihai 邱飞海

Ruan Lingyu 阮玲玉

Shao Jinying 邵锦英

Shen Siliang 沈嗣良

Shi Ruixia 石瑞霞

Song Junfu 宋君复

Sun Guiyun 孙桂云

Sun Hebin 孙和宾

Sun Yu 孙瑜

Sun Zhenghe 孙征和

Tang Liangli 汤良礼

Tao Bolin 陶伯林

Tu Shaozhen 屠绍桢

Tu Yunsheng 涂云生

Wang Jianming 汪剑鸣

Wang Lan 王兰

Wang Longde 王隆德

Wang Rumin 王汝珉

Wang Yuan 王渊

Wang Zhaoming 汪兆明

Wang Zhengting 王正廷

Wang Zhixin 王志新

Wang Zimei 汪子美

Wu Bangwei 吴邦伟

Wu Chuanyu 吴传玉

Wu Dingpei 吴鼎培

Wu Kaisheng 吴凯声

Wu Meixian 吴梅仙

Wu Tiecheng 吴铁城

Wu Yifang 吴贻芳

Wu Yunrui 吴蕴瑞

Xi Jun 席均

Xi Yuquan 席与群

Xiang Dawei 向大威

Xiao Shuling 萧淑芩

Xiong Shihui 熊式辉

Xu Beihong 徐悲鸿

Yan Shuhe 严淑和

Yan Yangchu 晏阳初

Yang Changhua 杨昌华

Yang Ren 杨仁

Yang Sen 杨森

Yang Wanxing (Zhunan) 杨万兴 (柱南)

Yang Xiaorang 杨效让

Yang Xiuqiong 杨秀琼

Yang Xiuzhen 杨秀珍

Yao Ruifang 姚瑞芳

Ye Qianyu 叶浅予

Yu Xuezhong 于学忠

Yu Ziyu 于子玉

Yuan Dunli 袁敦礼

Yuan Liang 袁良

Yue Xiuyun 乐秀云

Zeng Zhongming 曾仲鸣

Zhai Lianyuan 翟涟源

Zhang Boling 张伯苓

Zhang Huilan 张汇兰

Zhang Jingsheng 张竞生

Zhang Shankun 张善琨

Zhang Zhizhong 张治中

Zheng Hongying 郑鸿英

Zheng Lixia 郑丽霞

Zhong Qi 钟骐

Zhou Gucheng 周谷城

Zhou Shuzhen 周淑珍

Zhou Xuan 周璇

Zhu Shifang 朱士方

Zhuang Shuyu 庄淑玉

Zong Weigeng 宗维赓

Zou Shande 邹善德

Other Terms and Phrases

Baidai changpian 百代唱片

bailian xiaosheng 白脸小生

Baofeijiao 保肺胶

bense biaoyan 本色表演

chang ti dun yi 倡体敦谊

dajia guixiu 大家闺秀

datui meiren 大腿美人

Dongnan nüzi tiyu zhuanke xuexiao 东南女子体育专科学校

Dongwu daxue 东吴大学

Dongya nüzi tiyu zhangke xuexiao 东亚女子体育专科学校

duanlian 锻炼

duxue 督学

feilao 肺痨

Fengyong daxue 冯庸大学

fudao 妇道

Funü xiejin hui 妇女协进会

guige zhi feng 闺阁之风

guofang dianying 国防电影

guohuo yundong 国货运动

Guoji meirong yuan 国际美容院

Guomin tiyu fa 国民体育法

guonan 国难

guoyu 国语

guoyu zhuyin yundong 国语注音运动

Hebei Tianjin nüzi shifan xueyuan 河北天津女子师范学院

huakui 花魁

ji 髻

jianmei zhuyi 健美主义

jianyue mingxing 简约明星

Jiaofang nüzi minzhong xueshe 教坊女子民众学社

jiaoxiao linglong 娇小玲珑

Jimei 集美

Jinling nüzi wenli xueyuan 金陵女子文理学院

jinshi nüquan fada 近世女权发达

jixing 畸形

Liangjiang hua 两江化

Lianhua 联华

lijiao 礼教

liuwang xuanshou 流亡选手

Lizhi she 励志社

luoti shenghuo yundong 裸体生活运动

maiguozei 卖国贼

meirenyu 美人鱼

Meirong guwen lan 美容顾问栏

mingyuan 名媛

Mingyue she 明月社

Minxin 民新

minzu zhilin 民族之林

Modeng pohuai tuan 摩登破坏团

modeng xiaojie/nülang 摩登小姐/女郎

nanxinghua 男性化

Nuchao jushe 怒潮剧社

Nüxuesheng xufa da tongmeng 女学生蓄发大同盟

qigong 气功

Qinfen shuju 勤奋书局

Qinhuai 秦淮

qipao 旗袍

qizhi 气质

qizhuang yifu 奇装异服

quanmin jianshen yundong 全民健身运动

renge 人格

rougan 肉感

ru Hua pian 辱华片

Saipao jie zhi quanwe: nan Qian bei Liu xiangying pimei 赛跑界之权威：
　　南钱北刘相映媲美

Shanghai jiangnan tiyu xuexiao 上海江南体育学校

Shanghai Zhonghua Jidujiao Nüqingnianhui Quanguo Xiehui tiyu shifan xuexiao
　　上海中华基督教女青年会全国协会体育师范学校

Shanghai Zhonghua nüzi lanqiu hui 上海中华女子篮球会

shidai shuxiang 世代书香

Sili liangjiang nüzi tiyu shifan zhuanke xuexiao 私立两江女子体育师范专科学校

siling qiu 司令球

Suhu qingnian yuan Ma rexue tuan 苏沪青年援马热血团

taiji cao 太极操

Tianyi 天一

ticao 体操

tiyu jia 体育家

Tiyu kaocha tuan 体育考察团

tiyu mingxing 体育明星

tongxing ai 同性爱

waiwu riji, guonan fangyin 外侮日急 国难方殷

Wang Kai 王开

Wanguo yundong hui 万国运动会

wanjin you 万金油

Wuben nüxiao 务本女校

wuxia shenguai pian 武侠神怪片

xiansheng 先生

xiaoshimin 小市民

Xinhua 新华

xiong jiujiu 雄赳赳

Yihua 艺华

Yilian 艺联

you ai zhenjie, you shang feng, hua you ru guoti 有碍贞节，有伤风化，有辱国体

yuanshi de jianmei shenghuo 原始的健美生活

yuanyang hudie pai 鸳鸯蝴蝶派

yundong jia 运动家

Zhengzhi yanjiu hui 政治研究会

Zhongguo nüzi ticao xuexiao 中国女子体操学校

Zhonghua buxing tuan 中华步行团

Bibliography

Archival Sources

Beijing Municipal Archives, vol. J2, no. 3, file 557.

James Yen Papers, Butler Library, Columbia University, New York.

Second National Archives of China in Nanjing, vol. 648, files 1574 and 1478; vol. 668, files 26, 34, 39, 87, 338.

Zhang Huilan, "Health Education in the Public Health Program" 1945, box 69, stack 14, James Yen Papers, Butler Library, Columbia University, New York.

Selected Chinese-Language Sources

An Shuqing. "Tianjin nüzi shifan xueyuan tiyu xi jieshi" [A brief history of the Tiyu Department at Tianjin Women's Normal College]. *Tiyu shiliao* 8 (September 1982): 47.

Cai Yangwu and Liu Yali, eds. *Shanghai tiyu zhi* [Gazette of Shanghai tiyu]. Shanghai: Shanghai shehui kexue yuan chubanshe, 1996.

Chen Bo. "Zhongguo zuoyi dianying yundong de dansheng chengzhang yu fazhan" [The birth, growth, and development of leftist cinema in China]. *Dangdai dianying* [Contemporary cinema] 4 (1991): 4-13.

Chen Cunren. *Kangzhan shidai shenghuo shi* [History of life during the anti-Japanese war]. Guilin: Guangxi shifan daxue chubanshe, 2007.

Chen Yongsheng. *Ouzhou tiyu kaocha riji* [Diary of observing *tiyu* in Europe]. Shanghai: Nansheng chubanshe, 1938.

Cheng Jun. "Zhongguo nüzi guanfei liuxue zhi shi" [History of Chinese women studying overseas on public funds]. *Minguo chunqiu* [Annals of the Republican China] 6 (25 November 1990): 38.

Chengdu tiyu xueyuan tiyu shi yanjiu shi, ed. *Zhongguo jindai tiyu shi jianbian* [Brief history of tiyu in early modern China]. Beijing: Renmin tiyu chubanshe, 1981.

Chongqing shi tiyu yundong weiyuanhui and Chongqing shizhi zongbian shi, eds. *Kangzhang shiqi peidu tiyu shiliao* [Historical sources on tiyu in the wartime capital]. Chongqing: Chongqing chubanshe, 1987.

Di liu jie quanguo yundong dahui wesheng zhu, ed. *Weisheng tekan* [Special issue on hygiene (during the Sixth National Games)]. Shanghai: n.p., 1935.

Di liu jie quanguo yundong dahui zhixu ce [Program of the Sixth National Games]. Shanghai: n.p., 1935.

Di liu jie quanyun shimo ji [Full record of the Sixth National Games]. Beiping: Pingbao tiyu bu, 1935.

Di wu jie quanyun hui teji [Special collections on the Fifth National Games]. 1933.

Di wu jie quanyun zhuanji [Special collections on the Fifth National Games]. Shanghai: Wenhua meishu tushu gongsi, 1933.

Dong Shouyi. "Aolinpike jiushi" [Memories of the Olympics]. *Tiyu shiliao* 2 (August 1980): 3-14.

Du Longyuan. "Tiyu jiaoyuan duiyu xiao xuesheng de zhuyi" [Suggestions to physical educators on working with elementary school students], recorded by Meng Pu. *Tiyu zhoubao* 28 (13 August 1932): 5.

Ge Min. "Yidai tianjing nüjie Qian Xingsu" [Track and field heroine of a generation Qian Xingsu]. In *Titan xianfeng* [Forerunners in sports], 35-38. Shanghai: Shanghai renmin chubanshe, 1990.

Hebei shifan daxue tiyu xueyuan yuanshi, 1931-2002 [History of the physical education department of Hebei Normal University]. Draft, 2002.

Hitomi, Kinue. *Nü yundong yuan linzhen zhiqian* [Female athletes before competition], translated by Liu Jiaxiong. Shanghai: Qinfen shuju, 1931.

Hu Die and Liu Huiqin. *Hu Die huiyi lu* [Memoirs of Hu Die]. Beijing: Wenhua yishu chubanshe, 1988.

Hu Die nüshi xiezhen ji [Photograph collections of Ms. Hu Die], vol. 12. Shanghai: Liangyou tushu yinshua gongsi, 1933.

Huang Shufang, Long Jingxiong, Yang Ren, Xiang Dawei, Cheng Baixue, Chang Mingzhen, et al., interviewed by Wu Zhiming. "Liangjiang nüzi tiyu zhuanke xuexiao xiaoshi" [History of the Private Liangjiang Women's Tiyu Normal School]. *Tiyu shiliao* 6 (April 1982): 7-8.

Jin Chuan. "Nü pao wang Li Sen" [Sprinter queen Li Sen], 32-34. In *Titan xianfeng*. Shanghai: Shanghai renmin chubanshe, 1990.

Li Jingchang and Li Fan, eds. *Shanghai tiyu jingcui* [The essence of tiyu in Shanghai]. Beijing: Dadi chubanshe, 1989.

Li Lili. *Xingyun liushui pian: huiyi, zhuinian, yingcun* [Free and easy pieces: reminiscences, recollections, and images]. Beijing: Zhongguo dianying chubanshe (private imprint), 2001.

Li Zhenzhong. "Zhongguo lanqiu daibiao dui canjia di shisi jie Aoyunhui jingguo" [The whole course of China's basketball team competing in the 14th Olympics]. *Tiyu shiliao* 2 (August 1980): 44-47.

Liu Jun. "Zhang Huilan yisheng zhili fazhan tiyu, jiushi gaoling huo Lianheguo rongyu jiang" [Zhang Huilan, who has devoted her whole life to tiyu, wins a UNESCO medal at the age of ninety], *Renmin ribao*, 3 January 1987.

"Liu Mei Zhongguo xueshenghui xiaoshi" [A brief history of the Association of Chinese Students in America]. *Dongfang zazhi* 14, 12 (December 1917).

Liu Yuhua. "Yi di shiyi jie Aoyunhui Zhongguo wushu dui fu Ou biaoyan" [Recalling the Chinese martial arts team going to Europe for the 11th Olympics]. *Tiyu shiliao* 2 (August 1980): 29-30.

—. "Duiyu Wang Xinwu de 'Tichang wushu de yixie jianyi' de yixie jianyi" [Some suggestions on Wang Xinwu's "Some suggestions on promoting martial arts"]. *Tiyu wencong* 7 (1957): 10.

Lu Lihua. "Fuxing hou de Liangjiang nüzi tiyu shifan xuexiao shinian qian de huisu" [Past decade of the recovered Liangjiang Women's Tiyu Normal School]. *Qinfen tiyu yuebao* 1, 10 (10 July 1934): 31-32.

—. "Jiankang de zhufu yu jiating" [Healthy housewives and families]. *Zhufu zhiyou* 1, 3 (1937): 5-8.

—. "Jie wo Huazhou" [Strengthening our China]. *Guoshu zhoukan* 158-60 (1936): 5.

—. "Jiqie xuyao zhi Zhongguo nüzi tiyu" [The urgently needed tiyu for Chinese women]. *Tiyu zhoubao* 2, 20 (24 June 1933): 1.

—. "Liangjiang nütishi lanqiu dui yuanzheng nanyang ji" [On the tour of the basketball team of the Private Liangjiang Women's Tiyu Normal School in Southeast Asia]. *Qinfen tiyu yuebao* 2, 10 (10 July 1935): 677-78.

—. "Liangjiang nüxiao canjia Wanguo Lanqiu Sai de jingguo" [On Liangjiang competing in the Multi-national Basketball Games]. *Shanghai tiyu shihua* 2 (1984): 15.

–. "Nannü jihui zhi jundeng" [Equal opportunity for men and women]. *Xing zazhi* 1 (1927): 1-2.

–. "Nüzi tiyu yu jiating xingfu" [Women's tiyu and family happiness]. *Funü yuebao* 3, 3 (1937): 8.

–. "Shanghai jidai juban de shiye" [The urgent causes in Shanghai]. *Zhongguo Hongshizihui yuekan* 37 (1938): 4-9.

–. "Shanghai nüzi tiyu yingyou de gaijin" [Needed improvements for Shanghai women's tiyu]. *Shanghai jiaoyu jie* 4 (1933): 26-27.

–. "Shejiao gongkai zhi zhen yiyi" [The true meaning of open socialization]. *Xing zazhi* 2 (1927): 1-3.

–. "Sichuan kaocha hou zhi yinxiang" [My impression after investigation in Sichuan]. *Zhonghua guohuo chanxiao xiehui meizhou huibao* [Weekly report of the Chinese National Goods Production and Distribution Association], 3, 37 (1937): 3.

–. "Tiyu yu jiating, renlei jiankang de xin faxian" [Tiyu and families: new discoveries on human happiness]. *Kuaile jiating* 1, 6 (1937): 90-92.

–. "Weixie de quxian" [Dangerous curves]. *Shaonü* 2, 1 (1949): 21-24.

–. "Woguo zuizao chuguo bisai de nüzi lanqiu dui" [Our nation's first women's basketball team that competed abroad]. *Tiyu shiliao* 3 (February 1981): 40.

–. "Zhongguo nü lanqiu zai quanyunhui geiyu women de yinxiang" [The impression China women's basketball teams left on us during the National Games]. *Qinfen tiyu yuebao* 1, 2 (10 November 1933): 7-8.

Lu Lihua, Duan Gangcheng, and Zhou De, interviewed by Chu Jianhong. "Shanghai Zhongguo nüzi ticao xuexiao jieshi" [A brief history of the Chinese Women's Gymnastics School in Shanghai]. *Tiyu shiliao* 6 (April 1982): 4-5.

Lu Xun. *Lu Xun wencui* [The essence of Lu Xun's work]. Beijing: Wenhua yishu chubanshe, 2003.

Ma Chongjin and Hu Bozhou, eds. *Di liu jie quanguo yundong dahui huabao* [Pictorial of the Sixth National Games]. Shanghai: Qinfen shuju, 1935.

Mai, Kele [McCloy]. "Di liu jie Yuandong yundong hui de jiaoxun" [Lessons from the Sixth Far Eastern Games]. *Tiyu jikan* 2, 2 (July 1923): 1-6.

–. "Nüzi jingzheng yundong" [Competitive sports for women]. *Tiyu jikan* 2, 2 (July 1923): 1-8.

Mao Ruiqing. "Zhang Huilan huo Lianheguo Jiaokewen Zhuzhi tiyu jiang" [Zhang Huilan wins tiyu medal from the UNESCO]. *Renmin ribao*, 6 June 1987.

Minguo ershi'er nian quanguo yundong dahui zong baogao shu [Official report of the 1933 National Games]. Shanghai: Zhonghua shuju, 1934.

Pan Gongzhan. "Wei ju chengbao sili Liangjiang nüzi shifan xuexiao mujuan fuxing xuexiao jianshe yi an zhunyu bei'an you" [Approval of Fundraising by the Private Liangjiang Women's Tiyu Normal School for reconstructing its campus]. *Shanghai shi zhengfu gongbao* 155 (1935): 83-84.

Pei Shunyuan and Shen Zhenchao, eds. *Nü yundong yuan* [Female athletes]. Shanghai: Shanghai tiyu shubao she, 1935.

Quanguo yundong dahui zong baogao: Shijiu nian si yue Hangzhou juxing [The general report of the National Games: held in Hangzhou in April 1930]. N.p.: n.p., 1930.

Quanyun hui teji [Special collections on the National Games]. Shanghai: Tiyu shenghuo chubanshe, 1948.

Shen Kunnan. "Zhongguo tianjing daibiaodui canjia di shiyi jie Aoyunhui bisai qingkuang" [The story of the track and field delegate who participated in the 11th Olympics]. *Tiyu shiliao* 2 (August 1980): 19-20.

Shi Xia. "Fu Baolu." *Tiyu shiliao* 4 (June 1981): 38.

–. "Hafu si jiemei" [The four sisters from Harbin]. *Tiyu shiliao* 4 (June 1981): 38.

–. "Qian Xingsu." *Tiyu Shiliao* 4 (June 1981): 44.

–. "Shijia xiongmei" [The Shi siblings]. *Tiyu shiliao* 6 (April 1982): 37.

Su Xiaoqing. *Xin minzhu zhuyi tiyu shi* [A history of the new democratic tiyu]. Fuzhou: Fujian jiaoyu chubanshe, 1999.

Tiyu huanghou – modeng mingge xuan [Queen of sports – selection of famous modern songs].

Wan Tianshi. "Yi ge nüzi duanpao mingjiang de zhaoyu – ji Li Sen" [The tragic experience of famous female dasher – Li Sen]. *Tiyu shiliao* 6 (April 1982): 33-34.

Wang Jianming. *Meirenyu Yang Xiuqiong* [The Mermaid Yang Xiuqiong]. Shanghai: Guanghua shuju, 1935.

Wang Jinsheng. *Bainian dongren* [The significant individuals during the past century]. Shijiazhuang: Hebei jiaoyu chubanshe, 2002.

Wang Zhenya. *Jiu Zhongguo tiyu jianwen* [The observations of *tiyu* in old China]. Beijing: Renmin tiyu chubanshe, 1984.

Wu Bangwei. "Zuiijin gexiang yundong guize zhi zhaiyao" [Digest of the latest rules for various sports]. *Tiyu yanjiu yu tongxun* 1, 2 (March 1933): 191-200.

Wu Wenzhong. *Tiyu shi* [History of *tiyu*]. Taipei: Guoli bianyiguan, 1962.

Wu Zhiming and Wu Jian. "Nülan wuhao – ji Chen Baixue" [Female basketball player no. 5 – the story of Chen Baixue]. *Tiyu shiliao* 6 (April 1982) 7-8, and 8 (1982): 41.

Xiao Zhongguo. "Tichang nüzi tiyu yu Zhonghua minzu zhi fuxing" [Advocating women's tiyu and revival of the Chinese nation]. *Tiyu jikan* 3, 2 (June 1937): 145-47.

Xu Songtao. "Woguo di yi wei nü tiyu jiaoshi" [The first female tiyu teacher in the nation]. *Tiyu shiliao* 3 (Feburary 1981): 30-31.

Yang Buwei. *Yi ge nüren de zizhuan* [Autobiography of a woman]. Taipei: Zhuanji wenxue chubanshe, 1967.

–. *Zaji Zhao jia* [Miscellaneous notes on the Zhao family]. Taipei: Zhuanji wenxue chubanshe, 1972.

Yang Hansheg, Shi Dongshan et al. "Guanyu guofang dianying zhi jianli" [On the establishment of the national defence films]. *Kangzhan dianying* 1 (March 1938): 2-5.

Yang Xiuqiong. *Yang Xiuqiong zizhuan* [Autobiography of Yang Xiuqiong]. Hong Kong: Xinhua chubanshe, 1938.

Ye Qianyu, ed. *Mingguo ershi'er nian quanguo yundong hui zhuankan* [Special journal of the 1933 National Games]. Shanghai: Shidai tushu gongsi, 1933.

Yu Chien-ming. "Jindai Huadong diqu de nü qiuyuan: yi baokan zazhi weizhu de taolun" [Female ball players on the east coast in early modern China: discussions mainly based on newspapers and magazines]. *Zhongyang yanjiu yuan jindai shi yanjiu suo jikan* [Journal of the Institute of Modern History, Academia Sinica] 32 (1999): 57-125.

–. *Yundong chang nei wai: Jindai Huadong diqu de nüzi tiyu, 1895-1937* [On and off the playing fields: a modern history of physical education for girls in eastern China]. Taipei: Institute of Modern History, Academia Sinica, 2009.

Yuan Congmei. "'Rexue zhonghun' zhi hua" [Thoughts on *The Patriotic Family*]. *Kangzhan dianying* 1 (March 1938): 15.

Zen Biao. *Zhongyang suqu tiyu shi.* [A history of tiyu in the Central Soviet District]. Nanchang: Jiangxi gaoxiao chubanshe, 1999.

Zeng Naidun. *Nü xuesheng shenghuo sumiao* [Sketches of lives of female students]. Shanghai: Nüzi shudian, 1936.

Zhang Ailing. *Zhang Ailing dianchang wenji* [Collection of classics by Zhang Ailing (Eileen Chang)]. Harbin: Harbin chubanshe, 2005.

Zhang Banglun. "Canjia di shisi jie Aoyunhui zhuiyi" [Recalling participation in the Fourteenth Olympics]. *Tiyu shiliao* 2 (August 1980): 32-43.

Zhang Huilan. "Pianren de jiaxiang: di shiyi jie Aoyunhui xiaoyi" [The fake decorations that fooled people: memories of the Eleventh Olympics]. *Tiyu shiliao* 4 (June 1981): 38-39.

Zhang Huilan, interviewed by Qiu Weichang. "Wo zai Zhongda tiyu xi shenghuo pianduan" [Pieces of memories of my life in the National Central University]. *Tiyu shiliao* 10 (October 1984): 85-87.

Zhang Huilan, interviewed by Qiu Weichang and Zheng Yuangao. "Shanghai Nüqingnianhui tiyu shifan xuexiao" [The Shanghai YWCA Tiyu Normal School]. *Tiyu shiliao* 9 (January 1983): 8-9; and in *Titan xianfeng* [Forerunners in sports], 188-91. Shanghai: Shanghai renmin chubanshe, 1990.

–. "Zaoqi peiyang nüzi tiyu shizi de xuexiao" [First schools that brought up female tiyu teachers]. In *Titan xianfeng*, 192-96. Shanghai: Shanghai renmin chubanshe, 1990.

Zhang Huilan and Sun Zhenghe. *Hehuan yundong* [Gentle exercise]. Shanghai: Qinfen shuju, 1935.

Zhang Jiwu. *Feichang shiqi zhi guomin tiyu* [Tiyu for citizenry during the national crisis]. Shanghai: Zhonghua shuju, 1937.

Zhang Yongjiu. *Minguo sanda wenyao jizhuan: shangxin de jitan* [Biographies of the three cultural demons in Republican China: the altar full of sorrows]. Beijing: Dongfang chubanshe, 2010.

Zhao Yukun. "Jijian xiaoshi" [Several minor events]. *Tiyu shiliao* 6 (April 1982): 36.

Zhejiang zhongdeng xuexiao di'er ci lianhe yundong hui baogao [Report of the second united games of secondary schools in Zhejiang Province]. N.p.: n.p., 1919.

Zheng Yongzhi. "Quanguo de yinse zhanshi qilai" [Rise, the soldiers of silver screen across the nation]. *Kangzhan dianying* 1 (March 1938): 6-7.

Zhongguo di'er lishi dang'an guan, ed. *Zhonghua Minguo shi dang'an ziliao huibian* [Selected archival materials from the Republican period], vols. 5 and 3. Nanjing: Jiangsu guji chubanshe, 1991.

Zhongguo dianying jia xiehui, ed. *Zhongguo dianying jia liezhuan* [Biographies of China's cinematic figures]. Beijing: Zhongguo dianying chubanshe, 1982.

Zhongguo Guomindang zhongyang zhixing weiyuanhui xuanchuan weiyuanhui, ed. *Tiyu yu jiuguo* [Tiyu and national salvation]. N.p.: n.p., n.d.

Zhonghua minguo ershi'er nian quanguo yundong dahui jinian ce [The program of 1933 National Games]. Shanghai: Zhonghua shuju, 1933.

Zhonghua minguo nian nian di shiwu jie Huabei yundong hui [The Fifteenth North China Games in 1931]. N.p.: n.p., 1931.

Zhonghua quanguo tiyu zonghui choubei weiyuanhui, ed. *Xin minzhu zhuyi de guomin tiyu* [New democratic tiyu for citizenry]. Beijing: n.p., 1949.

Zhonghua tiyu xiejin hui [China National Amateur Athletic Federation], ed. *Chuxi di shiyi jie shijie yundong hui Zhonghua daibiao tuan baogao* [Official report of the Chinese delegation to the Eleventh Olympics in Berlin in 1936]. Shanghai: n.p., 1937.

Selected Western-Language Sources

"Advisory Council on China Films." *China at War* 8, 1 (January 1942): 50.

Benstock, Shari, and Suzanne Ferriss, eds. *Footnotes on Shoes*. New Brunswick, NJ: Rutgers University Press, 2001.

Braudy, Leo. *The Frenzy of Renown: Fame and Its History*. New York: Oxford University Press, 1986.

Brownell, Susan. *Training the Body for China: Sports in the Moral Order of the People's Republic*. Chicago: University of Chicago Press, 1995.

Cahn, Susan K. *Coming on Strong: Gender and Sexuality in Twentieth-Century Women's Sports*. Cambridge, MA: Harvard University Press, 1994.

Carter, James H. *Creating a Chinese Harbin: Nationalism in an International City, 1916-1932.* Ithaca, NY: Cornell University Press, 2002.

Chao, Y.R. [Zhao Yuanren]. "Some Contractive Aspects of the Chinese National Language Movement." In *Aspects of Chinese Sociolinguistics: Essays by Yuen Ren Chao,* edited by Anwar S. Dil. Stanford, CA: Stanford University Press, 1976.

Chen, Tina Mai. "Proletarian White and Working Bodies in Mao's China." *Positions: East Asia Cultures Critique* 11, 2 (Fall 2003): 361-93.

"'China's Mermaid' Dies." *Vancouver Sun,* 13 October 1982.

"Chinese Mermaid." *Atlanta Constitution,* 12 November 1935.

Clarey, Christopher. "Li Na Dethrones Schiavone at French Open," *New York Times,* 4 June 2011.

Cong, Xiaoping. *Teachers' Schools and the Making of the Modern Chinese Nation-State.* Vancouver: UBC Press, 2007.

Croll, Elisabeth. *Feminism and Socialism in China.* London: Routledge, Keegan and Paul, 1978.

Cui, Shuqin. *Women through the Lens: Gender and Nation in a Century of Chinese Cinema.* Honolulu: University of Hawai'i Press, 2003.

Daley, Arthur J. "On Basketball Courts: Chinese Play Basketball." *New York Times,* 21 January 1939, 10.

Dikötter, Frank. *Exotic Commodities: Modern Objects and Everyday Life in China.* New York: Columbia University Press, 2006.

–. *Sex, Culture and Modernity in China: Medical Science and the Construction of Sexual Identities in the Early Republican Period.* Honolulu: University of Hawai'i Press, 1995.

–. *Things Modern: Material Culture and Everyday Life in China.* London: Hurst, 2007.

Dong, Madeline Yue, and Joshua Goldstein, eds. *Everyday Modernity in China.* Seattle: University of Washington Press, 2006.

Dong Jinxia. *Women, Sport and Society in Modern China: Holding Up More than Half the Sky.* London: Frank Cass, 2003.

Duara, Prasenjit. *The Global and Regional in China's Nation-Formation.* New York: Routledge, 2009.

–. "The Regime of Authenticity: Timelessness, Gender, and National History in Modern China." *History and Theory* 37, 3 (October 1998): 297-99.

–. *Sovereignty and Authenticity: Manchukuo and the East Asian Modern.* Lanham, MD: Rowman and Littlefield, 2003.

Edwards, Louise, and Elaine Jeffreys. eds. *Celebrity in China.* Hong Kong: Hong Kong University Press, 2010.

Edwards, Louise, and Mina Roces, eds. *Women's Suffrage in Asia: Gender, Nationalism, and Democracy.* London: Routledge, 2004.

"Eleanor Holm Whalen, 30's Swimming Champion, Dies." *New York Times,* 2 February 2004.

Faderman, Lillian. *Odd Girls and Twilight Lovers: A History of Lesbian Life in Twentieth-Century America.* New York: Columbia University Press, 1991.

Fan Hong. "Blue Shirts, Nationalists and Nationalism: Fascism in 1930s China." In *Superman Supreme: Fascist Body as Political Icon-Global Fascism,* edited by J.A. Mangan, 205-26. London: Frank Cass, 2000.

–. *Footbinding, Feminism and Freedom: The Liberation of Women's Bodies in Modern China.* London: Frank Cass, 1997.

–, ed. *Sport, Nationalism and Orientalism: The Asian Games.* New York: Routledge, 2007.

Farquhar, Mary, and Yingjin Zhang, eds. *Chinese Film Stars.* New York: Routledge, 2010.

"The Feminist Movement in China." *People's Tribune* 25, 5 (1 June 1935): 301-14.

Feng, Jin. *The Making of a Family Saga: Ginling College.* Albany, NY: SUNY Press, 2010.

Finnane, Antonia. *Changing Clothes in China: Fashion, History, Nation.* New York: Columbia University Press, 2008.

–. "What Should Chinese Women Wear? A National Problem." In *Dress, Sex and Text in Chinese Culture,* edited by Antonia Finnane and Anne McLaren, 3-36. Clayton, Australia: Monash Asia Institute, 1999.

Frederick, Sarah. *Turning Pages: Reading and Writing Women's Magazines in Interwar Japan.* Honolulu: University of Hawai'i Press, 2006.

Freedman, Estelle B. *Maternal Justice: Miriam Van Waters and the Female Reform Tradition.* Chicago: University of Chicago Press, 1996.

Frost, Dennis J. *Seeing Stars: Sports Celebrity, Identity and Body Culture in Modern Japan.* Cambridge, MA: Harvard University Press, 2011.

Fu, Poshek. *Between Shanghai and Hong Kong: The Politics of Chinese Cinema.* Stanford, CA: Stanford University Press, 2003.

Fung, Edmund S.K. *Intellectual Foundations of Chinese Modernity: Cultural and Political Thought in the Republican Era.* New York: Cambridge University Press, 2010.

Gamson, Joshua. *Claims to Fame: Celebrity in Contemporary America.* Berkeley: University of California Press, 1994.

Gao, Yunxiang. "China and the Olympics" and "2008 Olympics." In *Encyclopedia of Modern China,* 4 vols., edited by David Pong. Detroit: Gale/Scribners, 2009.

–. "Sports, Gender, and Nation-State during China's 'National Crisis' from 1931 to 1945." PhD diss., University of Iowa, 2005.

Garrett, Shirley S. *Social Reformers in Urban China: The Chinese YMCA, 1895-1926.* Cambridge, MA: Harvard University Press, 1970.

Gerth, Karl. *China Made: Consumer Culture and the Creation of the Nation.* Cambridge, MA: Harvard University Press, 2003.

Gilmartin, Christina K. *Engendering the Chinese Revolution: Radical Women, Communist Politics and Mass Movements in the 1920s.* Berkeley: University of California Press, 1995.

Glosser, Susan, "'Women's Culture of Resistance': An Ordinary Response to Extraordinary Circumstances." In *In the Shadow of the Rising Sun: Shanghai after Japanese Occupation,* edited by Christian Henriot and Wen-Hsin Yeh, 312-25. New York: Cambridge University Press, 2004.

Goldman, Merle, and Elizabeth J. Perry, eds. *Changing Meanings of Citizenship in Modern China.* Cambridge, MA: Harvard University Press, 2002.

Goldstein, Joshua. *Drama Kings: Players and Publics in the Re-creation of Peking Opera, 1830-1937.* Berkeley: University of California Press, 2007.

Goodman, Bryna, and Wendy Larson, eds. *Gender in Motion: Divisions of Labor and Cultural Change in Late Imperial and Modern China.* Lanham, MD: Rowman and Littlefield, 2005.

Graham, Gale. "Exercising Control: Sports and Physical Education in American Protestant Mission Schools in China, 1880-1930." *Signs* 20 (Autumn 1994): 23-48.

Grundy, Pamela, and Susan Shackelford. *Shattering the Glass: The Remarkable History of Women's Basketball.* New York: New Press, 2005.

Guo, Yingjie. "China's Celebrity Mothers: Female Virtues, Patriotism, and Social Harmony." In *Celebrity in China,* edited by Louise Edwards and Elaine Jeffreys, 45-66. Hong Kong: Hong Kong University Press, 2010.

Gutman, Allen. "Sports Crowds." In *Crowds,* edited by Jeffrey T. Schnapp and Matthew Tiews, 111-33. Stanford, CA: Stanford University Press, 2006.

Hahn, Emily. *China to Me: A Partial Autobiography.* Philadelphia: Blakiston, 1944.

Hau, Michael. *The Cult of Health and Beauty in Germany: A Social History, 1890-1930*. Chicago: University of Chicago Press, 2003.

Hayford, Charles. *To the People: James Yen and Village China*. New York: Columbia University Press, 1990.

Hershatter, Gail. *Dangerous Pleasures: Prostitution and Modernity in Twentieth-Century Shanghai*. Berkeley: University of California Press, 1997.

–. "State of the Field: Women in China's Long Twentieth Century." *Journal of Asian Studies* 63, 4 (November 2004): 991-1065.

Hodges, Graham Russell Gao. *Anna May Wong: From Laundryman's Daughter to Hollywood Legend*. New York: Palgrave Macmillan, 2004.

Hoh, Gunsun. *Physical Education in China*. Shanghai: Commercial Press, 1926.

Hu, Jubin. *Projecting a Nation: Chinese National Cinema before 1949*. Hong Kong: Hong Kong University Press, 2003.

Hung, Chang-tai. *War and Popular Culture: Resistance in Modern China, 1937-1945*. Berkeley: University of California Press, 1994.

Johnson, Walter. "On Agency." *Journal of Social History* 37, 2 (Autumn 2003): 113-24.

Jones, Andrew F. *Yellow Music: Media Culture and Colonial Modernity in the Chinese Jazz Age*. Durham, NC: Duke University Press, 2001.

Judge, Joan. *The Precious Raft of History: The Past, the West, and the Woman Question in China*. Stanford, CA: Stanford University Press, 2008.

–. *Print and Politics: "Shibao" and the Culture of Reform in Late Qing China*. Stanford: Stanford University Press, 1996.

–. "Talent, Virtue, and the Nation: Chinese Nationalisms and Female Subjectivities in the Early Twentieth Century." *American Historical Review* 106, 3 (June 2001): 765-803.

Kazuko, Ono. *Chinese Women in a Century of Revolution, 1850-1950*. Stanford, CA: Stanford University Press, 1982.

Ko, Dorothy. *Cinderella's Sisters: A Revisionist History of Footbinding*. Berkeley: University of California Press, 2005.

Kotlach, Jonathan. *Sports, Politics and Ideology in China*. New York: Jonathan David, 1972.

Kirby, William C. *Germany and Republican China*. Stanford, CA: Stanford University Press, 1984.

–. "The Internationalization of China: Foreign Relations at Home and Abroad in the Republican Era." In *Reappraising Republican China*, edited by Frederic Wakeman Jr. and Richard L. Edmonds, 179-204. Oxford: Oxford University Press, 2000.

Knipping, Paul August. "Clair E. Turner and the Growth of Health Education." PhD diss., University of Wisconsin, 1970.

Kwok, Daniel W.Y. *Scientism in Chinese Thought, 1900-1950*. New Haven, CT: Yale University Press, 1965.

Leary, Charles. "Sexual Modernism in China: Zhang Jingsheng and 1920s Urban Culture." PhD diss., Cornell University, 1994.

Lee, Leo Ou-Fan. *Shanghai Modern: The Flowering of a New Urban Culture in China, 1930-1945*. Cambridge, MA: Harvard University Press, 1999.

Li, Danke. *Echoes of Chongqing: Women in Wartime China*. Urbana: University of Illinois Press, 2010.

Li, Hongshan. *U.S.-China Educational Exchange: State, Society, and Intercultural Relations, 1905-1950*. New Brunswick, NJ: Rutgers University Press, 2008.

Li, Laura Tyson. *Madame Chiang Kai-shek: China's Eternal First Lady*. New York: Atlantic Monthly Press, 2006.

Lin, Yutang. *My Country and My People*. New York: Reynal and Hitchcock, 1935.

Link, E. Perry Jr. *Mandarin Ducks and Butterflies: Popular Fiction in Early Twentieth-Century Chinese Cities*. Berkeley: University of California Press, 1981.

Little, James R. "Charles Harold McCloy: His Contributions to Physical Education." PhD diss., University of Iowa, 1968.

Lu, Hanchao. *Beyond the Neon Lights: Everyday Shanghai in the Early Twentieth Century.* Berkeley: University of California Press, 1999.

Lu, Sheldon H., and Emilie Yueh-yu, eds. *Chinese Language Film: Historiography.* Honolulu: University of Hawai'i Press, 2005.

Lu, Suping, ed. *Terror in Minnie Vautrin's Nanjing: Diaries and Correspondence 1937-38.* Urbana: University of Illinois Press, 2008.

Lutz, Jessie G., ed. *Pioneer Christian Women: Gender, Christianity, and Social Mobility.* Bethlehem, PA: Lehigh University Press, 2010.

MacDonald, Sean. "Li Lili: Acting a Lively *Jianmei* Type." In *Chinese Film Stars,* edited by Mary Farquhar and Yingjin Zhang, 50-67. New York: Routledge, 2010.

Mandell, Richard D. *The Nazi Olympics.* New York: Macmillan, 1971.

Mangan, J.A., ed. *Superman Supreme: Fascist Body as Political Icon-Global Fascism.* London: Frank Cass, 2000.

Marshall, P. David, ed. *The Celebrity Culture Reader.* New York: Routledge, 2006.

McCloy, Charles H. "A Study of Landing Shock in Jumping for Women." *Bulletin of the State University of Iowa,* 15 August 1931, 101-11. Found in Box 2, Charles H. McCloy Papers, Special Collections, University of Iowa Libraries.

–. "New Wine in New Bottles." *Journal of Physical Education* 25 (October 1927): 43-52.

–. *Philosophical Bases for Physical Education.* New York: F.S. Crofts, 1940.

–. "Some Fundamental Considerations in Physical Education." *Physical Training* 17 (November 1919): 4-11.

–. "What Is Modern Physical Education." *University of Iowa Extension Bulletin* 505 (1 April 1941): 2-16.

Morris, Andrew D. *Marrow of the Nation: A History of Sports and Physical Culture in Republican China.* Berkeley: University of California Press, 2004.

–. "Native Songs and Dances: Southeast Asia in a Greater Chinese Sporting Community, 1920-48." *Journal of Southeast Asian Studies* 31, 1 (March 2000): 48-69.

Mosse, George. *The Image of Man: The Creation of Modern Masculinity.* New York: Oxford University Press, 1996.

–. *Nationalism and Sexuality: Respectability and Abnormal Sexuality in Modern Europe.* New York: Howard Fertig, 1997.

Mitter, Rana. *A Bitter Revolution: China's Struggle with the Modern World.* New York: Oxford University Press, 2004.

–. *The Manchurian Myth: Nationalism, Resistance and Collaboration in Modern China.* Berkeley: University of California Press, 2000.

Pang, Laikwan. *Building a New China in Cinema: The Chinese Left-Wing Cinema Movement, 1932-1935.* Lanham, MD: Rowman and Littlefield, 2002.

Pickowicz, Paul G. "Melodramatic Representation and the 'May Fourth' Tradition of Chinese Cinema." In *From May Fourth to June Fourth: Fiction and Film in Twentieth-Century China,* edited by Ellen Widmer and David Der-wei Wang, 295-326. Cambridge, MA: Harvard University Press, 1993.

–. "The Theme of Spiritual Pollution in Chinese Films of the 1930s." *Modern China* 17, 1 (January 1991): 38-75.

Ponce de Leon, Charles L. *Self-Exposure: Human-Interest Journalism and the Emergence of Celebrity in America, 1890-1940.* Chapel Hill: University of North Carolina Press, 2004.

"Progress despite Difficulties: China's Young Movie Industry." *China at War* 7, 4 (October 1941): 67-9.

Radway, Janice. *Reading the Romance: Women, Patriarchy, and Popular Literature.* Chapel Hill: University of North Carolina Press, 1984.

Reed, Christopher A. *Gutenberg in Shanghai: Chinese Print Capitalism, 1876-1937.* Vancouver: UBC Press, 2004.

Riefenstahl, Leni. *Schönheit im Olympischen Kampf. Mit zahlreichen Aufnahmen von den Olympischen Spielen 1936.* Berlin: Deutscher Verlag, 1937.

Rogaski, Ruth. *Hygienic Modernity: Meaning of Health and Disease in Treaty-Port China.* Berkeley: University of California Press, 2004.

Sang, Tze-lan D. *The Emerging Lesbian: Female Same-Sex Desire in Modern China.* Chicago: University of Chicago Press, 2003.

Saussy, Haun. "Crowds, Number, and Mass in China." In *Crowds,* edited by Jeffrey T. Schnapp and Matthew Tiews, 262-65. Stanford, CA: Stanford University Press, 2006.

Schnapp, Jeffrey T., and Matthew Tiews, eds. *Crowds.* Stanford, CA: Stanford University Press, 2006.

Shen, Vivien. *The Origins of Left-Wing Cinema in China, 1932-37.* New York: Routledge, 2005.

Shih, Shu-mei. "Gender, Race, and Semicolonialism: Liu Na'ou's Urban Shanghai Landscape." *Journal of Asian Studies* 55, 4 (1996): 934-56.

Silber, Cathy. "From Daughter to Daughter-in-Law in the Women's Script of Southern Hunan." In *Engendering China: Women, Culture, and the State,* edited by Christina K. Gilmartin et al., 47-69. Cambridge, MA: Harvard University Press, 1994.

Spence, Jonathan. *The Search for Modern China.* 2nd ed. New York: Norton, 1999.

"Sports in China: Enthusiasts Face Lack of Equipment." *China at War* 7, 4 (April 1944): 60-62.

Steele, Valerie. *Shoes: A Lexicon of Style.* London: Scriptum Editions, 1998.

Stevens, Sarah E. "The New Woman and the Modern Girl in Republican China." *NWSA Journal* 15 (Autumn 2003): 82-103.

Stiffler, Douglas A. "Creating 'New China's First New-Style Regular University,' 1949-50." In *Dilemmas of Victory: The Early Years of the People's Republic of China,* edited by Jeremy Brown and Paul G. Pickowicz, 288-308. Cambridge, MA: Harvard University Press, 2007.

"Successful Field Day by Local Chinese: Happy Social Function." *Manchuria Daily News,* 15 May 1923.

Sudo, Mizuyo. "Concepts of Women's Rights in Modern China." In *Translating Feminisms in China,* edited by Dorothy Ko and Wang Zheng, 13-34. New York: Blackwell, 2008.

Tang, Xiaobing. *Chinese Modern: The Heroic and the Quotidian.* Durham, NC: Duke University Press, 2000.

The Modern Girl around the World Research Group, eds. *The Modern Girl around the World: Consumption, Modernity, and Globalization.* Durham: Duke University Press, 2008.

Thurston, Mrs. Lawrence, and Ruth M. Chester. *Ginling College.* New York: United Board for Christian Colleges in China, 1955.

Urbain, Jean-Didier. *At the Beach.* Minneapolis: University of Minnesota Press, 2003.

Wakeman, Frederic Jr. *Policing Shanghai, 1927-1937.* Berkeley: University of California Press, 1995.

Wakeman, Frederic Jr., and Richard L. Edmonds, eds. *Reappraising Republican China.* Oxford: Oxford University Press, 2000.

Wang, Zheng. *Women in the Chinese Enlightenment: Oral and Textual Histories.* Berkeley: University of California Press, 1999.

–. "Feminism: China." In *Routledge International Encyclopedia of Women: Global Women's Issues and Knowledge,* edited by Cheris Kramarae and Dale Spender, 2: 736-37. New York: Routledge, 2000.

Warner, Patricia Campbell. *When Girls Came Out to Play: The Birth of American Sportswear.* Amherst: University of Massachusetts Press, 2006.

Wilbur, C. Martin. "The Nationalist Revolution: From Canton to Nanjing, 1923-1928." In *The Cambridge History of China*, vol. 12, pt. 1. Cambridge: Cambridge University Press, 1983.

Wiltse, Jeff. *Contested Waters: A Social History of Swimming Pools in America*. Chapel Hill: University of North Carolina Press, 2007.

Winchester, Simon. *The Man Who Loved China: The Fantastic Story of the Eccentric Scientist Who Unlocked the Mysteries of the Middle Kingdom*. New York: HarperCollins, 2008.

Wu, Chih-kang. "The Influence of YMCA on the Development of Physical Education in China." PhD diss., University of Michigan, 1956.

Xiao, Zhiwei. "Film Censorship in China, 1927-1937." PhD diss., University of California at San Diego, 1994.

Xie, Bingying. *A Woman Soldier's Own Story*, translated by Lily Chia Brissman and Barry Brissman. New York: Columbia University Press, 2001.

Xu, Guoqi. *Olympic Dreams: China and Sports, 1895-2008*. Cambridge, MA: Harvard University Press, 2008.

Yao, Ming. *Yao: A Life in Two Worlds*. New York: Miramax, 2004.

Ye, Weili. *Seeking Modernity in China's Name: Chinese Students in the United States, 1900-1927*. Stanford, CA: Stanford University Press, 2001.

Yeh, Catherine Vance. *Shanghai Love: Courtesans, Intellectuals and Entertainment Culture, 1850-1910*. Seattle: University of Washington Press, 2006.

Yeh, Wen-Hsin. *Shanghai Splendor: Economic Sentiments and the Making of Modern China, 1843-1949*. Berkeley: University of California Press, 2007.

Yen, Hsiao-pei. "Body Politics, Modernity and National Salvation: The Modern Girl and the New Life Movement." *Asian Studies Review* 29, 2 (June 2005): 165-86.

Yep, Kathleen S. "Playing Rough and Tough: Chinese American Basketball Players in the 1930s and 1940s." *Frontiers: A Journal of Women's Studies* 31, 1 (2010): 123-41.

"Yvonne Tan Sau King." *Globe and Mail*, 14 October 1982.

Zamperini, Paola. *Lost Bodies: Prostitution and Masculinity in Chinese Fiction*. Leiden: Brill, 2010.

Zhang, Huilan. "A Colligation of Facts and Principles Basic to Sound Curriculum Construction for Physical Education in China." PhD diss., University of Iowa, 1944.

–. "The Development of a Program of Hygiene for the National Teachers College for Women." Thesis for a Certificate in Public Health, Massachusetts Institute of Technology, 1941.

Zhang, Yingjin. *Chinese National Cinema*. New York: Routledge, 2004.

–, ed. *Cinema and Urban Culture in Shanghai, 1922-1943*. Stanford, CA: Stanford University Press, 1999.

Zhang, Yingjin and Xiao Zhiwei, eds. *Encyclopedia of Chinese Film*. New York: Routledge, 1998.

Zhang, Zhen. *An Amorous History of the Silver Screen: Shanghai Cinema, 1896-1937*. Chicago: University of Chicago Press, 2005.

Index

Note: "(f)" after a page reference indicates a figure

Contemporary Chinese Studies

Kimberley Ens Manning and Felix Wemheuer, eds., *Eating Bitterness: New Perspectives on China's Great Leap Forward and Famine*

Helen M. Schneider, *Keeping the Nation's House: Domestic Management and the Making of Modern China*

James A. Flath and Norman Smith, eds., *Beyond Suffering: Recounting War in Modern China*

Elizabeth R. VanderVen, *A School in Every Village: Educational Reform in a Northeast China County, 1904-31*

Norman Smith, *Intoxicating Manchuria: Alcohol, Opium, and Culture in China's Northeast*

Juan Wang, *Merry Laughter and Angry Curses: The Shanghai Tabloid Press, 1897-1911*

Richard King, *Milestones on a Golden Road: Writing for Chinese Socialism, 1945-80*

David Faure and Ho Ts'ui-P'ing, *Chieftains into Ancestors: Imperial Expansion and Indigenous Society in Southwest China*

Printed and bound in Canada by Friesens

Set in Futura and Warnock by Artegraphica Design Co. Ltd.

Copy editor: Frank Chow

Proofreader: Mary Newberry

Indexer: Pat Buchanan